The
Impossible
Country

BRIAN HALL

The Impossible Country

A Journey Through the Last Days of Yugoslavia

Secker & Warburg LONDON

First published in Great Britain in 1994
by Martin Secker & Warburg Limited
an imprint of Reed Consumer Books Limited
Michelin House, 81 Fulham Road, London, SW3 6RB
and Auckland, Melbourne, Singapore and Toronto

A catalogue record for this book
is available from the British Library
ISBN 0 436 20032 5

The quotation on pp. 184–5 is from *The Epic in
the Making* by Svetozar Koljević, and is included
by kind permission of Oxford University Press;
the quotations from *Marko the Prince* translated
by Anne Pennington and Peter Levi are included
by permission of John Johnson Ltd

Printed in Great Britain
by Mackays of Chatham plc,
Chatham, Kent

To the people of Sarajevo

May God make you live in interesting times.

Chinese curse

Acknowledgements

I would like to thank Dan Franklin for rescuing this book, and Vicki Harris for improving it; Margarett Loke, for providing moral and material support at the time when I most needed it; Gert Bregman, for cheerfully fighting an uphill battle; Mark Polizzotti, for giving the exile an American home; and most of all, Pamela, for indulging me no more than I asked, but far more than I deserved.

The enormous debt of gratitude I owe to the people who appear in this book will be obvious to the reader. I have repaid their generosity unkindly, by turning their stories into my own. I cannot make amends, I can only apologize.

A Guide to the Pronunciation of Serbo-Croatian Words

c is pronounced 'ts', as in 'pits'
č is 'ch', as in 'church'
ć is a slightly softer 'ch', like the 'tu' in 'nature'
dž is 'j', as in 'judge'
dj is a softer 'j' like the 'du' in 'verdure'
j is 'y', as in 'yell'
lj is a liquid 'l', like the sound in 'million'
nj is like the 'ny' sound in 'onion'
š is 'sh', as in 'shout'
ž is like the 's' in 'measure'
all vowels are continental

Usage Note

In my choice of the words 'Croat' or 'Croatian', 'Serb' or 'Serbian' and 'Slovene' or 'Slovenian', I have adapted a system proposed by the historian Ivo Banac. A person is a Serb, Croat or Slovene. When used as adjectives, 'Serb', 'Croat' and 'Slovene' refer to ethnicity: Slovene soldier, Croat leader, Serb viewpoint. 'Serbian', 'Croatian' and 'Slovenian' refer to the language, the land and attributes of the state: Serbian history, Slovenian independence, Croatian Parliament.

This distinction can be quite useful. A 'Croatian Serb' means a Serb who lives in Croatia, whereas a 'Croat-Serb' means a person of mixed Croat and Serb ancestry. 'Croatian territory' means land that belongs to Croatia, regardless of who is living on it. 'Croat territory' means land where Croats are living, regardless of which state it belongs to.

Foreword

I travelled in Yugoslavia from May to mid-September of 1991. Although my arrival and departure were determined principally by personal matters, they coincidentally marked off a distinct period in the country's slow and agonizing slide towards its bloody demise. There had been isolated incidents of violence between Croats and Serbs after Croatia elected a nationalist government in free elections in the spring of 1990, but the current period of civil war more or less began with the massacre at Borovo Selo on 2 May 1991, a week before my arrival.

During my time in Yugoslavia, the conflict grew gradually in intensity, but remained confined to comparatively small territories in Croatia, so that I was able to move about easily in other parts of the country. I should note, in particular, that the fighting had not yet begun in Bosnia-Hercegovina, and I had the opportunity to travel there during what neither I nor the inhabitants knew would turn out to be the last days of peaceful coexistence between its three religious communities.

At the end of June, Slovenia and Croatia declared their independence, which led to a ten-day war in Slovenia, sharper fighting in Croatia, and a three-month moratorium imposed by the EC on the independence declarations. When I left what was no longer a country, the moratorium was drawing to a close and the Croats had begun blockading Yugoslav Army barracks on their territory. The fighting had consequently intensified dramatically. At the same time, fuel shortages and blocked transportation routes were making travel difficult everywhere. By then, people had only one thing on their minds. The story had shifted from one that a travel writer could follow in his own desultory way to one better suited to a war correspondent.

Throughout my journey I avoided the war areas, certainly because I did not want to put myself in danger, but also because I did not consider the war as such to be my story. Wars require a dehumanization of the enemy. The Serbs, Croats and Muslims of Yugoslavia had done this before and were doing it again. They did it efficiently. The best opposition to this process I could envision was to concentrate, wherever I went, whether far from the battle lines or close, on the individuals I met – how they behaved in what was left of their normal lives, what they thought about themselves and their history, what they thought about the other ethnic groups and their histories. I wanted to present them as whole, irreducible, even while they turned each other into caricatures, monsters. I wanted to see the enemy through their eyes, then meet the enemy and turn around to look back.

Try as they might, the peoples of the late Yugoslavia will not be able to kill all of the Other. When wars are over there remain the groups that waged them, made up of real people, likeable people, with their personalities, their histories and their hatreds still whole.

Part One
Zagreb

1

The Wall had come down, the Eastern Bloc was rubble, and Vienna was newly rich. Export/import businesses and joint enterprises were opening almost daily. On every street it seemed that half the neo-Renaissance apartment buildings had just been renovated, while the other half were under tarpaulins. New gilt on the Hofburg friezes gleamed in the May sunshine. Above Joseph II Square, you could hardly see Atlas for the balloon of bullion on his back.

The first night after the scaffolding had come down at Michaelerplatz, some traditionalist with a short memory had spray-painted DON'T TURN OUR HOFBURG INTO DISNEYLAND across the sand-blasted façade. Personally, I appreciated this new Vienna, even though I could no longer afford it. I was headed for some of the greyest cities in Europe, and I drank in the clean cream colours, the tidy flowering parks filled with dogs but free of dogshit.

The engine of this prosperity was abundant cheap labour. My friend Eric's new apartment in a spanking Ringstrasse-style building near the German Embassy had been renovated by Hungarian black-market workers, and the same men were now fixing the floor above. They were cheerful, hard workers. When Eric wanted to dispose of a decrepit cast-iron coal-burning stove, they arrived at his door *en masse* to wrestle the five hundred pounds of metal down the stairs and into the back of a diminutive pick-up, which headed off towards Budapest in a cloud of unregulated exhaust.

Today's Viennese despised the Hungarians as materialists and hustlers who crowded the shopping district around Maria Hilfer

Strasse, looking for deals on leather boots and VCRs. The Czechs were thought to be more cultured. In the days after the Velvet Revolution, thousands of them came to Vienna, apparently to sightsee more than to shop. The city handed out free transit and museum passes to anyone with a Czech passport and the street trams flew the Czech flag. The Brueghel Room at the Kunsthistorisches Museum was wall-to-wall Czech.

I had only known Vienna as a backwater, marooned underneath the Eastern Bloc, farther east, in fact, than Zagreb or Prague. Now it felt like the centre, or at least one centre, of exciting developments, of the movement of peoples – of history. Placards along the Ring no longer burbled about the local opening of an English musical or an American movie. Instead, they debated a pending referendum on whether or not Vienna and Budapest would jointly mount a World's Fair. The Hungarians would be junior partners, as they had been under the Austro-Hungarian Empire, only this time they were joining willingly. Meanwhile, the cheap labour from the east had supplanted a certain amount of expensive labour at home, and Jorg Haider, the leader of the Austrian Progressive Party, was garnering twenty per cent in the polls in his run for Chancellor by publicly expressing admiration for the labour policies of the Nazis and calling for a ban on immigration.

The inequalities of West and East were poignant, and so stark that, if anything, the terms 'West' and 'East' had become more significant in the previous two years, deepening from political terms into sociological ones. Eric played French horn in the Wiener Simfoniker, and he described to me a production of *The Flying Dutchman* mounted at the Bregenz Festival in the summer of 1990. The stage was a platform built out over the water of the Boden See, and a lighthouse had been erected on it so that in the opera's final scene the heroine, instead of jumping off the usual cliff, could run into the tower and up the spiral stairs, until a stunt double emerged at the top and flung himself into the water. At the first performance, the stuntman was a Hungarian, who broke his arm in the fall. 'Probably an out-of-work nuclear physicist,' Eric speculated.

4

The next night another Hungarian made the plunge, and cracked a rib. After that the festival employed an Austrian professional, but with his perfect swan dive he didn't look nearly as convincing as the two Hungarians, who had gone off the roof flailing madly, as if thrown by the stage manager.

2

Recent events in Yugoslavia – bomb attacks on railways, scattered shooting throughout Slavonia – were in all the Viennese newspapers, not merely because they were nearby, but because they concerned Croatia, which had once belonged to the Austro-Hungarian Empire. If the Hungarians and Czechs were turning again towards Vienna – you could almost think of them as coming home, couldn't you? – then why not the Croats?

I called a Serb friend in Belgrade to ask her if the trains from Vienna through Zagreb to Belgrade were running normally. She said they were. I called a Croat friend in Zagreb to wonder out loud about the safety of travelling through the country – if we could still call it a country? He said he didn't know, adding, 'Anyway, even if it's dangerous, you're a journalist, right?'

'Uh . . . right,' I said.

But I wasn't. And I had no experience in, nor predilection for, inserting myself into dangerous situations. My wife had assured me that if I got myself killed she would never forgive me. I knew some journalists, and knew the mental attitude that enabled them to work on stories like this one: Only a few people are dying, and I won't be one of them. By contrast, my gut feeling was that if any bullet was fired within a mile of me, it would find me.

I had first visited Yugoslavia in 1989, when I spent a month researching a magazine piece on the rise of Serb nationalism. I returned for two months in the spring of 1990 to cover the multi-party elections in Slovenia and Croatia, the first in Yugoslavia in over half a century. The friends I had made during those trips could be forgiven for thinking I was a journalist since I had, in fact, been doing journalistic work. But it was the first I had ever done, and as it turned out I did it badly, since I didn't much like pursuing stories. I preferred to drift, being confident that stories, like bullets, would find me.

Through the rest of 1990 I studied Serbo-Croatian while finishing a novel. I was contemplating a walking tour through Yugoslavia, and I saw myself camping in the mountains, hiking on sunny mornings into a Catholic Croat village, or an Orthodox Serb village, or a Bosnian Muslim village. What had fascinated me about Yugoslavia from the beginning was its nationality question, in which adherents of three different religions, with a long history of enmity, were forced to live in close proximity. The potential for future conflict would, of course, form a background to my observations of the various ethnic groups.

But as 1990 became 1991, the 'potential for conflict' began to look more and more like actual conflict. Serbs who formed a majority in a Croatian region called Krajina had set up armed blockades on the roads into their territory, held a referendum and proclaimed autonomy. Serb militants occupied the national park at the Plitvice Lakes, and two Croat policemen were reported killed. In the village of Pakrac, Croat security forces attacked Serbs who had seized the police station, and the Yugoslav Army had to be sent in to separate the sides. A solo walking tour started to look like an unwise idea for a physical coward.

Still, this was not a war, and I did not believe a war would break out. The rhetoric on both sides was bloodthirsty, even apocalyptic, but Balkan rhetoric is noted for that. My optimism was based on nothing, and I knew it was based on nothing, yet I nursed it. Two days after finishing the novel, I was in New York City with a ticket to Vienna. A week had gone by with no alarming news, but on the night before my flight, newspapers reported that twelve Croat policemen and three Serb villagers had been killed in a shoot-out in the Slavonian village of Borovo Selo.

On 9 May I boarded the train for Yugoslavia at Vienna's South Station. I shared a compartment with an elderly Slovene and a Serb family: a mother, her uncle and her infant daughter. The uncle borrowed my *Kurier* and disappeared behind a photograph of a bloody-headed Croat policeman lying in the Borovo Selo morgue. His niece told me she feared the nationalist leader of Serbia, Slobodan Milošević. Unfortunately, she feared the principal opposition leader, Vuk Drašković, even more. She and her uncle were Serbs from Bosnia and, like many natives of that impoverished central republic, they had found work in the more developed northern republic of Slovenia. Only the Croats were a problem, the uncle told me, casting a quick glance at the old Slovene gentlemen across from him. Serbs and Slovenes got along just fine. The Slovene made no comment.

By then we had entered Slovenia. Yellow fields of rape slid past the window. At Zidani Most I changed to a local train heading towards Zagreb, and fell into conversation with a tall Slovene student. He was well-turned-out in a long fawn raincoat, with gold-rimmed glasses and the gangsterish slicked-back hair popularized by Giorgio Armani. In contrast to the Serb uncle, he was worried about future Serb–Slovene relations. In two months, the Slovenes were set to declare independence from Yugoslavia, and he was not entirely sure the Yugoslav Army would not move in.

And if it did, would the Slovenes fight?

He laughed ruefully, and paused for several seconds before answering only that it was a difficult question. The stereotype of the Slovenes, which the Slovenes also accepted, was that they were pacifists, more interested in earning wages than waging war. The only thing the student knew was that if the Army moved in he would move out.

'I am young,' he offered as sufficient reason, as if both he and I knew that young men never fight wars. 'I want to eat! To live!'

After he got off, I found myself in the company of two Croats. They were friends, but were arguing bitterly over Tito. The short one, with a broad, bald head and a solid moustache that seemed to press his mouth half-way down his chin, maintained that the lingering Tito cult was embarrassing. His friend expressed shock. Tito, he argued, had at least kept the ethnic groups from killing each other.

The bald man had a simple method for judging moral character: Franjo Tudjman, the nationalist who had been elected President of Croatia the year before, had been jailed under Tito, and was therefore good. Alija Izetbegović, the Muslim who had been elected President of Bosnia-Hercegovina, had also been jailed under Tito, and was therefore also good. Slobodan Milošević, the President of Serbia, had never been jailed under Tito. QED.

I had told the bald man I was researching a book, and when we parted at the station in Zagreb after a round of Turkish coffee, he had only one piece of advice, which he delivered gravely, almost warningly, his hand on my arm and his moustache descending farther down his chin:

'Write the truth.'

3

Even intellectuals in Yugoslavia tend to think the truth is not only knowable, but obvious. The idea that people of good will could disagree on important issues is foreign to them. If you disagreed, you had a motive. Perhaps you were someone's agent. The most charitable interpretation – the one they usually bestowed on me, as they were kind to visitors from the admired west – was that you had been duped by the other side. You were an innocent, a western sheep among Balkan wolves.

An irony here was that I had never been in a country where the truth was more complex, more fundamentally unknowable, than in Yugoslavia. A truism among foreign reporters covering the area held that the western media had under-reported the region for years, and the explanation they gave for the failing seemed plausible. Any article would have to begin with five thousand words explaining terms (who was who, where they lived, how they got there, what they spoke) and by then the article would be over. Among editors it was a given – not only knowable, but obvious – that no one wanted to read ten thousand words on Yugoslavia.

Yugoslavia as a subject had a tendency to swallow its students whole. When Rebecca West set about explaining the country after a brief visit in 1937, she found herself drawn into research on the Roman, Byzantine, Ottoman, Austro-Hungarian and Russian Empires, on early Christianity, the Catholic–Orthodox schism, the origins and rise of nationalism, on Fascism and Nazism, on the nature of heroism and the nature of Evil (emphatically with a capital E). She came to believe that in Yugoslavia's urgent moral questions could be glimpsed – and perhaps grasped! – keys to understanding all mankind, all human history and God, and after four years of writing, she loosed on the world what must surely be the longest travel narrative in the history of literature, the 1,100 densely packed pages of *Black Lamb and Grey Falcon*. And even within that cavernous space, she succeeded only in representing the Serb viewpoint.

Did it ever make sense to call Yugoslavia a country? Or was Tito, as A. J. P. Taylor once said, the 'last Habsburg'? The 1991 census showed the largest percentage ever of people calling themselves 'Yugoslav', and that was only 6.6 per cent, and most of those were children of mixed marriages. (The fact that they were called 'mixed marriages' is telling.) Intellectuals occasionally called themselves Yugoslavs, but that was a political stance, as an American might say he was a liberal.

When the Serbs and the Croats first appeared on the Balkan peninsula towards the middle of the seventh century, they were closely related tribes, speaking various dialects of the same language, but because they happened to settle on either side of the Valentinian–Valens line dividing the Western and Eastern Roman Empires, they developed different orientations, the Croats towards Rome and Catholicism, the Serbs towards Constantinople and Orthodoxy. (Today, they still speak basically the same language, although the Croats insist continually and bitterly that there is a separate language called Croatian, which was deliberately under-represented by the Serb chauvinists who created the common literary language, called Serbo-Croatian by the Serbs, and Croato-Serbian by the Croats.) For 250 years after the Turks conquered Serbia, a steady stream of Serb refugees moved north into territories that until then had been principally occupied by Croats and Hungarians. The Austrians, wanting fortified garrisons in southern Croatia and Hungary to hold back the Turks, offered tax relief, freedom from feudal obligations and protection from religious persecution to these Serb refugees if they would settle the border region as a permanent military force. One garrisoned district was established in Slavonia, another in the area around Karlovac. (Today's term for the latter, Krajina, derives from *Vojna Krajina*, which means 'Military Border'.) Thus it happened that a significant population of Serbs came to live on what the Croats considered Croatian land.

The Croats and those Serbs living on ancient – or was it now 'former'? – Croatian territory got along together just once, just barely, and just long enough to dream up Yugoslavia. In the nineteenth century they found themselves in league against their mutual overlords, the Hungarians, who in a prolonged frenzy of romantic nationalism were attempting to Magyarize Croatia. Croats and Serbs responded with a romantic nationalism of their own, which they called, for want of a better term, Yugoslavism ('South Slavism'). When the Serbs of Serbia expelled the Turks and established an independent kingdom, Yugoslavism had a magnet, romantically conceived. Croatia would detach itself from Austria-Hungary and unite with free Serbia. The chaos at the end of World War I brought added impetus. The starving Croat peasantry had started looting the towns and estates, and the only nearby army strong enough to stop them was Serbia's.

But it had already been apparent for some time that 'Yugoslavia' meant different things to Croats and to Serbs. To Croats it meant a mutual-defence relationship – a pragmatic impulse. To the Serbs, who considered it only natural that Croats would want to join a people as glorious as themselves, it meant a fraternal relationship, that is, big brother Serbia and little brother Croatia – a sentimental impulse. The Croats demanded a sovereign Croatia within a federal structure. The Serbs rammed through a centralist constitution. The Croats – partners, right? – boycotted the assembly. The Serbs reacted sentimentally, which is to say, harshly. The large-hearted big brother was forced to discipline the ungrateful little one.

Other peoples that had been folded into this 'Yugoslavia' hardly made the hoped-for development of a 'Yugoslav' consciousness more likely. The Catholic Slovenes had more cultural affinity with the Austrians than they did with any of their Slav cousins, and they spoke Slovenian, which Serbs and Croats could only half understand. The Orthodox Macedonians were called 'Serbs' during the inter-war period, but that did not change the fact that they spoke a dialect (or perhaps a language, not yet recognized) that was closer to Bulgarian than Serbian. The sizeable southern minority of Albanians – part-Muslim, part-Catholic and speaking a language that was not even Slavic, but Illyrian – tended to feel that the areas they lived in should be part of newly formed Albania. And then there was this population of Islamicized Slavs in Bosnia, whom the regime officially called 'Serbs', and whom the average Serb called 'Turks', and not as a compliment.

The only thing that kept the country from falling apart during the inter-war period was the royal dictatorship of the Serb King Aleksandar I and, after his assassination by Croats in Marseille in 1934, the pure power of a police state. Both Serbs and Croats grew to hate the government, and for largely the same reasons, but tragically, and quite naturally, Serb opposition was political, whereas Croat opposition was national. When Germany, Italy and Bulgaria invaded and dismembered Yugoslavia in 1941, they found the Croats happy to help them. Within days, the Independent State of Croatia, a Fascist puppet regime, was proclaimed.

A three-cornered civil war of sickening ferocity broke out on Yugoslav territory. On one side were the Croatian Ustashas and the Domobran, the SS and regular army of the Independent State of Croatia. On a second side were the Chetniks – Royal Army officers and soldiers, virtually all Serbs, who had regrouped in the central Serbian mountains after the collapse of the Army in April 1941. On the third side were the Communist Partisans, a multi-ethnic guerilla movement which managed temporarily to channel nationalist hatred into class hatred, a neat trick in a peasant country virtually without classes.

At a Partisan summit meeting in 1943 in the Bosnian mountain town of Jajce, the second Yugoslavia was born. In view of the fratricidal war in full flame at the time, Partisan leader Josip Broz Tito and his comrades took as their slogan 'Brotherhood and Unity'. They decreed that when the war was over the country would be re-established as a federation of six republics: Slovenia, Croatia, Serbia, Bosnia-Hercegovina, Montenegro and Macedonia. The proposed structure deliberately weakened Serbia by carving out of it the two autonomous provinces of Vojvodina and Kosovo, because Tito was worried about a re-emergence of Serb dominance. A Communist he may have been, but even Communists have mothers, and Tito's was a Slovene, his father a Croat.

Neither the Chetniks nor the Ustashas considered another Yugoslavia conceivable after four years of blood-letting. The Chetniks wanted a Greater Serbia, the Ustashas a Greater Croatia. But the Partisans won the three-cornered war, and impossible Yugoslavia was reborn, midwifed by the ideology that even more than most ideologies ignored the complexities of human nature. Since the constitution of Yugoslavia II never worked, the Communists rewrote it more or less constantly during the next forty-seven years. They redefined the rights of the republics *vis à vis* the federal government and upgraded, and then later downgraded again, the autonomy of Serbia's two provinces, trying to apply the stick, and then the carrot, and then a carrot-coloured stick, on the resolutely untameable nationalities.

It was relentlessly creative, but it was never a solution. The only thing that kept the second Yugoslavia from falling apart was more pure power – the royal dictatorship of Supreme Commander Tito.

Tito died in 1980, and the most surprising thing since then is that Yugoslavia survived for eleven years without him.

4

All the stores in the centre of Zagreb had GOD PROTECT CROATIA in their windows, in identical white stick-on letters.

'I didn't notice when it started,' Nino shrugged at my question, dodging people on the packed sidewalk. 'One store probably did it first, and then the rest had to do it or they wouldn't look patriotic.'

We were hurrying to a VE Day demonstration in the Square of Great Croats, but we arrived just as the crowd was dispersing. Posters on the columns of the circular building in the middle of the square invited us to light candles and lay flowers on its marble steps, which were already sloppy with melted wax and crushed petals. The police directing traffic wore the same grey uniforms I remembered, but the old red star on their caps had been replaced by the *šahovnica*, an armorial shield bearing a red-and-white chessboard pattern. This had been the medieval coat of arms of Croatia, but it also happened to have been the symbol used by the Ustashas. Displaying the šahovnica had been forbidden for forty-five years on pain of long imprisonment, and its appearance on posters in the previous year's election campaign had titillated my acquaintances. Now the šahovnicas were everywhere, including on the republican flag, but unlike the sex magazines, which were also everywhere, they still evoked a hormonal response.

Croats could agree on the šahovnica. It had been a symbol of Croatian statehood centuries before the Ustashas used it, and surely everyone, even the thin-skinned Serbs, could understand its legitimate role in current events. Even Nino, who was wary of Croat nationalism, considered the Serbs' outrage over the reappearance of the šahovnica wilful and perverse.

Some other actions taken by the Croatian Democratic Union, or HDZ, the party that won the elections in the spring of 1990, did not enjoy such consensus. Today's demonstration had been a protest against one of them, the square's new name, this awkward reference to 'Great Croats'. It used to be called 'Square of the Victims of Fascism', and during the election Croat intellectuals, who tended to look down on the HDZ as a party of primitive nationalists, had joked that the HDZ never held its rallies in this square because the name made its leaders uncomfortable.

As indeed it did. Belgrade did not have a Square of the Victims of Fascism. The leader of the HDZ, Franjo Tudjman, had considered the name a provocation thought up by federal (i.e. Serb) Communists, an implication that all Croats had Fascistic tendencies. Tudjman and his cronies lacked nothing if not imagination, and they could not see that changing the name only made them look *more* like Fascists.

The intellectuals were appalled – and old Partisans were insulted. 'There was no referendum about the change,' said Marin Gergković, the head of the League of Social Democrats, whom Nino buttonholed for me in the dissolving crowd. 'The HDZ was drunk with victory. They forgot they only got forty-two per cent of the vote. Croats were also victims of Fascism! More Croats were Partisans than they were Ustashas.'

'Really?' I said. 'How many?'

'That I don't know. You should ask an expert. But I know for a fact that more were Partisans.'

Nino meant something different by 'victim'. 'I consider that my grandfather was also a victim of Fascism,' he said. Nino's grandfather had been a Fascist – an Ustasha judge in the Croatian city of Karlovac. 'He was a victim of that ideology.'

We came away from the square. The controversy over the name was only the latest in a colourful history. The circular colonnaded building had originally been an art pavilion, designed by the Dalmatian sculptor Ivan Meštrović in the abstract classical style of the 30s which now looked, indeed, Fascist, or Social Realist, depending on the context. During the war, Ante Pavelić, the Poglavnik – 'Head Man' – of the Independent State of Croatia, turned it into a mosque as part of his policy of rapprochement with the Bosnian Muslims, in the hope that they would help him kill Serbs. Today, the building was still flanked by the fountain

Islam requires for ablutions before prayer, and the people living near by still called it 'the mosque', although – or perhaps because – since the war it had been the Museum of the Revolution. And now, enthroned amid this grandiose new name, it was nothing. The exhibition had been closed by the new government, because it was Communist history. Ex-history.

Last year, Nino had voted for one of the intellectuals' parties. A dozen of them had come together in a grand coalition occupying an office that always bustled with bright young people, where the party leaders wandered in and out, talking a blue streak, their interview schedules in disarray. Foreign reporters needing background information were invariably steered towards historians, legal experts and economists working for the Coalition. They had the famous dissidents of Croatia's last twenty years, and the statesman-like leaders of the abortive nationalist movement of 1971. All the HDZ had was Tudjman, who with his heavy dark glasses and florid face looked like a Mafia don, and a bunch of young *émigré* footsoldiers speaking Croatian with wide Australian accents.

The Coalition's rallies had well-known comedians to warm up the audiences and eloquent, tart speeches by Vlado Gotovac, a playwright-cum-politician who was always introduced with poignant longing as 'the Croatian Havel'. The HDZ rallies were notable mainly for the phalanx of bodyguards surrounding a visibly frightened Tudjman – there had been a murky episode with a Serb and a gun a few months before – and speeches by a frisky gnomish monk in habit who screamed invective against the Serbs and wondered aloud what the Croats had done to deserve God's having blessed them with Dr Franjo Tudjman.

To his footsoldiers, too, he was always 'Doctor'. You had to know that he was a university professor, a historian. He had been kicked out of the Communist Party in 1968 for signing a declaration on Croatian language rights. In one of his books, he had set out to prove that not nearly as many Serbs had died in Croatian concentration camps during World War II as was usually claimed.

Supporters of the Coalition sniffed. He was not a good writer, they said. And 'Doctor'? Surely you'd heard that he got his degree by stealing someone else's work. They did, however, credit him for having told the truth about the concentration camps.

Come election day, the HDZ bulldozed the Coalition, which collapsed like a house of cards and vanished overnight. Tudjman spent the evening watching the returns on television and laughing incredulously. The Communists, who had shamelessly renamed themselves the Party of Democratic Change, came in a distant second. True, the HDZ had only won forty-two per cent of the vote, but it took over sixty per cent of the seats in Parliament. That was the Communists' fault. They had rigged the election rules to assure parliamentary dominance to the largest party, since, in a field of over thirty parties with themselves controlling the media, it had never occurred to them that they would not be the largest.

Tudjman had won by keeping the message simple, wrapping himself in red and white, making promises without worrying about whether or not he could keep them, and calling into question the patriotism of his opponents. (When he was at untelevised rallies he simply called them traitors and claimed later that he had been misquoted.) He had also organized in Australia before he did so at home, because he knew that if he had the émigré community on his side, the Croats still living in Croatia – that is, the voters – would tend to follow the émigrés' lead, because they were western and therefore understood democracy better.

This insecurity in the face of all things western ran deep. When I was watching the pre-election debates on Zagreb TV, people kept turning to me and saying ruefully, 'To you, this must seem like the playing of little children.' I did not have the heart to tell them that precisely what made it so touchingly innocent was the fact that the participants actually discussed the issues, forgetting the camera, turning in their seats to argue directly with their opponents.

Nino and I had reached the attic apartment he shared with his girlfriend Nataša and their mutual friend Silvija. 'Nice,' I murmured, opening the rattly steel-framed doors on the two bed-rooms and the long room under the eaves that must have been the kitchen, judging from the quartet of gas eyes and the metal sink at one end. The herringbone parquet floors in the bedrooms had been badly glued to the concrete slab, and clattered xylophon-ically as you walked across them. There was a terrace with a view of the hills to the north; and a clothesline placed so that if you dropped anything it would fall three storeys.

I could understand how proud Nino was of it. Last year he, Nataša and Silvija had been living with their respective parents, even though all three had had decent jobs for years. Privately owned apartments were scarce and exorbitant, while 'social' apartments (ones owned by companies and leased to their employees) had waiting lists of years, sometimes decades – and in any case were being phased out.

Nino told me the rent was $650 (a common labourer in Zagreb made $200 a month, a lawyer perhaps $600), and it had to be paid in hard currency, which meant he had to trade on the black market and risk getting ripped off by the itchy hustlers who hung out below the cathedral. Requiring payment in hard currency was illegal, but virtually universal for private apartments. There were no leases. The rent could go up by any amount, any month.

When the two women got home from work the four of us went out and caught up over a pizza. Silvija was the News Director at Zagreb's Radio 101, which until the previous year had been officially a 'youth' station. A small woman, she dressed entirely in black, and the thick bars of her jet-black eyelashes contrasted with her short hair of vivid plum. Tonight she looked tired and sad, as she often did in the couple of days preceding her Saturday news programme.

Nataša was a researcher and reporter at the same radio station. Also small, she tended towards rumpled sweatshirts and wore no make-up, which was unusual for a Yugoslav woman. She spoke with a slight rasp that fell pleasantly on the ear.

Nino wore his usual tweedy sports jacket and trousers ending above the ankle. Sandy-haired, with ice-grey eyes and a strong nose, he was good-looking except for his bad teeth, which he covered with his upper lip as he talked, giving a slight whiffling intonation to his speech.

Our conversation turned inevitably to Borovo Selo. Before 1 May no one had heard of this small village on the Danube near Vukovar, but the name by now had acquired the punch of Lockerbie for Americans, or Munich for Israelis. Maps accompanying news reports on Zagreb television about fighting in Slavonia now always marked Borovo Selo prominently, even if the fighting was elsewhere, as if the village were the area's root of conflict, of evil. It was a Serb village.

But in Croatia. And therefore it was legitimately under the jurisdiction of the Croat police, the Croats argued, despite the Serb militias and 'defence committees', all illegal, that had sprung up in Serb-populated regions of Croatia since the previous summer.

According to the official version in Zagreb, on the night of 1 May two patrol cars had driven into the centre of Borovo Selo. When two policemen climbed out of one of the cars, villagers immediately opened fire, wounding both. The second car fled. Not daring to go in again that night, the police the next morning called the head of the defence committee in Borovo Selo, a man named Vukašin Šoškočanin, to demand an explanation. He said he had no personal knowledge of an incident, but he would investigate. He called back a short while later saying the villagers had the two policemen, and someone should come to pick them up. A second car was sent, this time backed up by a bus full of policemen, and when the two vehicles reached the centre of Borovo Selo, the villagers again opened fire. In the mêlée, twelve policemen and three villagers were killed. Three of the dead policemen were mutilated.

But my three interlocutors were sceptical. Were the numbers right? Why did the police go into Borovo Selo in the first place? Why did this little village have so many Serb gunmen?

Across the Danube from Borovo Selo lay Serbia. Nataša said 'people were saying' that specially trained Serb irregulars had been ferried across the river. None of the three dead Serbs were from Borovo Selo. Perhaps more Serbs had died – the shooting had gone on for two or three hours – but their bodies had been spirited away.

The mutilations were the first atrocity of this new war. I sensed everyone had been waiting for this. People had frequently told me the year before that, if fighting broke out, I, Europe, westerners – all civilized people – would be astounded at how brutal it would be. Yugoslavs said things like this with a strange, grim satisfaction. Perhaps it was the satisfaction of having your worst doubts about yourself confirmed. This was the Balkans, Yugoslavs liked to say, shrugging. The single word explained: corruption, chaos, cruelty, genocide.

Yet much about this atrocity was confused. The first reports had said the two policemen wounded in the night had had their eyes gouged out and their throats cut. Now it was said they had been sent, alive, with gunshot wounds but no other indignities, to a hospital in Novi Sad – presumably by the Serb villagers, although I suspected few Croats would be interested in specifying that. Instead, they concentrated on the mutilations, which now they claimed happened to *other* policemen, the next day.

During the shoot-out? I asked. Would there be an opportunity in the middle of a firefight?

Perhaps afterwards, Silvija said. The Serbs won the battle, taking hostages. They were in control of the situation for several hours before they handed over the twelve bodies.

'Perhaps more than twelve,' Nino said. 'They might be under-reporting the dead.'

'Who?'

'The authorities.'

'Why?'

'Maybe it looks bad.'

Silvija was sure of one thing. There *had* been atrocities. As News Director at the radio she had been invited to a press conference given by the Croatian Interior Ministry and shown photographs that had not been released to the public. 'I couldn't recognize these bloody bits and pieces as parts of people. Heads, arms . . .' She trailed off.

'You're sure the pictures were accurate?'

'They were photographs! And the Serbs are capable of it. A friend of mine was trapped for ten days behind the blockade near Vukovar. She saw a policeman wounded. The Serbs pulled off his helmet and beat his head with their rifles, destroying his face. He is alive, but brain-damaged. She saw this with her own eyes.'

I thought of the old adage that you could tell something about a nation by its vocabulary, Inuit having a dozen words for snow, Bedouin for sand, Meso-Americans for tubers, and so on. Serbo-Croatian had a disturbingly large number of words for butchering. One of them was *kundačiti*, which meant 'to beat with the butt end of a rifle'.

'I think Borovo Selo was a Croatian game,' Nino said. 'Those police boys were set up. Why would they be sent right into the middle of a Serb village without reinforcements? The Croatian government wanted to show what the Serbs are capable of.'

'Then why under-report the dead?'

He shrugged. 'Maybe they didn't.'

I asked Nino, Nataša and Silvija if they thought the Serbs living in Croatia had any legitimate concerns.

'Of course,' Nino said. 'Tudjman did some very stupid things at the beginning. You know I don't like the HDZ.'

'I know.'

'They changed the constitution to say that Croatia was the nation-state of the Croats. That offended the Serbs. As it should have! They are citizens of Croatia. If we don't make them feel like citizens of Croatia, how can we ask them to support us?'

'We thought the constitution should just say, "Croatia is the country of its citizens,"' Silvija said, Nataša nodding. 'It's wrong even to talk about nations in the constitution.'

One heard this frequently from Yugoslav intellectuals, this plaintive call for a 'country of its citizens'. They had their fingers exactly on the problem. Yugoslavia, like other countries that had staggered out from the rubble of the Ottoman and Habsburg Empires waving the bullet-riddled standard of national self-determination, had never developed a legal concept of the citizen. Individuals were granted rights on the basis of their nationality, not because of any notion that every human being possessed

20

inherent rights. Politicians might promise 'equal rights' to a minority, but the fact remained that those people were constitutionally *defined* as a minority, as guests in someone else's nation-state. This made it extremely difficult to allay their fears, for the simple reason that their fears were well founded.

'But the HDZ insisted on this new wording,' Nataša said, 'and the Serb delegates walked out of the Parliament. That was it. They never came back.'

'Other things?' I asked.

'Oh,' Nino replied a little reluctantly, 'the new flag, with the šahovnica, sure. I wouldn't have picked it. And Tudjman made a big mistake by never going to the Serb areas after he was elected.'

'Why should he?' Silvija expostulated. 'They tried to shoot him!'

'Because it is part of Croatia,' Nino said. 'Tudjman is the President of Croatia.'

'How about the policy of replacing Serbs on the police force with Croats?' I asked.

'That merely makes sense,' Nino said. 'Under the Communists the Croatian police force was more than fifty per cent Serb, even though they make up only fifteen per cent of the population. And almost all the senior officers were Serbs. OK, that was somewhat natural. It's a cultural thing. Serbs love to order other people around. But we have to make the police force reflect the population.'

'And the oaths?' The new government had demanded that Serb policemen and other state employees sign an oath declaring loyalty to Croatia, and renouncing the 'bandits and terrorists', that is, the Serbs who were blockading the roads and demanding autonomy in the Krajina.

'Bad idea,' Nino conceded. 'But the point I wanted to make is, sure, HDZ did some stupid things. They are primitive people, I know that. I agree completely. You remember I said that last year.'

'I remember.'

'But the Serbs kill us for this! That's all I'm saying. Do you kill people just because you don't like this oath, because you don't like the new flag?'

'Serbs aren't normal,' Nataša said, screwing an index finger into her temple. 'They were right to be angry, but not like this. You bump into a Serb and he pulls out a gun and shoots you.'

Back at the apartment, we watched the news on television. Vojislav Šešelj was on again. Zagreb TV devoted a lot of air time to him, because he was a scary Serb. He led an opposition party in Serbia that was really a private army. His followers called themselves Chetniks.

To appreciate the horror this word evoked in Croats, one had to remember that the Chetniks had occupied the loser's place alongside the Ustashas in the post-war textbooks of Yugoslavia, which had pictured them both as having been slavering lunatics, baby killers, drinkers of blood. The Chetniks and the Ustashas had been the twin national demons – one Serb and one Croat – haunting Yugoslavia's past, ready to rise ghoulishly from the grave and unleash racism and genocide the moment the Communist Party ceased its internationalist vigilance, its ritual chanting of 'Brotherhood and Unity!' Anyone under fifty years of age had grown up with those teachings, and though the Party might now have been discredited, you never forgot what you learned in first grade.

And here they were, night after night, on television. They wore the familiar brimless olive wool Chetnik cap, which had been standard issue in the old Royalist Army before it acquired horns. They sported the trademark Chetnik coiffure of long, unkempt hair and beard. They waved Bowie knives in the air and held them in their teeth. The demon was loose. Šešelj had a bullet head, an academic's soft body, the bland unshakeable gaze of the deepest sort of fanatic. He was saying that he had sent his men to Borovo Selo, and he would send more. He had five thousand men now under arms, and would have ten thousand by June. Like Tudjman, he had a PhD, but no one said he stole it. Even Croats admitted he was intelligent. But in the 80s he had been imprisoned in Bosnia, which had always been known for its particularly harsh police methods. Something had happened to him in prison. He had come out a different man.

Had Borovo Selo been the beachhead of a Serb invasion? There it blinked on the map on the screen. Reports were coming in of scattered shooting in Slavonia. Nataša said Šoškočanin, of the Borovo Selo defence committee, had boasted on Novi Sad TV that he had personally killed six Ustashas, and would kill six hundred more to defend his village.

'They always call us Ustashas,' Silvija said. 'They call *them-selves* Chetniks, but no Croat today would call himself Ustasha. That was madness, and we know it. The Serbs don't.'

5

It was curious that Silvija had never noticed the Ustashas who gathered every day in Jelačić Square, in the centre of the city. They clustered clubbishly, like the youth group they were, on granite tiers at the base of a lamppost. They wore Ante Pavelić T-shirts and sold *Independent State of Croatia*, a Croatian-language Toronto newspaper, while a boombox blared '*Ustaški bećarac*', a street-fighting song, and *Ustaška budnica*, a call to arms.

I bought a copy of the paper from a young bearded man, commenting that I could sympathize with their desire for an independent state, but wondered why they chose to honour Pavelić, who was hardly an exemplary historical figure.

A visible bristle spread through the group.

'What?' another man barked. 'What did he say?'

'He's got something against Pavelić,' the bearded man answered.

A woman in a red windbreaker called from the other side of the circle, 'Where are you from?'

'The US.'

'A stupid American!' 'Stupid' was the formulaic epithet in Zagreb for Americans. 'Well, Reagan and Bush aren't any good

either! We're tired of fucking Americans who don't know anything, who don't understand Croatia and won't help us! The
Russians are better! At least the Russians are our Slav brothers!'

I moved around to her side, as the men turned away with
gestures of derision: Let the woman deal with him. She wore dark
glasses shielded at the sides, goggle-like, although it was not a
bright day.

'Aren't Serbs also Slav brothers?' I asked.

'Nah, Serbs are different. They aren't real Slavs, they have Arab
blood, or something. You can tell by the shape of their hands.'
She held out her own hand, which had exceptionally long, narrow
fingers. 'Serbs have square fingers. Let me see your hand. That's
not a Serb hand either. Where is your family from? Do you have
Croat background?'

'English.'

'Puh! Too bad for you.' She said it rather kindly, with genuine
pity. 'Look, another way you can tell Serbs are not real Slavs is
that their church isn't really Orthodox. It's got some difference
from the real Russian church, I can't remember what.'

'But Croats are Roman Catholic!' I said.

'Yes, Croats and Poles. And why? Because Croats and Poles
are the stupidest Slavs in the world. If Hitler had won, Pavelić
today would be considered a great man. But Hitler lost, and so
Pavelić was dragged down with him. That was how stupid we
were, counting on the Germans. You Germans are a degenerate
race.'

'I'm not German.'

'The English are German. You don't even know your own
history.'

'So I'm degenerate?'

'Yes. I'm sorry to tell you that, but it's true.'

'How am I degenerate?' I spread my arms, so that she could
examine me. Since she was standing on the tier, I was looking up
at her, a supplicant. 'Can you tell just by looking at me?'

Could she tell I wore contact lenses? My eyesight was terrible.

She glanced away. 'I don't like to talk about it directly to you.'

She pointed to the crowds in the big square. 'Just look at these people! They're all good-looking!'

She was right. But so were the Serbs. Yugoslavs in general were a handsome people. And if you believed short people were inferior, you might also notice how tall they were. I was six-one, and in Montenegro I was always finding myself talking into other men's shirt buttons.

'Do you see a single sick person?' she was saying. 'Anywhere else in Europe you would see sick people.'

I had allergies. Grass gave me hives.

'And look how you English talk. This mushy, wowsy –' She manipulated her lips, making a noise that sounded like a German imitating an Englishman, or an Englishman imitating an American, or an American imitating an Australian – that universal clownish braying that went back beyond the Greeks' 'bar bar' to deride the speech of the barbarians.

'Look at this girl!' A woman was passing. 'Nice girl, huh? You should marry this girl.'

'For the genes?'

'Do you some good. Have better kids.'

Sometimes my back hurt. I had calcium deposits in my teeth. My thumbs were double-jointed.

'But they wouldn't respect their degenerate dad,' I said. I had begun to suspect she was pulling my leg. But she seemed puzzled by my attempt to answer in kind, and only shrugged. 'Back to Pavelić –' I said.

'A great man!'

'Isn't there anybody else to admire in Croatia today?'

'Only Pavelić.'

'But Pavelić is dead!'

'Yes. Unfortunately.'

'If it really comes to a fight between Serbs and Croats, who do you think would win?'

She squatted, to look me in the eye, a one-way communication since I could not see hers. 'It won't happen. Croats won't fight Serbs. Look at what Serbia did to us in Borovo Selo, and still Croats didn't fight.'

Interestingly, this was exactly what Serbs would have said, their lips curling into a sneer. The year before, the leading opposition figure in Serbia, Vuk Drašković, had growled to me, throwing back his long Chetnik-style hair and dilating his equine nostrils, 'Never in history have the Croats fought the Serbs alone! They have the souls of hyenas. This time they wouldn't have Uncle Hitler to help them.'

'Why won't you fight?' I asked her.

'Croats aren't so stupid. A civil war is just what Europe wants, because then we will be in their pocket. We won't fight a war just to be in Europe's pocket.'

'So if you can't rely on Europe, and the US won't help, and Croats won't fight alone, how will Croatia ever be free?'

For the first time, she paused. 'Perhaps God will help,' she said.

I tried to end the conversation on a jocular note, which, however, came out queasily. I offered to shake her hand, a very American and not at all Croatian way of parting. (The Croats kissed each other twice on the cheeks. The Serbs did it three times.) 'You're not afraid to touch a degenerate hand, are you?' I was overworking a feeble joke.

She shook to oblige me, and I realized my palm was moist. The bristling of the crowd against me had caused it. I recalled how I always felt a mild disgust at the touch of a clammy hand. Her long-fingered hand was cool and dry.

6

I sat on a bench farther down the square to look through the paper I had bought.

> The fact is that the young generation in Croatia is slowly
> uncovering the secrets of the recent past, gradually
> realizing that they have been brainwashed; they are

26

realizing that Pavelić, the Ustaše and the defenders of the
Independent State of Croatia had absolutely nothing to
do with Nazi-Fascism . . .

In a photo, beaming women dressed in Croatian folk costumes
stood beneath a banner reading LONG LIVE THE 10TH OF APRIL.

On 25 March 1941, the Yugoslav government, encircled by the
Axis powers and their allies, signed the Tripartite Pact with
Germany, allowing Hitler to transport war matériel through
Yugoslavia to aid the Italians bogged down in Greece. But two
days later, Serb Army generals overthrew the regency of Prince
Pavle and put the seventeen-year-old Petar II on the throne. When
news of the *putsch* spread through Belgrade, Serbs poured into
the streets to support it, shouting, '*Bolje rat nego pakt! Bolje grob
nego rob!*' – 'Better war than pact! Better death than slavery!'
They waved French and English flags and sang the Serb national
anthem. They spat on the German minister's car. The whole
spontaneous convulsion was a characteristic Serb gesture, valiant
but reckless, something good for a story, but perhaps only for the
beginning of one.

Hitler remarked later that when the news of the putsch was
brought to him he thought it was a joke, so little could he believe
that a small nation, and a Slav one at that – the Germans were
the people, after all, who had made the word 'slave' out of 'Slav'
– would dare to stand up to him. On being assured the putsch
was real, he was, as Winston Churchill wrote, 'stung to the quick.
He had a burst of that convulsive anger which momentarily
blotted out thought and sometimes impelled him on his most dire
adventures.'

In a meeting with the German High Command, Hitler
announced Operation Punishment. Preparations would begin
immediately 'to destroy Yugoslavia militarily and as a national
unit'. No ultimatum would be sent. The attack would be 'carried
out with unmerciful harshness'. The minutes of the meeting noted,
'It can be assumed that the Croats will come to our side when we
attack.'

Churchill, again:

> On the morning of April 6 German bombers appeared
> over Belgrade. Flying in relays from occupied airfields in
> Rumania, they delivered a methodical attack lasting three
> days upon the Yugoslav capital. From rooftop height,
> without fear of resistance, they blasted the city without
> mercy . . . When silence came at last on April 8 over
> seventeen thousand citizens of Belgrade lay dead in the
> streets or under the débris. Out of the nightmare of
> smoke and fire came the maddened animals released from
> their shattered cages in the zoological gardens. A stricken
> stork hobbled past the main hotel, which was a mass of
> flames. A bear, dazed and uncomprehending, shuffled
> through the inferno with slow and awkward gait down
> towards the Danube.

Belgrade was still burning on 10 April when Zagreb,
untouched, flags fluttering, welcomed the German Army, and
Slavko Kvaternik, arriving from Italy, announced the foundation
of the Independent State of Croatia (or NDH). On 13 April Ante
Pavelić, a nationalist extremist who had been carrying out terrorist operations against Yugoslavia from bases in Hungary and Italy
throughout the 30s (his proudest achievement had been the
assassination of King Aleksandar), entered Zagreb with an escort
of Italian tanks.

As leader of the NDH, Pavelić promised, 'Blood will be shed
and heads will fall.' Ironically, this arch-nationalist had agreed
when he made common cause with Mussolini to allow Italy to
take more than half of Dalmatia. In recompense Croatia was given
Bosnia-Hercegovina. But whereas Dalmatia was eighty per cent
Croat, Bosnia was less than twenty-five per cent Croat, and along
with the new territory came about a million Serbs, making the
total Serb population in the NDH about two million, a rather
large minority within a Croat population of four million. The first
concentration camps were set up within days. Hitler's representative in the Balkans, Hermann Neubacher, reported later:

The recipe for the Orthodox solution of the Ustasha-führer and the Poglavnik of Croatia, Ante Pavelić, reminds one of the bloodiest memories connected with Religious Wars: 'One third must be converted to Catholicism, one third must leave the country, and one third must die!' The last point of this programme was carried out. When leading Ustashi state that one million of Orthodox Serbs were slaughtered, this, in my opinion, is a boasting exaggeration. On the basis of reports I received, I estimated that three quarters of a million defenceless people were slaughtered.

Hitler was concerned about these numbers, saying to Neubacher, 'I also told the Poglavnik that it is not so simple to annihilate such a minority, it is too large.' The Poglavnik called his policy 'cleansing'.

The Nazi records of World War II are punctuated by reports from German witnesses declaring disgust at the massacres carried out by the Croats. One senses an almost hysterical relief in those accounts, as the observers gratefully embrace the moral high ground. The Germans wanted to believe that their own annihilation of the Jews was a civilized affair. It involved research and development, quotas, storage facilities, train timetables. Such an undertaking had never before been attempted on such a scale. It was like building a pyramid.

But the Ustashas were different. They were not motivated by high ideals. They simply hated Serbs. They did not go for industrial efficiency, for getting the victims out of sight. They preferred things up close and physical. They went into the next village and killed people they knew personally. They took photographs of each other chopping off a neighbour's head. They made a point of bayonetting pregnant women in the abdomen, shouting some slogan about killing 'the seeds of the beasts'. They hacked off noses and ears, and made holes in chests to pull out hearts while they were still beating. They had a brigade called 'the skullcrushers', which did unbelievable things to people's heads and then took photographs so that others could believe it.

In his World War II memoirs, *Kaputt*, the Italian reporter Curzio Malaparte described an interview with Pavelić:

> While he spoke, I gazed at a wicker basket on the
> Poglavnik's desk. The lid was raised and the basket
> seemed to be filled with mussels, or shelled oysters . . .
> 'Are they Dalmatian oysters?' I asked the Poglavnik.
> Ante Pavelić removed the lid from the basket and
> revealed the mussels, that slimy and jelly-like mass, and
> he said smiling, with that tired good-natured smile of his,
> 'It is a present from my loyal *ustashis*. Forty pounds of
> human eyes.'

On 30 April 1941, the NDH issued a decree called 'The Protection of Aryan Blood and the Honour of the Croatian People'. That took care of the Jews, but what about the Serbs, who were also Aryan? The field had to be narrowed – to Teutons, perhaps. So some Ustashas claimed that the Croats were direct descendants of the Goths.

At least today's Ustashas knew they were Slavs. Now that they despised Hitler, it no longer mattered that Hitler had despised them. And the Serbs, inferior in 1941 because they were not Goths, were inferior today because they were not 'really' Slav.

Long live the 10th of April.

I took a stroll around Jelačić Square. It was the most pleasant square in Zagreb, a city of pleasant squares, closed to cars and rimmed by handsome Habsburgian nineteenth-century buildings in cream and grey, marred only by the obligatory skyscraper of which every Yugoslav city, to prove its modernity, had at least one, always spectacularly ugly and always printed on the city maps as a tourist attraction. The trams converged here, clanging their bells, and the cathedral and main market were nearby, so the square was always bustling with people. The news kiosks were here, and the balloon sellers, and the skateboard boys with their fluorescent watches and sneaker-laces, and the money changers veering to intercept you before you reached the door of the exchange office, and the huge Gradska Kavana, or City Café, an

Austrian municipal institution like the Bavarian *Ratskellers*, where elderly *zagrepčani* waltzed to a band of three old men playing '*Que será será*' and talked in the old city dialect, which has almost as much Slovenian in it as Croatian. In their heavy loden topcoats and felt hats they looked Viennese, except that they drank Turkish coffee, and a young friend of mine who, unlike most young people, enjoyed the City Café, would lean towards me and whisper, 'Aren't they cute?'

The previous year booths representing the various political parties had lined the square, and the atmosphere had been exuberant. People had been thrilled just to see the Communists forced to hang out posters and man their booths like everybody else. Šahovnica badges were for sale, and šahovnica key rings, šahovnica bumper stickers and of course šahovnica flags, and aluminium cans chequered red and white and purporting to contain 'Pure Croatian Air'. Twin-engined planes flew high over the square and disappeared, and minutes later leaflets would spin out of an empty blue sky like some bizarre natural phenomenon. The HDZ posters pictured Tudjman above the words WE ALONE WILL DECIDE THE DESTINY OF OUR CROATIA, and Tudjman in his speeches sounded equally confident. He talked about the 'unnatural shape' of Croatia, 'like an apple with a bite taken out of it' – the bite being Bosnia – and how this 'clearly had to change'. (Croat nationalists' unshakeable conviction that Bosnia 'had always belonged to Croatia', as they invariably put it, was based on an interpretation of a somewhat obscure passage in the historical writings of the tenth-century Byzantine emperor Constantine VII Porphyrogenitus.)

Talk like this frightened some people. The shape of Croatia looked more like an open-mouthed crocodile than an apple. Somebody kept defacing the Tudjman posters at night, drawing on him a flop of hair and a square moustache, so evocative of Hitler in so few, sure lines, that it qualified as art. Some students and intellectuals found themselves, to their own amazement, supporting the Communists, because even the Coalition had taken on a glib nationalism in its attempt to head off the surging HDZ. Nino admitted to me that he liked the Communists' programme

31

better than anyone else's, and so did I. They sounded like Western-style social democrats – not accidentally, their new name, 'Party of Democratic Change', is spelled SDP in Croatian – and were headed by the leader of the reform wing, Ivica Račan, who had taken over at the previous congress. Born in a German concentration camp, he had the battered face of a bad boxer, and hair that looked like he had cut it himself, on a moving train. Quite plausibly, the opportunists among the Communists had jumped ship, leaving the hapless idealists behind to try to convince people that, honest, *this* time they would be as good as their utopian words. That was their painfully naïve slogan: 'We mean it seriously.'

Of course, people scoffed. Oh – *now* you're serious! People called Račan 'the Rat'. He looked like a drowning one.

Nino could not bring himself to vote for them, not after forty-five years of power. He voted for the Coalition and watched his vote disappear in a puff of smoke.

This year the square was still boisterous, but the mood had darkened. The latest issue of *Free Weekly*, a new publication that Silvija called 'a dirty paper' because of its hysterical style, was opened on the stands to a photo-spread of dead people with gaping gashes across their throats, beaten faces, eyes pulped or gone. 'Victims of wild beasts!' the caption read. On the cover, a mother grieved, and a child's pathetic letter to his butchered father was scrawled above her in lettering so childlike I suspected an adult author: 'Dear Daddy – Be careful and come back soon.' Now it wasn't intellectuals who complained about Tudjman, but parties to the right of him. They called him a traitor for having negotiated with the Army over Borovo Selo, and for having retreated in recent days from the word 'independence' for Croatia to 'sovereignty'. I wondered if they relished throwing back at him the word with which he had so liberally larded his campaign. More likely, no irony was intended.

The myriad šahovnica junk was still for sale, but attracting more attention now were bitter mementos, like the hastily pro-duced books on Partisan atrocities. One man had set himself up by a lamppost to sell posters of an artist's rendition of the massacre at Bleiburg, an incident in which a quarter of a million Croats who had fled to Austria to surrender to the British in the final days of the war were turned back, and made to surrender to the Partisans, who disarmed them, machine-gunned tens of thousands of them and sent the rest off on death marches to various parts of Yugoslavia. Since Bleiburg was in Austria, there had been a memorial there for years, but the word had never been spoken publicly in Yugoslavia until last year. The man's posters, as cheaply gaudy and badly drawn as the prints of saints in the Catholic and Orthodox churches, showed a multitude being attacked from all sides, women and children shot through the heads, blood gushing from severed limbs, lines of bodies falling before the massed guns. Above it all planes circled like vultures, the RAF symbol clear on their wings. The man was asking 300 dinars, or a day's wages.

That was one common element of the nationalist bric-à-brac – its exorbitant price. These men, working out of briefcases, were as itchy as the money changers, and they had no trouble reconciling their hard-eyed extortion with their patriotism. What was the national dream all about, but the right to be nakedly capitalistic? This was the free market, right here in Jelačić Square. You want it? Three hundred dinars.

Two men who had invested in instamatic cameras would accost anyone dallying near the statue of Ban Jelačić on its spanking new granite base, with an offer to take his photograph along with the good *ban* for 120 dinars. Despite the price, they were each selling about a dozen pictures a day, because the ban (governor) was a national hero of Croatia. So national that after the Second World War the Communists had removed the statue and redubbed the square Republic Square, which was the name it had carried until the day the HDZ assumed power. The old story asserted that the Communists had planned to melt down the statue and recast it as tram rails. But this was doubtful, not least because the statue was bronze and tram rails were steel. But it was true that the statue had been rescued from destruction by being cut up and hidden, either in a hayloft in the countryside by a farmer, or in the basement of the Glyptotek in the Upper Town by a professor of art – I had heard both.

Ban Josip Jelačić was one of the few military heroes the Croats had. The Hungarians' almost genocidal nationalism in the 1840s had made them so obnoxious to the Croats, their nominal subjects, that when in 1848 the Hungarians revolted against their own rulers, the Austrians, Ban Jelačić headed across the Drava with fifty thousand men to confront the rebels, perfectly encapsulating the hopeless muddle of the sprawling empire in which they were all entwined by declaring war on Ferdinand V, King of Hungary, in the name of Ferdinand V, King of Croatia.

It was the oldest of stories: a low vassal helping the lord to defeat a middling one. With additional help from the Russians, Jelačić won, and the hated Hungarians were routed, and the Croats, for their pains, were handed back to the Hungarians as a sop in the Ausgleich of 1867.

But Jelačić in his cockaded hat and frogged uniform had sat proudly on his horse and pointed his sword in the direction of Budapest. And there he had remained, a meeting point and a sentimental favourite, until the Communists took him down and made him even more of a favourite. The most popular song during the elections the previous year, the one that kicked off every rally and blared from every fast-food stand on its bed of jangling Dalmatian mandolins until you wanted to rip out the speaker cords (but, if you had, you would have been beaten up as a Serb *provocateur*), began: 'Rise up, Ban! Croatia calls you!' Meanwhile the HDZ leaders were promising to roaring cheers that the statue, which had been found, would be returned to the square. Once there, like a combination of Holger Danske and the Commandant's statue in the Don Juan legend, perhaps Jelačić would come to life, bounding with his horse down to the paving stones and brandishing his sword, now as steely as tram rails.

The joke around town asked which way the statue would be pointing. He could hardly point north to Budapest any more – especially not since, as it later turned out, Croatia was secretly buying arms from Hungary. But even Tudjman had enough sense not to yield to temptation.

34

'Why is he pointing south?' I asked a woman in the tourist office on the square. 'I thought he was going to point east, towards Serbia.'

But I had made her angry. 'We were careful not to make any political statement,' she said. 'He is pointing towards *our* coast.' She mastered her irritation enough to wonder why I was there. Was I actually a tourist?

When I told her I was writing a travel book, she, like most people, thought I meant a guidebook. She laughed at the absurdity of it. 'You've come at a . . .' she trailed off.

'Bad time,' I suggested.

'No,' she said reflexively, and then repeated it more firmly. 'No. An unusual time.'

I asked her about the history museums, which I wanted to see. But she said that both the Museum of the Revolution and the History of Croatia Museum were closed. The exhibitions were being 'updated'. They were going to fold the history of World War II (which used to be covered in the Museum of the Revolution) into the exhibition on general history. 'So there won't be such an unnatural stress on it,' she said.

'Good idea,' I said.

How about the City History Museum? I asked.

No, that was being reorganized. 'Why do you want to see museums?' she asked. 'History is out there.' She pointed through the window to the square.

I went out again, past the posters of Bleiburg, the Ante Pavelić T-shirts. I was approached by one of the men with instamatics. He was Albanian, tall and blond, young, with a shy smile full of long teeth and receding gums, a forestry student from the university in Kosovo, who came here during vacations to make a little money. He slept on the floor of his cousin's apartment. He had no idea who Jelačić was, the only statue he cared about was the one of Skanderbeg, in Tirana.

He had heard me talking with the Ustashas and, though he had been friendly when we had first met the day before, he was now wary, a little hostile. 'How can you defend the Serbs?' he demanded of me.

'I wasn't defending the Serbs. But I do have Serb friends.'

'How can that be possible?' He squinted at me, baring his teeth. 'That is very strange to me.'

He told me how the Serbs were oppressing his people. All the Albanians in Kosovo wanted was a better life, a little democracy, but the Serbs kept them down. I had to write about Kosovo. The world had to know.

'I will be going there,' I assured him.

'Write the truth,' he said.

7

The walk from Jelačić Square to Radio 101 took me past a new company, Croatia Airlines. The office had no travel posters, no customers and hardly any office workers, but the airline did lease two planes which made flights to Split, Pula and other Croatian cities, in case you didn't want to patronize the Yugoslav carrier, JAT. A photograph in the window showed Tudjman on a maiden flight, looking almost panic-stricken, perhaps with bombs on his mind.

I reflected on the curious extent to which airlines had become symbols of nationhood, like national birds. Of course the most spectacular way to strike at a nation was to blow a few of its citizens out of the sky, as Croat separatists did to a JAT flight over Czechoslovakia in 1972. But this scapegoat status spilled over into other areas, where airlines were no more vulnerable than other businesses: in Zagreb, after a particularly hard-fought soccer game between the home team Dynamo and Belgrade's Red Star, the 'Bad Blue Boys' (as the Dynamo fans called themselves) would head straight for the JAT office downtown, smash the windows and set the place on fire.

So it probably should not have surprised me when Croats in the 1990 elections, arguing that they wanted to replace the

Yugoslav federation with a 'confederation', specified the kind of confederation they wanted by pointing to Scandinavia.

Scandinavia is a confederation? I asked.

Sure, they said. It has SAS.

Perhaps the Scandinavian countries were 'mature' enough not to need their own airlines. If so, they were the only ones. An airline proved you existed in places that counted, like Frankfurt and London. It was a fleet of carrier pigeons delivering the national message. Romania had no food, and practically no government, but it had the airline Tarom, and in every airport in Europe you could look at the arrivals board and feel that somehow the essence of Romania was perfectly evoked by the fact that the two-hour flight from Bucharest was eleven hours late. JAT had the suggestive habit of seldom being able to assure you in advance whether your flight from, say, New York would land first in Zagreb and then go on to Belgrade, or vice versa. Sometimes the landing order would be switched in mid-flight, screwing up everybody's connections, and you had to wonder if the Serb pilot and the Croat co-pilot had been arm-wrestling for the honour in the cockpit.

So now Croatia had an airline before it had airspace. The company's logo was a šahovnica shaped like a B-2 bomber.

Radio 101 was a block farther on, above the kind of youth centre you could still find in many European cities — a tattered café, a smoke-fogged bar below ground, a video-game room, a courtyard of posters and cigarette butts where students wearing scarves talked earnestly and punks with black teeth and exploded sneakers nursed their morning beers. In this case, the youth centre had technically been under the aegis of the Communist Youth League. It had functioned like a red-light district, where the illicit was sanctioned, within limits.

Naturally, the youth of Zagreb had wanted to test those limits, and the best place to do it had been the dinky radio station upstairs, so in the mid-80s they had started broadcasting iconoclastic news coverage mixed with the latest music from the west and irreverent satires of Titoism, the Army, the current leaders and the taboo ethnic issue. One of their most popular weekly satires was called 'Naughty Boys', in which each 'boy', speaking in the appropriate dialect and playing on the accepted stereotypes, represented one of the nationalities. Part of the humour was that the Naughty Boys fought all the time. Nino was one of them.

As an early punishment, the city council summarily changed the station's assigned frequency, apparently hoping that listeners would have trouble finding Radio 101 if it was not actually at 101 on the dial. In addition, the station was consistently refused its application for an AM permit, despite huge swathes of space on the airwaves.

One might ask why the authorities didn't just shut it down. For one thing, that wasn't Yugoslavia's style. Among the European Communist countries, Yugoslavia had always specialized in an absurd, half-assed sort of harassment, which appeared to spring from a knee-jerk repression response unbacked by the will to carry through. (If Dubček represented 'Communism with a human face', Titoism was Communism in a fright wig.)

But there was another reason. Radio 101 made tons of money. Advertisers knew that, at least within the limited area in which 101 could be heard, it enjoyed a ninety-two per cent audience share among eighteen- to forty-year-olds. This was not only because of its politics, but because it played David Byrne and Public Enemy and Red Hot Chili Peppers while the big stations played assorted lounge lizards named Darko and Željko crooning 'new-composed folk music'. None of 101's reporters, announcers or DJs were paid well, so all that money was disappearing into the coffers of the Communist Youth League. This was a gadfly that laid golden eggs.

The radio station's rooms consisted of two cluttered studios, the General Director's office and a single small loft space for news preparation, divided into compartments for culture, sports and politics by cabinets of gouged blond wood with sagging shelves. The two phones were constantly busy, and both had locks that made it impossible to call long-distance without authorization. There were no computers, of course, nor even electric typewriters, but a fleet of stripped-down reel-to-reel manuals — sticking keys, filled-in 'e's and all – made in Sarajevo, on which reporters pounded out news items in duplicate, using carbon paper.

Silvija ran in, scrabbled through a sea of sheets on the work table and disappeared again reading an item. I knew better than to bother her the day before her weekly programme, but Nataša had a few spare minutes, and Nino was waiting for the smaller studio to open up, so we went down to the café next door to the youth centre. I saw that the Archaeological Museum across the street was open and thought somewhat snidely that perhaps history that far back did not have to be rewritten.

I noticed as we talked how much angrier Nino was than last year. Back then, he had still called himself a Yugoslav, and talked about his Serb friends in Belgrade. He had argued that Croatia's best hope for becoming 'European' and 'mature' lay in its middling position between east and west, between Catholicism and Orthodoxy, its Habsburg legacy of cosmopolitanism. In that sense, Croatia was the most central country of Central Europe, he had argued. But the HDZ was moving in the opposite direction, towards isolation and 'purity'. The nationalists who dressed up in costumes were in danger of becoming like Scots with their kilts and bagpipes, transforming themselves into wax-work tourist kitsch, something quaint and marginal.

But that was last year. Now he said he wished he could be Yugoslav, but the category no longer existed. 'The Serbs killed it,' he said. 'To say you are a Yugoslav now is to say you are pro-Serb. When Serbs say they want to save Yugoslavia, they are playing dirty. "Yugoslavia" sounds nice, but it is the perfect playing field for Serbs.'

And his friends in Belgrade?

'I can't talk to them. Nobody understands Croats now.' The last time he had gone to Belgrade he had drawn on his talents as a mimic and spoken in Ekavian, the predominantly Serb dialect.

Last week he had gone to Spain to attend a convention of the Jeunesse Européenne Fédéraliste, and when the story of Borovo Selo broke, the delegates to the International Seminar on Regionalism sent a cable to 'the people of Yugoslavia' and the various presidents, urging in a young, self-important way that 'finally' a solution be found for this 'absurd situation' – namely a 'federalist solution'. Nino showed me a photo of the delegates to the seminar, he among them. They stood on a sidewalk in Madrid with happy smiles, young people from all over Europe, bright and hopeful and federalist. They seemed to be thinking, *We* get along. Why don't you?

Nino would have agreed with them last year, but this year he kept thinking of the Catalans. 'They don't even have the rights that Croats did in Yugoslavia,' he said, amazed. 'I kept telling these people, "Look around you! Wake up! You've got the Basques, the Corsicans, the Flemish . . ." For the past two years we've seen a movement of western democracy east. Very nice. Now we'll start to see a wave in the opposite direction, from east to west, of nationalism. Europe will find out that making a federation is only the beginning of its problems.'

He had argued a similar point last night, and it occurred to me that behind his insistence lay a desire to believe that the Balkans were not a special case. That is, they were no more primitive than the next powder keg. And of course he may have been right.

Silvija hurried by, looking for someone, then consented to join us for a quick coffee. We talked about changes at the radio station since the HDZ took over. Nino, Nataša and Silvija all agreed that things had been better under the Communists.

'The old ones were corrupt and inept,' Silvija said, 'but they were also tired. Communism meant nothing to them but an easy job. But these HDZ people actually *believe* in their programme, so they're much harder to deal with.'

'You'll never guess who the new General Director is,' Nataša said.

'Gamilec is out?' I asked.

'On the street,' Nino chuckled happily.

The Communists' appointee, Nikola Gamilec, had been a tweedy man with a bushy beard and small round wire-rimmed glasses, who had looked so much the part of a politically engaged radio director that I was several minutes into an interview with him before I realized he knew nothing about the radio, and

40

apparently nothing about politics. He delivered platitudes one after the other, with pained concentration, as if struggling to give birth to great ideas. He came to work late every morning and sat in his dim bare office and had people bring him coffee while he read the paper, and slipped out early. He scrupulously avoided me after the interview. He seemed a timid man.

As for the new director, since Nataša's question implied it was someone I knew, and not the best choice, I automatically thought of the worst – one of the junior reporters last year, a thin man with paranoid eyes who had always stared at me obliquely out of corners and from behind door jambs, but refused to speak to me directly and warned everyone that I was a CIA agent. He had fought with Nino, accusing him of bias against the HDZ, saying, 'We won't put up with that after the elections.'

'Igor Ćopo,' I said jokingly.

'Somebody already told you!' Nino said.

'You're kidding! He's really the Director? How did that happen?'

'Quietly,' Silvija said, fatigued.

'Couldn't you do anything about it?'

'What to do?' Nataša asked.

'It just happened,' Silvija shrugged.

They were resigned. This was how things worked.

'But couldn't you . . . protest?' I was being a western sheep.

'I just don't talk to him,' Silvija said. 'I haven't spoken to him in five months.'

That was not strictly true. Only a couple of days ago she had threatened to resign when Ćopo told her she couldn't air an interview with the leader of one of the opposition parties, saying, 'We can't have just anyone off the street on the radio.' This had come on the heels of a disturbing incident in which Silvija had noticed that a report she had written had been altered by the announcer. For every instance in which she had written 'Croatian politics', the announcer had read 'the democratic politics of the Republic of Croatia'. For a later broadcast, Silvija told Nataša to change the phrase back, after which an order came down from Ćopo. Whoever had tampered with the text was to be suspended for a month. He meant Nataša, not the original announcer. Nataša had returned to work only last week.

'We never had suspensions under the Communists,' Silvija said.

That the HDZ had proved to be even less tolerant of free speech than the Communists surprised no one at the table. Radio 101 had had trouble from HDZ supporters during the elections. One of the HDZ candidates for the Parliament had died – of natural causes – after the first round of voting, and Nataša, reporting the news half-asleep at two in the morning, accidentally read out the name of the wrong HDZ man. Dimly suspecting mockery, or a 'provocation' (to use Communist terminology), or who knows what, half a dozen HDZ gorillas (as Nino always called them) showed up at the station the next day and physically threatened the reporters. For the next few days Nino stayed late at the offices to accompany Nataša home.

At around the same time, self-appointed HDZ watchdogs started patrolling their own apartment houses, demanding of anyone who came or went what he was doing. 'These people are like the brownshirts,' one friend told me after he had been accosted by a particularly truculent stranger outside his room. 'The police might have hit you over the head, but at least they always showed you their ID.'

Nino said bitterly, 'My father had to live down the fact that *his* father was Ustasha. Now I have to live down the fact that *my* father is Communist.'

At this point, I could write something condescending about traditions of democracy not developing overnight, except that some of the people with the most totalitarian leanings during the elections had been the émigrés from Australia and Canada, and the self-appointed 'election monitors' from the US. These latter were people from private organizations with names like Lawyers for Democratic Reforms who held the solipsistic belief that a free election could not occur anywhere on the planet unless at least one American was present to observe it. They did not speak a word of Serbo-Croatian and did not seem to know that the election commissions they so mistrusted were made up of representatives from all the parties. Knowing only that the western

42

media had anointed the HDZ as *the* party opposing the Communists, they would have viewed any outcome other than a sweeping HDZ victory as highly suspicious, and if you expressed any opposition to the HDZ it meant you were a Communist, which, in the best of all possible worlds, would disqualify you from voting.

Why not? The Communists were not people, but a malignant abstraction. I remembered Jim, a tidy young American conservative whose speciality was interfering in Central America but who was moonlighting, excitedly telling me how he had 'actual photographs – incredible! an exclusive! – of *Communists* counting ballots', as if he had seen monkeys typing *Hamlet*. When confronted with Nino, who lost no time saying he thought the HDZ and the Communists had a lot in common, Jim literally backed away, pulling me with him. Then a group of Australians who had heard I was from the *New York Times* wondered if I was the correspondent who had written something critical of the HDZ the previous week, and Jim had to clear a path for me, assuring them I was somebody else, while they growled, '*That's* good,' and massaged their knuckles.

Did they know that Tudjman, too, had been a Communist? Did they know that almost everyone now heading a party had been? Tudjman used to brag that he had been the youngest Partisan general in World War II, although now his followers insisted that he had met Tito only twice. (Tudjman himself, when I asked him, modestly demurred, 'Well, three or four times.')

Silvija had to get back to work, so we all returned to the offices. When we reached the top of the stairs I saw Ćopo for the first time this year. He was a new man. No longer lurking in the corners, he stood full in the doorway of the newsroom, surveying his workers, tapping a pair of dark glasses against his thumb. When he caught sight of me he swept the glasses over his eyes with a suave gesture, turned on his heel and headed for the Director's office with what could only be called a swagger.

Radio 101 still made good money, some of which went into Ćopo's generous salary, and the rest into the HDZ coffers. The newsroom had not been improved, and the reporters were getting

43

paid no more than before. One difference from the previous era was that the reporters had begun to fight among themselves. As relations with Serbia grew worse, more of them believed it was their patriotic duty to support the HDZ and, if necessary, screen the news. Some of them no longer recognized their own filters. In that way 101 had, indeed, become westernized. Censorship was becoming an unconscious process.

The same hardening of views had occurred among the Naughty Boys, and although Nino was still in the show – it had moved to a bigger radio station and was paying much better, about $650 a month – he was disgusted with it, and continued only because he needed the money. Like the reporters, the Naughty Boys now fought for real, both over the tone of the show and over money matters. There had been a falling-out over a recording contract.

Nino much preferred a programme he had started at 101 during the elections the previous year, even though it paid him only half what Naughty Boys did. In 'The Piček Saga' he played an old Croat man called Dida ('Grandad') while his friend Jadranka played Dida's daughter-in-law, a Muslim. The series had begun with the two of them breaking into a broadcast as though they were real people who had come to Radio 101 looking for help in locating Dida's son, a man named Eogen Ćiro Piček, who had disappeared a few days before during one of the Serb nationalist rallies that Milošević was orchestrating around the country at that time. As with 'Naughty Boys', the humour centred on ethnic issues, and the show became very popular. Like a hapless everyman lost in the whirl of his disintegrating country, Piček was glimpsed briefly at HDZ rallies, anti-military protests, polling stations, or having his picture taken next to Ban Jelačić. But he always disappeared again.

Then something unexpected happened. People started calling in to the radio to report that they might have spotted Piček too. Others called to ask if he had been found yet, and expressed concern for the family. One man called to announce, with all apparent seriousness, that *he* was Piček, and they could stop looking for him.

Nino was stunned. He found it funny and exhilarating, but

also somewhat sobering, that people could believe something so patently fictional just because it was on the radio. (For one thing, the name 'Piček' should have been a giveaway, since *pička* in Croatian is a common swearword meaning 'cunt'.) I appeared briefly that year on Nino's show as a stupid American reporter from the *New York Times* doing a piece on the missing Piček, and Nino told me later that the episode had convinced even more people that the show was real. If anything had more power to convince, to mesmerize, than the (non-Communist) local media, it was the western media.

8

In Belgrade in 1990 I had watched the Eurovision Song Contest one night on television with Serb friends.

For the first time, the contest was being held in Yugoslavia, because a singer from Zagreb had won the previous year, and my friends, acutely aware that all Europe was watching, were anxious that the production go off without embarrassing glitches. As the broadcast began, as the camera swept dizzyingly down from the ceiling of the specially designed hall in Zagreb and across a stage lit by flashing floor panels while computer graphics swirled across the screen, a sigh of relief went around the room. It looked professional. It looked like Europe.

In Yugoslavia's pantheon of national stereotypes, Slovenes were honest but cold. Serbs were simple and impulsive. Muslims were slippery and untrustworthy. And Croats were the smartypants, the talkers and complainers, the ones with the superficial shine. The Croats were the right ones to be hosting the contest, the Serbs conceded. Also right, as Yugoslavia's entry, was the singer from Zagreb who had won the year before. There remained enough fellow-feeling then that the Serbs could feel she represented all of Yugoslavia. And how western could you get? She made herself up to look like Marilyn Monroe.

45

I had never seen the Eurovision Song Contest before and had imagined it was a celebration of the diverse musical heritage of Europe – German *Lieder* about forests and mushrooms, twanging Greek dances with howling clarinets, Bosnian love songs in stark unison. I was amazed, perhaps naïvely, to find that all the groups sang the same kind of plastic commercial-jingle music that made American or English pop sound gritty and vital – if you could believe that.

But technically, anyway, the show proceeded without a hitch. The M.C., a popular quiz show host in Zagreb, was suave and capable, speaking English, French, German, and Italian fluently. None of the lights exploded, nobody tripped over a cord and killed the power, the mikes never squealed. My friends breathed more easily. The proudest moment came during the judging, when panels from every country in Europe called in with their point tallies. One by one, countries like France and Germany and England were on the line, beginning with 'Greetings to Yugoslavia!' The signals were loud and clear. What better proof than this crystalline reception that Yugoslavia was not a primitive Balkan backwater, but a part of Europe? France sounded like it was calling from the next room.

Then came the turn of the Yugoslav jury, which had gathered in Zadar, a city on the coast. 'Hello?' said the MC in Zagreb. 'Hello? Zadar, are you there?'

Nothing.

My friends groaned.

'Zadar, hello?'

A crackling came over the line. The pale voice of a ghost murmured sadly.

'I couldn't hear that, Zadar. Hello, are you there?'

A low moan. The line went dead.

My friends' heads were in their hands.

Eventually the call came through, but the mood of relief and pride had been broken. What had they expected? my friends asked each other in anguish. Just go out to the main pedestrian zone of Belgrade, the *capital of Yugoslavia*, and try the public phones. None of them worked!

46

The kind of music we had heard that evening was all of a piece with what the contest represented, so poignantly, to my friends. The Eurovision Song Contest was an affirmation of togetherness, not only because all of Europe sat down at the same time to watch the same programme, but because the contestants, when they opened their mouths, all sang the same thing. Marilyn Monroe had done it, too, and had sounded to me no worse than the others, and had come in seventh out of some two dozen – not bad, but not good enough to erase the Zadar débâcle.

The Italians won that year, with a song called 'Europe: 1992'. It was about the European economic union.

A year had gone by. The Song Contest was back, hosted by Italy. The contest had actually taken place the previous week, but the Borovo Selo massacre had just occurred, and Zagreb TV decided to postpone the broadcast. If the Yugoslav jury had been in Zadar again, its calls would have gone nowhere. Zadar was surrounded by Serb insurgents, and had had no water or electricity for days.

I watched the contest with Nino and a friend of his, an engineering student named Vesna. The Yugoslav entry was a singer from Serbia, and Nino and Vesna expressed disgust.

'In the last few years Yugoslavia has always done pretty well,' Vesna explained, 'because the singers were always from Zagreb. But the Serbs couldn't stand it any more, and they forced this "Baby Doll" on us.'

'She's bad,' Nino said.

'You won't believe how bad she is.'

'It's embarrassing.'

As this was a delayed broadcast, Nino and Vesna already knew that Baby Doll (instead of making herself up to look like Marilyn Monroe, she used an English stage name) had finished in second-to-last place. 'Of course,' Nino grumbled. 'Stupid Serbs.'

Part of Nino's disgruntlement arose, I sensed, from the fact that, just the week before, a Spanish delegate to the Jeunesse Européenne Fédéraliste convention had laughed to him in an easy manner about the lousy Zagreb production the previous year, as if both he and Nino knew that the very idea of holding the contest in Yugoslavia was a 'hoke'. (The delegates spoke to each other in EuroEnglish, and he had meant 'joke'.)

'OK,' Nino said to me, trying to neutralize the insult by agreeing with it, 'the show was terrible, I know that.'

'It wasn't terrible,' I said, and meant it. It had been put together at least as well, if not better, than the Italian production we were now watching. But I would have said it even if I hadn't meant it. Nino didn't even like the contest. He hated the music. But the Spaniard's comments had obviously hurt his feelings.

I pointed out that the Italian host this year was an utter klutz who could only speak Italian. But Nino still fretted. Baby Doll came on in a loud aquamarine costume, and Nino and Vesna could hardly watch, they were so mortified. The voting began, and Baby Doll headed for her predetermined spot at the bottom.

Then there was a mechanical glitch. Nino and Vesna crowed with delight, cat-called and threw things at the screen. 'What a hoke!' Nino cried.

But somehow it wasn't enough. No matter how badly the Italians screwed up, they didn't look embarrassed. And like Americans, they considered it perfectly natural that they couldn't speak a word of any language but their own.

Perhaps the polyglot display by the Zagreb MC the year before had been a little *too* suave. The vulgar showing-off of the upstart, perhaps?

9

Silvija never allowed me to make coffee in the mornings. Even Nino and Nataša could not brew it as well as she did, because her family came from Bosnia, where the Turkish legacy was the strongest, the coffee the most authentic. When the water boiled, she added it to the dust-fine grounds in the *džezva*, a truncated brass cone with a straight handle, and returned it to the fire until it frothed to the lip, removed it for a few seconds, and returned it to froth a second time. It was so thick it slithered into your cup, with a foaming crown of mud that slowly submerged. Strictly speaking, Bosnian tradition required that you dip a sugar cube into your coffee and suck on it, then drink the coffee bitter, but Nino, Nataša and Silvija all preferred, a little shame-facedly, to drop in pinhead tablets they called 'diabetic sugar', which they assured me was healthier.

Sometimes Silvija's boyfriend Robbie joined us. He was a short, solidly built man of striking handsomeness who did not sleep at home because he was hiding from the reserves. All men in Yugoslavia, at the end of their compulsory year of military service, were assigned to a reserve unit, either in the Army or in the various territorial defence forces. Nino had been lucky. He had been assigned to a Croatian territorial defence reserve unit near Karlovac that the Croatian government probably would not mobilize, because a lot of Serbs were living in that particular area. Robbie had been assigned to the army reserves, and since the Army was still trying to preserve an image of neutrality it was calling up soldiers from all the republics. When Robbie was at home, he never answered the phone until friends shouted through the answering machine, 'Robbie! It's not the Army! Pick up the phone!'

Breakfasts consisted of cheese and bread, spring onions and pale rose sausage slices oozing water, which Nino brought up from the privately owned grocery at the bottom of the street. Being American and, when at home, a vegetarian, I added leafy greens, which I munched on one morning while reading an article in the paper about the high levels of lead in Zagreb's produce owing to the fact that so much of it came from private gardens planted on unused strips of public land, such as the dividers of highways. (There was no such thing as unleaded gasoline in Yugoslavia.) Breakfasts started mid-morning and lasted long, until Nino was an hour or two late for his job at the Student Club, and Silvija or Nataša had a meeting in two minutes at the radio station. At the last second Silvija would call a taxi, which cost ten times as much as the tram, turning to me and saying, 'We

49

have a problem with taxis,' the way you might say you had a problem with alcohol.

Silvija usually spent the mornings in a slow smoulder of fatigue and disgust, her small mouth quietly miserable. She was sick of the radio, sick of press conferences, sick of fighting with the director above her and the new converts to Croatism below. Nothing was clear any more. I ventured one morning that she looked nice, as she did, in creamy pink lipstick, a silver jacket and skirt with black stockings patterned with flowers, and she answered in a monotone, her eyes invisible behind the black bars of her lowered eyelashes, 'Very. I feel very nice. I feel like killing someone today.' Later, Nino confided to me that he and Nataša were worried about her. She had started to hate the Serbs too much.

The sunnier days I spent walking around the city, seeing what had changed since last year, what was new. The fruit trees in the suburbs and the horse-chestnuts in the parks were in full bloom. Zagreb still had no McDonald's, the acquiring of which was considered to be an essential milestone on the road to becoming convincingly European (that is to say, Americanized), even though Belgrade now had three. The explanation was that Genex owned the franchise and Genex was a Serbian company.

'Hum-Hum and Humby are better anyway,' sniffed Silvija. But it seemed to me like she was putting on a brave face.

Here and there, tattered posters of Tudjman and his slogan, 'We alone will decide the destiny of our Croatia,' still hung on walls, all the colours except blue burned out of them by the sun. In nearby cafés, people read newspapers with headlines such as ARMY HAS SECRET PLAN FOR SURROUNDING ZAGREB. The irony was so cheap I hesitated to note it down. But there it was.

People seemed to do little but read the papers. I walked from one café of rustling pages to the next. People read the respectable paper, *Vjesnik* (*Herald*), or the tabloid *Večernji List* (*Evening Paper*) or the 'dirty paper', *Slobodni Tjednik* (*Free Weekly*), all of them Croatian, and peddling, in their varying styles, the Croatian point of view. I never saw anyone reading the Belgrade daily, *Politika*, which had been the most respected paper in Yugoslavia before Milošević turned it into his personal mouthpiece, a hate-mongering rag. More disappointingly, I also never saw anyone reading the magazine *Vreme (Time)* which was written by Serb journalists whom Milošević had purged, and which Nataša and Nino called 'the best magazine in Yugoslavia' (although Silvija, smouldering, refused to read it), or *Oslobodjenje (Liberation)*, the Sarajevo paper, both of which might have offered them a different perspective on events.

Nor was anyone reading *Borba (Struggle)*, the paper of the Yugoslav Communist Party. In what seemed an apt symbol for the balancing act that has always been Yugoslavism, *Borba* mixed Cyrillic (the script used by Serbs, Montenegrins and Macedonians) with the Latin script, according to a complicated formula. The front page alternated from day to day, and if it was in, say, Cyrillic, then the following two pages would be in Latin, the fourth in Cyrillic, the fifth Latin, the sixth and seventh Cyrillic, and so on.

Wandering into bookstores, I noted the new titles on Croatian history, Croatian folk customs. I admired the fat Croatian–English and Croatian–German dictionaries. (The older dictionaries, which admitted the existence of a language called Croato-Serbian, had all disappeared.) In the display windows lay Tudjman's books: *The National Question in Contemporary Europe*, *The Nation-State: Key to the Peace of Europe*, and, of course, *Wasteland: The Historical Realities*, the book in which Tudjman argued that only about thirty-five thousand Serbs had died in Jasenovac, the worst of the World War II concentration camps, not the half-million or million that Serbs claimed.

It was impossible in Yugoslavia to escape this counting of corpses. Nataša had shown me a book she kept in her bedroom, *Yugoslav Population Losses during World War II*, which consisted almost entirely of graphs and tables – census reports, records from post-war refugee camps, emigration statistics, birth rates, natural death rates – which the author crushed, combined and mixed to produce, like alchemical gold, the final table of grand totals of the dead:

237,000 Partisans (from all ethnic groups)
285,000 peasants killed in village massacres (all ethnic groups)
216,000 murdered in the camps, including Jasenovac (mainly Serbs and Jews)
209,000 quislings and collaborators (mainly Croats).

For Nataša, the truth of the book was self-evident. How could anything so detailed be inaccurate?

And perhaps it *was* accurate. How could I know? But my suspicions were aroused by a simple fact: the numbers were more or less equal. It was exactly what made me sceptical of Tudjman's estimate of thirty-five thousand for Jasenovac. Jasenovac, for the Serbs, was *the* symbol of the genocide committed against them. For the Croats, that symbol was Bleiburg. Some Croats said half a million had been executed at Bleiburg, but Tudjman, interestingly enough, had told me that was a wild exaggeration. (Bleiburg was a Partisan crime, and Tudjman had been a Partisan, and he was still proud enough of that fact to assure me he had met Tito thrice, not twice.) And how many people did Tudjman estimate to have died at Bleiburg? Thirty-five thousand.

The competing death tolls from fifty years ago were not merely cold statistics. As the Serbs shouted their own figures louder and louder, they sounded more and more to the Croats like *guidelines*. There was a far more urgent reason than mere historical accuracy to balance the sheets.

When I walked, I kept returning to Jelačić Square. It was considered the centre of the city, but that only dated to the nineteenth century. The older core was the Upper Town, situated on two low hills, Kaptol and Grič, just north of Jelačić Square, where the bulky embossed buildings of Franz Josef's reign gave way to Baroque palaces and churches, cobblestoned streets and staircases, a few remnants of medieval walls and gates. In the Middle Ages, each hill had had its own settlement with its own fortifications, the canons and lay clerks settling around the cathedral on Kaptol, the craftsmen living on Grič in a walled enclosure known as Gradec. In 1242, the Hungarian King Béla

IV conferred on Gradec the status of a Free Royal City in gratitude for its walls having protected him at one stage in his headlong flight from the Mongols the year before. The churchmen of Kaptol never got used to the new civil rights of their neighbours on Gradec, and the two groups battled each other so often down at the stream separating the two hills that the crossing became known as Bloody Bridge. Only the Turks brought them together.

The stream had long since been enclosed, and Bloody Bridge was now a narrow street between a café and a jewellery store, from which I headed up towards Gradec. On the left, I passed the building where the intellectuals of the Coalition had thrown their party on the night of the elections, before they realized no one had voted for them. While Tudjman's hordes roasted entire cows out in the housing projects where the HDZ's main strength was to be found, the Coalition drank home-made wine out of a fifty-gallon plastic drum and spent the evening on the phone to an émigré radio station in Canada. One after another, they speechified in pendulous tones, as though their words were going straight into the history books, while some old-guardist at the telephone exchange kept cutting the line.

I passed into Gradec proper through the Stone Gate, a dark passageway which was also a chapel, the central icon being a representation of the Madonna and child which had miraculously survived a fire in 1731. In my visits of previous years, there had usually been one or two elderly worshippers in the dark, but this year I was always a little stunned by the shimmering bank of candles, the press of young people on their knees in the pews or on the cobblestones, or caressing the iron grating that protected the Madonna, the young soldiers kissing the crosses hanging from their necks. When I walked through with Nino, he sneered, once we were out of earshot, saying that for most of those people it was just the fashionable thing to do, a way to feel like Croats.

'Why didn't they go to church before?' he asked. 'It has never been illegal here. Even in the 50s, the only people who couldn't go to church were Party members.' Christmas services, on the other hand, had always been packed. When they ended at midnight, with the ringing of the bells, some of the worshippers would invariably go around smashing the windscreens of any cars with Belgrade plates.

At the centre of Gradec lay Stjepan Radić Square, named after the head of the Croat Peasant Party in the 1920s, a respected and popular figure and perhaps the best leader the Croats had ever had, who was shot to death along with two other Croat deputies on the floor of the Parliament in 1928 by a representative from Montenegro. The Croats said the Serbs killed him, while the Serbs responded heatedly that the assassin was not Serb, but Montenegrin, thus upholding an ethnic distinction whose existence they otherwise denied.

On the north side of the square I checked the door of the old Information Ministry, where in past visits female press liaison officers had served me coffee and politely steered me away from things I wanted to know, but the door was locked and the brass plaques removed. On the east side stood the Croatian Parliament, and on the west, the Baroque palace which had once housed the Croatian ban and had become, under Tito, a hall for the grander sort of receptions. Tudjman, who had a good nose for swank, had turned it into his presidential palace.

The thirteenth-century church of St Mark occupied the middle of the square, and when I went into its crypt-like interior I saw that it, too, was full. Women were saying the rosary. One sat in the gallery at the west end chanting the Hail Mary, while the others huddled in the choir responding with the 'Holy Mary' in unison. The sound of their voices glowed in the stony dark, a soft, tuneful, eerie muttering, like rain puttering on a hollow block. On the wall, a muscular Jesus emerged warrior-like from the baptismal stream.

Several of the Catholic churches in Zagreb were being renovated. Scaffolding surrounded the tower of St Mark's, and in the next square plasterers were restoring the interior of the high Baroque church of St Catherine to its pink and white sugary splendour. On the other hill, stonemasons were replacing acid-worn finials on the neo-Gothic façade of the cathedral. One of them told me that the cathedral's patron, St Stephen, had been a Croat, which was nonsense. He had been the son of Geza and

Sarolta, both Magyars, and became the first Christian King of Hungary. His crown, virtually a religious relic for the Hungarians and a symbol of their statehood, lay in state in Budapest.

But a little confusion was natural at a time when the Croats were busily reclaiming their own. Inside the cathedral I came across a marble bas-relief by Ivan Meštrović of Cardinal Alojzije Stepinac, who had been Archbishop of Zagreb during the Ustasha regime. He had proclaimed the foundation of the Independent State of Croatia from the pulpit of this very cathedral on Easter Day 1941. Throughout the war he gave his public support to the Ustashas, referred to Ante Pavelić as 'our glorious leader' and disingenuously welcomed, as a wholly coincidental working of God's grace in the hearts of Serbs, the suddenly high number of conversions of the Orthodox to Catholicism on Croatian territory, which he estimated at 240,000. (Mass conversions were held with armed Ustashas present. Jews were not allowed to convert; as neither were most intellectuals, students, priests or village leaders. Their conversions were considered 'insincere', and they were shot instead.) In the last days of the war, Stepinac appealed over the radio for the populace to rally against the advancing Allies, and a year later he explained to a British officer that he had chosen to support Fascism because the alternative had been Communism, and he hoped that the West would 'use its atomic power to impose western civilization on Moscow and Belgrade before it was too late'. In 1946 he was tried and convicted for wartime collaboration and sentenced to 16 years in prison, of which he served five. He died in his native village in 1960.

And here he was on the wall of his cathedral, in Meštrović's stiff, polished style, kneeling in front of Christ, who bent over him protectively, His hand stretched to the cardinal's head in blessing. A guide was showing the work to a group of tired, blank-eyed French tourists, and he pointed out that the work had been executed in Detroit, explaining simply: 'All the intelligent Croats left Croatia after the war.'

The Communists had renamed one square in every city and town in Yugoslavia 'Brotherhood and Unity', and in Zagreb that square, significantly, was the one that abutted the Serbian Orthodox church. Also significantly, the *zagrepčani* never called it Brotherhood and Unity Square, but Flower Square, after the flower market that took place there daily, or Preradović Square, for the Croatian poet whose statue stood in it. On the evening that I attended a vespers service in the Orthodox church there were perhaps two dozen worshippers – pretty good for vespers, and especially for Serbs, who fiercely identified with their church as a national symbol, but didn't actually attend services in anything like the numbers that the Catholic Croats did.

Some twenty thousand Serbs were living in Zagreb, and, as Nino had pointed out to me, the Serbs who were establishing *de facto* autonomy with their militias in the Krajina were doing no favours for their brethren living here, who had to face the deteriorating relations with the Croats all around them. In fact, although the Krajina had a large Serb majority, most Serbs living in Croatia did not live in the Krajina. In the Catholic sermons of Zagreb I had heard 'Croatia' or 'Croatian people' so often it became comical, if also mildly revolting. For the prayer portion of the Orthodox vespers service the two priests never once mentioned Croatia, nor for that matter the Krajina. They prayed for Yugoslavia. Chanted in the dark mode of Orthodox hymn melodies, their words sounded appropriately sad and other-worldly, like a prayer for the dead. Then the older priest swung the censer.

Although the history museums were closed for 'updating', there were several shows celebrating the glories of Croatian culture. At an exhibition of 'One Thousand Years of Croatian Sculpture' in a huge gallery in the Upper Town, the guards were on duty, the garderobe was open, the long rows of rooms were well-lit and waiting, and not once in three hours did I see another person. That evening I returned to find the apartment locked and empty, so I wrote notes on the terrace of the restaurant at the bottom of the street and there, too, I was utterly alone. Now and then the waiter would stand in the doorway and gaze into the quiet darkness, and at eleven he went around folding, with great care, the spotless tablecloths and napkins. For some reason, the fact that he did this without saying a word to me seemed especially sad. That night Milan Paroški, a member of the Serbian Parliament (and another favourite of the Croatian media, since he was as nuts as Šešelj), appeared on TV saying, 'If anyone now says Krajina is part of Croatia, you can kill him like a dog,' and Nino, bitter and frightened, responded, 'Yes, this is how they will kill us like dogs, by taking tourists hostage, by scaring them all away. So that there will be no witnesses.' That is, no western witnesses. As the Nazis had known, only western witnesses counted.

Evenings in the apartment lasted until two or three, in a thick haze of cigarette smoke, propelled by conversation, coffee, an orange-flavoured vitamin drink, and the propolis drops Nino and Silvija added to it as another health measure. On no account could the television news be missed. Silvija watched it with her pocket tape recorder turned on.

Dominating the broadcasts for the moment was the issue of the upcoming rotation in the Yugoslav collective Presidency. The current President of the Presidency, Borisav Jović, a Serb, was due to yield his place in a few days to Stipe Mesić, a Croat. The one-year position had never held much power, but in unexpected situations constitutions – even never-neverland constitutions like Yugoslavia's – could create unexpected powers. The Federal Presidency happened to be Commander-in-Chief of the Yugoslav Army, and the President of the Presidency, who could wield only one vote like any other member, happened to enjoy one small, extra power. He was the only member who could call an emergency meeting.

Every time a Serb militia clashed with a Croat police force, Jović called an emergency session and the Presidency, following a close vote, directed the Army to intervene and restore order. The Army was still officially neutral, but the way the Croats perceived it was that a Serb militia would attack an area, and after a couple of days of fighting the Army would roll in to 'separate the sides'. Then the Army would stay where it was, while the militia penetrated deeper – after which the army would roll forward again to 'separate the sides'.

Stipe Mesić had already promised he would not be calling

emergency sessions at the drop of a hat. He had also predicted that he would be 'the last President of Yugoslavia'.

'The Serbs won't allow the rotation to happen,' Nino said with certainty.

'How?' Nataša asked. 'It's automatic.'

'They'll think of something. They'll do what they want.'

Later in the evenings came the multi-part docudrama on the Bleiburg massacre, which everyone watched as avidly as they did the news. Finally, very late, only after all other programmes had ended, Zagreb TV broadcast the news from Yutel, a new station in Sarajevo that drew on reporters from all over Yugoslavia in an attempt to provide, if not objective coverage, at least competing biases. Tudjman had recently threatened to ban the broadcasting of Yutel in Croatia, citing a general anti-Croat slant. When asked at a press conference to specify his complaint, the only thing he could think of was that Yutel used too much Cyrillic.

10

On a bright Sunday afternoon, Danko and Nika picked up Nataša, Nino and me and drove us out of town. As we crossed the Sava into New Zagreb, Nino pointed out a large glass building under construction.

'The new national library,' he said. 'We'll be able to fit all Croatian literature in there when we're done.' I turned to look at the cranes and girders as we passed. 'And when the Serbs are done,' he added, 'we'll be able to fit all of Croatia in there.'

The others in the car snickered, but Nino didn't seem to register it. He was in something of a funk because Silvija and Nataša had listened to his Piček broadcast that morning without laughing once. Perhaps he had realized that, in fact, the sketch was too close to the truth to be funny. He was finding himself confronted by the comedian's classic dilemma – a reality nearly indistinguishable from parody.

58

We left the serried ranks of New Zagreb's apartment complexes behind. Lush hills rose on the left. Danko hit a button and the power windows of his Honda Accord slid up. He slipped in a tape, and Aretha Franklin demanded respect from four hidden speakers.

'Nice, huh?' Nino said, running his palms over the nap of the slate-blue seats.

'Very,' I obliged.

In Yugoslavia a car like this cost an astronomical amount, but as a professional basketball player Danko could afford it. His team, Cibona, had once belonged to an all-Yugoslav league, but a new Croatian league had been formed, with ties to other European leagues. Now, instead of going to Belgrade or Sarajevo to play, Danko flew to Italy. Nika was his girlfriend, a tall, dark-complexioned twenty-year-old who liked to wear gold bangles, and copper earrings the size of pocket watches to set off her swan's neck. People mistook her shyness for hauteur. A student of American literature, she spoke perfect English on the rare occasions when she could be coaxed into saying anything.

'If I ever have the money to buy a car,' Nino was saying, from far down in his seat, 'I'll register it in Vienna, so it'll have Austrian plates. If you have a ZG on your plate, you can kiss the car goodbye if you go to Serbia, or even try to get through to the coast. You have Zagreb plates, don't you, Danko?'

'Yes.'

'You'll notice he's driving north-west,' Nino said to me.

We were headed for Mokrice, a castle about twenty-five kilometres out of Zagreb, just across the Slovenian border. I asked Danko what he thought would happen when Slovenia declared its independence from Yugoslavia in six weeks.

'They'll get away with it,' he said confidently. 'For them, the Serbs say, "You want to go? Then go! Get the fuck out of here!"'

'Not for us,' Nika said.

'There aren't any Serbs living in Slovenia,' Danko said.

'All power to 'em,' Nino said, referring to the Slovenes. 'They've done it right from the beginning.'

The Slovenian government had been clear ever since the elections of 1990 that if no progress was made towards talks on the future of Yugoslavia, they would declare themselves independent on 27 June. Needless to say, no progress had been made. The Serbs had refused to discuss anything substantive. The republic had already passed the laws laying the groundwork for a split. The careful preparations, the announcement long in advance, were typical of the Slovenes. Just as typically, the Croatian government had talked and squawked and proposed and threatened an independence move for some time now, but no clear ultimatum had been sent to Belgrade, no date had been set. Instead of constructing a legal framework for secession, the Croatian Parliament had spent its time passing laws on the new national anthem, the new flag and the new presidential seal.

'The West says Slovenia would be too small to survive on its own, but look at Luxembourg,' Nino said.

'Look at Lichtenstein,' said Nataša.

'Look at Monaco,' said Nika, who, come to think of it, would not have looked out of place at a baccarat table.

'Look at Vatican City,' I said.

'The Slovenes will do very well on their own,' Nataša said. 'They are a very hard-working people. Harder-working than Croats.'

The conversation turned to Yugoslavia's varied work ethic, i.e. the somewhat offputting industriousness of the Slovenes, the middle ground occupied by the Croats and the corrupt laziness of the Serbs, who had learned it from the even lazier Turks. Croatia had always paid more into the federal coffers than it ever got out in terms of federal investment, everyone agreed. Belgrade sucked up money and spent it on repressing the Albanians in Kosovo. Kosovo was a black hole of funds, and Serbs, in their pathological hatred of Albanians, were dragging the whole country towards Third World conditions. The standard of living in Yugoslavia had dropped thirty per cent in the past three years.

'Ante Marković is the only decent politician in all of Yugoslavia,' Danko said. Marković was the Federal Prime Minister, a Croat, whose economic austerity programme had reduced the federal deficit and cut the inflation rate of 2,000% in 1989 to 100% in 1990. 'And to show how hopeless Yugoslavia is, everyone is against him.'

'His hands are tied,' Nino said. 'Croats are against him because he's still for Yugoslavia.'

'And in Belgrade, people told me he is a CIA agent, because of his western economic policy, and his work with Jeffrey Sachs,' Danko said, referring to the man who had designed Poland's economic 'shock' transition to a free market.

'There!' Nino expostulated. 'That's the primitive Serb mentality! Everything is CIA!'

'So the Serbs sabotaged the programme,' Danko said simply.

Unlike so many assertions about Yugoslavia, Danko's was unarguable. The cornerstone of Marković's programme had been such a tight rein on the money supply that state enterprises were paying their employees a month or more late, and banks had put restrictions on withdrawals from hard-currency accounts. But in the weeks leading up to the Serbian elections in December 1990 (Milošević's reluctant response to the elections in Slovenia and Croatia), not only was there no shortage of money, Serbian workers' wages were actually rising. No one knew where the money was coming from. I spoke with an opposition leader who postulated that Milošević was running a Ponzi scheme, funnelling money ostensibly raised for investment in patriotic 'Serbia Bonds' and 'National Loans' directly into wages.

But the truth was even worse. After the elections, the Serbian legislature admitted that it had secretly passed a law allowing the National Bank of Serbia to take − steal, really − 1.3 billion dollars' worth of dinars from the National Bank of Yugoslavia. This was fully half the money allotted for the whole country for all of 1991. Even for Milošević, it was an almost unbelievably selfish, provocative and destructive act. He had been re-elected, and Marković's economic policy lay in ruins. If Croats and Slovenes had still entertained any doubts about the necessity of seceding as soon as possible, they evaporated.

'So Sachs isn't coming any more,' Danko said.

Gloom settled over the car. Sachs personified the west. He was

61

young and energetic and smiled all the time, and he gave the impression of never in his life having doubted for a second a single one of his ideas. He came from *Harvard*, for Christ's sake. What more of a *deus ex machina* could you ask for? He had saved the Poles. And now he had given up on Yugoslavia. He had thrown up his hands and walked away.

'A decent life,' Nino was saying. 'That's all people want. Serbs and Croats can't live together? Bunch of shit. We got along fine when the economy was better. I had Serb friends. Danko spent half his life in Belgrade.'

'From eight to seventeen,' Danko confirmed.

'The 70s, man,' Nino said, sinking into a reverie, 'those were the good old days. It was normal to go travelling. Normal! You'd go to Hungary or Czechoslovakia, and you couldn't believe how poor they were. They looked on us like we were kings. We had money for clothes – nice stuff. You know what I mean, nothing too fancy. But nice.' He touched an imaginary lapel, kissed his fingers. 'Nice. That's when people were building holiday homes on the coast.'

That was also when Tito ran up the enormous foreign debt that was helping to ruin the economy today. In 1971, the so-called Croatian Spring had developed secessionist overtones, causing Tito to crack down on the republic's leaders. After the pill came the sugar, in the form of foreign funds pumped into the economy – a policy not unlike Milošević's theft of federal money, only on a country-wide scale. Nino knew this as well as I did, so I didn't bother to say it.

'I've got simple desires,' Nino was saying. 'All I want is a house, a car, a Land Rover and a cottage on Susak.' Susak was the tiny northern Dalmatian island where Nino and Nataša had spent their last two vacations. 'Well . . . Maybe not just on Susak. I tell you what would be perfect. One cottage on Susak, one in the middle Dalmatian islands, and one in the south. And a yacht to go between them. A house, a car, a Land Rover, three cottages and a yacht. That's all! I'd be completely satisfied!'

'Here it is,' Danko said. 'Slovenia.'

We passed the sign. Danko slipped in a tape by Dr Voice, a

Slovene singer who held concerts called 'Slobo parties', in mock salute to Slobodan Milošević.

'Slobo! Slobo! Proud name!' blasted from the speakers, first as heavy metal, then reggae, disco, hip-hop, funk, rap, Slovenian folk (wheezing accordions), and grand opera. Dr Voice sang them all out of tune. Like the Slovenes, the Croats used to make fun of the 'primitive' hero-worshipping of the Serbs, who held up framed photographs of Milošević at their rallies. But then Croats starting holding up photos of Tudjman.

At Mokrice, we joined the rest of the Sunday crowd in admiring the picturesque rusticity of the old stables, the restored pomposity of the fifteenth-century château (now a hotel and restaurant). While we ambled through the wooded grounds in cool damp sunshine, Nika told me about the American books she had read, elucidating her judgements with extreme caution, while Nino hung behind, making Nataša and Danko laugh with his imitation of Serbs.

'You said it, brother. Beautiful day, mother! Now, listen to the words of an old woman, son . . .' Serbs did address each other that way, whether they were related or not. 'They're all brothers down there,' Nino said, catching up with us. 'One big happy family. That's why they only need one party.'

Croatian hoke: Three Slovenes make a choir. Three Serbs make an army. Three Croats make six political parties.

The restaurant was open, but empty. Few people these days could afford a restaurant meal, especially one at such an elegant establishment. I knew this outing had been arranged especially for me, and I also knew the restaurant was exactly the sort of place Nino loved – definitely Austrian, with heavy green curtains on wooden rods, cream wainscotting, steamed-wood chairs with upholstered seats, and menus in leather jackets with floral script. So I offered to treat them, which contravened the hospitality code, and was a mistake. Now I had admitted I was hungry, which meant we had to eat, but of course I would not be allowed to pay. After some haggling, I got the others to agree that I would pay half, and they could split the rest. But all this accomplished was that they ordered less than I did, insisting they were not

63

hungry. If I was going to pay half the bill, then by God I was going to eat half the food.

Danko ordered a beer, Nika a tonic and salad. Nino and Nataša shared a steak tartare, and the sight of their obvious delight as they watched our suave Slovene waiter wheel in the cart covered with crisp linen, the silver platter with its mound of purple flesh, the ring of capers, anchovies, onions, mustard, pepper, salt and egg yolks, each in its own cup, dispelled the lingering dismay I was feeling over my maladroitness. With silver tongs the waiter transferred the beef into a silver bowl and cut in the ingredients one by one with such sure strokes that I imagined he was counting them. His gold cufflinks flashed.

This was Europe, in all its painful unattainability. The linen, the silver, the view from the bay windows through lindens down to beds of flowers and a sloping lawn. This was what all Slovenes would be able to enjoy once they had cut themselves away from the putrid corpse of Yugoslavia.

Nika asked what 'cucumber' was in Slovenian, and the waiter, who spoke, of course, perfect Serbo-Croatian, told her, with a little smile that was either suave or frosty. Was he wondering why Croats who lived twenty-five kilometres from his border could not speak a word of his language? He shot his cuffs, and wished us *bon appetit* with an aide-de-camp's incline of his head. Did he click his heels? I wasn't sure. He rolled the cart away.

The portion of steak tartare turned out to be so large that Nino and Nataša could not finish it, and I asked if there was such a practice in Yugoslavia as taking extra food home.

'In Croatia, never,' Nataša said, colouring at the mere thought of it. 'It would be considered very cheap, very crass.'

'Yes, I've heard about that,' Nino said curiously. 'The Germans do it too, carrying out these little bags. It seems so ridiculous. You say it's for your dog, but then you eat it yourself.'

'No!' Nataša exclaimed.

'It's true,' Nino insisted. 'But it makes sense. Why waste food? Of course. But we wouldn't do it, as Nataša says. Maybe in Slovenia they do it, I don't know. We'll ask.'

He did ask, but with evident embarrassment, citing the American at the table who wanted to know, and retreating into a joke: 'If you don't give us a doggy bag, our government will communicate its displeasure to the Independent State of Slovenia.' The table of Croats laughed, perhaps a little too noisily, while the waiter responded with the same tiny smile. Perhaps it *was* sauve. Wasn't it suave to be unreadable? Taking home extra food was not uncommon in Slovenia, he said in the discreet voice a maître d'hotel might use in answering a guest's question about escort services. Nataša raised her eyebrows at me.

As he disappeared to wrap the meat, my table companions wavered between derision at the Slovenes' penny-pinching ways (but as this would imply derision of Americans, they were gentle about it) and chagrin at the thought that this, too, might be Europe, this common sense about money. Was there something foolish about the value Croats placed on appearing careless about money even when they were poor? Something not unlike potlatch, perhaps? Something . . . primitive? After all, the Serbs placed an even higher value on open-handedness than the Croats did.

On the return trip to Zagreb, Danko took the back roads. On a small street outside a village he stopped the car exactly on the border, so that he and Nika, in the front seats, were in Croatia, while Nataša, Nino and I were in Slovenia.

'Stupid Slovenes!' Danko and Nika yelled at the back seat.

'Fuck you, Croats!' Nino and Nataša yelled back.

11

Silvija's mother's earliest memory was of invaders in her Bosnian town. She was three years old. The men had guns, and they said to her, 'Tell us, little girl, who do you fear the most?' Her parents looked down at her with intense interest.

Years passed before she realized why the armed men had asked *her*. Her parents had only told them what they had wanted to hear. If her parents had spoken hostilely or fearfully of these men in this household, the child would have known.

'Come, tell us,' they coaxed. 'Who do you fear the most?'

'Chepniks,' she said.

The men laughed, and her parents laughed too, loudly. She had meant Chetniks. The men stroked her hair and went away. They had been Ustashas.

Silvija's grandfather came from a Catholic family so devout that he was the only son to have married, all five of his brothers having entered the priesthood. This was not unusual in Hercegovina, where the Catholic population was renowned for its militant devotion. One of his brothers became Archbishop of Bosnia after the war. Another spent several years in jail.

'But none of my family was Ustasha,' Silvija declared. A clarification was natural at this point, since much of the Catholic clergy in Bosnia supported the Ustashas during the war.

One night her grandfather, taking his constitutional with his wife, met on the street a gentlemanly, handsome man, elegantly dressed, who was in fact a notorious Ustasha, known to be a torturer and murderer. He greeted them pleasantly and offered Silvija's grandfather a cigarette from his gold case.

'My grandfather said, "I won't take a cigarette from bloody hands,"' Silvija told me proudly. 'My grandmother was very angry with my grandfather for that. It was a very dangerous thing to have done.'

Families lovingly passed down stories like this through the generations: the confrontation, the moral stand, the quotable line. Common, too, was the element of subsequent recrimination, which served to underline the risk involved. One had to wonder, perhaps uncharitably, about the truth of them. Perhaps, in this case, it had happened exactly as stated. Or perhaps her grandfather had merely declined the cigarette gruffly, and had thought up the line later. Or perhaps he had accepted the cigarette with a servile smile, hating himself. Or perhaps he had been Ustasha too, and the two of them had stood together for some time, smoking cigarettes and laughing about the people they had tortured and killed.

66

No one's family had ever killed anyone, yet millions had died.

Eventually, the family came to live in Zagreb, where Silvija's mother met Silvija's father. He lived with his parents in a fine old house they had owned before the war, and in fact still owned, but had been forced by the Communists to divide into five apartments. The tenants paid rent, but not to them. For a while, they had even been required to share their apartment with a woman, an insolent stranger, a peasant, who never cleaned anything and treated them like servants.

Hundreds of thousands of people in towns and cities throughout Yugoslavia lived like that for years after the war, sharing toilets, dividing rooms with sheets, taking turns at the stove or the hotplate, growing to hate each other, inflicting devious damage on each other's possessions. Everyone could tell a story of this or that tenant who had not spoken a single word to his room-mate or hall-mate for five years. Gradually, as the thousands of 'social' apartments of New Zagreb rose above the sandy soil on the far side of the Sava, the tenants drained away, or died, and the tales of flats shared by antagonists now seemed almost as far away and strange to Silvija as they did to me.

Silvija was on good terms with her parents. She no longer went to church, but let her parents believe this was only because she was too busy. Actually, she no longer believed in God. Her parents wanted her to finish the law degree she had begun years before. She had completed most of the degree requirements when she took her first job at Radio 101, but soon she was caught up in politics, in fights against the nebulous censor, in new friends and new music. She stopped studying. Now she was News Director, and last year had won a prestigious award for her work. But when she was depressed, as she was tonight, she told herself she had just been playing, refusing to grow up. She tried to remember when she had liked politics. The degree hovered reproachfully. But she had been studying *law*. Which law? The HDZ had rewritten the constitution last year. She tried to remember when she had liked law. When she saw her favourite professor in the street, she crossed to the other side to avoid him.

Nino and Nataša were at a Pet Shop Boys concert, but Silvija had no money for a ticket. I had offered to treat her, but she declined. She had felt worse when she got home, and found a message on the answering machine from Nino's mother, asking him to call her. It was about the Army.

At times like this Silvija wondered how people kept going. She wondered about ordinary workers, who were paid $150 or $200 a month. How did they survive? She had heard of families who lived entirely on bread. She had never seen homeless people until this year. It used to be that only Gypsies begged. Now Croat children and lame men went through the cafés trying to sell a single flower. Three of her friends had committed suicide.

'They weren't crazy,' she told me. 'They had good reasons.'

When I had first got back to the apartment she had been too subdued to talk, so we had tried to watch an old Gary Cooper movie on television, but it was so execrable we gave up. Yet the badness of it had cheered her a little. So she talked about her mother in the war, her grandfather who told off the Ustasha, the apartments she grew up in. 'Would you like to see my photographs?' she asked unexpectedly.

I would.

She spilled them out of a pleated cardboard folder. Small greenish photos of her as a child, big glossy black-and-whites from a year or two ago. A friend of hers was a professional photographer, and he had composed arty shots of her under black-and-white-striped awnings, in broad-brimmed hats, in strapless evening gowns. One had her all in black, crouched against a wall, staring stonily into the camera. She was beautiful. And in all of them, even when smiling, sad. Even as a child, she had the same disappointed eyes.

As soon as Nino came through the door, still high on the concert, we told him his mother had called about the Army. 'Oh shit!' he said. He ran to the phone.

Nataša waited in the kitchen, looking sick.

After a minute, Nino came back. 'It's all right, it's all right!' He swept his hair off his forehead with a nervous gesture. 'It was about two books I borrowed from the army library two years ago. They were sending the final notice.'

'Only *now*?' I said.

He laughed, giddy with relief. 'That's the Army!' He knocked his knees together and collapsed in a histrionic heap on the floor.

12

On 15 May the terse announcement came over the radio at noon. Stipe Mesić had not been confirmed as President of Yugoslavia.

'I fuck your mother!' Nino was on his feet. 'What did I say? I knew it!'

'They never had to be "confirmed" before!' Silvija said.

'This is what they mean by Yugoslavia!' Nino yelled, pointing a trembling finger at the radio. 'Yugoslavia by *their* rules! Serboslavia!'

'But how did they block him?' I asked, ovine. 'What does the constitution say about the rotation?'

'Brian, Brian,' Nino said, struggling for patience, 'don't hoke with me about the constitution! Who cares about the constitution?'

But on the way to the Student Club, the taxi driver exclaimed, aggrieved, 'The Serbs just walk all over the constitution!'

I looked at Nino. 'He worked in Germany for five years,' Nino shrugged. 'What does he know?'

Later that day, I visited Marija and Ante, a brother and sister who lived with their parents in a run-down little stone country house beyond the end of a tramline, part of an old village that was now a suburb, where the lindens were pine-green from the thick black grit thrown up from the busy commuting road.

We sat down to view a tape of the session on television. Maria had heard that the Muslim representative from Bosnia had voted against Mesić, and she expressed disgust.

'What crafty game are they playing now? There is an old Croat proverb: "Muslims change their caps as the wind changes."'

But we saw that Marija's source had heard wrong. Slovenia,

Croatia, Macedonia, and Bosnia-Hercegovina voted for Mesić. Serbia, Vojvodina and Kosovo voted against him. Montenegro abstained, on the grounds that its new representative to the Presidency had not been confirmed yet by the Montenegrin Parliament.

Afterwards, we argued about what had happened. Had Mesić lost because he needed five votes? Or had the election been held up because Montenegro's missing man was due to become vice-President, and the Vice-President had to be elected before the President? If the latter, you could be sure it was a set-up. Montenegro was in Serbia's pocket, everyone knew that.

In virtually all cases, Serbia could count on four of the Presidency's eight votes, because the men were hand-picked by Milošević. Two years ago, he and his followers had overthrown the governments of Montenegro and Vojvodina, and last year he had annulled the autonomy of Kosovo. The Kosovo representatives always had Albanian names, but they voted like good Serbs. The previous Kosovo marionette had not supported Milošević on one vote, and had been instantly dismissed. But it had appeared for a while as though he could not be replaced, because only the Kosovo Parliament could pick a representative, and Milošević had dissolved the Parliament. Briefly the Croats gloated over the Serbs' self-created predicament – proving that they, too, could be caught now and then taking the constitution seriously. The Serbs knew better. They simply put in a new man and dared the other republics to do something about it. And there he was, with his Albanian name, voting as he was supposed to.

'Everyone gets one vote,' Ante said. 'Serbia gets four votes. That's democracy!' (That was also the crux of an old Croat joke. A Serb and a Croat were about to share a cake. The Serb said, 'Let's share it like brothers!' And the Croat responded, 'No, let's divide it half and half.')

But in a way, the constitution *had* made itself felt. It had forced Montenegro's President Momir Bulatović, whom Croats called 'the waiter' for his servile attendance on Milošević, to go on television and make obvious his lickspittle toadying. It had forced Serbia's representative Jović to show himself as the fox he was, demanding this extraordinary vote and then sitting through it impassively, his eyes hooded under eyebrows peaked like circum-flex accents, as if it were normal procedure.

Mesić had sat pale and tight-lipped, and had left as soon as the vote was over. He had promised he would be the last President of Yugoslavia, but apparently Jović wanted that honour.

Ante could not believe there would be war. Serbs did not want war either, he said. He had been in Belgrade and Niš recently, and he knew the morale there was low.

'Write good things about everyone,' he urged me. 'Things will be solved soon.'

Perhaps that was only the optimism of a new father. Ante's ten-month-old son sat on his sister's lap, bald and balloon-headed, a smiling buddha, but with upside-down ears, not the fat earlobes indicating wisdom, but swollen *tops*. The seat of dumb cheeriness?

The baby looked uncannily like his bald grandfather, who also grinned vacantly, though more from alcohol than ignorance. Ante and Marija considered themselves entirely Croat, but their father was a Serb. He had not called himself that in many years, but no matter, the neighbours had recently taken to doing it for him. They telephoned his wife to report they had seen him hanging around this place or that, and didn't she think he might be spying? She knew he was no spy, but she did not defend him. He was a drunk, which was worse.

His brother, who lived near by, had never stopped calling himself a Serb. He marked on a map where Serbs were fighting Croats in Slavonia, labelling the Serb-held areas 'Serbia'. He was one of those loud talkers who enjoyed the obnoxiousness of his own opinions. Marija told me matter-of-factly that someone would probably kill him.

As I walked to the gate the dog tried to kill me, as he always did, but the rope held. A local tramline was due to be extended right through their living room, but the political emergency had put all such projects on hold. Marija was disappointed almost to tears. She would have been given her own flat in recompense, far away from her parents.

13

At midnight on 15 May Yugoslavia ceased to have a presidency. Slovenia, Croatia, Macedonia and Bosnia-Hercegovina claimed that Mesić was already President. Jović called a meeting of the Presidency, but only Serbia's three men and Montenegro came.

Mesić responded by saying to the press, 'What meeting? I didn't call a meeting.'

Croats feared a military coup, but the generals were saying that the Yugoslav Army had always obeyed the constitution, and would continue to do so. But the Army had no commander-in-chief. The Federal Prime Minister, Ante Marković, famous for his optimism (who but an optimist would take on that economy?), was still smiling. Yugoslavia would survive, he said, whether or not all of its parts functioned. He had said the same two years ago, when the League of Communists of Yugoslavia had fractured, and his popularity had soared. Now people sneered. Would he still be smiling when the water covered his mouth, his high, ingratiating eyebrows?

On the day the Presidency died, so did Vukašin Šoškočanin, the leader of the Serb defence force in Borovo Selo. The boat in which he and five others had been crossing the Danube was overturned by the wake of a Bulgarian barge. Radio 101 announced, 'The only good news today is that Vukašin Šoško-čanin died. Unfortunately, the other five in the boat were saved.'

Silvija was incensed. 'See the problems I have! That is totally unprofessional! OK, it's good he died. But you don't say it on the *radio*!'

Nino wondered who had killed him. The Croats? Or perhaps the Serbs, angry that he had bragged on Novi Sad TV about killing Croats, making them (Serbs) look like animals. Or perhaps he wasn't dead, but removed to some place safe from Croat reprisals. His body had not been recovered.

72

'Then again, it might really have been an accident,' I said.

Nino ignored me.

Meanwhile I was getting ready to go to Belgrade, and people were sincerely frightened for me. Serbs were angry at Americans right now, they said, because of Senator Robert Dole's support for the Albanians. I might be assaulted.

This was not like Hungarians warning me that Romanians would rob me, knife me, bugger me. Romania, to them, had always been beyond the pale, literally trans-sylvania. But, not long ago, Croats had visited Belgrade frequently. They used to go on holiday in Montenegro.

Croats talked to me about the threat of the east – eastern totalitarianism, eastern cruelty, eastern corruption. I did not like this East–West dichotomy, which came so easily to everyone's tongue. When the Ottoman Empire had extended to Belgrade, both Serbs and Croats in Austria's Military Borders had fought what they considered the barbarian east. Then Serbia became free, and Croats redefined the east. They made it Byzantium, Orthodoxy. The totalitarian, cruel and corrupt Serb. In 1945, the Croats fled north to surrender to the west, in the form of the British Army, but were handed back – betrayed – to the east: the totalitarian and cruel Partisans. What was Stalin but a throwback to Ivan the Terrible? You would think from the way Croats talked that Tito had been a Serb.

When one man beat another to death, when a politician absconded with millions, when ballots were rigged, when imbecilic sons of Party leaders became company directors, Croats' explanation lay nestled in a defeatist shrug and a single word: 'Balkan'. In the Croats' Manichaean world-view, 'Balkan' was the principle of darkness, 'Europe' the principle of light. You could see vestiges of Europe all around you in Zagreb, in the Habsburg buildings, now black with Balkan dirt, in the parks of sycamores and lindens, now littered with Balkan trash. Croatia had belonged to Europe, before being carried into the Balkan Captivity by the Serbs. The Croats were struggling to cut themselves free, frantic to do it before the *Evropska Zajednica*, the European Community, opened its internal borders and slammed shut its external ones. Like a balloon, Europe was taking off, a bright round promise of salvation floating away with the Wizard of EZ. Europe would become so buoyantly prosperous that Croatia, running below, its broken shackles clanging behind, would never be able to reach it.

Poignantly, Croats half believed they did not deserve to. They knew Europe looked on them as a Balkan race, and could anything Europe thought be wholly wrong? They conceded that Slovenes were harder workers, more honest. Croatia had belonged to the Habsburg Empire, but the Slovenes had actually lived on Austrian crown lands. Like Germans, Slovenes furiously swept dirt off dirt courtyards. Like Germans, they waited for the little green man before they crossed the street. Slovenes actually *did* speak a different language from the Serbs. Did no Serbs live in Slovenia because the Slovenes did not deserve them?

Everywhere, I talked to people who protested against opinions I had never held, never expressed. 'We are not barbarians!' they cried. 'We are a cultured nation! We had one of the first parliaments in Europe! We had a code of laws before the Serbs did, before the Magna Carta!' Being Slav was not good enough, because the Slavs dated back only 1,500 years. No, the Croats (*Hrvati*) descended from an Iranian tribe, the Harahvatis, first mentioned in 200 BC.

I had to wonder. Did they really mean to imply that a nation with fewer writers and simpler buildings – perhaps with no parks at all! – did not deserve to be free? Or that a young nation had no rights? As they were speaking to an American, the absurdity of the proposition hung heavy around us.

On my last night in Zagreb there was a comedy show on Nino's television. A man stood on the stage with the long hair and unkempt beard of the Chetnik, and the Chetnik's tall winter fur cap adorned with the medallion of the Serbian double-headed eagle. But his clothes were barbaric, a hilarious collection of skins and horns evoking Attila the Hun. He was smiling and waving to the crowd, trying to be a statesman, like a king in his motorcade. A 'new' Chetnik, perhaps, like a 'new' Nixon, a respectable Chetnik purged of his pathologies. But from offstage came the

74

bang of rifle fire, and at the sound of each shot our respectable Chetnik looked disconcerted, mildly embarrassed, but recovered in a moment and returned to waving, with smiles and nods, until another shot rang out, causing another moment of mild embarrassment.

My friends laughed at the sketch, not bitterly but with true delight, and it occurred to me that here was one genuine difference between Serbs and Croats. Serbs would not laugh at a sketch about Ustashas. The Serbs were far too earnest a people – Croats would say 'primitive' – to have much talent for irony. In the irony of the Croats, Serbs saw heartlessness. Croats could laugh at a sketch about murder because Croats did not value life as Serbs did.

The next morning Nino offered to share a taxi with me on his way to the Student Club, and he was so late getting ready that I almost missed the train. He had a eurocheque for 800 Deutschmarks in his pocket, his pay from the Jeunesse Européenne Fédéraliste for having organized a Croatian chapter, despite his loss of faith in federalism. As no Yugoslav bank would pay out hard currency on a foreign cheque any more, he would have to travel to Austria to cash it, and so he and Nataša and his mother would make a day of it. They would cross the border to Graz, and drink coffee in an Austrian coffee shop and eat chocolate torte. He kissed his fingers. I left him with his visions of heavy curtains and leather-clad menus, of a country where waiters were waiters and politicians were politicians.

Part Two

Belgrade

14

Vlado shared the space at the end of the carriage with me. His room in Zagreb was exactly this size, he said, gesturing to the four corners at our feet with his cigarette. He had a bed, and a chair to sit on when he put on his shoes. DM100 a month, payable in hard currency. He made about DM250 – in dinars – as a construction worker. Not that he was actually getting paid. He hadn't seen his wages in four months.

He was clad entirely in faded Levis, the *ne plus ultra* of Yugoslav fashion, except for his pointed black slipper-like shoes. He kept his thick wavy black hair swept back, where it fell below his shoulders. He was twenty-six years old.

He wasn't married. How could he marry? No room for a wife or kids, and no money to get more room. His brother worked in Stuttgart, and his sister in Vienna. They both had families.

Why didn't *he* go abroad? I asked.

Europe was trying to throw out the foreign workers it already had. He was the baby of the family, born too late.

Vlado had no ticket. 'I don't have any money,' he told the conductor. 'You know how it is.' Some conductors did know, but this one seemed unforgiving. He told Vlado testily that he would have to get off at the next station and moved on, squeezing sideways through the press.

A man poked his head out of the toilet. 'He's gone,' Vlado assured him. The man emerged and bummed a cigarette.

Vlado was going to his parents' place for the weekend. They had two acres, two cows and a pig in a village near Djakovo. They gave him pocket money and stuffed him with food so that he didn't have to eat much during the week. When he got thrown off a train, he would wait and board the next and ride it until he got thrown off again. By this method, a trip that normally took four hours could take as much as twenty-four. The last leg, a branch line, was the worst, because the trains consisted of only two wagons and stopped at every village. Both discovery and ejection occurred quickly. He often ended up walking the last fifteen miles.

Vlado did not get off at the next station. The man who had hidden in the toilet went back in, and five minutes later the conductor came by. 'You didn't get off,' he pointed out in a reasonable voice.

'No, I guess not.'

The conductor allowed himself a small smile. 'Well, you got away with it, then.'

After the conductor had disappeared I gave Vlado enough money to cover his round-trip ticket on the branch line, which minimal courtesy led us into that conversational staple of bad times, as fundamental as coffee and cigarettes: most people everywhere were good, but unfortunately a small number of bad people – we decided it was somewhere between one and five per cent – were enough to cause all the problems of this world. But Vlado was optimistic. He more or less had to be. He was a 'real Yugoslav', as he put it, with a Serb father and Croat mother living in an area claimed by both Serbs and Croats, not thirty miles from Borovo Selo.

After Vlado got off, I found a seat in a compartment where the people were handing round an article in the day's paper.

'Ah, Pintarić!' a middle-aged man said, chuckling with slow, thick relish. 'So he's done it again!'

Others repeated the name with happy sighs.

Pintarić was a bandit.

'The worst in Yugoslavia!' the middle-aged man, Pero, said proudly.

And a Croat!

In the days of the Turks, the *hajduks*, or mountain bandits, were also the revolutionaries. Or the revolutionaries were all bandits, depending on how you chose to look at it. Most of them cut the throats of both Slav and Turk – anyone who had money and not enough bodyguards, basically – but in the popular tradition only the Turkish dead were remembered.

The tradition had no trouble surviving in a modern society in which people grew up despising the government, and Pintarić knew how to play his role. As the article described his latest escapade, he had entered a bar in a Croatian village with a pistol in his hand, a rifle over his shoulder, and provided his own identification scene in the classic epic manner, thundering, 'Do you know who I am?'

'Pintarić!' the barman quaked, as deep in his role as the bandit, while the clientele dived for cover. Pintarić held everyone hostage for two hours while he drank the best liquor in the house, his pistol resting on the bar. As he savoured each glass, he paid, insisting that the barman deposit his money in the register. At the end, he emptied the register and put a bullet through it. This progression – the deadpan observation of form, the equally deadpan contravention, the concluding explosion of scorn – was particularly admired by the people in my compartment. It showed a certain sly wit.

Pintarić disappeared 'without a trace'. How else?

He had his hajduk scruples. 'He only kills men,' Pero told me.

And where did he operate?

The compartment smiled. 'Everywhere!' an old woman crowed.

One of his arms was paralysed, which naturally reduced his firepower. And yet when, several months ago, he had been run to ground in a forest and surrounded by a thousand policemen with helicopters, dogs and machine guns, he escaped, killing two cops on the way out. 'That's why I don't count much on our police protecting us,' Pero concluded.

At Vinkovci, the last town before Serbia, the train emptied and I found myself alone with Miroslav, a student of mechanical engineering at Zagreb University. He dressed tidily, and had an air of unflappable conviction.

On the station platform strolled policemen in bullet-proof vests, camouflaged for jungle warfare, cradling submachine guns. I asked Miroslav if he knew what kind of guns they were.

81

'Sure,' he said. 'M-70-A Kalashnikovs. The Yugoslav Army also uses Kalashnikovs, but a different model, the M-70, with a wooden clipcase instead of the metal ones you see here. That's how you tell the difference. These are better. Each one costs about 1,800 Deutschmarks, but actually you have to pay a lot more if you want to buy one. Two thousand nine hundred or so.'

'People can buy them?'

He gave me a knowing look. 'People can buy anything.'

We had pulled out of Vinkovci and were running between flat fields, low scattered farmhouses. Miroslav gestured out the window. 'I guarantee you, every family out there has a gun. Yugoslavia has always been a well-armed country. Like America! After the war, people kept their guns. For "hunting".' His nudging smile put quotes around the word. 'But that was only pistols, old rifles. People have much better stuff now.'

Something about the image of Kalashnikovs under farmers' beds deeply appealed to Yugoslavs. Bullets in the breadbox, chickens in the coop brooding on hand grenades. As a Soviet diplomat once complained to *Washington Post* correspondent Dusko Doder, Yugoslavs were 'anarchists, anarchists; there's no other word for them!'.

Tito had accommodated this trait in his doctrine of General People's Defence, which he formulated after the 1968 Soviet invasion of Czechoslovakia (he feared Yugoslavia was next), taking the Swiss model of an armed citizenry and adding a strong army. Communist history taught that the Royal Yugoslav Army's capitulation to the Germans in April 1941 had been treasonous – in a way, quisling – and the post-1968 constitution formally outlawed a repetition. According to the constitution, *no one* had the right to sign the capitulation of the armed forces. Local defence militias were therefore constitutionally directed to ignore cease-fires. This was ratification of a mentality that would assume huge importance in the coming months.

We were approaching the Serbian border. 'Not many people going to Belgrade,' I observed, after walking up and down the empty train.

82

'Village people!' Miroslav said scornfully. 'They think Belgrade is like the countryside, where someone will cut your throat.'

He was on his way to see his girlfriend, a Serb. 'My girlfriend and I are city people. City people have a broader outlook. They are not anti-Croat, or anti-Serb. I feel completely normal in Belgrade.' He added, 'There won't be war. I am sure of that. People have too much to lose.'

His was not the optimism of the young father, nor of the 'real' Yugoslav, nor of the weekend miscegenator, nor, I thought, of the self-styled cosmopolite, but of the entrepreneur who profited from unsettled times. I wasn't so sure about 'people', but certainly Miroslav had too much to lose.

He had explained his activities to me. After last year's elections, Serbia had slapped a tax on Croatian goods, and Croatia had retaliated by lowering its tax on foreign cars. (Yugoslav cars were manufactured in Serbia, and they could only compete in the domestic market by virtue of the ninety per cent tax levied on imported cars.) Miroslav would fly to Copenhagen on a student ticket and buy a Mazda through a Danish friend, to benefit from the lower taxes on intra-EC trade. Then he would drive the car to Yugoslavia via Hungary, so that he could enter Croatia directly, pay the new low forty-one per cent Croatian automobile tax at the border, and drive on to Serbia, where he could sell the car for more than twice what he had paid for it. In the past three months he had sold ten cars in this way, clearing about DM7,000 on each car. He did not know how much longer this delightful situation would last, so for the time being he had given up his studies to devote himself to profiteering full-time. Yugoslavia had never been so good to him. He had even postponed going to America, where he had been planning to work for his uncle.

Probably because I have no talent for it, I tend to dislike people who make money in ingenious ways. Miroslav sat with his tidy haircut, his leather briefcase, his smug glee, and was no exception. But perhaps his kind was Yugoslavia's best hope. People often made the argument that an interrelated economy was the only lasting solution to regional conflict – that it no longer mattered, say, whether Alsace belonged to France or Germany once German workers could commute to France and work in a German-owned company whose products were sold free of tariffs in either country – and Yugoslavia's hope lay in attaining that point where borders became irrelevant.

The Communists had never been true internationalists. The Soviet Union had been built on old-fashioned Russian hegemonism, and in Yugoslavia the League of Communists had comprised various republican factions, each jealous of its turf. The Communists in the Balkans who had most favoured a break-up of Yugoslavia after the war, for purely proletarian reasons of course, were – surprise! – the Bulgarians.

Capitalists were the real internationalists. They were the secular heirs to the incestuous European nobility which knew no borders except the impermeable ones between classes. A Deutschmark was as good as a dollar. And Yugoslavs were not only like Americans in being absurdly well-armed anarchists. They were also natural hucksters.

We crossed into Serbia. Outside the window stretched green fields dotted with crimson poppies so bright the eye could not focus on them. The farmhouses had ochre walls of straw mud, tiled roofs weathered to the colour of dried blood. We had passed within ten miles of the war area around Vukovar, but the shooting and shelling still occurred mostly at night, and we had heard nothing. I made a mental note to start referring to the language as Serbian, instead of Croatian.

15

Serbs like to say that Belgrade has been destroyed forty times. That strikes me as a conservative estimate.

In the third century BC, on the high ground overlooking the confluence of the Sava and Danube Rivers, the Celts built Singidunum: 'Round Fort'. When the Romans overran it, they adopted the name but destroyed the fort, and constructed in its stead their usual rectangular *castrum*. Singidunum became one of the fortifications along the border of the Roman Empire, facing across the Danube into trackless forests from which Roman generals shrank and out of which felt-capped, long-haired Dacians poured every winter, crossing the frozen Danube to ravage Moesia. Downriver, on the walls of Tomi, some nameless barbarian clashed swords with the exiled Ovid, who wrote pitifully to friends in Rome that the Moesian winters were so cold that wine froze in the jars and was served in glittering pieces, like garnet.

When Valentinian divided the empire with his brother Valens in 364, the boundary between east and west ran along the Sava, directly beneath the walls of Singidunum. The fort on the high ground between the rivers became 'the east'. Across the Sava, the plains of Pannonia Inferior were west. And across the Danube, the limitless forest remained neither: shelter no longer for Dacians, but for Huns, Goths, Sarmatians, Gepids.

The Western Empire declined and fell. Now Singidunum faced the barbarians across both rivers. The Huns, Goths, Sarmatians and Gepids each had their turn at destroying the fort on the hill. Justinian regained it on his way to reconquering Italy. The Avars took it away fifty years later. Charlemagne's Franks routed the Avars. The Bulgars drove out the Franks. The Byzantine Emperor Basil II Bulgaroctonus ('Bulgar-Slayer') slew the Bulgars.

By then the settlement was known as Beograd, a Slav word meaning 'White City'. Flat, defenceless Pannonia was nearly deserted, and the Magyars marched over the Carpathians to fill the void. They came south and destroyed Belgrade. The Bulgars, recovered from Bulgaroctonus, came north and took it back. The Western Empire had also rebounded, in the persons of Germanic emperors who could barely read or write, and the Crusaders stopped to sack Belgrade on their way to the Holy Land. The fact that the barbarians were by now all Christians made little difference to the fortunes of the town.

In 1284 the Serbs conquered Belgrade for the first time, but held it only briefly before the Magyars destroyed it again. Then the Byzantine Serbs and the papal-crowned Magyars formed a shaky alliance against a new enemy: the Turks. Like everyone else, the Turks wanted Belgrade because it controlled access both north into the plains of Hungary and west into the plains of Croatia. For eighty years they tried to take the town, finally succeeding in 1521. They burned it to the ground and built it anew. Roman Singidunum had not been round, and Slav Beograd had never been white. The Turks gave the town a better name, as pungent as its past: Darol-i-Jehad, 'the Home of Holy Wars'.

The age of the great migrations was over. Belgrade became a Turkish town with a hundred mosques, Hungary a Turkish dependency. Kara Mustafa led the Sultan's army to the walls of Vienna in 1683, but failed to take it and was brought back to Belgrade and beheaded, his head presented to the Sultan on a silver dish. The Austrians pressed their advantage and captured Belgrade in 1688. The Turks surged back and destroyed it in 1690. Prince Eugen of Savoy took it again in 1717, along with northern Serbia, and the Austrians converted the mosques to churches. When the Turks returned in 1739, they changed the churches back into mosques.

For the first time in a thousand years Belgrade stood again on a recognizable border, part of the Ottoman fortifications holding back the Habsburg hordes. The two empires were losing their vitality, ossifying. A stalemate across the Sava suited them both. From the fortress on the rock the Turks could see the Habsburg-yellow church towers of Zemun. They could hear the bells that seemed to them a brutish 'bar bar', a blasphemy, compared to the Koranic lucidity of the muezzins' call.

At this juncture, as it happened, the great age of European travel writing dawned, and the cliché of Belgrade as the gateway to the east was born, digging itself deeply into the collective consciousness of Europe. One after the other, travellers in search of the exotic, the cruel, the opulent — images Europe conjured for itself and imposed on the east like a suitor on the object of his desire — took their last meals and night's lodgings in Austrian Zemun and in the morning crossed the Sava as though it were the Styx.

They saw what they had come to see: vice and sensuality, as

86

if Europe had no opium dens, no brothels; riches, as if the Vatican had no treasury; cruelty, as if the iron maiden, the stake and Vasco da Gama were not western. They also saw the Serb *rayah*s, uneducated and uncouth, brutalized to the last extreme by the janissaries, being born bit by bit into that excruciating vitality, the fire of desperate zeal, that the Austrians and Turks had lost.

The Serbs south of Belgrade rose in 1804. In 1806 they besieged and took the town. The Turks reconquered it in 1813, and massacred the male inhabitants. The Serbs rose again in 1815 and drove the Turks out of all northern and central Serbia.

But if Turkey had become the Sick Man of Europe, Austria was degenerating into the muddled, punch-drunk Shitland described by Robert Musil, and neither of them wanted a strong, free Serbia. Nor did Russia. The Serbs were forced to accept a Turkish garrison in Belgrade. It was not until the Congress of Berlin in 1878 that Serbia was granted full independence.

But even after Belgrade had become entirely Serb, the Turkish quarter effaced, the mosques torn down and replaced by five-storey apartment houses that would not have looked out of place on Vienna's Ringstrasse, it retained, in the European mind, the queasy, suspect status of the Other – non-Habsburg, non-Catholic. Literary clichés do not die easily, especially when reinforced by superficialities. The man who had driven out the Turks in 1815, Miloš Obrenović, built for himself in the middle of Belgrade an opulent Turkish house, with light-filled rooms and patterned wooden ceilings, and a divan on which he could smoke a *čibuk* and take his ease, cross-legged on a cushion. Many of his Serb subjects wore fezes, and stippled their conversation with Turkish words. They placed great value on making, once in their lives, the pilgrimage to Jerusalem, which they called the *hadž*.

Zemun was still Austria, and the Sava was still the edge of the civilized world. Austria annexed Bosnia-Hercegovina to extend that civilization. Gavrilo Princip protested against the slight by shooting Franz Ferdinand. World War I began with the Austrians in Zemun bombarding Belgrade.

What number were we up to now? Thirty-six, if the Serbs were right, because they took Belgrade back and lost it again in 1915, and World War II would bring the final two: in 1941, when the Germans began the war in Yugoslavia by reducing Belgrade to rubble, and in 1944, when the Allies ended it the same way. In between, Zemun belonged to the Independent State of Croatia, and the Ustashas established a camp between the yellow Catholic churches, in which thousands of Serbs died, within sight of the city on the hill.

No wonder that Belgrade today is not an attractive town – a hodge-podge of lone, crippled remnants from past eras, held together by the cement of post-war housing blocks, and all so grimy grey that the city's name is a reproach, if you are sympathetic, or a joke, if you are not. On grey days I was convinced I could shoot a roll of film in Belgrade and no one, looking at the pictures afterwards, would be able to tell whether I had used colour film or black-and-white.

But Belgrade partakes of that enthralling character shared by all cities that have an obvious reason for being where they are. Their brute topological functionality gives them a shape, no matter how large they sprawl. You walk straight to the heart, and can pronounce it the heart as surely as if you stood with a sextant at the North Pole. Belgrade's heart, of course, is the fortress on the rock, now called by its Turkish name, Kalemegdan. Below, the Sava flows into the Danube, and one defenceless plain stretches north into Hungary, and another points east towards the heart of Croatia, where pretty Zagreb lies.

To the Serbs, Zagreb's prettiness is Zagreb's shame. It has no obvious strategic reason for being where it is. The Romans built no city there. The Turks never tried seriously to take Zagreb, because they did not need it. They simply bypassed it. In 1941 the Germans left Zagreb untouched because it turned quisling so quickly. And although the Serbs sided with the Allies while the Croats fought for Hitler, the Allies bombed the hell out of Belgrade and scrupulously spared Zagreb, because Belgrade quartered the German command whilst Zagreb, turning coat again as the Germans fell back in Russia, had secretly promised

88

the Allies that Croatia would not fire on planes heading north to bomb Germany if those planes did not bomb Croatia.

Today, the Sava is no longer a boundary, but the frontier is still close. Croatia lies only sixty miles west. Perhaps one finds it amazing that the fourth-century line dividing Rome and Constantinople along the Sava and Drina Rivers, down the middle of what would become Yugoslavia, held for so long, through Justinian's reconquests to the border of France, the Franks' incursions to the walls of Byzantium, the Turks' drive to Vienna, Prince Eugen's charge to the middle of Serbia. Every time the line moved, after a few years it returned, finding again a point of equilibrium that never shifted. The simple reason for the tenacity of that line was the great fortress of Belgrade, the key to the Balkans, the Home of Holy Wars.

One evening I walked with Mirjana along the quays of New Belgrade. The sun, low ahead, blurred and sagged into a Danubian haze, so that the sloppily strewn houses and frowning ministries and blowsy parking garages of the old town were colourized momentarily from their usual smog-grey to a faint, dirty pink. Mirjana, who had lived in Belgrade far too long to be sentimental about it, said, 'From a distance it's not *that* bad-looking a town, is it?'

16

Mirjana lived on the Danube side of the spine of old Belgrade, where the regular streets still reflected the grid laid down by the Romans for their fort. From 1815 to 1867, when Serbia had been autonomous but a Turkish garrison remained in the fortress, this slope had been the Turkish town, under Turkish administration, while the Serbs had lived under their own government on the other side of the ridge, overlooking the Sava. The border between east and west had thus stood briefly, not at the Sava but down the middle of the high rock itself, as though Serbs and Turks both owned half a border post. But not quite. The Turks held the whole fortress.

Three blocks above Mirjana's apartment, on the sidewalk under the sycamores, a bronze youth as beautiful as Narcissus lay dead beside a broken pot, out of which real water flowed into a basin. The monument covered a natural spring to which, on a hot June day in 1862, a Serb youth had come to draw water. He fell into an argument with two Turkish soldiers lounging by the fountain, and they killed him. The Serbs on the far side of the ridge rioted, causing the Turkish commander in the fortress to bombard the Serbian town for four hours. After – let's see – thirty-four destructions of Belgrade, the thirty-fifth was inflicted by its own fortress, which showed that having the border along the rock might be logical, but was hardly reasonable.

Five years later the English persuaded the Turks to leave, and today the people who frequented the one remaining mosque, four blocks away, were not Turks but Albanians, and the woman who swept the floor of Sheik Mustafa's tomb, a little brick beehive dwarfed by the Belgrade University buildings around it, was a Bosnian Muslim. The family that lounged by the fountain every fine day as I passed were not Turks either, but Serb villagers who retained a country appreciation for sitting outside and listening to the gurgle of water, even here, where the parked cars so crowded both sidewalks and the narrow street that the trolley-buses sometimes got stuck. The woman crocheted white table covers which she later tried to sell to the rare tourists in Kalemegdan, while her children chased each other around the bench. They occupied the ground-floor apartment opposite and even on rainy days seemed to live half outdoors, as they kept their windows thrown open and leaned out to greet passers-by. You could stop on the sidewalk and watch their television with them. Mirjana sniffed a little, because this failure to distinguish properly between inside and out was a mark of the peasant.

Mirjana came from a well-connected Belgrade family. When she was a girl in the 30s, she had loved to visit the villas of her two aunts who had married industrialists and lived with the other elite on Topčider, a hill above Belgrade. 'At least in those days

90

you knew where people's money came from,' she told me a trifle defensively. 'People earned it.'

Her own parents had lived a little more modestly. When the seamstress came to work for them one week of the year, she not only made new dresses but repaired old ones, and cut the worn middle third out of sheets in order to sew the outer two-thirds together, so that parental bedding could find new life on the beds of the children.

Mirjana's father had fought in both Balkan Wars and in the Great War. He had been a captain in the Serbian Army when it was defeated by the combined forces of Austria, Germany and Bulgaria in 1915, and forced to make its famously punishing winter retreat through the Albanian mountains to the Adriatic. The Serbs had transformed that catastrophe, through their epic imagination, into something awful but glorious. It had become, like their defeat by the Turks on Kosovo Field in 1389, one of the treasures in their storehouse of national myths. They had been defeated, but had refused to surrender. Rather than give up their arms to the enemy, they had opted to abandon their own country, as the Russians had done before Napoleon.

In one of Mirjana's books, I could pore over the photographs: the driving snow, the knife-edged mountains, the soldiers wound in rags like mummies, their faces veiled, ghost-like. The dead horses, the frozen feet, the teeth falling out from scurvy. The paralysed King Petar was drawn on a caisson, while the Prince-Regent Aleksandar, who had had his appendix removed in a mountain cottage, was carried next to him, strapped to a stretcher. Monks laboured up the cliffs with coffins containing the sacred relics of Serbia's medieval kings. Rebecca West writes, 'It is like some fantastic detail in a Byzantine fresco, improbable, nearly impossible, yet a valid symbol of a truth, that a country which was about to die should bear with it on its journey to death, its kings, living and dead, all prostrate, immobile.' Of the 250,000 soldiers who began the journey, one hundred thousand perished, from exposure and starvation, and from the attentions of Albanian snipers.

As for Mirjana's father, he had never talked about it much. He had gone through the mountains, and he had survived. With the remnants of the Army he made it to Corfu, where he recovered and re-equipped. In 1917 he and 150,000 other Serbs, as part of a three hundred thousand-man Allied force, invaded his own country, fighting up from Salonika into Macedonia, driving the Germans and Bulgarians back.

'The conduct of the Serbian Army in World War I is in all the military history books,' the captain's daughter proudly told me. 'It's taught at West Point! It's a unique example of a defeated army evacuating its country en masse in order to regroup and return.'

Like many Serbs in 1918, Mirjana's father considered Yugo-slavia a fitting monument to the suffering of his people, a just reward for their heroic and selfless efforts. In the First Balkan War the Serbs had driven the Turks out of Kosovo, the heart of the medieval Serbian kingdom, and had fallen to kiss the holy ground where their ancestors had died in 1389. In the Second Balkan War they had driven the Bulgarians out of Macedonia and called it, in their triumph, South Serbia. World War I was their third straight victory and part, by now, of a pattern. In the Serb view, Croatia and Slovenia had not been *conquered*, although one certainly could look at it that way, since Croats and Slovenes had fought in the Habsburg armies. They had been *liberated*, just as Kosovo and Macedonia had been liberated. Uncounted Serbs had died to give Croats and Slovenes a better life in – well, in 'Yugoslavia', if that's what they wanted to call it.

Conquered peoples could be forgiven for being sullen. You even had to respect them for showing the gumption to rebel. But liberated peoples were supposed to be grateful, and recalcitrance was merely despicable.

In the inter-war years Mirjana's father rose to the rank of lieutenant-colonel in the Yugoslav Army. He was widely respected and liked. 'A real gentleman,' Mirjana said, 'with all the social graces.'

A unique custom of the Serbian Orthodox Church was that families shared a patron saint, on whose day they were 'at home' to their friends, and Mirjana remembered with great fondness the

St George's Day every November when her mother and she would bake for a week and clean the house in preparation for the scores of people who would stream through all day to pay their respects to her father. Many more would send telegrams or flowers. Her father would scrupulously record in a notebook who came, what they brought and which was their family saint, so that he could return the compliment at the appropriate time. But to be both popular and conscientious was problematic, because more than half of all Serbs had as their family saint either St Nicholas or St George. (The latter, a fertility figure, was so popular he had two days, and you belonged to either a May St George family or a November St George family.) Mirjana especially remembered, laughing her raspy smoker's laugh, the St George's Day in May, when her father would venture out in the early morning, note-book in pocket, and drive like a madman all over town, returning to pick up more presents, crossing names off his list and heading out again, not forgetting to return telegram for telegram, flower for flower, and not coming home until late in the evening, unhappily stuffed with cakes and *slatko* (a spoonful of jam traditionally served to guests, and not refusable) and jittery from coffee.

By 1941, he had been appointed the Commander of Belgrade. He did not participate in the officer's coup that ousted Prince Pavle, but he was summoned to an emergency session of the military command that followed it. He telephoned from the meeting to order his family to leave the city. A war would be starting, he said. On 4 April, Mirjana and her mother and brother went to stay with relatives in central Serbia. Two days later, Belgrade was flattened.

By the time they returned in May, the Yugoslav Army had been defeated, and Belgrade was occupied by the Germans. They found the family house quartering German soldiers, so they moved in with one of the aunts on Topčider. No one had any idea whether Mirjana's father was alive or dead. All they knew was that he had marched out of Belgrade with the Army to fight his fourth war. The Yugoslav Army had gone north to protect the Croats when it would have made more military sense to draw south to protect

Serbia, and the Croats had betrayed the Serbs, and the Army had quickly been surrounded and overpowered. Many had died, and tens of thousands had been taken prisoner and transported to camps in Germany.

In Belgrade, proclamations in German and Serbian ordered Jews to wear the star. The buildings of the military academy south of the city were turned into a camp where hostages were kept until it was time to shoot them. August brought exceptionally fine weather, and Mirjana strolled with other Belgraders along Terazije, the handsome central avenue in front of the Hotel Moscow. From the elegant wrought-iron Art Nouveau lampposts, bodies were hanging.

'You didn't know what to do,' Mirjana said. 'Cross to the other side of the street? Stare at them? Was ignoring them worse?' Today, in her memory they were heavy but peripheral, blind spots in the corner of the eye. She thought they had been young men, but was not sure.

Then bodies started to float down the Sava, out of Croatia. At times they came so thickly they clogged the piers of Belgrade's bridges, one of which would later be renamed 'Bridge of Brotherhood and Unity'. They came in two waves, the first in 1942, when the Germans were winning everywhere and the Ustashas were confident they would be able to clear their territory of Serbs, and the second in 1944, when the Germans were losing and the Ustashas were trying only to clear their camps, to destroy evidence. On summer days Mirjana would go boating and the bodies would float by her as she rowed. Then for years after the war, when she went swimming out to one of the wooded islands in the Sava she would occasionally happen upon skeletons by the shore, the hands tied behind with wire, the backs of the skulls bashed in.

Mirjana moved down into the city with some friends. The Allies began bombing runs, but often she would not bother to go down into the cellar. She would stand at a window and watch the planes as they dived to release their loads and climbed away. The searing whistle of the bombs ended in muffled whumps you felt in your knees, and you located the strike by the rising clouds of

94

cement dust. One day people were talking about a really big raid coming, but Mirjana did not believe it. Then she heard a sound she had never heard before: not the angry insect buzz of dive-bombers, but a deep distant thunder roll, and she went out on the roof and looked up and saw, high up, more planes than she imagined an army could possess, Flying Fortresses, so high they were silver flecks fanned across the sky.

The Americans.

Later came the siege of Belgrade. The Partisans were fighting up from the south, and the Russians from the east, coordinating their assaults so that they would arrive in the city together. Shooting broke out between the apartment buildings. Mirjana and her friends would stand out on the balcony and compete to see who could spot the snipers first, until they themselves were spotted and bullets pinged against the wall around them and they ducked behind the skirting, shrieking girlishly. Mirjana was sixteen. Belgrade was liberated in October 1944.

Mirjana's father, as it turned out, was alive, a prisoner of war in Germany. He was released in 1945, but not allowed to see his family until the Partisans had interrogated him, because they, like the Soviets, considered prisoners of war traitors until proven innocent, and a colonel in the Royal Yugoslav Army was particularly suspect. Communists ransacked the family house. Among other things, they took away photos that Mirjana's mother had taken of the bodies in the Sava. (Mirjana had always assumed the photos had been destroyed in the name of Brotherhood and Unity, but apparently they had only been filed away until the day they might again become useful. Several weeks ago one of them had shown up in a Belgrade newspaper doing a series on Ustasha atrocities.) Fortunately, the colonel's soldiers all vouched for him. He had not collaborated. He was allowed to come home.

He was sixty-three years old. Serbia had won again, and Yugoslavia was bigger than ever, having picked up Istria and a couple of islands, and bits here and there of Bulgaria. But the Serb king in whose name the colonel had fought was in exile, and this 'Tito', a former locksmith and a Croat, had divided Serbia into three parts.

Mirjana's father did what many energetic people do late in life when they cannot accept what their lives have become. He wrote his memoirs. He died in 1982, at the age of a hundred.

17

By the time of her father's death, Mirjana was a widow.

After the war, the English she had learned from a governess landed her a job as translator and correspondent for a western newspaper whose office was a room in the Hotel Moscow. She married, and with her husband found an apartment in an inter-war building of brick and crumbling stucco three blocks down from the fountain of the dead youth. They were lucky, in that none of the strangers with whom they shared the apartment became their mortal enemies. They stayed on year after year while the other tenants slowly drained away, until they had the apart-ment to themselves and their two children. Mirjana's husband, a psychiatrist, had become well-known and respected, and they were doing pretty well for themselves until one day he was killed in a car accident. The children were not yet in school. Mirjana worked hard for the newspaper and raised the children on her own, into two intelligent and charming young people, the twin delights of her life, the son a medical student and the daughter a translator.

The son had pains, which the doctors did not take seriously, saying it was usual for a medical student psychosomatically to reproduce what he was studying. He died of cancer. When I met Mirjana through a mutual friend a year later she was living alone with her son's aged pointer, Leni. Her daughter was living in New York City, studying at NYU and translating at the UN. Mirjana generously offered me a room in her apartment, but worried that my sleep might be disturbed by Leni, who would crawl into my bed at night and steal the covers, or by herself, who since her son had died could not sleep, but instead wandered through the apartment, or read through the piles of newspapers on her dining-room table, or watched the interminable late-night news programmes covering the Yugoslav crisis.

Her newspaper had cut the room in the Hotel Moscow out of its budget years ago, so the 'office' was now the second phone and the fax machine in Mirjana's apartment. Whenever a fresh crisis of constitutionality or a spectacular enough outbreak of violence seemed to warrant a couple of days' attention in its pages, the paper would send a correspondent from Paris or Warsaw, and Mirjana would patiently direct him or her where to go, and sometimes go along to translate. In that capacity, she had gone to Borovo Selo.

The official Croat version, as she related it, was almost identical to what I had heard in Zagreb. Two Croat police cars had driven at night into the centre of Borovo Selo, and two policemen left their car to speak to the men in the other car. Villagers, plus assorted trigger-happy Chetniks ferried in from training bases in Vojvodina, opened fire with automatic weapons, wounding the two men. The second car escaped. In the morning the authorities in Vukovar telephoned Village Defence Commander Šoškočanin, who said he knew nothing about an incident, but would look into it and call back. When he did so, he said, 'We have the two men; come pick them up.' Another patrol was sent, consisting of a patrol car in front and a bus full of policemen behind. As they pulled into the centre of the town, the villagers again opened fire. Twelve policemen and three villagers were killed. The bodies of three policemen were mutilated.

Mirjana had interviewed Šoškočanin, whose version, not sur-prisingly, differed. According to him, the policemen in the two patrol cars on the first night had opened fire as soon as they had driven into Borovo Selo. A few armed villagers were keeping a vigil, because history had taught them to guard against just this sort of Ustasha atrocity. But there were no reinforcements from Serbia, and the villagers had only their old hunting weapons. In that first exchange of fire, the defenders of their homes wounded two policemen, who were immediately sent to a hospital in Novi Sad for treatment. Vukovar called the next morning at ten, but as

97

yet Šoškočanin knew nothing of what had happened the previous
night, so he said he would investigate and report back at twelve-
thirty. At no time did he call and tell the authorities to pick up
the two wounded policemen. Why would he have done that,
when they were already in Novi Sad? At twelve-seventeen two
Land Rovers, a police car and two buses roared into the village.
Three hundred policemen poured out, firing, and killed an
unarmed man standing by the door of the infirmary. The villagers
fired back with their old hunting guns. The police stormed the
infirmary, taking doctors and patients hostage. They ordered
everyone to lie on the floor and trained their guns on the backs of
their heads. The shooting outside lasted for three hours. The
death toll was only one villager, not three, and twenty-five
policemen, not twelve. No mutilations occurred. Only Croats did
that.

Mirjana had a third version, which was based on certain
rumours she had heard while talking to people in Borovo Selo.
This was the version she believed.

On the first night, the Croat policemen had come to the village
on account of a bet. They would sneak in under cover of darkness,
take down the Serbian flag (a tricolour with a red star, unchanged
from the Communist days) on the pole outside the town hall, and
run up the Croatian šahovnica. But a villager spotted them and,
either fearing an attack or outraged at the insult to his flag, rashly
fired. The policemen who escaped in the second car would not, of
course, have admitted to their superiors that they had been in the
village on a prank, attempting a provocative act, but instead
would have reported that they had been attacked out of the blue.

Mirjana believed Šoškočanin when he said he did not call the
authorities in Vukovar and tell them to come and pick up the two
policemen. Vukovar probably made that story up to justify what
was more likely a hot-headed decision by the local militia
commander to reclaim his wounded – perhaps dead, perhaps
monstrously mutilated – men. Certainly the one thing he would
not have guessed was that the Serbs, wild beasts on two legs, had
sent the men to a Novi Sad hospital.

So the reinforcements came. Every person in the village swore to Mirjana that the police fired first, and she believed it. She also believed that the man standing outside the infirmary *had* been armed. Of course he'd been armed, she argued, he was guarding the building. The buses and cars full of policemen roared into the village, the man outside the infirmary was startled and raised his gun, a policeman shot him, and the villagers, arrayed at points around the square, shot back.

And not with hunting guns. Mirjana scoffed at that claim. The number and size of the holes she had seen in the buildings pointed to much more powerful weapons. And anyway, how could villagers with hunting rifles go into battle against policemen with automatic weapons, killing twenty-five and suffering only one casualty? Serbs were good fighters, but they were not that good. She believed that the villagers had not been alone, and that three Serbs *had* been killed, and that all three of them had been outsiders. Šoškočanin had had to admit to one, because the body had been recovered – and that man had not been a villager. Šoškočanin said he had been visiting friends.

Mirjana did not believe that the police 'stormed the infirmary to take hostages'. Fire was coming from the town hall and the back of the square, and they ran into the infirmary to protect themselves. They did not order the patients to lie on the floor because they were sadistic, but because they were afraid and did not know who might have a gun.

Other policemen had been pinned down in a ditch across the road. Their commander threw a grenade and ordered his men to rise out of the ditch, which they did, only to be mown down by machine-gun fire. Here occurred the twenty-five Croat casualties. The policemen in the infirmary were allowed to leave after the Army rolled in.

On the alleged mutilations, Mirjana repeated to me what a doctor had told her: that a high-powered rifle bullet to the head could do all sorts of things, including cause the eyes to pop out. And as for the cut throats, Mirjana had looked at the photographs, and was sceptical. She had seen a few cut throats in her life and in her experience the marks left were slits. The gaping gashes in the photographs looked more like bullet wounds to her.

(The question that interested me, but apparently no one else, was why slitting someone's throat was an atrocity, while blasting it open with a bullet was not.)

Mirjana's pieced-together account sounded plausible to me because, unlike either the official Croat or official Serb version, it did not rely on a characterization of the opposing side as maniacally homicidal, only homicidally frightened. The bet involving the flag sounded exactly right. Most of the new Croat policemen were young village boys. A jejune prank, a startled shot, a weapon raised reflexively, a volley in self-defence – and when the smoke cleared, thirty people lay dead. I had not seen a single newspaper article or television report on Borovo Selo that had done anything but repeat the vein-popping diatribes of the politicians, or expand on them with incendiary images and rumours of their own, and so the consequences were much greater than thirty dead. Borovo Selo was infecting the country. The next time, with the fear greater, a raised weapon would not be necessary to spark the volley.

Mirjana had a television antenna on the roof of her building that allowed her, unlike most people in the city, to get both Belgrade and Zagreb TV. That night Belgrade TV reported that Serb truck drivers carrying food and medicine to beleaguered Slavonian villages had been stopped by Croats and badly beaten. The attackers had bragged to the bloody men at their feet, 'That is how Australian Croats beat.'

Meanwhile, Zagreb TV was showing more clips of Šešelj. 'We do not want an Ustasha president,' he was saying, his eyes as blank as dead fish. 'If Mesić becomes President, we will cut his throat.'

Mirjana took a drag on her cigarette, staring meditatively through the rising smoke. 'That man needs a psychiatrist,' she said judiciously.

18

A question about Borovo Selo remained. Why did Zagreb maintain that only twelve policemen had died, if the villagers had actually killed twenty-five?

The Serb newspapers had an answer. Only twelve of the twenty-five dead were Croats. The rest were Albanians.

It all made perfect sense. The Croats had been enlarging their militias at precisely the time when the Serbian government had been firing Albanian policemen in Kosovo and replacing them with Serbs. The out-of-work Albanians – who were known, by the way, for their oriental cruelty – were being transported secretly to Croatia. The villagers in Borovo Selo had seen numbers tattooed on the wrists of many of the dead policemen. These, surely, were Albanians. The Croats must have registered them in the police rolls as numbers rather than names to conceal their ethnic identity.

The thirteen Albanian dead, then, had been secretly shipped back to Kosovo. The same sort of thing must have happened at the Plitvice lakes, and at Pakrac. Rumours now had it that many more Croats had died in those two incidents than Zagreb was admitting to. These rumours jibed with the Serbs' unarticulated assumption that any battle in which they fought would naturally result in ten or twenty times as many casualties among the enemy as among themselves. Doctors from Belgrade who had been posted down to Kosovo to serve the Serb community had come back saying that unmarked graves were popping up all over the province.

This story had a wonderfully lurid quality, with its image of nameless Albanians, serialized like robots, coming north to do the Croats' bidding. It was a folk tale about the walking dead, which belief, as a matter of fact, originated in Serbia. ('*Vampir*' has been the only Serbian word so far to enter into international usage. Although can 'kundačiti' be far behind?) The too-clever Croats made perfect Frankensteins, the subhuman Albanians perfect monsters.

19

On a cold wet day I walked south from the centre to the low hill of Vračar where, next to the National Library, the Serbs were building the largest Orthodox church in the world.

It would be consecrated to their patron saint, Sava, the founder and first archbishop of their church. St Sava died on a pilgrimage to the Holy Land in 1235 and was buried at Mileševa monastery, where, in 1595, his body was disinterred on Sinan Pasha's orders, brought to Belgrade and burned on this hill. Serbs say the pasha was provoked to this deed by the fact that Sava's saintliness was so renowned, the perfume of his incorruptible body so ambrosial, that Muslims had begun making pilgrimages to his burial place. It was also said that when fire was touched to the miraculous corpse a huge flame rose up over Belgrade, making the city visible from miles away. The Turks roared in triumph, the enslaved Serbs wept, and the free Serbs across the Sava sharpened their swords. Troublesomely for the legend, in 1595 the Serbs across the Sava were not free.

The idea of building a memorial church on the site dated to 1895, the three hundredth anniversary of the immolation, but as money and organization were lacking, and as two Balkan wars and the Great War intervened, an architectural plan was not approved until 1927, and construction began only in 1935. The walls stood barely ten metres high when the Germans invaded in 1941, and after the war Tito never gave permission for building to continue, despite repeated requests by the Patriarch of the Serbian Orthodox Church. Then in 1984, for no obvious reason, the government reversed its policy, and when Slobodan Milošević came to power in 1987 he aggressively supported continued construction as one of his opening salvoes in the new round of Serb nationalism.

I took one of those tours in which the guide reeled off numbers while his innumerate flock gazed vacantly at the vaults. The central dome weighed a gazillion tons and took four cranes a month to raise. Six gigahillion cubic feet – or was that metres? – of concrete had been poured for the walls.

Suffice it to say that the place was extremely large. The central dome, the height of which equalled the width and length of the building, in proper Roman fashion, was flanked by four cupolas below which four half-domes, flush against the main walls, were flanked each by two cupolas over the porches. Interestingly, although medieval Serbian Orthodox architecture is inter-nationally celebrated, the design for this church had little in common with it. Inspiration seemed to have sprung at least as much from the Hagia Sophia in Istanbul, whose pile-of-turtles look this building shared, in a more tucked-in form.

The importance the Church of St Sava had assumed in the past couple of years as the Serbs grew more aggressively nationalistic could be inferred from the fact that special services had already been held in it. In 1989 thousands had packed inside – if you can call it 'inside' when the central dome had not yet been raised – for a service celebrating the six hundredth anniversary of the Battle of Kosovo. In 1990, the Patriarch presided over another service marking the three hundredth anniversary of the great Serb migration led by Archbishop Arsenije out of Turkish Serbia into Hungarian Vojvodina. (In brief, the reason why Vojvodina is part of Serbia today.)

The floor was still dirt. The concrete was a particularly gloomy shade of grey, but the domes were being sheathed in copper, the outside walls would be faced with Carrara marble, and the inside would be splattered with mosaics. All of this would cost hexadil-lions. (Medieval Serbian churches had all been frescoed, because it was cheaper.) I wondered if the facing would start falling off after a year or two, as it always did on Yugoslav hotels and banks.

In the visitors' centre at the edge of the grounds I picked up a reprint of a sermon delivered by a German pastor in Osnabrück in May 1945, entitled 'These are the Serbs!'.

> Our Fatherland has lost the war. The victors are
> Russians, Americans, English. Perhaps they had better
> arms, more soldiers, better leadership. But this is, in fact,
> a pure material victory . . .
> But there are, among us, a people who have won
> another, more beautiful victory – a victory of the soul, a
> victory of the heart and of honour, a victory of peace and
> Christian love. These are the Serbs! . . .
> We have known that here, among us, have been 5,000
> Serb officers, who once represented the social élite of their
> country and now resemble skeletons, exhausted from
> hunger.
> We knew that among the Serbs burns a belief: he who
> does not take revenge, does not earn heaven! And we
> were really afraid of the vengeance of these Serbian
> martyrs. We were afraid that they would do to us, after
> our defeat, the same things which we had done to
> them . . .
> However, what happened?
> When the barbed wire of the camps broke and when
> 5,000 living Serb skeletons appeared freely among us,
> these skeletons caressed our children, giving them sweets!
> They spoke to us! The Serbs were hugging the children of
> those who had caused the greatest misfortune to their
> Fatherland.
> Only now do we understand why our great poet
> Goethe learned the Serbian language. Only now do we
> understand why Bismarck's last word on his deathbed
> was – 'Serbia!'

The piece sounded so quintessentially Serb that I wondered if a German had really written it. The reprint was sourced to an April 1989 issue of *Politika*, which was not bound by any awkward standards of truthfulness. I had trouble imagining the line about revenge and heaven being spoken in German, in which it had no more ring than in English, whereas in Serbian it possessed exactly the sort of ditty quality Serbs preferred in their proverbs: *Ko se ne osveti, taj se ne posveti!* But the reference to Goethe, who learned Serbian because he admired Serb epic oral poetry, sounded a genuine German note, implying as it did that the Serbs were redeemed by being noticed by Goethe.

But why *did* Bismarck say 'Serbia' as he died? The pastor seemed to imply he had been struck by a vision of heaven; if a Serb were to paint the scene, the Iron Chancellor's face would be bathed in a shaft of light. But perhaps by 'Serbia' he meant, 'Go south, young man!' or 'The horror! the horror!' After all, wasn't it Bismarck who also said, albeit not from his deathbed, that the petty feuds of the Balkans were 'not worth the balls of one Pomeranian grenadier'?

Another question: How on earth could the skeletons, just out of the camps, have had sweets to give to the children?

And: Was one of the skeletons Mirjana's father?

As I turned to go, I heard a man who had been on the tour with me speaking to his two sons half in Serbian and half in English. He was tall and mustachioed, with a long nose that swelled, then tapered, then ended in a protuberant capsule like the chamber at the end of a condom. He told me he had lived for five years in England, where he was married to an Englishwoman, but he had been born in the Krajina. Every time he visited Belgrade he came to the St Sava church, and he had made two pilgrimages to the Hilandar monastery on Mt Athos.

I valued talking to people from the mixed areas of Croatia – which I was now afraid to visit, owing to the fighting – because they tended to express more bluntly and passionately the feelings that others hid behind obscurantist phrases. Even in 1989, when most Serbs and Croats were still paying lip service to Brotherhood and Unity, the teenage boys from the Serb villages of Lika fantasized to me about the 'provocation' they eagerly awaited, so that they could ride on their mopeds into the neighbouring Croat villages and mow people down with machine guns.

Every family from those mixed areas had stories, and this man,

Ante, was no exception. The Ustashas had killed eighteen members of his mother's family. They had buried his grandmother alive. They had plucked out his grandfather's eyes, and killed him by jamming a stick down his throat.

Ante had lowered his voice so that his sons would not hear. He shrugged, and explained in a reasonable tone, 'Croats seem to enjoy that kind of thing.' He went on. 'World War II was only the latest outrage, you know. Have you heard about the massacres of Serb civilians in World War I during the Austrian occupation?'

'Yes.'

'The perpetrators were not Austrian soldiers, but Croats. The bloodthirstiness of the Croats has been known throughout history. The Germans used to have a saying: "God save us from war and from the Croats." A word in Serbian for a really bad character is a *bitanga*. That's a conflation of *bitte-danke*. During the crusades, the Germans were returning from the Holy Land through Croatia, and the Croats would come to their camps, begging, "Bitte, danke. Bitte, danke."' Ante scrunched his face into a servile grimace. 'They would beg for knives, for pieces of glass. For something shiny, the ways Indians do. Then they would creep back at night and cut the Germans' throats with the knives they had been given. That's a bitanga.

'And it's all starting again.

'But what I'm really afraid of is that this time around the Serbs will be the same. The people I know in Krajina are sounding as bloodthirsty as the Croats. People are getting killed every day. My family is exhausted. They work all day, and then have to man the barricades all night.'

Ante had a simple question. 'Why do the Croats want to hold on to the Krajina? It is a poor region. And the Serbs there are ten times worse than the Serbs in Serbia. The Serbs in Serbia were serfs for five hundred years, while the Krajina Serbs were *Grenzer* for the Austrians – border guards against the Turks. Primitiveness and aggression are bred into them.'

Imagine, he said, the conditions along the Austrian Military Border for centuries. He bowed his shoulders and assumed a craven expression, darting glances up towards the expected blow.

Imagine the poor Croat peasant in his cheap homespun, with his feudal obligations, his lack of culture, creeping through the village streets. Now comes the Serb – Ante straightened and slapped his chest – a free man, well-fed and armed, proud, a fighter, with his bristling moustache and his honest laugh, his clothes richly embroidered with vibrant folk motifs. He must have swaggered unbearably, that Serb, taking all the women, drinking and fighting, a warrior among worms.

'No wonder the Serbs were hated,' Ante concluded.

And no wonder that the Serbs, through the years, bred stronger and stronger, while the Croats were naturally selected for servility and cunning. No wonder, at Borovo Selo, the Serbs had only suffered three casualties while killing thirty-five Croats. 'They're absolute beginners,' Ante scoffed.

'Thirty-five?' I said. 'I thought it was twenty-five.'

'That's the official version.'

'I thought the *official* version was twelve.'

'No one believes that.'

'Who do you think started it?'

'I don't have to think. There are the facts. One policeman climbed the flagpole while the other one started shooting.'

'And the unreported dead?'

'Albanians. They used to have numbers tattooed on their wrists; now they're stamped on with a special ink.'

'And have more Serbs been killed than reported?'

'Probably. The Croats arrested seventeen in the Krajina, who are probably all dead. They keep postponing the trial because they have no one to bring. A Croatian doctor said no surgeon would ever be able to rebuild the men's faces.'

I wondered if anyone outside the Balkans talked like that. People here had a genius for squeezing the last drop of horror out of violence. While American military sharpshooters talked about 'servicing the target', Serbs and Croats would explain that when you shot a man in the head his skull exploded and brain matter showered down on his wife and children. Was it admirably straightforward? Or did it indicate a bloodthirsty imagination?

It was six o'clock, and the man had to leave. His boys would not forgive him if they were late getting home for *Ninja Turtles*.

'It seems to be the favourite show of boys all over the world,' I observed. We stood in the doorway, watching the light rain come down, Ante's boys playing at kick-boxing in the street.

'I suppose it could be worse,' Ante said. 'It teaches them to eat pizza, which is better than hotdogs.'

'Sure. Bread, tomatoes, cheese . . .'

'And perhaps when they all grow up and run across a painting by Donatello or Raphael, they will like it, without knowing why.' Ante thought about that for a minute, watching his boys. 'Perhaps that's how peace will finally come,' he said. 'This generation will grow up and instead of eating Serbian *ajvar* and Croatian *kulen* they'll all eat pizza, and they'll agree too much on what's really important, like their favourite TV shows, to fight. Those turtles, you know, don't actually ever hurt anybody.'

He rounded up his kids.

'Cowabunga,' I said to them.

Delighted, they keened it back at me, twirling invisible nunchaks.

20

Mirjana's silvering sepia hair flopped uncombed past ears as large as Abraham Lincoln's. Her seamed face, naturally scowly, was occasionally broken by a sideways smile that seemed to have twisted loose from an internal grip, trapping one prominent tooth against her lower lip like a hard nub of pain sandwiched in humour. She would clap her knuckly hands together as she leaned over to talk babytalk in her smoky, wood-grained voice to Leni, who would dance a youthful jig on his stiff legs and croon back at her.

Yugoslavia had the highest traffic-fatality rate in Europe. The drivers − 'Anarchists!' − played chicken so unthinkingly they would have been surprised to learn that people elsewhere distinguished it from normal driving. I could understand why an overtaking car kept accelerating towards a head-on collision, since it had to complete the pass to get out of the way, but I could not understand why the opposing car did not brake. No matter how many times I saw it, I did not believe it. The car honked, but did not brake, it honked as it closed in until the passing car cut at the first and last possible second back to its own lane. Or it honked all the way into the collision, with the invariably seatbelt-less drivers – I had never met a Yugoslav who did not despise me for wearing a seatbelt – catapulting through both windshields, passing each other on the left as they had failed to do on the right.

Car-accident deaths were like war-atrocity stories; every family had them. Mirjana's husband had been a passenger when he was killed. Her closest friend's husband had been a pedestrian, run down on a Belgrade street. In many parts of Belgrade you had to walk in the streets despite the danger, because parked cars hogged the sidewalks. Belgrade seemed like some futuristic dystopia in which automobiles had invaded from another planet and enslaved humans, and were altering the Earth's atmosphere to suit themselves.

Mirjana hated driving, and for the moment she hadn't the option, in any case. She owned a car which her son had bought third- or fourth-hand, but he had still been fixing it when he died. Thereafter it passed into the care of a mechanic friend who, because he did the work for free in his spare time, was still at it more than a year later.

Everyone in Yugoslavia had to be a handyman, or had to know one. It was the only way to get anything done. Mechanical ability was assumed to be sex-linked, so women proposed, men disposed. Mirjana had once relied on her son, and now relied on a network of her son's friends. Two of them one day rewired the phone jacks in pursuit of some minor increase in convenience, and when I came in that night, Mirjana was in a panic. 'My God, the phone isn't working!'

In the library a body lay sprawled on the couch, its feet splayed grotesquely, its head dangling towards the floor. I thought one of her newspaper's correspondents had died and Mirjana was upset because she couldn't call the ambulance. But the body turned out to belong to her upstairs neighbour, who had the jack open and was reconnecting wires. He tried every possible combination, but could not get the phone to work.

'I'll strangle those boys,' Mirjana vowed. As long as the phone was down, there was no Belgrade office for the paper.

Unfortunately, I was useless. I had had the luxury all my life of never learning how anything worked. I wasn't even sure whether you could touch a phone line without getting electrocuted.

But Mirjana was even less mechanical than I was, so I did manage to help her one day, after the phone was fixed, by reading the manual for the answering machine her daughter had recently brought from New York and explaining to her how to erase the old messages which, by then, amounted to about forty-five minutes. Mirjana had got into the habit of hitting 'playback' and reading the newspaper while waiting for the new messages to come around.

I slept in her son's old room. His hockey sticks and helmet still hung on the wall, his medical books gathered dust on the shelves. Framed photos throughout the apartment kept him in mind, a curly-haired boy with bushy eyebrows. I wondered where those eyebrows had come from until I saw Mirjana's wedding pictures. They had once been hers. The bride beamed unrestrainedly next to the debonair groom, who slouched in his capacious suit, holding his cigarette Russian-style, palm-up between thumb and index finger. His smile was cooler.

Representations of him around the apartment were even more numerous than of his son – not photos but sketches, fond caricatures, professionally done, which suggested the distinguished circles in which he had moved. In the library, a large bust of him with a psychiatrist's goatee and sternly cocked eyebrows frowned over our shoulders when we watched the nightly news. The brass plaque on the front door still identified the apartment as his, not hers.

Even on the brightest days the flat was dark. Daylight was something you glimpsed through a scrim of leaves and heavy curtains at the far end of the room beyond the one you were in. That was another world – the present. I read under little lamps with browning shades that cast a brown light. The plaster walls were painted a Victorian dusky rose. The parquet floors groaned. Half-ton mirrors with bevelled edges and flaking backings presented me with milky images of myself. On the back of the front door hung a board covered with messages written in felt-tip marker. Like the messages on the machine, they were old, but Mirjana would not want to erase these. Her son's friends had written them during a party, the last one before he died.

Heirlooms from both Mirjana's family and her husband's filled cupboards, sideboards, tables, corners. In the glass cases in the dining room I could identify the ornate silver servers, enamel-tipped spoons, porcelain cups and gold-rimmed dishes that I had seen in the wedding photos gleaming on the presentation table behind the couple. Now they were filmed, furry with dust, unused for years, if ever. The enormous carved-wood dining table was lost under stacks of magazines and papers. Mirjana's typewriter seemed to have died in a landslide.

Her icons were on the wall over the sideboard. She had hung a sprig of lavender on St George. But her prize was a *hadžijska ikona* which her husband's grandfather, a Russian, had ordered on his return from a hadž to Jerusalem in 1820. Some three feet by five, the wooden board was painted with a profusion of little chapels, under whose vaults biblical scenes were jumbled together without chronology or coherence, in the exuberant, unselfconscious way of folk art: a Madonna and Child, St George killing the dragon, the Crucifixion, Abraham with his knife to Isaac's throat, Jonah standing imperturbably in the mouth of the whale, Judas hanging on the Judas tree, the Deposition from the Cross, the scourging of Jesus, the Transfiguration. The figures had large heads, hanging forward with regretful eyes. They all looked guilty of something. In the little leftover areas the artist had painted sailing boats, either alluding to the Fisher of Souls or conforming to the often observed phenomenon that when people are asked to draw anything at all, twenty per cent will draw sailing boats.

The room beyond had been the psychiatrist's inner sanctum, the consultation room. Crimson velvet upholstery still sound-proofed the door. If the other rooms were crowded, this one was jammed. Flowered wing-chairs, a *chaise-longue*, more glass cases. No room to walk anywhere, except to one of the near corners where Mirjana slept, when she managed to sleep, on a couch. Perhaps *the* couch.

She wore sweaters and trousers made dingy and shapeless by extreme age, soiled running shoes that looked too big on her. Her daughter was always telling her to buy herself something nice but Mirjana would huff at me, indignant, and speak as though I were her daughter, since the genuine article was thousands of miles away. 'What do I need new clothes for, frankly? You tell me.'

I couldn't. I dressed like a slob too.

Leni would come with us on the daily trips to the bakery or the open-air market. As soon as he got out to the street, he would head up the hill because that was the long route, the one that took him by the bakery where they always gave him a roll. He would stop at the first corner looking back hopefully at us, and if we took a step in that direction he would be off, in his swinging, straight-legged gait, his large head low, skimming over the ground.

His route was obstacled by 'good dogs' and 'bad dogs'. A good dog on the corner was a medium-sized mongrel of silken curls, to whom Leni would crawl up on his stomach, simpering. There was often a bad dog at the grocery store next to the market, a dachshund bitch who was such a – well, such a bitch, that Mirjana didn't like to leave Leni alone while she went in to shop. I would stand with him and we would both watch left and right, worriedly.

At the market on Fridays, Mirjana always bought seventeen pink roses. She visited her husband's grave every Saturday, and he had been dead seventeen years. However, she would bring only sixteen roses to the grave, leaving one in the apartment. In

Yugoslavia you never brought an odd number of flowers to a cemetery because that would cause someone you knew to die, to even out the number.

Back in the apartment she washed the grime off Leni's feet in the 'tubbie' and threw for him his 'hedgie', a green plastic hedgehog. 'But what? But what?' she asked of him, feigning ignorance, as he stood over his toy and groaned at her to throw it again. 'He talks,' she said to me.

He bucked, turned around with a clatter of toenails, crooned.

'He's such a strange dog. He's like a little child. But what? But what?'

I cringed at the thought that he would die on her.

Later, she put the seventeen roses in water. She patted them from the sides with her large hands as you would fluff a pillow, and bent to inhale. She straightened with that sideways smile which in this case signified worldly regret.

'Everything is grown so artificially now,' she said. 'Even roses have no scent.'

21

Brief, perfect spring came to Belgrade. Fluff from hidden cotton-wood trees sailed in hordes along the boulevards, incongruously white against the grime of the buildings, the haze of car exhaust. As tufts flew by me, I wondered if their filaments were gathering lead particles like krill on baleen, if after a block or two they would drop with a clatter to the ground.

But I left the pollution behind me as I ascended Topčider Hill. There the villas, the high hedges, the manicured grounds were as clean as the cotton.

Mirjana: 'After the Communists came, there were so many *more* rich people! When my aunts lived on Topčider, all the wealthy people of Belgrade fitted on a single street.'

That was Užička Street, down which I walked. The Communists had confiscated Mirjana's aunts' villas for themselves, but eventually they and many of the other houses on Topčider became residences for ambassadors, who, even more than high Communist officials, considered swank their due. I admired the Swedes' Tudor with its Volvo, the Iranians' Contemporary with its Mercedes, the Americans' Georgian with its two-masted barge of a Lincoln. Tito had given the Americans the second-largest manor on the hill, in gratitude, it was said, for emergency relief aid sent by the Truman administration in 1950 after a catastrophic drought. (Tito's break with Stalin had occurred two years previously, and the Cominform was still maintaining an economic blockade of Yugoslavia.) Many Yugoslavs still remembered the yellow powder in bags stamped with the US seal that they called *Trumanova jaja*, or 'Truman's eggs'. Something of a joke, since the phrase also meant Truman's balls.

The largest villa on the hill became Tito's residence, along with three neighbouring villas, and others were torn down to enlarge the grounds. I bought a ticket for the complex, now a clutch of museums. Most of all, I wanted to see the collection of relay batons in the 25 May Museum, a concrete and steel building in a style much favoured by Yugoslav Communists, having two wings whose rooflines rose gradually from a central hall. The idea was to evoke optimism and uplift, the same subliminal message a watch seller sends when he sets all his watches to ten-past ten.

By the time the war was over, the Tito cult was already in full swing, and the first of the annual *Štafete Mladosti*, or Youth Relays, took place in 1945. In a *štafeta*, scores of young people chosen for their running ability would carry a baton through the entire country. The relay would take over a month, and each night the television news would report on the location of the baton. The last runner would enter Belgrade on 25 May, Tito's birthday, and proceed to the Red Star Stadium, where he would present the baton to Tito, to the cheers of tens of thousands of young people.

Every year a different baton was designed. In addition (lest one conclude this official homage was hollow), ordinary Yugoslavs began making their own batons and sending them to Tito.

114

Eventually, there were forty official batons and twenty-one thousand unofficial ones. The 25 May Museum was built to hold them all.

'I love some of the home-made ones,' the museum guide told me. 'They're so imaginative, with heart in them. Real folk art.' Unfortunately, they weren't there. They had been taken out two weeks previously to make room for a non-Tito exhibition.

'We're planning to turn this into more of a general-interest museum,' the guide explained. She conceded that the plans arose from the fact that so few people came to the museum any more.

I would have been fascinated to see the batons, both as folk art and as social commentary, but Yugoslavs had a Tito hangover. It would be quite some time before they could be interested in Titoism as a political phenomenon divorced from the question of whether he was God or the Devil, or – hardest to accept – neither.

The štafetas continued after Tito died, although you had to wonder whom the runner handed the baton to at the end. I also wondered: Tito died on 4 May 1980 at five-past three p.m. and every 4 May after that, exactly at 3.05, air-raid sirens sounded throughout the country, and all traffic came to a stop, all pedestrians stood stock still on the sidewalks, farmers stood next to their cows, children stopped running in the playgrounds. For three minutes the country stood to attention. The year's youth relay would already have begun, and an essential element of the spectacle was that the baton should never stop moving. One runner handed it over to the next with the kind of ostentatious continuity displayed by the Pony Express or – the obvious inspiration – the Olympic torch. So now on 4 May at five-past three, did the runner stop and spoil Tito's memorial? Or did he keep running and insult Tito's memory? The dilemma reminded me of Ban Jelačić declaring war on Ferdinand V of Hungary in the name of Ferdinand V of Austria.

In 1986 the Communist Youth Organization of Slovenia killed the štafeta mladosti by refusing to participate in it, arguing that it was, in a way, adolescent. The father was dead and it was time to grow up. Their refusal provoked a storm of controversy, but also made them so popular in Slovenia, which had always been the republic in the vanguard of reform, that when they ran in the elections in 1990 under the name of the Liberal Party, they came in third out of a field of more than a dozen.

The leader of the Liberal Party proudly kept in his office the baton that was supposed to have been used in 1986 – his ticket into the new parliament – and when he handed it to me I burst out laughing. The designer, whoever he was, had anticipated the Communist Youth in debunking the relay, in his own sly way. The baton consisted of a black base surmounted by a rod of clear lucite, down the length of which several parallel holes had been drilled, so that they resembled a bundle of rods tied around a central shaft. In other words, the baton was a *fasces*, the Roman symbol of authority and the etymological inspiration for Mussolini's *Fascisti*. The Liberal Party leader had never heard of a fasces.

I had to content myself with the other collections. A cylindrical building next to the 25 May Museum housed six floors of state gifts to Tito.

Tito had always lived exceptionally well, even in the years before the war when the Communist Party was illegal in Yugoslavia. He liked to say that during his years of undercover work he escaped the attention of the Yugoslav secret police because they expected Communists to be stubbly men in shabby suits, whereas he dressed impeccably and always travelled first-class. In the midst of the most primitive conditions during the guerilla war in Bosnia in World War II, Tito rode, whenever he could, in a diminutive steam train (the British liaison officer Fitzroy MacLean dubbed it 'the Partisan Express') even though it could hardly go anywhere, and, to get it to the few places it *could* go, the Partisans had to repair tracks they themselves had sabotaged, and its noise and smoke made their position conspicuous.

After the war, with Tito's predilections unchecked, villas, yachts and antiques mounted. He owned – or rather 'the people' owned for him – seventeen castles and villas around the country, far more than had belonged to the Karadjordjević dynasty. Like the Russian tsars, he ate not off mere sterling, but solid gold.

It came to be understood that any state visit to Tito, if it were to succeed, had to be accompanied by a lavish gift, and here they all were, a marvellously eclectic assortment of pricy items, such as lacquered Thai tea-sets, English silver services, Ming vases and African gongs. I noted with particular interest Stalin's garish gewgaw of 1945, a porcelain lump like a melted polychrome candle entitled 'The Duel', in which a knight on horseback with a red cape was a split second away from burying his axe in another knight's face. Mao Zhedong had given an ivory piece of elaborately carved spheres nested snugly one inside the other. Richard Nixon's gift was a Federal bureau – probably not an intentional pun – of cherry wood, with brass locks and handles. Quasi-state visits were best represented by the ornate silver tray and cover adorned with a dead bird, inscribed HAPPY XMAS, WITH MUCH ADMIRATION AND AFFECTION, ELIZABETH AND RICHARD BURTON.

On the top floor, on dressmakers' dummies in glass cases, were arrayed Tito's various uniforms, which he loved as much as his *objets d'art*: his sober evening uniform of navy blue; his ice-cream admiral's whites; the royal blue suit with the red sash that only he, as Supreme Commander and Marshal of Yugoslavia, could wear.

Western observers meeting Tito for the first time during the war invariably noted his ramrod posture, and the fact that he wore his neatly pressed woollens buttoned to the throat, even in the hottest weather. A photograph of Tito and Churchill at their first meeting on Capri in 1944 shows the British Prime Minister sloppily poured into open-necked pyjama-light linens, a heat rash in bloom across his dazed face, while the Partisan grins composedly from the straitjacket of his martial tunic. Clearly, the head of the Allied Forces has come to visit his dotty grandfather at a convalescent home. In his later years Tito grew stout and dyed his coiffure a Reagan orange. He took on the androgynous, mummified look one sometimes sees in vain old men.

The guide led me and a handful of other visitors through the grounds. Tito's peacocks milled under the trees, uttering cries like women falling off ledges.

Here was Tito's hunting lodge, a *faux*-rustic log cabin lined with hunting rifles and shotguns, inlaid with silver and mother-of-pearl, and Tito's own trophies – antelope heads and bear skins, horns and tusks and open jaws, whole lion skins tacked to the ceiling.

A few steps farther on was his game house, with its comfy blond-wood 50s styling: his billiard table, his machine shop, his darkroom, his outsized chrome blender and coffee maker, his TV with its round-edged screen and rabbit-eared antenna. The guide informed us that this was Tito's favourite place, and I could imagine him in his ascot and boater, mixing daiquiris and slaughtering his guests at billiards. Beating him was probably as bad an idea as arriving empty-handed.

The main residence was a large villa in the Spanish style. Period chairs huddled around matching tables looking lost in the over-sized rooms. The boss's desk remained as he left it, as neat as his tunics, with a yellowed newspaper from 4 May 1980.

'You will note,' the guide said solemnly, 'that the clocks are stopped at five-past three.'

'You mean they all stopped exactly when he died?' I asked, getting into the mood.

The guide gave me a strange look. 'Of course not,' he said.

The others had had enough, so I went on alone to the 4 July Museum, a stucco villa a short walk down the hill. Tito and other Communists met here in secret on 4 July 1941 – three months after the bombing of Belgrade – and decided to call for a general uprising. I looked at the table around which the decision was made. I looked at the camp-bed on which Tito slept. A map showed me exactly which streets Tito had walked down in order to get to the meeting. The text on the wall informed me that the people's uprising against the Fascist occupiers and their quisling lackeys duly began on 7 July, in the village of Bela Crkva.

Mirjana: 'What's the word? Oh yes. Bullshit.'

The uprising, in fact, had already begun, having been called by Royal Army officers – soon to be Četnici, a word they borrowed from the old days when bands (čete) of Serbs harried the Turks – on 12 May, in the hills of Ravna Gora in Serbia. The plaques in the 4 July Museum of course did not mention Ravna Gora, nor did they explain the perhaps puzzling delay of two months before the Yugoslav Communists, in their turn, called for resistance. But the answer was simple. Hitler did not invade the Soviet Union until 22 June.

Tito's exhortation was almost funny: 'Proletarians from all parts of Yugoslavia – to arms! . . . You cannot stand idly by while the precious blood of the heroic people of Soviet Russia is shed.'

A final observance remained: the House of Flowers, in which Tito lay buried. It had once been a greenhouse in which the amateur yachtsman, pilot, photographer, machinist and horticulturalist had grown orchids. I walked up the deserted paths, which were marked with arrows to control the flow of the crowds, past bronze sculptures with names like 'The Wounded Courier' and, as the English translation ran, 'The Pigeon of Peace'. The guard by the glass door ushered me in silently with a suave semaphore of his white-gloved hands. A megalith of white marble lay among anthuriums, coleus and mother-in-law's tongue. Soldiers stood crisply at attention at the four corners.

No one but the guardsmen of Tito's tomb were allowed to wear the royal-blue uniform with the red braid that the Marshal himself had worn. The clear implication was that they belonged to him. In the old days, slaves were strangled by the graves of their masters, but today they only had to play dead. At least these young soldiers, unlike the Buckingham Palace automatons, had the indiscipline to follow me with their eyes. ('Anarchists!') None the less, I felt under-dressed and awkwardly at-ease, an atheist at a religious service. The gold letters on the marble block said JOSIP BROZ TITO.

He was born simply Josip Broz, in a village on the Croatian–Slovenian border in 1892, a subject of the Habsburg Empire. His official biographies say he fought on the Russian front in World War I, where he was taken prisoner in 1915 and later exposed to the ideas of the Russian Revolution. They never mention that before he fought on the Russian front he had fought as a sergeant-major against the Serbs. He had been one of the bitangas. Even today, most Serbs do not know this.

Why 'Tito'? Fitzroy MacLean said the name came from the way he parcelled out orders to his Partisans: 'You do this. You, this. You, this.' (In Serbo-Croatian, '*Ti, to.*') My guide in the 4 July Museum had scoffed at that theory, saying 'Tito' was derived from Titus. During the war, rumour had it that there were several Titos, the word being a title that each Partisan leader assumed on the death of his predecessor. Some hypothesized that TITO stood for Third International Terrorist Organization. Tito himself gave the simplest explanation: he claimed that it was a common name in the area he came from. It seemed superbly indicative of Yugoslavia that something as easily verifiable as this last explanation had never been verified.

Tito lived on after death in the portraits that were hung, according to an unwritten but iron rule, in every public place. He lived on in the štafetas, in the blowing of sirens on 4 May. He lived on in the 5,000-dinar bill (as Johnny Hart observed, good animals are reincarnated as humans, whereas good humans are reincarnated as money), which the National Bank promised would always be the highest.

But then came hyper-inflation, caused largely by Tito's debt-financed economic policies, and his legacy devalued as drastically as his dinar note. Eventually, the bank was forced to issue a 10,000-dinar bill. Then a 50,000. Then a 1,000,000. (It solved the blasphemy problem by not putting real people on the higher notes, only idealized types of miners and farm girls.) Serbs demonstrated against Tito, ripping up his image on the 5,000-dinar notes, which they could afford to do because by then the notes were worth less than five cents. When a shopowner first took a portrait of Tito off his wall, it was big news on television. Then suddenly, one day, you realized you could hardly find his picture anywhere in Belgrade.

But the dead man lingered, haunting the wild imaginings of his people. He had been married only three times, but they said he had had many mistresses, siring dozens of illegitimate children. Who knew where all those young Titos were? Perhaps one worked next to you.

A few years back, an old gravestone had been found in Vojvodina on which was written JOSIP BROZ. Some people concluded that the real Josip Broz had died in the war, and this

Tito was a substitute, an imposter. Some said this Tito was actually a Russian. (That's what the World War II Chetnik leader Draža Mihajlović thought, perhaps because Tito spoke a rather peculiar dialect of Croatian.) Others pointed to his love of uniforms, his stocky build, his age, his fondness for hunting, his title of 'Marshal', and to an undeniable facial likeness, and drew the obvious conclusion. The post-war Tito was really Hermann Göring. But by this point they were joking.

I think.

State secrets had turned sinister. The god had become a vampire. He wasn't even buried in a cemetery, like real dead people, but Dracula-like in his own walled fortress. And four doll-Titos jerked stiffly around the coffin. Or were they his sons?

The leader of the new Chetniks, Šešelj, wanted the bloodsucker excorcized. 'They should offer the body to his widow,' he said. 'If she doesn't want it, then they should offer it to the Croats. If *they* don't want it, then they should bury it in the cheapest possible way.'

I came out of the House of Flowers. The deserted plaza of fountains and walks sloped away towards the city. Grass was growing up between the cobblestones. Somewhere – believe it or not – a cock was crowing.

From this particular vantage point, the Church of St Sava dominated the Belgrade skyline. The golden cross on the dome glowed in the sun.

22

Down the hill, I wandered into a *zadužbina crkva* – an Orthodox church built privately as charity or in fulfilment of a vow. In this case an infertile couple had finally had a child, and had built the church as thanks to God. The simple and appealing exterior – brick, with the traditional small and high central dome – dated from 1939, but the frescoes inside had recently been redone. The man I spoke with was immensely proud of the new interior, and I smiled and nodded, keeping to myself the over-educated person's preference for art that is cracked, faded and sooty.

The church smelled pleasantly of the cut grass strewn across the floor, and a lone woman sat on a stool, plaiting blades into a tiny wreath. Today was the Orthodox Pentecost, and grass covered the floors of all the Orthodox churches in Serbia. Women wove three wreaths, for the Trinity, and placed them beneath the main icon in their homes, burning the dried wreaths from the previous year.

I met an old man sitting outside the church. 'A hundred years!' he said, getting up.

I looked at him, astonished. 'You?'

'No, you!' He shook my hand.

He wore a woollen jacket with black braiding around the pockets, a rare remnant of folk costume. The felt fedora, too, was old-fashioned. You could see such hats in the grainy World War II photographs of peasants digging their own graves while armed Ustashas posed and smiled. He had a peasant's boiled hands. Crocodile skin covered the upper half of his face. He gestured for me to sit by him in the sun and he talked to me, phlegm rising periodically into his throat to strangle him, bringing tears to his eyes. Or was it emotion?

He had fought for four years as a Chetnik, and then one year as a Partisan. That made five years in a four-year war, but he insisted on it. He had been wounded by a grenade, and still carried shrapnel in his back and right leg. But did he have a pension? No, not a cent. And meanwhile that whore up the hill, she had a pension as fat as her behind.

A middle-aged man came out of the church. 'A hundred years!' the old man said, rising and taking his hand. (Mirjana later told me it was an old country greeting, meaning, 'May you live a hundred years.')

'A Chetnik for four years,' the middle-aged man said supportively, gesturing to his friend, who took the compliment with studied impassivity.

'So I heard.'

122

'And one year a Partisan.'

'That makes five years a fighter.'

'Amazing, isn't it?'

'Quite.'

The old man described his war experiences, but I could not understand much of it through the sticky gurglings in his throat. He choked and spat, his eyes brimmed. Startling bits emerged. Something about a comrade, who had to go back. They were leaving a battle, fleeing perhaps, or marching towards another one, and this colleague went back. A couple of hundred metres, or was it two kilometres? Just to cut someone's head off. A woman's apparently. The old man removed his fedora to gather his hair and pull upward, and drew his finger across his throat. I looked around for the middle-aged man to interpret for me, but he had disappeared into the church.

The old man rearranged things in his chest. With his boiled hands on his knees, he leaned forward hawking. He was speaking of some heroic act he had performed. (Had he saved the woman? Or was this a different story?) But there had been no witnesses, and so he never got a medal. He had gone to the commission, and there the officers, the bastards, had sat, their own chests covered with medals they had given themselves, but they would not give one to him. And they also hadn't given him a pension, whereas – he looked to make sure his friend wasn't there, he lowered his voice – whereas that whore up the hill . . .

I realized he was talking about Tito's last wife, Jovanka, who still lived somewhere on Topčider, in a small apartment. A pension she may have had now, but she complained bitterly to the newspapers of the villas, yachts and artworks that had been taken from her, reclaimed by the state. For years she had been virtually under house arrest.

'Pa da,' the old man sighed. And then the war was finally over. Almost two million dead. And here it was coming again. I should tell him why. He didn't know.

He ran a hand roughly across the crocodile skin and I uneasily imagined it splitting along the baked-earth crevices, bleeding down the deep channels.

In the good old days under King Aleksandar, there wasn't all this Croatia for Croats, Slovenia for Slovenes. Everyone was a Yugoslav. The phlegm was surging again. Did I know that good King Aleksandar had had three sons, and that he had given the first a Serb name, the second a Croat name and the third a Slovene name? That was how good a Yugoslav he was. And they killed him.

The old man gasped for air. The tears in his eyes were so rheumy they seemed of the same substance as the glue that throttled him. An ancient crusted handkerchief took on a new load of snot.

The old man was thirteen when Croats shot his king.

And King Petar defied the Germans, and yet the Communists never let him back. He died in exile while the whore up on the hill . . .

The middle-aged man came back and clucked his tongue. Had he told me about the grenade?

He had.

And no pension!

23

Dimitrije, a friend I had known for the past two years, had bought a Chetnik cap.

'It's not a Chetnik cap!' he protested. 'It's the old Royal Army cap.'

'But you bought it because it's a Chetnik cap,' his wife Snežana said.

They were both Serbs. But two years ago, he would call himself a Serb, she would call herself a Yugoslav, and when he insulted Croats she would yell at him, 'That's exactly the mentality that's going to destroy this country!'

Now they only argued about why she was too busy being an

architect to bear him any children. On the subject of the Croats, she shrugged angrily and said, 'They are Nazis.'

'The reason we want all Serbs together in one state is that we fear for the Serbs outside Serbia,' Dimitrije said. 'There are Romanians outside Romania, Hungarians outside Hungary, and so on. That's OK. Because no one bothers them. But Serbs outside Serbia? They are not safe.'

Everywhere in Belgrade Serbs explained to me why they were convinced the Ustasha terror was starting again.

First and foremost, there was the return of the šahovnica. In a country with sensibilities to symbols so finely tuned that some people saw an Ustasha cap in the abstract blob on the 5,000-dinar bill, the šahovnica had burst on the scene like an atrocity in and of itself. Croats said it was their medieval coat of arms, but Germans might just as well argue, in bringing back the swastika, that it was an ancient sun symbol.

Then there were the loyalty oaths, and the fact that Serb policemen and judges who did not sign them were fired. There was the change in the Croatian constitution, demoting Serbs from a 'nation' to a 'minority'.

The Serbs described to me a sickening feeling of *déjà vu*. Nothing, to them, was coincidental. The Ustasha regime had been intensely Catholic. Ante Pavelić and his ministers had appeared often in the company of the Papal Nuncio and the Archbishop of Zagreb. They had obtained the blessing of Pope Pius XII. Now here was Tudjman, with his screaming monk, his requests to meet with John Paul II, his followers cramming the churches.

To the Serbs, accustomed as they were to the autocephalic, national status of Orthodox churches, the Roman Catholic Church was a foreign agent, worse than a mere international conspiracy bent on their destruction. Just as 'internationalist' Communism had really been disguised Russian hegemonism, Roman Catholicism covertly advanced Italian objectives. This was no small concern when Italy was your neighbour. The last time the Italians had their way on the Balkan peninsula they took Dalmatia, Istria and half of Slovenia, and created a Greater Albania out of chunks of southern Yugoslavia, including Kosovo.

Yugoslavia and Italy had been struggling bitterly over territory around Trieste as late as 1975.

Neither was it a coincidence that Germany was leading the fight in the EC to recognize Croatia. Only a year reunited, and the Germans were panting to get their tentacles once again around all of Central Europe. The Serbs talked bitterly about the Fourth Reich.

Even small things had returned to haunt them, with a sinister, almost uncanny predictability. Tudjman was changing the language, as Pavelić had done, to accentuate the differences between Croatian and Serbian. He was even resurrecting the same words.

'They say they're more western than we are,' Snežana said. 'But they love these fake words that sound like Slavic grunts. Like this *zrakoplovna luka* – "air-swimmer-port" – for *aerodrom*. It's a Nazi word. It's their obsession with racial purity.'

Not least important was the fact that this was 1991. Peoples who are obsessed with the past feel the demagogic pull of those fat round numbers around which inchoate pride and hatred can coalesce. So the Croats celebrated 'One Thousand Years of Croatian Sculpture', or the nine hundredth anniversary of Zagreb. The Independent State of Croatia made much of the fact that it was founded exactly 1,300 years after the Croats displaced the Avars in Illyricum.

For the Serbs, the round numbers were on the march.

1989. Six hundred years before, the Serbian state had died trying to save Europe from the Turk, in the Battle of Kosovo.

1990. Three hundred years before, Serbs had tried again to rid the west of the Turk, and had failed, were abandoned by the Austrians who had promised them support, and were forced in their tens of thousands to leave their homeland, to die on marches northward and in the foreign land called 'the Duchy' – Vojvodina. A hundred and twenty-five years later they tried to get rid of the Turks a third time, and succeeded, and when Novi Sad television neglected one night to lead off its evening news with a story about the 175th anniversary of that uprising, instead placing it after a report on the just-held Slovenian elections, Milošević fired the entire news team.

1991. Fifty years ago the Serbs had 'flung their reckless, heroic defiance at the tyrant and conqueror in the moment of his greatest power', as Churchill admiringly put it, and had one day to dance in the streets before the bombs fell and four years of darkness followed.

The only part that did not fit was that the English and the Americans were not supporting Serbia. Even the French, with whom the Serbs had a long tradition of mutual admiration, were not supporting them. Serbs on the street asked me plaintively, or angrily, why America did not understand. Serbs and Americans had been allies in both world wars, whereas Croatia had been our enemy.

I pointed out that Americans no longer considered Germany or Japan our enemies either. I said it might be worth thinking about trying to get beyond that. But it didn't wash.

'Historians have recorded the disastrous fact', Tito once said, 'that not one of fifty generations on our territory has been spared the devastation of war and heavy losses.'

Serbs had been waiting all their lives for this. They learned their history by listening to the oral epic poetry that Goethe had so admired, and they believed in the eternal return. A man with the ancient one-string instrument called a *gusle* sang about the Battle of Kosovo in the pedestrian zone.

> Miloš Obilić heard Prince Lazar,
> his living heart was loaded with sorrow,
> he took up cold wine in a golden cup,
> he drank to Lazar from the golden cup:
> 'Health, Lazar, father-in-law, my health and yours!
> And by that God who has created me,
> by Danica, my young and betrothed love,
> may she have great glory and pride from me,
> I will keep faith with you on Kosovo;
> and I promise before all these barons,
> before tomorrow's sun touches his east

I shall come to the tent of the Sultan
and strike this knife into his living heart,
and I shall trample him with my right foot.'

America and England were violating the sacred space at the heart
of the epic. Only the Serbs, faithful to their history, stood ready
again to do battle. If they had to, they would stand alone.

Serbs often compared themselves to the Jews. Like the Jews,
they had historically suffered from the twin scourges of militant
Catholicism and aggressive Islam. Like the Jews, they had died by
the hundreds of thousands in concentration camps. Posters in the
Independent State of Croatia, in offices, restaurants, shops and
trams, had read, NO SERBS, JEWS, NOMADS OR DOGS ALLOWED.
Jews on the streets wearing their yellow stars passed Serbs
wearing blue armbands marked with a P, for *Pravoslavac*, or
'Orthodox'.

Serbs looked at Israel's policy of militant vigilance against its
Arab neighbours, its reliance on offence as the only trustworthy
defence. They had even borrowed the Jews' rallying cry: Never
again! *Nikad više!* They would make absolutely sure of that.

'I was never interested in politics,' Snežana said. 'Everyone has
the right not to have to think about politics. But you can't any
more. I read recently that the Krajina was always a part of Serbia
until World War II, that it was split off from Serbia when the
Partisans drew the republic lines.'

I told her about the Military Border. She had never heard of it.

Dimitrije put away his Chetnik cap and settled with me in front
of the television with a bottle of *šljivovica*. Soon he was indignant,
almost in tears. Belgrade TV was broadcasting *The Simon Wie-
senthal Story*.

24

Vanja – tall, curly-haired, with restless eyes – had been born and raised in the Croatian coastal city of Split, where I had met him in 1990, but he lived most of the year in Belgrade, where he was a student of art history at the university. His father was a Serb and his mother a Croat, and he had Serb friends in Belgrade and Croat friends in Split. An agnostic with agnostic parents, he thought of himself as neither Roman Catholic nor Orthodox. In other words, he was another superannuated Yugoslav.

But, surrounded by frenzied flag wavers, he felt he had to wave something. He had to have *some* answer to the increasingly common challenge as to who he was.

'Vanja', clearly, was not enough. Was he Vanja, son of Milan, or Vanja, son of Marija? All he had by way of a group identification was his Split slang, his taste for seafood and dark red wines, his experience around boats. So on the day we got together he was wearing in his lapel a pin adorned with three crowns, the coat of arms of Dalmatia.

Vanja's father spoke Ekavian – meaning he said *mleko* and *breg* where most Croats would say *mlijeko* or *mliko* and *brijeg* or *brig* – and to make matters worse he lived in army housing. Not that he had anything to do with the Army; he had swopped apartments. But the people who telephoned in the middle of the night did not know, or they did not care. 'Time is running out for you,' they said, if he answered. If his wife answered, they called her a Chetnik whore. I remembered Vanja's father as a small, dapper old gentleman in a crisp panama hat who liked to walk his dog.

Someone in Split was bombing the *Borba* news-stands. Presumably there were no *Politika* news-stands to bomb, and *Borba*, the paper of 'Yugoslavism' published in Belgrade, was the next best thing. Vanja had responded to a *Borba* classified ad, and had been offered a correspondent's job, quite a plum, in his home town. But his mother was begging him not to take it. I wondered out loud what had happened to the last correspondent, but Vanja had not asked.

Serbs said that only Croats showed such intolerance towards others. Here in Belgrade, they said, you could read whatever paper you wanted, whereas in Croatia they allowed only Croatian papers. No one was bombing news-stands in Belgrade. Even now, they said, a Croat would be perfectly safe anywhere in Serbia. Not only safe, but treated well. That was the way Serbs were.

Certainly one way the Serbs were was that they tended to end boasts with that phrase.

Since last year Vanja had bought his first car, a twenty-three-year-old Audi which he had had to rebuild from the engine outward, and which he kept going with ingenuity, paper clips and occasional genuine spare parts found among the split-open carburettors and distributors at the edges of outdoor food markets. 'My Gypsy car', he called it, since when you saw Gypsies on the roads of Yugoslavia they were often not in their cars but behind them, pushing.

Now that Vanja had a car, he could risk his life in it. Last month he had visited a sick relative in Zagreb before heading to Split. His mother had urged him to drive to Rijeka and then down the coast, so that he would bypass the Serb-held Krajina, but that particular route was twice as long, and Vanja was young enough for this sort of consideration to carry considerable weight. Instead, Vanja drove through the barricades: first the Army's, then a Serb roadblock on the way into the Krajina and another on the way out, then a second army checkpoint, then a Croat checkpoint, then a third by the Army and a second by the Croats. He had made it, and he had saved time, and he had belied the Croat papers that said the Serb blockaders would kill him and the Serb papers that said the Croats would kill him. But he had also had an automatic rifle pointed at his chest when he reached for his identification, which was underneath his coat. At that moment, the knowledge that a single careless move could kill him stopped being merely intellectual and settled concretely behind his sternum, about where the steel-jacketed bullet would tear through him. He was not planning to drive that route again.

Now that Vanja had a car, walking in Belgrade was out of the question, and after meeting his girlfriend, Maja, we wound through the streets until he found his Audi, then drove for twenty minutes through the heavy traffic, stopped twice to look under the hood, inched up and down narrow cobblestoned streets behind cars looking for parking places, got into a shouting match with another driver who objected to Vanja's heading the wrong way up a one-way street, squeezed into a minuscule space, and walked several blocks to a restaurant that we could have reached on foot in one-third of the time.

It was an old neighbourhood *kafana* that Vanja liked, where the smoke was thick and the food heavy, and the roving band played *stara gradska* ('old city') songs on accordion, guitar and double bass. Stara gradska music was a Belgrade speciality that Vanja, despite the pin on his lapel, much preferred to Dalmatian music. The latter involved banks of mandolin-like instruments called *tamburice* jangling until your nerves jangled with them, while stara gradska songs were slow and sappy, each line ending on a long-held note, during which the accordion or the guitar would execute aimless, melancholy riffs, fading off into the contemplative murmurs of the bass. It was the kind of music that made you feel like spending hours watching smoke drifting upward and light reflecting off the wine in your glass, while you mused over love affairs you had screwed up many years ago.

'Stop the Danube, stop the clocks,' the singer crooned. 'You're my love!'

A man at the table next to us kept slipping dinar notes into his glass at the ends of songs to keep the band from wandering off. One of his companions, a gold-toothed wolfman whose beard spread up to his eyes, sang along, standing in a sort of tai-chi crouch, with his hands out in front of him making gentle caressing motions as if he were balancing invisible forces, blissed out on the music and the amber fluid he was drinking. Later on, the singing would be communal and boisterous, and some people would be falling down. In one such place, I had had the tablecloth pulled right out from under my notebook by a collapsing patron. Nino would have called it primitive. But I was most reminded, in fact, of Austria. Not Nino's cafés, but the *Heurigen* of Grinzing and Heiligenstadt, where accordionists sang of getting drunk, and people got drunk, and men pulled waitresses into their laps to stuff their faces between their perspiring breasts.

'Don't touch my guitar,' the guitarist sang, 'or I will kill you in front of witnesses.'

While I ate pork stuffed with cheese and bacon on a bed of *kajmak* — a tasty sludge made from the scum of boiled milk — Vanja informed me that the band's violinist, who always ate here, had recently died of a heart attack. His violin hung on the wall. The accordionist, during a break, sat with us and remembered him tearfully. Vanja himself was getting tipsy enough to speak at unseemly length about the woman he had loved last year, over whom he had been moping when he was supposed to be guiding me around Split for an article on Diocletian's palace. She was living now with 'some yuppie asshole lawyer', as Vanja put it, and he was trying to remember the line from *The Tempest*. Was it 'First we kill all the lawyers'? 'Whatever we do, we have to kill the lawyers'? 'Time to go and kill the lawyers'?

We drove to a different kafana for more drinks, but Maja thought it was too crowded and smoky. Vanja called her a snob. Back in the car, we passed the Church of St Sava, mountainous in the dark, and Vanja poured out his frustration: 'The whole Byzantine tradition developed towards smallness. The monasteries are tiny, beautiful buildings. This one will hold twelve thousand people! That's for a stadium, not a church. All the money going into this, and no money for the medieval monasteries we already have. It has fifty-two bells, they say. So I said to them, why does it need fifty-two bells? Is it going to ring a different bell each week?'

We ended up behind the Belgrade Radio and TV building, in an abandoned lot, drinking *lozovača*, a brandy made from grape stalks, at Fratelli's. The establishment was an ancient double decker bus which two brothers — *i fratelli* — had bought from a junk dealer in London, driven down in seven days, remodelled and parked where the radio and television technicians could easily find a drink at two a.m. Their style was jukebox retro: yards of curved chrome, gleaming yellow counters, green walls, a purple rug. My head touched the ceiling, Vanja stooped. I fratelli talked to me about their future, their eyes shining like the chrome. They would give tours of Belgrade. One would drive, the other would man the microphone and the bar. All they needed was tourists.

25

Republic Square was only a ten-minute walk from Kalemegdan, but well into the nineteenth century this spot had still been part of the moat around the city walls. Here had stood the Stamboul Gate, where the Turks, after insurrections, would line up the heads of rebels on stakes. Today the square was bounded by the National Theatre and the National Museum. In front of the museum stood the equestrian statue of Prince Mihajlo, on whose pedestal people were placing flowers and lighting candles. VUKA-ŠIN ŠOŠKOČANIN, VICTIM OF USTASHAS one sign read. Another, DEATH TO USTASHAS.

Prince Mihajlo, pointing his sword towards Turkey over Šoš-kočanin's memorial, was also a martyr, but he had been killed by Serbs. He was an Obrenović, one of the few able leaders of that family, and partisans of the rival Karadjordjević dynasty stabbed him to death in Topčider Park in 1868. The dynasties had hated each other ever since the founder of one, Miloš Obrenović, leader of the 1815 revolt against the Turks, ordered the death of the other, Karadjordje Petrović, leader of the 1804 revolt against the Turks. Karadjordje ('Black George') had been a hell of a fighter, but no diplomat, whereas Obrenović demonstrated his consider-able political skills by presenting Karadjordje's head to the Turks.

Serbs often complained that their greatest liability, as a people, was their inability to act together. They said that the four Cyrillic Cs on the old Serbian coat of arms – a cross with that letter, which is pronounced 's', nested in each quarter – stood for *Samo sloga Srbina spašava*, or 'Only unity saves the Serbs.'

On this subject, Serbs viewed Croats with that mixture of envy and disdain which is really a single emotion, and so common that we ought to have a single word for it. They talked about 'the Croatian lobby' in the west, and particularly in America, which they said was so well organized compared to the honest but inexperienced efforts of the Serbs. (The Croats, by the way, had complained about 'the Serbian lobby'.) They talked about the uncanny way in which the Croat nation could act as one, as when they hailed, to a man, the founding of the Independent State of Croatia, and turned, to a man, to slaughter the Serbs.

Meanwhile, out of the western media's handy store of constantly repeated epithets came 'democratic, westward-leaning Croatia' and 'hard-line Communist Serbia'. 'But we have a real opposition here,' Serbs complained. 'The Croats don't! They all support HDZ!'

With Mirjana, I went to a press conference called to announce the formation of a new 'United Opposition'. This was the third or fourth attempt. As soon as the room was full, Vuk Drašković, the leader of the largest opposition party, deflated expectations by announcing that only four of Serbia's sixty-two parties had agreed to join the union. Mirjana put her head in her hands.

Vuk – everyone called him by his first name – had the long unkempt hair and beard that to Croats meant Chetnik. He was handsome in an exaggeratedly masculine way, his face all jutting nose and brow, his voice a commanding contrabass. He preferred flowing white shirts open at the neck so that his abundant chest hair was visible, and wore his coat without putting his arms in the sleeves, so that it could be swept on and off like a cape. He had been a journalist (detractors said he had been a Communist lackey living in a perk apartment) who had become famous writing bestsellers, grisly historical novels about – what else? – the massacres of Serbs during World War II. He had told me the year before that if Croatia wanted to secede, that was fine, as long as it left behind all areas with Serb majorities and paid Serbia 350 billion dollars in war reparations. He also talked about re-establishing Serb majorities in all parts of Yugoslavia that had had them before 10 April 1941 – areas which he calculated to comprise about half of Croatia and nearly all of Bosnia-Hercegovina. As a novelist, Vuk imaginatively relived the horror of the last war, and as a politician he seemed determined to erase it. He would remake Yugoslavia as if World War II had never happened.

But Vuk was more novelist than politician. He made up his positions like plots, and rewrote them whenever he saw more dramatic possibilities. He said what sounded good, and believed it as he said it. Today, he stressed peace and reconciliation, because he was after Milošević, and Milošević was leading the country into war. But he also vowed that Croatia would not leave Yugoslavia with the borders it had been granted at the founding of Yugoslavia II, in 1943, which was a point that struck a chord in all Serbs. The 1943 republican borders had been drawn in the context of a federation, it was argued, and they only made sense – if even then they made sense – as part of a federation. As soon as Croatia abrogated the federative contract, it gave up its right to the federal borders.

The press conference went much as others had done in Croatia. Half of the audience consisted not of reporters but of various claques, who gave the event the feeling of a revival meeting as they called out, '*Tako je!*' ('That's it!' or, if you like, 'Amen!') at the words of their favourite speakers. The speakers, for their part, had not yet learned to introduce themselves, and the reporters vainly called out, 'Name! Name!' as they droned on and on, staring fixedly at the table. Speeches had not changed with the coming of democracy. Like American ones, they were largely devoid of content, but at least American ones were shorter. The Communist regime in Yugoslavia, following the tendency of Communist regimes everywhere, had inflated the country's word supply until the currency was nearly useless, and the psychology lingered. Politicians papered the walls of meeting halls with ten-dollar words worth nothing.

When questions were called for at the end, there followed the usual pained silence. Reporters in Yugoslavia were not yet accustomed to asking questions. They looked at each other and fidgeted. After some urgings by the party leaders, a few questions dribbled in, of the 'could you clarify your position on . . .?' variety, which let everyone relax through another long speech. The single mildly challenging query – Did the united opposition support Stipe Mesić, the Croat, as President of Yugoslavia? – drew shocked murmurs from the crowd, as though the question was unfair, or impolite, or impudent. The party leaders and vice-leaders, mostly colourless old apparatchiks or rabbity academics, hid behind Vuk, who replied that Mesić ought to be allowed to become President, so that the world would see 'who is really breaking Yugoslavia apart'.

Then Vuk read the opposition's list of demands, and the claques took over, some of the reporters joining them. Only tepid applause greeted the demand that Belgrade TV2 be turned over to the control of the opposition, and TV3 made independent of any political control. Nor did the demand that certain of Miloše-vić's ministers be replaced cause much enthusiasm. But the crowd went wild over proposals to change the Serbian flag (i.e. get rid of the red star and substitute the Serbian coat of arms) and reinstate the Serbian national anthem.

(After World War I, the Yugoslav anthem, significantly, was nothing more than the old Serbian, Croatian and Slovenian anthems strung end to end, and after World War II it was something nobody liked called 'Hey, Slavs!'. The tune was stolen from the Polish anthem.)

The press conference ended with a call for a demonstration on 9 June in Freedom Square, to demand new elections. But the opposition had no leverage. Milošević and the Parliament which he controlled each had fresh mandates as of the year before, good for four more years.

On the way out, I asked Mirjana if she thought Vuk might some day be President of Serbia.

'Never!' she snorted.

'Why not?'

'With all that hair? And he doesn't even wear a tie!'

26

Before the last war, the boxy building in the park south of the city had been a military academy, as now it was once more, but during their occupation the Nazis had used it as a detention camp. Two rooms in the north end had been preserved as a museum. The exhibition was clearly not designed for foreign tourists, as the only texts were in calligraphic lower-case Cyrillic, a difficult script to make out. Even many Croats would have had trouble reading it, which was perhaps the idea.

Belgrade's Jews had spent only a brief time here before being entrained for the death camps farther north. The Germans had used this camp primarily as a holding pen for hostages, who had been either people they wanted to kill anyway – Communists, liberals, student leaders, any citizens with integrity who might command a following – or simply those unlucky enough to have been out on the street during one of the round-ups the Germans conducted whenever the numbers in the camp were getting dangerously low. The system was simple, and placards on the Belgrade streets patiently explained the rules and ramifications, as though giving arithmetic lessons to children. Fifty hostages would be shot for one dead German. Twenty-five would be shot for one wounded German. Therefore, if for example two Germans were wounded, fifty hostages would be shot. If they both later died, then fifty more would be shot. If only one died, then only twenty-five more hostages would be shot. Now, if two Germans were killed and one wounded, then how many . . .?

A series of photographs showed guards marching prisoners out to a field outside the city; lining them up in front of a ditch; doing their duty. There was no Ustasha-like brandishing of knives, no gloating. The Germans never got carried away. They always shot exactly the right number.

One of the museum's rooms re-created a typical cell: a shitpot and a cauldron in the corner, an iron stove, a low wooden platform along the wall on which the prisoners slept in a long row. Extending across the entire length of the opposite wall were photocopies of the camp records, beginning with prisoner number 40, admitted in April 1941. The clerk had probably been a Serb, or perhaps a *Volksdeutscher* from the Banat, in Vojvodina. The records were in Serbian. Only a couple of lines were devoted to each entry: name, birthplace, date of birth, and the date the prisoner 'came into the camp'. Next was written STRELJAN ('shot'), with another date, usually a few days later. Here and there were those who had somehow made themselves useful, perhaps as clowns, or servants, or informers, so that several months separated their date of entry and date of execution.

The word STRELJAN was written by hand until prisoner number 5247 (20 August 1942), when a stamp was finally made: STRELJAN _____ 194_ U BEOGRADU. This made the record-keeping less tedious when large numbers of prisoners (three dead Germans, two wounded) were executed at once. But the stamp did not, in fact, much help, because it could only be used for men. A shot woman was 'streljana', not 'streljan', and the clerk now had to stamp the men and write in the women. In the big batches, you could even see how his irritation eventually got the better of his grammar: he would always begin both stamping and writing, but eventually he would stamp everybody, and the dead women became male.

The last entry on the wall was dated 8 July 1944. The number was 23,233. There had been more – the work had continued until October, when Belgrade was liberated – but the display had run out of wall. A wooden plaque carved by survivors of the camp claimed a total of forty thousand dead. By the time my brochure for Belgrade's museums was printed in 1989, the number had risen to eighty thousand. The irony seemed perfect: the Germans had been so very careful about the numbers, but the Slavs had become emotional and messed them up. Nothing was more unknowable in the Balkans than numbers.

In the other room, objects in a glass case reminded one that the numbers were people. Faced with oblivion, some prisoners had filled the few long days of their stay by responding to a creative impulse. Some women had constructed dolls of themselves out of cloth and straw, familiars that would survive them. The dolls sat in a row in the case, all with severe, clamped-down expressions, as though refusing to answer questions. Only one woman had dressed her doll in a camp uniform. All the others had preferred an afterlife in their peasant smocks.

Pictures had been scratched into tin belt buckles, sewn in cross-stitches, engraved on silver cigarette cases and tin canteens, created out of fake inlay by gluing straw to the tops of wooden cases. The prisoners might have sketched anything – their homes, their spouses, open fields, woods, their saints, their king – but nearly all of them had chosen to picture the same thing: the camp. And it was always the same view, of the main building, with its two flat wings and central narrow spine, and its yard wall with corner watchtowers. Within this tiny artistic community, where the artists had rarely met the other artists, but had only seen the work they had left behind, there had even developed a trademark of the school, a wan joke: the use of a chain border around the pictures.

Some seemed oddly cheerful. The building looked handsome, imposing. A sampler included pink clouds over the prison, as though lit by a setting sun, trees in bloom, birds in the air. The watchtowers were picturesque, like castle keeps. One inevitably thought of a postcard: Wish you were here! And perhaps it was not an inappropriate sentiment, in a way, since the vantage point in all of the pictures was from outside the walls.

After the war, the field outside Belgrade where the hostages had been shot was dug up, and the thousands of bodies were reburied in cemeteries, with names on their tombstones. Of course the bones were rarely the right ones, but you could forget that. You had a place to lay flowers, and a chiselled name to talk to, and *someone* was buried there, perhaps not your wife, but someone who had suffered like her, perhaps spoken to her, perhaps seen her marched out. Then the museum opened, and you could go and see what it had been like, and grieve, and hate the Germans, until you slowly got used to hating them, and perhaps eventually even got tired of hating them.

There were no museums for those killed by the Ustashas. There were a few memorials, but, in the name of Brotherhood and Unity, they did not go into details. In the name of Brotherhood and Unity, you did not hate the Croats. In the name of Brotherhood and Unity, you did not even rebury the dead. The karst uplands of Croatia and Bosnia were riddled with natural limestone caves and pits into which thousands of corpses had been thrown during the war. Not just Croats killing Serbs, but everybody killing everybody else. Everyone still knew where the pits were. Families usually knew to which particular pit a father or brother or sister had been led, to have his or her throat cut at the rim.

But Tito's post-war government had not exhumed those dead. It had sealed the pits with concrete.

27

The Chetniks hawked their wares on Prince Mihajlo Street, the pedestrian zone along the spine of Belgrade's ridge. From fold-out tables they sold Orthodox crosses, Vuk buttons, Chetnik caps and posters of the World War II Chetnik *vojvoda*, or leader, Draža Mihajlović. A Vuk clock had his handsome, hairy face on the dial, with the Serbian coat of arms at 12, 3, 6 and 9.

The paper for Šešelj's Serbian Radical Party – THE WILL OF THE PEOPLE IS OUR HIGHEST LAW!; SERBIA WILL EXTEND TO THE LAST SERB! – was being sold alongside Vuk bookmarks even though the two men, who had begun in league, had fallen out over who would get to be the new vojvoda, and now insulted each other in public. (Samo sloga Srbina spašava!) New music groups, or washed-out ones angling for a comeback, had recorded old Chetnik songs, just as their counterparts – or were they the same groups? – had done with Croatian songs in Zagreb. The members of one posed on the cassette cover brandishing machine guns in some Slavonian village, presumably of mixed ethnicity – a teenage boy's heavy-metal fantasy come to gruesome life.

The Croats had been right when they said many more Serbs were now openly calling themselves Chetniks than there were Croats calling themselves Ustashas. But although Tito's post-war government had demonized both of its former enemies, the Chetniks had had, on the whole, a more understandable rationale for their actions. Whereas the Ustashas had been enthusiastic collaborators with the Nazis from the beginning, and had begun the ethnic slaughter, the Chetniks, though anti-Croat – especially after what they considered the Croatian betrayal of their Yugo-slavia – concentrated at the beginning on fighting the Germans. However, they viewed as their sacred mission the preservation of the Serb nation, so, when the Germans started shooting fifty Serb peasants for every dead German, they pulled back.

The Partisans, on the other hand, drew most of their fighters, at least in the beginning, from Serbs living in the Independent State of Croatia, who did not have the option of cooperating with the authorities in order to save their own or their families' lives. They were going to be slaughtered anyway. Moreover, the Partisan leadership was planning a fundamental transformation of Yugo-slavian society, and the more the war disrupted traditional pat-terns of living, the more desperate the populace became, the easier that transformation would be. So the Partisans kept killing Ger-mans, the Germans slaughtered entire towns, and the survivors fled to the hills where the Partisans recruited them. The Chetniks, suspicious of a conspiracy among the Partisan leadership to weaken the Serb nation, and loathing in any case the prospect of a Communist Yugoslavia, first began to fight the Partisans on their own, and then began to help the Germans fight them.

The Chetnik argument made sense. It was the Danish argu-ment: we will accomplish nothing by fighting so powerful an enemy except our own destruction. And if it were true, how simple it would make the world. The Partisans' heartlessness could be condemned along with the Germans', and, by a logical extension, pacifism held up as a universal ideal.

Unhappily, it was not true. Denmark would have killed an

insignificant number of Germans, and in doing so it would have suffered horribly. But Hitler would have lost the prestige of his 'model' protectorate, the security of the Danish rail lines bringing food and Kiruna coal, the luxury of holding Denmark with a handful of troops. Yugoslavia did suffer horribly, unimaginably, and at every pointless death, for death after death after death, it must have been clear to most Serbs that the resistance as a whole was pointless, or at least of such little import that their suffering made for a bitter farce.

But those German soldiers who were lining up villagers and mowing them down with machine-gun fire were needed at the Russian front. So were the bullets. By 1943, Hitler had poured some two dozen divisions into the Yugoslavian theatre, and he still only controlled the main towns. He mounted seven major campaigns to root out the Partisans, and never succeeded.

When Fitzroy MacLean reported to Winston Churchill in 1943 on the activities of the Partisans and Chetniks in Yugoslavia, Churchill had only one question: which group was killing more Germans? But he might as germanely have asked, Which group is forcing the Germans to kill more Yugoslavs? It was an uncomfortable truth – uncomfortable because it could not properly be asked of anyone to act on it – that forcing the enemy to kill you, if there were enough of you to be killed, would eventually, pebble by tiny pebble next to the mountain of your suffering, exhaust him. Perhaps not morally, as in Gandhi's optimistic argument, but at least materially. The spirit may be willing, but the flesh was weak.

In resurrecting the memory of the Chetniks today, the Serbs were creating for themselves something of a dilemma, because they were extremely proud of their role in resisting the Germans during the war. They insisted that the Chetniks had in fact fought the Germans more than the history books said – a new book by an English intelligence officer entitled *The Rape of Serbia* made just this case, alleging a conspiracy by crypto-leftist British liaison officers to credit Chetnik resistance operations to the Partisans – but they also accepted as historically true the Chetniks's eventual rationale that to fight the Germans brought death and ruin on innocent Serb women and children. And although this rationale had been humane, and had probably reflected the gut instincts of most Serbs, it did not conform to the Serbs' image of themselves, as warriors to whom honour was an absolute, something irreducible and uncompromising.

So Serbs combined the two traditions. The humane Chetniks were Serbs, and the uncompromising Partisans were also Serbs. Since Chetniks and Partisans slaughtered each other, this brought the Serbs back to – Samo sloga Srbina spašava!

But this raised another problem. Saying that the Partisan movement was essentially Serb supported the Croats' and Slovenes' charge that the post-war Yugoslavia was as dominated by Serbia as the inter-war one had been and, moreover, allowed them to lay the responsibility for Communism – such a dread word now that even Milošević had renamed his party the Socialists – largely at the Serbs' door.

But there was a way around this dilemma, too. The rank-and-file Partisans had been Serbs, but the leader – never forget! – the leader had been a Croat. And, like most Croats, he had been a talker, a natural strutter and chest-beater in his glittery uniforms, but – like most Croats – he had not been a fighter. The Serbs had fought for him, which was so like the Serbs, who never could learn to watch out for themselves, whose honest impulsiveness was always being manipulated by others.

One of the founding legends of the Partisans and their war concerned the time German forces had surrounded Tito and a band of Partisans at Užice. As the tale used to be told, the Partisan men so loved their god-like leader that they fought to the last man, holding the Germans at bay while Tito escaped. Now Serbs told it a different way: the Serbs died while the Croat fled.

Stupid Serbs, Nino would say. And in a way, the Serbs would agree. In their eyes, they were stupid the way Siegfried was stupid. The Croats were clever like Mime.

Farther down the pedestrian zone, I met a handsome, hawk-like young man with long hair and piercing blue eyes, selling a student newspaper. He was not a Chetnik. He did not like Vuk or Šešelj or Milošević. With a Macedonian mother and a Serb father, he called himself a Yugoslav. But he also said, 'The world is betraying Serbia.'

How so?

'It is not supporting us in Kosovo, or in Croatia. It is telling lies about us. There is an old saying: "The Serbs win in war and lose in peace."'

An older man stopped. 'The Communists are betraying Serbia!' he shouted at us. 'Tell him that!' he ordered the younger man.

'I understood it,' I said.

'Tell him that!' the man yelled again, and walked on.

'Who is he?' another man asked.

'A reporter,' the student said.

'From where?'

'America.'

'Why is America against Serbia?' the man challenged me.

'I'm not sure it is,' I said.

'This Senator Dole comes to Kosovo for one day, and then he tells lies about us.'

'He got a hundred thousand dollars from the Albanian lobby,' a fourth man said.

'They're very well organized,' the third man said.

'America and Serbia were allies in two world wars,' the fourth man said to me. 'Now they are against us. How can this be?'

'The world is disgracing itself,' the handsome student said, his handsome blue eyes flashing. 'If the world continues to betray Serbia, the world will be sorry.'

At the end of the pedestrian zone lay the fortress of Kalemegdan, now an extensive park in which you could stroll under the lindens, or climb from the ruins of one battlement to another, or get lost in the maze of dry moats. The oldest walls were of stone, but most were brick, straggling this way and that, half dismantled where Austrians had changed a Turkish plan, or Serbs an Austrian one, and some broken-down at the places where lovers found it convenient to clamber up into the bushes on the redoubts. People used the diminutive pepperpot-shaped corner watchtowers, which otherwise were charming, as outhouses. Women sitting on benches offered beautiful crocheted tablecloths which they displayed by spreading them across their very wide bodies. People played tennis and volleyball on the courts built along the flat bottoms of the moats.

The acacias were in bloom. Here and there were graves. I stopped to read one stone which told of Vladimir Djeković, a soldier, who had died in Kuršumlija on 26 December 1872, fighting the Turks. He had been brought here to be buried where so many Serbs had met a similar end, fighting the same enemy. His image, not a personal one, but a folk motif, stood stoutly front-on, in his soldier's uniform and cap, the rifle at his side pointing upward to signify readiness, his eyes round, lidless, clear and undoubting.

Kalemegdan was filled with military memorials. The place of honour, at the head of a short avenue leading from the main entrance, was occupied by one of the largest monuments, a massive robed figure rushing forward out of a maelstrom or a wild sea. The monument commemorated French help during World War I. The inscription read WE LOVE FRANCE AS SHE LOVED US.

It occurred to me, gazing at this statue, that there was something distinctly French about the Serbs. Like the French, and unlike the Croats, Serbs never doubted who they were. Their history, from the Turks to the Ustashas, had forced them to define themselves, and to clutch that definition to their chests. Like the French, they believed that the word 'glorious' could only, strictly speaking, refer to themselves. Like the French, they were possessed by an unassailable conviction that the greatest blessing they could confer on another people was to allow them to become Serbs. From this conviction followed an inability to distinguish between Serbia and Yugoslavia (France and her empire) and a sort of muddled, angry hurt, an outrage over ingratitude, when the colonies (Croatia, Algeria) rejected the embrace.

I thought of a poem quoted from a Serb author by Rebecca West that seemed to me best to capture the attitude of Serbs towards themselves. Was it only a coincidence that the poem was in French?

Le ciel serbe est couleur d'azur
Au dedans est assis un vrai dieu serbe

Entouré des anges serbes aux voix pures
Qui chantent la gloire de leur race superbe.

28

I was preparing to go to Sarajevo.

Both Serbs and Croats had a way of smiling when they referred to the Muslims. It seemed to mean, 'Those sly dogs.' A Croat sociologist smiled that smile when he assured me, 'You will never understand Bosnia unless you understand Islam.'

Mirjana smiled it when she said to me, 'Virtually all Bosnian Muslims come from Serb families. That's a *fact*. Moreoever, they know *which* Serb families they came from.'

I had an argument with Dimitrije. He had read recently in a Serbian paper that most of the Bosnian Muslims had not converted in the fifteenth century, when Bosnia was occupied by the Turks, but as late as the seventeenth century, or even the eighteenth. What kind of nation was that? he asked me. I argued that as long as your parents and grandparents were Muslims, I could not see how psychologically it made any difference to you whether the orientation went back farther.

But we got nowhere. I was basing my argument on the individual, and he on a mystical view of the nation as a superpersonality, with its own memory. But I left, thinking that, if there was such a thing as national memory, how come *Politika* could report that the Croatian Krajina had been part of Serbia until World War II, and the Serb nation believed it?

On my last night in Belgrade, Mirjana pulled out her photo album. She showed me pictures of her visit to her daughter, Marina, in New York City. She had been there during the Serbian elections, which had suited her just fine, since there was no one in any of the sixty-two parties she considered worth voting for.

New York looked cold and wet. Marina was stylish in her coiffure, her drapy clothes.

'She's beautiful, isn't she?' Mirjana prompted me.

Marina, despairing of her mother's wardrobe, had bought her a brilliant red cape, and my favourite picture was of Mirjana wrapped in it, hugging herself as a bat wraps its wings around its body, and smirking histrionically with closed eyes as if to say, 'Mine.' Above, in the distance, was the cable car to Roosevelt Island, and below, protruding from the cape, were her usual shapeless and worn trousers, her over-sized, cracked and filthy sneakers.

Mirjana gave me some parting advice. 'The west has to learn not to pay any attention to Yugoslavia. The west has to understand that Yugoslavia is not a serious country.'

When I left in the morning, Leni was subdued.

'Ah,' Mirjana muttered, looking down at him, 'now he will be sad.'

29

Yugoslav trains had always been packed, but now no one was going anywhere. No one had money, and no one wanted to be caught away from home, especially outside his own republic, in case the fighting suddenly spread.

I sat in the long empty train to Sarajevo. The flat fields of Srijem and Slavonia gave way to Bosnian hills. At the border, Bosnian policemen checked my passport.

I read the English-language weekly edition of *Politika*, a year-old effort by the Serbs to get their viewpoint out to a wider audience. The propagandizing thrust of the two *Politika*s differed. The Serbian-language edition was hysterical and intolerant, directed towards Serbs to make them hate non-Serbs. The English edition was measured and reasonable, directed towards non-Serbs to make them love Serbs.

News:

There was still no President of Yugoslavia. Sejdo Bajramović,

Milošević's toady from Kosovo, had been named 'Coordinator' of the Presidency, although both Serb and Croat lawyers agreed the post was unconstitutional.

With the Presidency not functioning, no one knew who had control over the Army.

Jovan Rašković, a leader of the Serbs in Croatia, said, 'The relation between Serbs and Croats may be apolitical, amoral and psychopathic, but its breaking-up would lead to bloodshed.'

Danica Drašković, the wife of Vuk, said to another Serb leader at a lunch given by the Patriarch of the Orthodox Church, 'The only true Serb is Vuk Drašković,' to which the man responded, 'If Vuk Drašković is the only true Serb, then I deny my Serbian-ness.' Danica replied by hitting the man on the head with a bottle.

Through the window, on the green hills, I saw white minarets. In the Serbian magazine on my lap was a photograph of a minaret, with the caption WHERE IS THIS MISSILE POINTING? A few minutes later, I saw a church with the central dome and exfoliated cross of Orthodoxy, and a few minutes after that, a Catholic church with a steeple and straight cross.

First I had said, 'How do you say that in Croatian?' Then I had said, 'How do you say that in Serbian?' Now, alone in the compartment, I practised saying, '*Kako to kažete na vašem jeziku?*'

'How do you say that in your language?'

Part Three
Sarajevo

30

If Yugoslavia was a microcosm of the resurgent nationality question world-wide, Bosnia-Hercegovina was a microcosm of Yugoslavia.

Of the 4.3 million people living in Bosnia-Hercegovina, forty-three per cent were Muslim, thirty-one per cent were Serb and seventeen per cent were Croat. They were not distributed evenly. Serbs formed majorities along a wide arc of western Bosnia called Bosanska Krajina (the twin of the Hrvatska, or Croatian Krajina, across the border), in parts of eastern Bosnia along the Serb border, and in eastern Hercegovina. Although the Croats were the smallest group, western Hercegovina was almost entirely Croat. The Muslims were concentrated in central and eastern Bosnia, and central Hercegovina.

But this was only a rough breakdown. Throughout the republic, pockets of Croats lived among Serbs, Serbs among Muslims, Muslims among Croats. People liked to say that an ethnic map of Bosnia looked like a leopard skin, but it was more fractal than that. There were pockets within pockets. In the Serb region, the Croat village had a Serb street in which lived a Croat family.

Yugoslavs called Bosnia 'the bomb of Yugoslavia'.

Tito had kept the ethnic groups from killing each other, and on Tito's birthday, two days before I arrived, Sarajevans had marched in the streets with his photograph raised above their heads and shouted the old slogans: 'Mi smo Titovi! Tito je naš!' 'We are Tito's! Tito is ours!'

In Belgrade, Mirjana had said, 'I would like to tell them, "Tito is six feet under, and if you want to be six feet under, too, that's your choice, but . . ."'

Through an agency, I rented a room from the Andrić family, on Marshal Tito Street. Mr Andrić, a husky, clean-shaven man with a shy demeanour, managed a cooperatively owned seafood restaurant in the pedestrian zone. He told me that they went days without a single diner.

Sanja, his daughter, had glowing green eyes so large they had to be cushioned on crescent bulges of flesh. She had wanted to go to art school, but her mother had deemed it impractical, so she was studying economics, which she hated. It sometimes seemed that all the young Yugoslavs I met yearned to live in lofts and paint or write poetry while they laboured for law, economics and engineering degrees. Meanwhile, laws meant nothing, economic theory was in disarray and there was no money to build anything.

Sanja told me her mother was a Serb and her father a Croat. She hastened to add that she and her sister were both Croats.

Intrigued, I asked her what she meant by that. (Had a potential 'Yugoslav' been turned into a Croat by a preference for a gentle father over a mother who had forced her to study economics?)

But no. She had meant only that her sister and she had both been baptized as Catholics. To Sanja, 'Croat' and 'Catholic' were synonymous.

Did she go to church?

Now and then.

So she went to the Catholic cathedral in the pedestrian zone?

No, she went to the Orthodox church near it.

Why?

She liked the building better. It was darker, more atmospheric. And her mother's father used to take her there when she was a little girl.

Going to an Orthodox church did not make her Orthodox?

No, as she said, she had been baptized a Catholic. For that matter, she had been baptized with a Muslim name. Sanala.

Why?

She had no idea. She had changed it at the first opportunity to the Croat name, Sanja.

Why?

She didn't like the sound of Sanala.

152

Because it was Muslim?

Because it had three syllables.

'Do you believe in God?' I asked.

She shrugged. 'I don't know.' Her expression suggested she considered it a silly question, or an uninteresting one, or even an irrelevant one. Or perhaps she thought I was being nosy.

Lest I continue, Sanja assured me she hated politics as much as she hated economics. She had been to Italy and Switzerland, but never to Belgrade. She had no idea what was going on there. Surely it was better to live in the United States where, she had heard, no one ever talked about politics, or worried about or even knew what the government was doing, or remembered the past.

My window looked down on the point where the central pedestrian zone debouched into Tito Street. At the junction of the two, a flame was burning. The first night, I went down to inspect it.

It was an 'eternal flame' – although in the next few days it kept going out – flickering from a grate set inside a metal wreath enamelled green. Behind, between columns in a semicircular niche, a text in the blue, white and red of the Yugoslav tricolour dedicated the flame to 'the courage, and the blood which they spilled together, of the fighters of the Bosnohercegovinian, Croatian, Montenegrin and Serbian Partisan brigades'. As it continued its eulogy, the text was careful at all appropriate points to list all the ethnic groups, a practice common throughout Yugoslavia, but it made for especially long texts in Bosnia because only here did they include references to 'Bosnohercegovinians'. None of the other republics admitted of such a group.

People had thrown coins on the grate, and these sat in the flames, blackened. I could only think how hot they were, and wondered if members of one ethnic group had burned members of another with red-hot pokers during the war.

I went back to my room. Mr Andrić sat expressionless at the dining-room table, TV-news light shifting across his face. Another truck filled with weapons had been discovered on a Bosnian road, origin and destination unknown.

The apartment was uncluttered. The white walls of my room

were bare except for a diminutive sampler of a village scene – not a Bosnian village, but a Croatian one, with Catholic steeple and lindens, executed by Sanja's Serb mother. The only other sampler hung in the kitchen: Tito, in his royal-blue cap.

31

At times in the Middle Ages, the Croat state ruled parts of Bosnia. At other times, the Serb state did. But most of the time, in fact if not in name, Bosnia was autonomous.

It was also peculiar. Mountainous, forested, criss-crossed with gorges, it was ideal rebel country, a haven for outcasts, a staging area for last stands that dragged on for centuries.

When Manichaeism, the Babylonian doctrine based on the eternal conflict of Light and Darkness, began to move west in the fifth century, it mixed with Christianity and produced the dualist Paulicians of Armenia. Byzantium tried to stamp out the heresy, and failed. Paulician missionaries penetrated into Bulgaria, where the religion took the Slav name Bogomilism, meaning 'love of God', or 'God have mercy'. In Byzantium itself, some of the leading families were infected with the doctrine. Bogomils were tortured to make them give up the secrets of their sect, tortured some more for good measure, and burned at the stake. Many fled to Serbia, where the doctrine continued to spread. In the twelfth century, Stevan Nemanja, the founder of the Nemanjić dynasty, expelled the Bogomils, and they retreated into Bosnia.

There, protected by the forests and mountains, Bogomilism fought off Catholicism and Orthodoxy for three hundred years, faring so well that it became more or less the state religion, and was sometimes called the Church of Bosnia. Occasionally, the bans or kings of Bosnia openly allied themselves with the creed, but even when they were nominally Catholics they were often secret Bogomils, and even when they were not, they realized the heretics were too entrenched to be opposed. Around 1200, even the Bishop of Bosnia, Daniel, became a Bogomil, and invited his new co-religionists to tear down the cathedral and bishop's palace at Kreševo.

With Bosnia as its secure headquarters, the doctrine marched west, where its eventual enemies knew it by different names. The Italians called the heretics Patarenes, after Pataria, a suburb of Milan where their influence was first noted. In Provence they were known as Albigensians, after the town of Albiga; and in the Rhine valley as Ketzers, or Cathars (from *kathairein*, 'to purify').

The heretics never used any of these terms. They called themselves 'Christians' or, if pressed, 'good Christians'. Like Manichees, they believed in two principles, one of Good and one of Evil, which were in perpetual conflict. To a lot of simple people, this seemed to explain what they saw around them better than the doctrine of an omnipotent Goodness that suffered Evil to hang around causing misery.

But Christian elements prevented the Bogomils from being strict dualists. They believed (or anyway, it is *thought* they believed – the only accounts to come down to us are the scurrilous ones of their persecutors) that God, the Principle of Goodness, had a son named Satanael, who rebelled against his father and created the world and everything in it. He also created Adam and Eve, but was unable to give them life, and was forced to appeal to his father for help. God agreed, and thus got His foot in the door (so to speak), through the medium of the spirit, to His son's evil, material world. The door was thrown wide open 5,500 years later, when God sent down his second son, Christ, to model for men the way to resist His Brother. Since all matter was evil, Christ could not have been incarnate, but was a phantom, and Mary was not a woman, but an angel.

In the eyes of Orthodoxy, the doctrine was bad enough, but its logical conclusions, in practical terms, were even worse. The Bogomils abhorred just about everything in the established Church as materialized corruptions of spiritual allegories: the cross, the Eucharist, the idolatry of saints' icons, priestly vestments, churches. Church bells were 'the trumpets of demons'. Priests were 'blind Pharisees'. The Bogomils met for their services in unadorned sheds, empty except for a table covered with a white cloth on which was laid a copy of the Gospels. They rejected the Pentateuch as the Devil's document, and discounted portions of the New Testament, but the books they did accept – by one account, the Psalms, the prophets, the Gospels, Acts, Epistles and the Apocalypse – they attempted to follow strictly. They prayed five times a day and five times each night. They strove to live a self-abnegating life, and those among them called the *perfecti* carried this endeavour to remarkable lengths, fasting perpetually and abstaining from marriage or sexual relations. Contemporary accounts describe the perfecti as having unkempt hair and beards, of walking bowed, of pulling long faces and groaning.

In short, 'Cathar' was the best of the names for them, because they were puritans – the first of a virtually continuous succession with which the opulent and corrupt Church was confronted. And the Church reacted to them the way it would towards all subsequent puritans. It did its best to exterminate them. When the blood-drenched campaigns against the Albigensians and Patarenes in the west succeeded, Ban Kulin of Bosnia offered asylum to the refugees. The Catholic kings of Hungary and Croatia, urged on by successive popes, conducted a series of cleansing campaigns in Bosnia, sacking cities and putting populations to the sword. But Bosnia's terrain protected its people too well, and after each campaign the heresy sprang forth anew. Some of the later and weaker Bosnian kings were persuaded to persecute the Bogomils themselves.

The eventual result had a certain poetic justice. Bogomilism was Christianity's eastern, spiritualized source come back to haunt it. In the fifteenth century another iconoclastic and austere religion – one that, as it happened, also abhorred church bells and required five daily prayers – came to the doors of Bosnia from that same spiritual source in the east. The Turks had defeated the Serbs at Kosovo Field in 1389 and had finished off the entire Serbian state by 1459. In 1463, they invaded Bosnia in

156

force. The fighting could have dragged on for years. Instead, they overran the region in eight days. The Bogomils handed the fortresses over to them.

Subsequently, many converted to Islam. The land-owning class undoubtedly did this partly to retain its privileges, but that did not mean Bogomilism had nothing to do with it. The same benefits accrued to conversions in Serbia, where virtually none occurred.

Bosnia became a unique possession of Turkey-in-Europe, with a renegade native land-owning aristocracy and a sizeable population of Muslim free peasantry. The converts passionately pursued an outward Turkishness in their dress and architecture, and adopted the Shari'a, or Islamic law, but their Slav heritage persisted in various ways, making them an oddity to the Anatolians. For one thing, they never learned Turkish. They also never went in much for polygyny, preferring to continue living in the old Slav extended households based on fathers and brothers, each with only one wife. They veiled only married women, and those incompletely, so that in some towns the women merely covered their faces by drawing across a corner of their kerchiefs, and in a few others they did not even bother to do that. The Turks had a saying for young men: 'Go to Bosnia, if you want to see your wife.'

And the Bosnians felt, as it turned out, little allegiance to the Turks themselves. The speed with which the landowners – now *begs* and *agas* – had converted suggested an easiness of conscience that allowed them to think of themselves, perhaps no longer as 'good Christians' but certainly still as good Slavs, fully deserving of their land. In their eyes, they might rule Bosnia with a little help from the Turks, but not by their leave.

They jealously guarded their local rights. Sarajevo, which had been an unimportant mining town before the Turkish occupation, became the centre of the new nobility and of the Bosnian Janissaries. The Janissaries – the standing army of the Ottoman Empire, made up of Christian children, principally from Bosnia and Bulgaria, carted off to Constantinople for military training and Islamic indoctrination – were troublesome to the Porte everywhere, but especially so in Bosnia, where they tended to support their fellow-Slavs of the local nobility in conflicts with the Sultan. As Rebecca West described the situation:

> Hence there grew up, well within the frontiers of the Ottoman Empire, a Free City, in which the Slavs lived as they liked, according to a constitution they based on Slav law and custom, and defied all interference. It even passed a law by which the Pasha of Bosnia was forbidden to stay more than a night at a time within the city walls. For that one night he was treated as an honoured guest, but the next morning he found himself escorted to the city gates.

The Bosnian nobles displayed the double fanaticism of converts and provincials. Bosnia was famous among the Ottoman possessions for the hostility its Muslims showed towards Christian travellers. When Mahmud II attempted a reform of the empire in the early 1800s, abolishing the corrupt feudal tax system and granting a few minuscule civil rights to the rayahs, the Bosnians denounced him as 'the Infidel Sultan', and rose in a series of revolts against the Porte, the most successful of which, in 1831, found them occupying Macedonia and parts of Bulgaria.

For the Catholic Croats and Orthodox Serbs of Bosnia, life was certainly miserable, but not necessarily more miserable than it was for the average sixteenth-century serf under a lord of his own religion. Indeed, the rayahs in the Ottoman Empire were allowed a certain freedom of movement that European serfs lacked, and moreover were not subject to military duty. But in the Ottoman Empire, sixteenth-century feudal conditions prevailed into the nineteenth century, and then actually worsened as the state descended into chaos. Serb historians write that the Muslims favoured the Catholics, who in return helped them keep down the Orthodox. Croat historians write that they favoured the Orthodox, who helped them oppress the Catholics. (Both go on to say that the favouritism showed to the opposing group caused members of *their* group to convert, and that those people should be converted back to their 'real' affiliation.)

Finally, the Ottoman Empire rotted away. Next door, the Serbs threw off the Turks, were massacred by them in reprisal, threw them off again and were massacred again, but achieved sovereignty in 1817. In 1875, the Christians of Bosnia-Hercegovina rose and, being mostly Serb, proclaimed their desire to join with Serbia. Serbia declared war on Turkey, but lost. The Great Powers intervened, and at the Congress of Berlin in 1878 Bosnia-Hercegovina was handed to Austria-Hungary. The same insurgents who had just tried to expel the Turks now tried to expel the Austrians, but in vain. The few Turks in Bosnia and the greater numbers in Serbia and Bulgaria melted away, and the Bosnian Muslims were left behind, an island of fezes and veils and mosques in a sea of Christians who had viewed the Turks as the arch-enemies of Europe and civilization for half a millennium.

The Austrians left the Muslims in their privileged position, partly to simplify the administration of Bosnia, partly to ensure that the Muslims and Serbs would not join forces against their Catholic masters. Muslims, in any case, were loath to make common cause with a people who told them they did not exist as a nation, and for whom anything Turkish aroused the soul-stirring hatred that a few centuries of slavery can produce. The Croats also thought the Bosnian Muslims did not really exist, but their opposition to Islam was diluted by an admixture of a strange sentimentality, perhaps traceable to 'Father of Croatia' Ante Starčević's Turkophilia (a result of his Austrophobia), or perhaps to the consideration that any system that managed to keep the Serbs down for so long could not be all bad. While Serb essayists railed against the 'bloodthirsty' and 'beastly' Turks (meaning the Muslims), Croat authors wrote novels under pseudonyms like Omer and Osman-beg in which noble Muslims fell in love with Catholic girls. Their point was no less clear for being implicit: the head might be Muslim, but the heart was Croat. (I am indebted to the historian Ivo Banac for elements of this analysis.)

Then Serb nationalists of the 'Young Bosnia' movement assassinated the Austrian Archduke Franz Ferdinand. The Bosnian government encouraged anti-Serb riots in Sarajevo and other

Bosnian towns, in which both Muslims and Croats took part. When the Great War began, Serbs were massacred in Bosnian villages. Others were forced to expatriate to Serbia, were relocated away from the frontier or were placed in detention camps, where as many as forty per cent died of maltreatment.

A Serb politician declared, 'As soon as our army crosses the Drina, it will give the Turks [again, the Muslims are meant] twenty-four – perhaps even forty-eight – hours to return to the faith of their forefathers [i.e. Serbian Orthodoxy] and then slay those who refuse, as we did in Serbia in the past.'

Then came 1918. After 450 long years, it was finally the Serbs' turn to dominate. Bosnian ex-rayahs and demobilized Serbian soldiers banded together to murder Muslims. Serb editorials continued the wartime call for Serbification or genocide: 'The singer of folk songs has foretold it and sung about it; he sings about it even today. We shall not repeat it here, because we all know it.' Because Muslims were the only landowners of Bosnia, the post-war land reforms fell on them. Some Muslims emigrated to Turkey, even though they did not speak the language.

Nor were the Bosnian Croats wooed to support Belgrade. Serbs were perhaps unique among hegemonists, in that they apparently had little conception of *divide et impera*. In their straightforward way, they made everyone hate them. Muslims and Croats bided their time, in a sullen alliance.

In 1941, after the Bogomils, the Muslims and the Serbs, it became the Croats' turn to rule. They did not, naturally, make the Serbs' mistake. They needed the support of the Muslims for the coming pogroms. (And if Serbs killed Muslims in retaliation, well then, so much the better.) In Zagreb, Ante Pavelić began calling the Muslims 'the flower of the Croat nation'. He turned Meštrović's Art Pavilion into a mosque.

So during World War II, Chetniks slaughtered Muslims, still calling them Turks. And Muslims, still loudly insisting they were *not* Turks, slashed their Slav brothers' throats with a nasty hooked blade that was their distinctive weapon. They called it a *handžar*, which meant 'knife' – in Turkish.

160

32

Benjamin and Miroslav were friends. Benjamin was a film-maker, and Miroslav a civil engineering student at Sarajevo University.

Benjamin was heavy-set, with a large head framed by a short stiff brush of beige hair and a beard clipped to stubble. His nose was a great two-sloped thing, neither hooked nor bent but simply changing direction half-way through its descent like a yatagan blade. Like many Sarajevans, he spoke Serbian, or Croatian, or Bosnian – at any rate, his language – with great force, his sentences peppered with guttural explosions, his Ks sounding like chicken bones going down a garbage-disposal unit. He changed subjects with an impatient 'Fuck that!' and disagreed with Miroslav with a good-natured 'Fuck you!' and ended his sentences with a concussive 'You know!' Whenever he made a point, which was about every ten seconds, he would glance away from his interlocutor and pull the two halves of his leather jacket decisively across his stomach like a curtain closing on the act, as if to say, 'That's all there is to it, and now I'm going, thank you.'

Miroslav was small and small-featured, swarthy, with neatly combed black hair and large black-rimmed glasses of the sort librarians in movies wear. His eyebrows seemed more or less permanently quizzically cocked, and he spoke about Yugoslavia's problems with a quietly humorous air, conveying the impression that he had deliberately chosen that tone because it was more dignified than crying.

Benjamin was a Muslim and Miroslav was a Croat.

When I had first met them the year before, they had introduced me to a third friend, Branko, a Serb. They had all grown up in Sarajevo and 'could talk about anything to each other', as Benjamin said.

'The people of Bosnia have learned, through enormous suffering, how to get along,' Miroslav added pointedly.

In the cities of central Bosnia, Muslims had Serb brothers-in-law, Croat best men. In some areas, the inter-marriage rate approached twenty-five per cent. Benjamin and Miroslav wanted that example to prevail in the coming months.

The coming months would be crucial. That same year, in the wake of the elections in Slovenia and Croatia, opposition parties had been legalized in Bosnia, but with the restriction, arising from naked fear, that none of them could be nationalist. Elections were promised but not scheduled. The security forces of Bosnia were renowned as the toughest and most vigilant in Yugoslavia. There was no leafleting in the streets, no booths, no banners. The Communists were confident they would do well in an election, since many people would be simply too afraid to vote anything else.

But no one expected the ban on nationalist parties to last. Intellectuals talked soberly about the probability that the Bosnian high court would find the ban unconstitutional. But more to the point, it was unenforceable. The largest opposition group carried an unimpeachable name, the Party of Democratic Action, but everyone knew it was the Muslim party.

My visit to Sarajevo that year assumed a comic-opera aspect. I was supposed to be a reporter, but I had tired of formal interviews in which members of the Central Committee or establishment editors-in-chief ponderously told me things like 'The history of ethnic relations is very complicated in this country.' The irony was that my liaison at the Ministry of Information, whose duty under a normal Communist system would have been to keep me as far away from information as possible, was a genuine convert to liberalization, and she chased me all over town, suggesting intellectuals and dissidents for me to interview. The dissidents wore sweaters instead of Central Committee suits, and the intellectuals smoked and looked sick, and the dissidents leaned forward and the intellectuals leaned back, and they all informed me that the history of ethnic relations in Yugoslavia was very complicated, very complicated indeed.

I escaped to drive around Sarajevo with Benjamin and Miroslav in Benjamin's car which, though tiny, was not small enough to navigate the tracks that counted for streets in the hills outside the centre of town. As Benjamin got lost, and eased his head out of a window barely big enough to accommodate it to hail passing boys with a machine-gun burst of Ks, and did hill starts backward from the vertiginous staircases the streets tended to turn into, and gunned the engine to slew up forty-five degrees around hairpins hardly larger than real hairpins, we talked about Bosnians. That is, whether they existed.

Miroslav and Benjamin, at any rate, called themselves Bosnians. But what was a Bosnian, I wanted to know? I was not asking about Muslims, but about some distinctive character that *all* inhabitants of Bosnia – Serb, Croat and Muslim – shared.

They groped for a way to explain it to me. 'It's a cultural thing . . .' Benjamin began.

'A feeling,' Miroslav said. 'A philosophy of life.'

'It's many things,' Benjamin said. He rubbed his fingertips together, caressing the gossamer-thin nuance of Bosnianness. 'A certain outlook.'

'Exactly!' Miroslav said. 'A unique outlook formed by the fact that the different groups live so close to each other.'

'Yes, our differences are what we have in common,' Benjamin said, happy to have formulated this paradox, this *bon mot*.

We stopped at a hillside community on the eastern edge of town where the old tollgate for caravans from Istanbul still stood. Benjamin wanted to buy a special Bosnian sort of bread at a bakery there, but they had run out, and we had to settle for rolls and Benjamin's description of what we were missing. We went into a kafana below the tollgate, built on the side of the hill so that the windows gave out on a vertiginous view of Sarajevo in the valley below and snow-capped mountains beyond.

'Do you have *smreka*?' Benjamin asked the dour woman behind the counter, and turning to me said, 'You'll love this. A Bosnian speciality.'

'Yes,' the woman said.

'Is it home-made?'

'Of course.'

'Three coffees and three glasses of smreka.'

Benjamin directed me to notice how the woman made the coffee. 'The little brass pot is a džezva,' he said. 'A Bosnian word. From Turkish.'

'Yes, I've seen them in Zagreb and Belgrade,' I said.

'Maybe. But they don't know how to make coffee there. Watch, watch.' He pointed surreptitiously, as if the woman with her traditional skills might flit away, bird-like, if we made any sudden moves. 'See, she puts the coffee grounds in the džezva and pours the boiling water on to it. In Serbia and Croatia, they first pour the water into the džezva and then stir in the grounds.' At the mere thought of it, Benjamin winced.

'It makes a difference?'

'Absolutely! Something doesn't . . .' Again the fingertips rubbed together. 'Ask my mother. It's hard to explain. Look!' He redirected my attention to the stove. 'Now she is returning the džezva to the fire until it boils up once, and now twice. There. It's done! That's the Bosnian way to make coffee.'

'Coffee-drinking is central to Bosnian culture,' Miroslav said.

'I can see that,' I said.

'It has to do with our idea of hospitality, of leisure. If you go out to the villages, that's where you'll really see it. A friend of ours was in a village last summer, in a kafana, and he drank his coffee quickly. You know, city-style. The proprietor got angry. "You don't know how to drink coffee!" he yelled at him. He threw him out. He wouldn't take his money.'

'That's a great story,' Benjamin said, beaming.

We sat on the cushioned benches running along the walls and drank our coffee from little handleless porcelain cups, each with a golden crescent and star in the bottom. The word for the cup was *fildžan*, Benjamin and Miroslav taught me, the sweet perfumed cubes of opaque jelly served with the coffee were *rahat lokum*. Both names were Turkish. The smreka was a drink of lemon juice, sugar and juniper berries.

But the smreka had been made from a powder. 'This always happens,' Benjamin sighed. 'If they don't say it's home-made, no one will buy it. You know!'

'You must go to the villages!' Miroslav said.

164

Serbs and Croats had already chorused this refrain to me, whenever the subject of their distinctive traditional cultures came up. Cities were the same all over the world, they had sighed — fallen from the paradise of folk dances and gardens out of which came šljivovica and smreka. Out in the villages I would find the *real* Serbia/Croatia/Bosnia.

We dipped our sugar cubes in the coffee and sucked on them, Bosnian-style. Benjamin was looking out of the window, down on the city.

'There is a place in Sarajevo,' he said, 'where an Orthodox church, a Catholic church, a mosque and a synagogue all stand within fifty metres of each other. There is no trouble between them. Isn't that amazing? That's what Bosnia is all about.'

'Zagreb is like the brain of Yugoslavia,' Miroslav said. 'Universities, rationality, and so on. Belgrade is the heart. Passion, anger. But Sarajevo! Sarajevo is the *soul*.'

I looked out over the minarets, the steeples, the domes, the old Turkish bazaar, the pseudo-Moorish town hall built by the Austrians, the corner where Franz Ferdinand was shot. Miroslav's designation seemed appropriate. While Belgrade thundered and Zagreb panicked, Sarajevo brooded. The brain and heart could be held in the hands, weighed. The soul was the most exalted, but many people did not believe it existed.

Miroslav and Benjamin talked to me for a while more about Bosnia's chance to play a 'historic role', as they put it, in reconciling the nations. They wanted to believe that Bosnia did not have to be the bomb of Yugoslavia. It could be the balm instead. I could hear the yearning in their voices.

But even then I could not help noticing that, although Branko was their good Serb friend, I had seen very little of him.

33

Since then I had visited some Bosnian villages. I had drunk real smreka and sat long over my coffee. But only the villagers of central Bosnia called themselves Bosnians, and they were mostly Muslims. In western Hercegovina, they all called themselves Croats and loved Tudjman, and were waiting for the ban on nationalist parties to be lifted so that they could organize a Bosnian branch of HDZ. In western Bosnia the Serbs looked across the border at Croatia and snarled, 'Krajina!'; and in eastern Bosnia they gazed across the Drina and sighed, 'Serbia!' It seemed to me then that Sarajevans were living a private dream of Bosnia, a Bosnia confined to urbanites like themselves.

And their dream had taken a beating. Shortly after I left the year before, the ban on nationalist parties had been lifted, and the Croats formed their HDZ, and the Serbs formed a Bosnian branch of the Krajina party, the Serbian Democratic Party or SDS. In the election at the end of the year the Communists, as usual, proved to have been pitifully over-confident about people's patience with them, and were trounced. The tallies for the three nationalist parties so closely paralleled the respective population percentages of the ethnic groups that one waggish columnist commented that the affair was less of an election than a census. Alija Izetbegović became the new President of the republic, since his Muslim party had garnered the most votes, and shortly afterwards announced a coalition government of all three parties. This made the rest of Yugoslavia sit up and take notice. Could the three nations actually govern together?

No, they couldn't. The government had been locked in stale-mate from the beginning, over issues such as its relations with other republics, reorganization of the police and the bureaucracy, control of the centre over the periphery, and the distribution and control of finances; in short, over everything of substance. While

Croatia and Serbia moved to more and more militant positions, Bosnia was paralysed.

Benjamin blamed the Serbs. 'Not the people,' he was careful to say. 'But their leaders. No compromise is possible. If their demands aren't met, and I mean in every last particular, they simply walk out of the meetings.'

Since last year Benjamin's wife Radina had given birth to a son, Mak. Radina's cousin had performed the delivery, a caesarian, in which he accidentally cut the baby. Mak would have a handsome duelling scar when he grew up, but now it was only an ugly pink wedge below his ear. 'The man was nervous, operating on his own cousin,' Benjamin said understandingly. Then, after a pause: 'All right, I'll admit it, I'd like to kill him.'

Benjamin and I strolled with Mak through the *baščaršija*, the old market of Sarajevo, down narrow cobbled streets which had been so tidied and restored that, without being inauthentic, they seemed touristy. The small shops used to function like packing crates, with a front wall like a large wooden shutter which was swung upward to open the shop. The shutters remained, but now they were raised to reveal glass doors and display windows. The coppersmiths and tinsmiths, leatherworkers and grocers had been relegated to the straggle of outer streets so that the main drags could be given over entirely to gold filigree, handbags, rugs and the ubiquitous oily little ground-meat lozenges called ćevapčići.

Since last year Benjamin had been allowed to make his first feature-length film. He was considered one of the most promising young film-makers in Yugoslavia, but sixty per cent of the money for a film came from the state, which still made personnel and allocation decisions according to a strict quota system. Bosnia was allowed only enough money for two or three films a year, and Benjamin would not have another chance at a full-length film for five or six years, even if this one was successful.

The script he was handed – *Holiday in Sarajevo*, about three rich Bosnian thiefs who return once a year to Sarajevo to spend their money – was not one he would have chosen, and I could sense, as he described it to me, his deep, almost bitter, disappointment. But he had worked on the script, and filmed it as best he could, and said he felt he had done a creditable job. At the moment he was recording the music in Sarajevo's best studio which, with typical government planning, had been built at one end of the airport runway and shared a wall with a basketball gym. He would have to get a finished print completed in time for the Yugoslav film festivals later in the summer. 'If they happen,' he said.

Mak spat out his pacifier.

'Fuck you, Mak!' Benjamin picked it off the ground and, since he was still a new father, grimaced at the dust, waggling his large head. He ran into a shop to have the pacifier washed off.

Once we were strolling again, he explained: 'In a normal summer the director and actors go around in a caravan from festival to festival. Like Gypsies! It's important to compete because Yugoslav films are shown in cinemas only in the autumn, right after the festivals. The rest of the year it's all American films. Pula is the main festival, with awards for all-round excellence. Then there's Herceg Novi for directors, Niš for actors, and so on. But Pula is in Croatia, so this year none of the Serbs will come. Herceg Novi is in Montenegro and Niš is in Serbia, so no Croats or Slovenes will come.

'It used to be a game. Every festival had enough prizes so that they could be handed out in the right proportions to the different republics. Now people suspect it will be a different game. The Croats will win in Pula, the Serbs in Niš, and so on. It's a real shame. What counts here has always been ethnic politics, never quality.'

'Do you think there *is* a republic that tends to make better films?'

'Oh, Bosnia has made the best films for years.'

Zagreb's and Belgrade's beggars were mainly Gypsy children who roamed the cafés. As you moved into Bosnia, or south into Kosovo, the beggars began to look more professional. They were adult, and maimed. We passed a woman by the Gazi Husrev-beg Mosque who raised a whole arm and half of another one at passers-by. Farther along, a man displayed a swollen and oozing leg on a cardboard sheet like a baked joint on a platter. A woman hidden under shawls, skirts and hanging kerchiefs hobbled doubled over, her masked head at knee level, knocking a foot-long cane against the pavement in front of her and dragging a frozen leg behind. She spoke the same phrases over and over, in a lulling mechanical rhythm that never varied, accenting the first word of every phrase and trailing off in flat chant-like intonation: 'DAJ mi para . . .'

'GIVE – me mon-ey, HAVE – some mer-cy, I – have no-thing, LOOK – at my trou-bles, GIVE – me mon-ey, HAVE – some mer-cy . . .'

She was not even a ghost. Everyone ignored her. The rare Slav beggars I had seen around the country seemed to be relatively successful, but I had yet to see a single person give a thing to a Gypsy.

'The film cost a million dollars,' Benjamin was saying, 'and raising our forty per cent was almost impossible. The producer takes the director around to meet people, and the director has to play the part. I was the Artist, the *rara avis*.' Benjamin slung his coat Vuk-style over both shoulders and donned dark glasses. He preened and sniffed. The nostrils of his parody of a Roman nose inflated like haemorrhoids. He looked great.

Mak spat out his pacifier.

'Fuck you, Mak!'

When he returned from washing it he said, 'If the state firms give money, they get a credit in the titles. But none of the state firms have any money. The director of one firm was a friend of mine, and he really wanted to help. So he gave us three thousand socks. You see what it is like. We're supposed to be making a movie, and we're selling socks.'

On the way to Benjamin's car we passed a news-stand. A special issue of *Pogledi* (*Views*), a Serb monarchist magazine, was emblazoned PARTISAN CRIMES IN SERBIA: 1944–45. 150,000 UNKNOWN GRAVES. Copies of a new book entitled *Genocide Against the Muslims* were stacked next to it. I bought the latest issue of *Globus*, a new Croat paper, headlined WILL BOSNIA BE DIVIDED? Tudjman and Milošević had recently met for the first time – a telling fact in itself, considering that Tudjman had been elected more than a year ago – and rumours were sweeping the country that they had sat down with a map of Yugoslavia to discuss who would get what.

'If I could ask Izetbegović just one question,' Benjamin said, strapping Mak into his car seat, 'I'd ask him what he knew about that meeting.' He eased the car into the traffic. 'What I've heard is, they agreed Tudjman would get western Hercegovina, Milošević would get the Croatian and Bosnian Krajinas and eastern Hercegovina, and the Muslims would be allowed to keep the area around Sarajevo, and would be given the Sandžak. Fuck me, roll up the windows.'

A warm breeze was finding its way to Mak's face. Benjamin subscribed to the common Yugoslav theory that moving air was bad for children. Parents on stiflingly hot trains conscientiously kept the windows shut while the other passengers smoked their cigarettes and nodded approvingly.

The Sandžak was an area in south-western Serbia with a heavy majority of Muslims. I did not say it to Benjamin, but I found it utterly unbelievable that the Serbs would ever agree to yielding an inch of their territory. Nor would the Croats ever consider giving up any of their Krajina.

I glanced through the *Globus* articles. Throughout, they referred to the republic I was in as Herceg-Bosna, presumably because the Croats lived mainly in Hercegovina. They howled that by all that was holy and historical Croatia should be bigger. The Banovina of Croatia – a short-lived entity of limited autonomy resulting from a last-ditch compromise between Serbs and Croats in 1939 – had been bigger than the post-war Croatian republic. A *Globus* map picturing the 1939 Banovina superimposed over the present-day republic satisfyingly showed how a return to these 'historical' borders would 'restore' to Croatia bits of western and northern Bosnia, all of western Hercegovina and a solid chunk of the central districts west of Sarajevo.

Yum. But the article went on. Everyone knew that the 1939 agreement was only temporary. Everyone knew that changes had already been planned, and all those changes were (naturally) in Croatia's favour. *Globus* printed a second map. Now Croatia was even bigger. It included a part of Vojvodina that 'until 1918 had been primarily a Croatian-Hungarian ethnic region'; more of western Bosnia; Sarajevo; areas south and east of Sarajevo that now had virtually no Croats but were, anyway, 'historically' Croatian.

Under this plan, Croatia would get 47.5% of 'Herceg-Bosna's' territory and 53.8% of its population. Of the people thus turned into Croatian citizens, 41.9% would be Muslims, 25.9% would be Croats and 21.6% would be Serbs. 'This . . . territorial division is based on the historical rights of Croatia. By it, Serbia would exceed its own historical rights. Therefore, although this solution appears acceptable to Croatia, it would in reality mean the acceptance of Serbian ethnic penetration into historical Croatian territory' – i.e. into any part of Herceg-Bosna, since historically it *all* belonged to Croatia. (See under: Porphyrogenitus, Constantine.)

I did not tell Benjamin that nowhere in *Globus* was there any indication that either the Serbs or the Croats would consider for a second letting the Muslims have any land of their own.

The sun poured through the closed windows. In the back seat Mak was gasping, as pink as his scar.

34

Benjamin's mother lived at the western end of Sarajevo, where the valley opened up, and where the post-war high-rises clustered in tremendous agglomerations of tens of thousands of people each. The access road felt like a ramp up to a gargantuan launching pad, where peasants had been gathered into ships and shot into the modern world.

One wondered if their former world had been so squalid. Had bands of teenagers lounged at the doors of their village homes to scrawl graffiti and smash bottles? In the twilit echoing staircases, tiles had fallen off the walls and potholes gaped in the concrete floors. Prison windows looked out on a wasteland of dirt and bulldozer tracks, where two children sat on a rubbishy hummock, unmoving, as if under the watch of a ring of guards three hundred feet tall.

But behind their doors, people created livable spaces, with rugs over the peeling linoleum and doilies in the windows that had stuck shut, or whose frames had splintered when an impatient hand had tried to force them open.

Benjamin's mother greeted us, a beaming, ample woman with permed hair tinted auburn, and costume jewellery of knuckly gold. Radina was there, lively-eyed and long-haired, but subdued from a cold. She and Benjamin lived a couple of towers away. Miroslav was also there. While the women prepared dinner and watched Mak and brought us whatever we needed in the way of coffee and juice, we men sat in the living room and talked politics.

I wondered if Miroslav had voted for the Croat party, and Benjamin for the Muslim party.

But no. Both had voted for some leftish greenish anti-nationalist party that had run a bearded professor or two, and put up clever, irreverent posters and had about three hundred members and got about 0.1% of the vote. Benjamin was the party's Vice-President.

'And how are things with Branko?' I asked.

'Oh, fine,' Benjamin said.

Miroslav quoted the party line. 'It's not the Serbs who are the problem, it's their leaders.'

'So you two and Branko can still talk about everything?'

There was a pained silence.

'I know he reads *Politika*,' Miroslav said delicately.

'He *does*?' Benjamin said, shocked.

Miroslav shrugged apologetically. 'I've seen him. So you see how it is, Brian. I know what he thinks. I don't need to talk politics with him.'

'So are there still any Bosnians?'

Benjamin was impatient, adamant. 'Whether we like it or not, we are Bosnians.'

'There is no other choice,' Miroslav said.

But over dinner, the talk was of differences, not commonalities.

172

'The non-Muslim politicians openly use insulting terms for the Muslims,' Benjamin's mother complained, as she went back and forth bringing out the broth, the dock leaves stuffed with meat and onions, the fried potatoes and roast beef and sour cream.

'They call us *balija*,' Benjamin said. 'An old word for a Muslim peasant, a man with shit on his boots, an idiot. This is not in private, this is in their regular speeches.'

'They also call us half-Turks,' Radina said from the corner, where she was dandling Mak.

'Or just plain Turks,' Benjamin's mother said.

Benjamin was not religious. Neither was his family, nor any of his friends. He had never been inside a mosque, and had little idea what went on inside one, other than that you could not wear shoes.

So what made him feel like a Muslim?

He pondered that for a long while.

Could I distinguish Muslims from Serbs or Croats by the look of their houses? I asked.

Oh no.

By the way they dressed?

No, no. (A laugh.) Did I think they still wore fezes? Nothing quaint like that.

Finally, Benjamin said, a trifle lamely, 'Women occupy an exalted place in Islam. The role of the mother is extremely important. The bond between a mother and her children is very strong.'

His mother beamed approvingly and took the dishes away.

'I've noticed neither of the women ate with us,' I said.

Benjamin laughed delightedly. 'And you are wondering if that's usual. Am I right? Miroslav, did you hear that?' They laughed together. Then the women laughed. 'Of course not!' Benjamin crowed. 'But you see, my mother has to do the cooking and Radina has to take care of Mak! *That's* why they're not eating! It's not a *custom*!'

I sensed that Benjamin was conscious that I, as a non-Muslim, would be likely to pounce on any signs of a 'typical' Muslim tendency to devalue women. That was the west's obsession with

Islam – that Sarajevo might have soul, but Muslim women did not. But I had raised the subject mischievously. I knew perfectly well that it was still a relatively common practice among all the peoples of Yugoslavia to have the women serve the men, and eat later.

'You asked about how to tell between Serbs, Croats and Muslims of Bosnia,' Benjamin said. 'I will tell you.' He smiled broadly and looked around, gathering attention. This was a favourite story.

'When the Austrians occupied Bosnia in 1878, the new governor visited a Muslim imam and asked him how to rule. The imam said, "You will only be able to rule Bosnia if you understand these three words: *akmaluk*, *jogunluk* and *fitniluk*."' Benjamin pronounced the words with gusto, his nostrils flared, a finger and thumb held out as if to hang each one in a row in the air. His Ks popped like firecrackers.

'These are Turkish words. Akmaluk describes the Muslims.'

Everyone at the table chuckled and nodded.

'And it means?' I said.

Benjamin waggled his head. 'It's difficult to translate.'

Everyone burst out laughing.

'It means . . . Miroslav, what does it mean?'

'*I'm* not going to say,' Miroslav said.

'It means . . .' Benjamin tried body language. He swayed loosely in his chair. He tilted his head one way, then the other. 'It means slow. Submissive. You know!'

'I'm not sure I do.'

'Waiting for the blow. Careful.'

'OK.'

'That's akmaluk. Jogunluk describes the Serbs.'

Louder laughter.

'Jogunluk means . . .' Benjamin looked pained. 'This is also difficult.'

'Stubborn,' Miroslav suggested.

Benjamin winced. 'Stubborn . . . maybe. But . . . Oppressive, maybe, is better. Obstinate. Bull-headed!'

'Yes, stubborn,' Miroslav said.

174

'All right, stubborn, but also . . .' Benjamin lifted his shoulders and bowed his arms. He hulked. 'Jogunluk is a big, stupid man, always bulling forward, waving his arms. He gets everything wrong, but refuses to listen, and keeps insisting on his own view in a loud voice. He drowns everyone else out. You always know what he thinks.'

'Exactly,' Miroslav said.

'Whereas, fitniluk – that's the Croats. Miroslav?'

'No, you, please.'

'All right. This is fitniluk.' Benjamin smiled sweetly, nodding. 'Yes, everything's nice, yes, yes.' He raised his eyebrows as if hanging on someone's every word. 'Mm, of course.' A knife was in his hand under the table. 'Mm, yes, of course.' He jerked the knife upward into that someone's guts, as his saccharine smile curdled into a grimace of hatred.

'That's fitniluk.'

'It's true!' Miroslav laughed. 'It's true!'

35

In the incessant Zagreb nattering about Croats and the Belgrade chest-thumping about Serbs, no one ever paused to wonder what exactly they were talking about. Nationalism is a collective egoism, but the more you gorge your own ego, the less collective it becomes. Were the Istrians Croats? They undoubtedly would have said so. But when Tudjman told them, during his election campaign, that they had to consider themselves Croats first and Istrians second, they were outraged, and Istria became the only non-Serb region of Croatia in which the HDZ lost. Vanja saw what Tudjman meant by 'Croat', and decided he was a Dalmatian.

Serbian Serbs said they had to protect Croatian Serbs. But were they the same nation? The two groups had had very different histories, the one as serfs, the other as military frontiersmen. The

Serbs in Krajina felt they were the truer type, a typical attitude of the frontier. The Serbs of Serbia had a more complex attitude towards the Krajina Serbs, a mixture of admiration and fear – the typical ambivalence of the centre. Perhaps Serbian Serbs agreed that Krajina Serbs were 'truer' Serbs, but they were not sure they liked themselves in this purified form. They half resented these men who took up arms so readily, who hated so easily, who were dragging Serbia into a war.

What extra wrinkle might have further confused Yugoslavia's nested national questions if the Krajina Serbs had started to call themselves Krajinans? Would they then have been as vociferous candidates for separate nationhood as the Montenegrins, who, like them, were culturally, linguistically and religiously Serb, but with a distinguishing political history? The worship of the Nation was the worship of the Word. One was a Croat because the term existed.

That was the Muslims' problem. They could not exist until a certain semantic confusion was cleared up. Both Serbs and Croats pointed out, blandly convinced that this put an end to all possible argument, that 'Muslim' was a religious term, not a national one. 'I am Catholic, but I am also Croat,' the Croat tendentiously argued, while his mirror image echoed, 'I am Orthodox, but I am also Serb.'

The Muslims, then, were Muslim, but *what else were they*?

In the Kingdom of Serbs, Croats and Slovenes, they had been counted as 'Serbs of the Muslim faith'. During World War II, the Croats called them 'the flower of the Croat nation'. After 1945 they had to register as Serb, Croat or 'undeclared'. Almost all of them chose 'undeclared'.

It was not until 1961 that they won the right to register as a separate nation. But they could not call themselves Bosnians because the Serbs and Croats of Bosnia, though not much liking the term for themselves, were hardly going to let the Muslims monopolize it. (Besides, a substantial population of 'Bosnian' – i.e. Slav, Serbo-Croato-Bosnian-speaking – Muslims lived outside Bosnia, in the Sandžak of Serbia.) Albanians were mostly Muslim, but they registered as Albanians. The word 'Muslim', when used alone, could refer to the religion of most Albanians and some Macedonians and all the Turks, but it could also refer specifically to the *nation* of 'Bosnian' Muslims. It was awkward, no doubt about it.

'So call us Eskimos!' Muslims told me in exasperation. Whenever discussions of Yugoslav ethnic complexities turned absurd, as they often threatened to do, someone invariably mentioned Eskimos.

Actually, many of the Muslims of Bosnia might not ever have been either Serb or Croat. Both Serbs and Croats passionately believed that their ancestors descended as Serbs and Croats into the Balkan peninsula in the sixth century (although, of course, the nations went back much further than that), but some scholars argued that the first incursion was by undifferentiated Slav tribes (whose self-identification as nothing more precise than 'Slavs' survives in the modern appellations 'Slovenia', 'Slovakia' and 'Slavonia'), whereas more powerful tribes calling themselves Serbs and Croats did not arrive until half a century later, when they were invited by the Byzantine emperors to come and help exterminate the Avars. The ur-Bosnians might have belonged to this first migration.

In addition, many present-day Bosnian Muslims were probably descended from peoples from all over Europe, since it was a fact well attested to in the historical records that, when Catholicism destroyed dualism in the west, the surviving Patarenes, Albigensians and Cathars – Italians, Germans, Frenchmen and Dutchmen – fled to Bosnia, where they found relative safety in numbers. This historical curiosity had occurred to me frequently as I walked the streets of a Bosnian town, noting the number of people with a striking coloration rare in the rest of Yugoslavia: tawny skin with vivid eyes of blue, green or shining grey.

Although I found these speculations intriguing, I considered them irrelevant to the question of Muslim ethnicity. But Balkan nationalists believed in blood. When they said the Albanians were the descendants of the Illyrians, they really seemed to mean that Illyrian blood flowed in Albanian veins, whereas none flowed in those of Croats, Serbs or Bulgarians. They seemed to believe that the Romans who colonized Dalmatia, and the Avars who harried them, had simpy vanished, along with their languages. The Serbs talked about people in Kosovo who spoke Albanian and considered themselves Albanian, but who were 'really' Turks, and therefore should be deported to Turkey. Albanians talked about Turks who had returned to Turkey who were 'really' Albanian, and should come back. Croats pointed to evidence that they had admixtures of Iranian or Gothic blood – satisfyingly ancient peoples – and seemed to believe Serbs did not. Serbs said that the Romance-language speakers of north-eastern Serbia were not Romanians – after all, that would legitimize Romanian irredentism – but Vlachs, and they said Vlachs were 'really' Serbs who had been romanized.

What did nationhood mean when you descended to this level? Were the English really Danish? Were the French (Franks) really German? What were Italians and Greeks today, Rome and Byzantium having operated for centuries as imperial slave markets?

Language, as opposed to genes, is usually considered one of the principal determining factors of a nation. Ethnologists would say that the Albanians are descendants of the Illyrians not because they have a monopoly on Illyrian corpuscles but because the Albanian language is thought to be a descendant of Illyrian. For centuries, a Vlach was anyone who lived in the Balkan mountains and spoke a form of Latin, whether his eyes were blue or brown, close- or wide-set. Romanians are those Vlachs who held on to their Romance language, while other Vlachs became Serbs, Croats, Bulgarians and Greeks by losing it.

Croats try to make language a distinguishing factor, often with nonsensical results. Yugoslavia, like any country, had a spectrum of dialects, flowing one into another as one moved north to south, west to east. The Croats living nearest Slovenia speak a dialect of 'Croatian' that sounds damn similar to Slovenian. The dialect of Zagreb and its environs – called 'Kajkavian', after *kaj*, its word for 'what' – is also Slovenian-influenced, and other Croats profess not to understand it, except when they are making fun of it. Istrians have their own dialect, called 'Čakavian'. The rest of the

Croats – which is most of them – speak 'Štokavian'. But so do all the Serbs.

Croats try to tackle this problem by dividing Štokavian into three subgroups, two of which I have mentioned elsewhere: Ijekavian (*mlijeko, brijeg*), Ikavian (*mliko, brig*) and Ekavian (*mleko, breg*). On the most simple-minded level of explanation – to give them the benefit of the doubt, perhaps they only said this to stupid Americans – Croats would tell me that Ijekavian is a distinguishing mark of Croatian, and Ekavian a mark of Serbian. But this is absurd. The Serbs in the Krajina speak Ijekavian just like the Croat neighbours they are trying to kill. The Monte-negrins speak a sort of super-Ijekavian, putting the *ije* vowel into more words than anyone else, which should make them super-Croats, but they happen to be super-Serbs.

Tudjman, who was once a Partisan, became a dissident under Tito solely because of the language question. He was kicked out of the Communist Party for signing a declaration on Croatian language rights. His own choice for pure Croatian is the Ikavian spoken in western Hercegovina.

But what does 'pure Croatian' mean? Is it any less of a fantasy than the explorers' habit of heading upriver, choosing one branch after another until they stood over a mountain rill which they called – heady with the Word – the headwaters of the Mississippi or the Missouri? Why is any dialect purer than another? Because writers of the earliest records happened to speak that dialect? Because that dialect happened to have been chosen as a basis for the literary language? Because that dialect is the farthest removed from dialects spoken by Serbs? Because the person defining 'pure' speaks that dialect?

In an interview, Tudjman told me that the Muslims could not be a separate nation because Islam was 'only a religion', whereas scholars knew they were all really Croats because when they saw milk they said 'mliko', and 'only Croats speak Ikavian'. I could only stare at him, at a loss for words. For one thing, it wasn't true. The Muslims of eastern Bosnia and eastern Hercegovina – at least half of the total population – speak Ijekavian along with their Serb and Montenegrin neighbours. And even if it were true, his argument, like so many nationalist arguments, was circular. The Muslims were really Croats because they spoke a dialect that only Croats spoke; but one could only say that only Croats spoke that dialect if the Muslims were really Croats. And even if his point were true and not circular, it was trivial.

Tudjman's mistake with the linguistic theory lay in not going far enough. When the Serbs had had their own infatuation with the language question in the nineteenth century, they had shown more *chutzpah*. Vuk Karadžić, the great Serb (and Great Serb) linguist and founder of the Serbo-Croatian literary language, reasoned simply and boldly: since all Serbs spoke Štokavian, Štokavian was the Serbian language. Therefore, anyone who spoke Štokavian was a Serb. This not only meant that all Bosnian Muslims were 'Muslim Serbs'; it meant that two-thirds of all *Croats* were actually Roman Catholic Serbs. Similarly, Croats who spoke Kajkavian were actually Slovenes. The only true Croats were those who spoke Čakavian. Thus did Karadžić cut the Gordian knot. And incidentally, he arrived at the satisfying conclusion that there were only eight hundred thousand Croats in the world, while there were 5.3 million Serbs.

This kind of argument represented the apotheosis of the Word. The Croats who spoke Štokavian needed to change nothing to become Serbs – neither their language, nor their religion, nor their history, nor their culture, nor their genealogies. They had simply to say 'Serb' and they would be Serbs, as Dorothy had only to say 'home' to find herself there.

The Father of Croatia, Ante Starčević, responded to Karadžić by going one step further. He claimed that, actually, there was no such thing as Serbs. All those people beyond the Drina were in reality Orthodox Croats. One wondered if either arch-Croat Starčević or arch-Serb Karadžić realized that their positions were nearly identical; the only thing they could not agree on was the name of the nation.

If only the Muslims had taken a new language, as the Vlachs – that is, highland Illyrians, Avars, Dacians, Gepids, Scythians, Goths and God knows what else – in becoming Romanized had adopted a form of Latin. But the peculiarity of the Ottoman

Empire left open the question: Which language? Turkish was the language of their new culture, but not enough Turks ever moved into Bosnia to make it even useful, let alone desirable. The language of the Bosnians' new faith, the language of their emotional allegiance, was Arabic, but it remained exclusively the language of worship, as it was to the Turks. Imams learned to read the Koran, while most Muslims memorized a few prayers and devout phrases. Outside the mosque they conversed in Bosno-Croato-Serbian.

Arabic and Turkish did leave their traces, of course. Serbs use plenty of Turkish loan-words, but Muslims use more. And the Muslim K that sounds like a vocal cord snapping, and an H that hisses gila-like from deep in the throat, are both Arabic consonants. (In the Bosnian towns, the Serbs and Croats have picked up the K, but have considerable trouble with the H.) Does this make for a separate Bosnian language, as some Muslims argue? According to the definition of 'language' most linguists use, no. According to the Croat definition – judging from their insistence that Croatian is a separate language from Serbian – then yes. But Croat nationalists are the most strident in insisting that the idea of a Bosnian language is absurd.

(One gradually came to be able to predict these furious about-faces. Croats told me Croatia had a right to autonomy, but the Krajina did not. Serbs said Vojvodina was once Hungary but now it was Serbia because Serbs lived there, whereas Kosovo would always be Serbia because it was once Serbia, no matter how many Albanians now lived there.)

Attempts to distinguish the three nations on non-religious cultural grounds ran into equal, and equally unacknowledged, difficulties. No cultural attributes – costumes, dances, marriage customs, food – were common to all Croats or all Serbs or all Muslims. This was the Istrian problem. Tudjman came with his costumed dancers, and they thought, 'Bah! Slavonian drivel.' The tamburicas played, and it was all Dalmatian jingle-jangle to them. Tudjman opened his mouth, and his 'pure' Croatian was not the dialect – excuse me, the language – that Istrians spoke.

Serbs had the one-string gusle and their national epics, but the Croats had the gusle too. The Muslims did not eat pork, but beyond that, people other than Benjamin could only answer my query about cultural differences by talking about the importance of mothers, before lapsing into fingertip-rubbing. The Muslims put water on their coffee while Serbs put coffee in their water, but Bosnian Serbs did it both ways, and besides, how could you even talk about it without laughing?

But they did, *ad infinitum*. I never thought I would consider folk dances sinister, but that is what they started to seem as they appeared night after night on television, in between scenes of war carnage. But even if there *were* a monolithic Croatian traditional culture, separate from Serbian culture, the final irony remained: the traditional cultures everywhere were moribund. City people commanded me to head for the villages, but the villages were depopulated except for the elderly and whichever of their children happened to be on vacation from their jobs in the cities, or in Germany. Television was virtually the only place you saw folk dances, or costumes, or heard the old songs. At the village fairs people wore blue jeans and played the radio and sold plastic toys from Taiwan. As little as fifteen years ago, the *kolo* – a traditional circle dance – was unavoidable at any gathering. In the past two years, I had seen it precisely once.

The Muslims were in a particular bind because, like the Serbs and Croats, they considered themselves European, and were desperate to assure Europe that they were as western as the next Balkan nation; but any attempt they made to stress their unique culture made them look eastern. Like it or not, that culture was Turkish. So Benjamin laughed in a cosmopolitan fashion at the idea of people wearing fezes, although in the small towns you saw fezes all the time, and a professor of Islamic law poured us both some excellent Scotch, saying, 'I am a Muslim, but I am also a man of the world,' and five minutes later cited the Muslim prohibition against alcohol as one of the primary distinctive traits of his people.

All of these issues – blood, language, culture – were masks, even if they were masks the Yugoslavs believed in. They were red herrings. The real distinguishing factor between Serbs, Croats and Muslims was, of course, religion.

Croats are Catholics, Serbs are Serbian Orthodox. During World War II, any Serbs that the Ustashas forcibly converted were subsequently called Croats, because with the change in confession the ethnic transmutation was considered complete. (Archbishop Stepinac, along with much of the Croatian clergy, subscribed to the convenient theory that these Serbs had once been Catholics – i.e. Croats – who had been forcibly converted to Orthodoxy, or Serbdom. The Ustashas were simply reclaiming their sheep.)

Today's Serb–Croat conflict, with its viciousness, its lack of distinction between soldiers and civilians, its lack of mercy towards women and children, certainly had the look of a religious war. Croat soldiers wore crosses into battle. The Chetniks, with their long hair and beards, looked like Orthodox priests. Serbs, at rallies and in photographs, flashed not the usual V, but the thumb and two fingers with which the Orthodox crossed themselves.

When the Thirty Years War finally ended in famine, depopulation and utter exhaustion on both sides, German Protestants and Catholics were supremely lucky that the word 'German' happened to exist. The Serbs and Croats had no Word to bind them. Their tendency to regard a religious difference as a national one was quadruply reinforced: by the unusual autonomy granted the Croats by the Roman Catholic Church, which allowed them their own Slavonic liturgy when all other western-rite Catholics could only use Latin; by Orthodoxy's organization, under which each church was state-based and autocephalic; by Islam's concept of the *umma*, a quasi-national community of the faithful; and by the Ottoman Empire's *millet* system, under which non-Muslim subjects were separated into communities according to religion, with each under the administration of its own religious authorities.

It was a tragic historical confluence of peculiarities. It allowed today's appalling spectacle of a people descending into a religious war in an ecumenical age, when their church leaders were for the most part trying to stop the fighting rather than egging it on, and when many of the fighters themselves were agnostic.

And it made for the supreme irony of Serbs and Croats complaining that Muslims could not be a separate nation because Islam was 'only a religion'.

If the war widened to include the Muslims, they would be in the worst position of all. They were weak. They had no home republic on which to depend for its 'territorial defence units', its 'security forces' and other paramilitary outfits. Bosnia's own such forces were in disarray, as the command structure splintered and the politicians stalemated.

The Muslims were also at a disadvantage on a deeper, psychological level. If Serbs and Croats had cast each other as the Other, the Muslims were even more Other. Fourteen hundred years of European fear and loathing of Islam confront them. Serbs and Croats alike look on them as mysterious, unknowable, devious – clichés the west has always imposed on the east. They speak of the Muslims with the smile of a man speaking of the supposed mysteries of Woman. When the sociologist told me I would never understand Bosnia until I understood Islam, he meant that I would never understand Bosnia.

How could Serbs call the Muslims Turks and not recall their five hundred years of humiliation, nor hum a few lines from one of their epic poems that taught them as children what all Turks deserved?

> 'Who was the hero, the good hero,
> who swept one sweep of his razor sword,
> his razor sword and his right hand,
> and carried away twenty heads?'
> 'That is Banović Strahin.'
> 'Who was the hero, the good hero,
> who thrust his lance through two and then two,
> and pushed and threw them into Sitnica?'
> 'That is Srdja Zlopogledja.'
> 'Who was the hero, the good hero,
> on the high chestnut horse

184

with a banner of the cross in his hand,
driving the Turks together into flocks,
herding them into Sitnica water?'
'That one is Bosko Jugović.'

And surely the Croats felt this Otherness as strongly as the Serbs. In their Manichaean world-view (a touch of the Bogomil in their background, perhaps?), if the Serbs were orientally lazy and corrupt, surely the Muslims were even more so. Who else were the Bosnians in the popular 'lazy Bosnian' jokes? For centuries the Croats had preached a holy war to free Bosnia of the 'Turkish yoke'. What Turkish yoke? There were virtually no Turks in Bosnia. And free Bosnia for whom?

Yet Tudjman, with chilling predictability, was calling the Muslims the 'flower of the Croat nation', as Ante Pavelić had done before him. Perhaps he was also saying, in closed council, what the Ustasha Prefect of Bosnia had said in 1941: 'After the Serbs, it's the turn of the Muslims.'

What was the word? Fitniluk.

Meanwhile, the Serbs walked out of every government meeting. Jogunluk.

And the Muslims, panic-stricken, were seized with paralysis. Akmaluk.

36

I made the pilgrimage to the spot where Gavrilo Princip fired the starting pistol for the First World War.

The fact that the Austrian Archduke Franz Ferdinand was assassinated at all is fairly incredible. It was the last act in a black comedy of errors that one could ascribe to the meaningless malignancy of blind bad luck à la Franz Kafka, to the dust-fine grindings of a malignant Fate à la Thomas Hardy, or to the shadowy manoeuvrings of a malignant conspiracy *à la* Oliver Stone.

Franz Ferdinand and the Military Governor of Bosnia, General Poćorek, decided that the Archduke would attend military manoeuvres in Bosnia on 27 June 1914. On the day after, he would be received by the Governor in Sarajevo.

This was a terrible idea. Austria's annexation of Bosnia in 1908 still aroused murderous passions in the breasts of young Bosnian Serbs, whose radical agitations the Sarajevo government was always busily suppressing, and 28 June was Vidovdan, or St Vitus' Day, which happened to be the Serbs' most important national day. The Battle of Kosovo had taken place on Vidovdan in 1389, and ever since then the Serbs had marked it with a mixture of deep mourning and fanatical pride. For them, Vidovdan represented blows struck – whether successfully or suicidally, it hardly mattered – against tyranny. It represented all that was recklessly glorious about the Serbs. Franz Ferdinand's visit to captive Sarajevo on Vidovdan would seem like a deliberate challenge – 'Shoot me if you can.' Matters were made worse by the fact that Poćorek and the civil administrator of Bosnia were hardly on speaking terms, so the visit was kept entirely in military hands. The civil authorities were not even notified – an astonishing omission, which resulted in virtually no police protection.

One would have thought the Archduke lucky, however, in his would-be assassins. The six students who mixed into the crowd along the route of the motorcade were reasonably good at staying up late in cafés and talking about Freedom, but they were bad shots and bad planners, with bad nerves. They had been fitted out with revolvers and bombs to kill the Archduke, and prussic acid to kill themselves, by a secret society in Serbia called the Black Hand, but it is hard to believe that any member of that organization expected the boys to do more than chicken out and throw their weapons away – as indeed some of them had done in their previous flirtations with violence – or get caught on their way to Sarajevo, or accidentally blow themselves up in somebody's attic.

On the morning of 28 June, the Archduke and his wife Sofia

drove into Sarajevo along the quay of the Miljacka, the little river that bisects the city. The six assassins were strung out along the quay. Two of them, one after the other, held their bombs under their coats and their revolvers in their pockets and simply watched the Archduke's car go by, in a sort of dreamy, stunned panic. A third did not notice until the last moment that he was standing next to a policeman. He also let the car pass. A fourth, a boy named Čabrinović, did throw his bomb, but too late, and it bounced off the back of Franz and Sofia's car and exploded near the car behind it, wounding the Archduke's aide-de-camp. Čabrinović swallowed his prussic acid and jumped into the river, but the poison did not kill him, or even make him ill, and he was arrested by the police. (Perhaps the 'Black Hand' had thought real prussic acid a little too dangerous for these boys.) The fifth and sixth conspirators, Princip and one Grabež, heard Čabrinović's bomb go off and concluded the job had been done. Princip was turning away when he saw the Archduke and his wife sail past, unharmed. It was too late to do anything, so, in a blue funk, he did what came naturally. He went to a café.

Meanwhile, the Archduke was in a rage. When he arrived at the Town Hall, he interrupted the Mayor's welcoming address by shouting, 'I come here to pay you a visit, and you throw bombs at me! It's an outrage!'

But for the Habsburgs, protocol was protocol. The Archduke subsided into grumbles, and the Mayor went back to his speech. Then the Archduke read his own prepared speech, full of diplomatic niceties, from a paper sprinkled with the blood of his aide-de-camp.

Next on the schedule was a visit to the Regional Museum. But Sofia suggested they visit the wounded aide-de-camp in the hospital instead. The Archduke agreed, and indignantly demanded of Poćorek if any more bombs would be thrown at them. Poćorek solemnly assured him there would be no more bombs. The royal couple could have waited for better police protection, but if protocol was protocol, a schedule was even more tyrannically a schedule. They were already some ten minutes late.

Although they could have reached the hospital via the planned route, they decided to change it, for safety's sake. Instead of turning away from the river at the second bridge from the Town Hall and going through the older part of town, the procession would continue straight along the quay, back the way it had come. The Archduke, Sofia and General Poćorek climbed into the second car in the motorcade, while an Austrian count drew his sword and jumped on to the running board with the gallant but rather mutton-headed idea of protecting them from further attacks. They set off.

Unfortunately, no one had told the chauffeurs about the change in the route. When the first car reached the second bridge it turned right. The chauffeur of the second car turned also, and was immediately berated by Poćorek. Confused, he stopped the car.

Princip, meanwhile, had finished his coffee and left the café. He was walking despondently along the sidewalk, still hardly able to believe that he and all five of his co-conspirators had failed so miserably. He heard a man speak sharply: 'What are you doing? We're going the wrong way!' He looked up, and right in front of him was an open car, stopped dead in the street. The chauffeur was turned in his seat, looking back towards the quay. A man with a sword crouched on the opposite running board. Another man was yelling at the chauffeur from the back seat. Next to him sat the Archduke, stiff and angry, an overstuffed, unmoving target in spotless white, three feet away.

It is hard to imagine what Princip thought. He was a free-thinker, so he probably did not believe in miracles. He raised the gun. No one paid any attention to him. He was a bad shot, but not bad enough to miss at that range. He shot the Archduke through the heart. He then tried to shoot Poćorek, but Sofia, lunging forward to cradle her dying husband, intercepted the bullet so exactly right that she died before he did.

The building on that corner in those days was a pretty little shop, with high rounded windows and stucco pilasters and stencilled advertisements on the glass. Trees lined the quay. But the trees were ripped out long ago, to make room for traffic, and

188

the building was remodelled between the wars in the blank grey style of Adolf Loos, so that you would never have guessed it was once attractive. Now it was the Young Bosnia Museum, a single room into which the exhaust from the rushing tide of cars and buses drifted, coating the walls with soot.

Here was a model of the quay, the route of the motorcade marked in black. Here was Sofia's schedule, printed on cream bond paper in floral script: Breakfast at the hotel in Ilidža, six miles from town. Holy mass in the chapel. Ten-thirty a.m., leave Town Hall. Ten-forty a.m., visit the museum. They had been late: they were shot at ten-forty-five.

Photos of the conspirators lined the walls. In glass cases below lay their tin watches, their steel glasses, their thumbed and broken-backed books. They stared out of the photographs with young, hollow eyes.

Princip looked the youngest of all. He could have been fourteen years old. He had an improbable wave of hair on the top of his head. His ears stuck out. He wore a too-small suit with a closed collar. A country boy. He had grown up in the hills, in extreme poverty. He had read about philosophy and socialism and revolution in the cafés, smoking instead of eating. A large bust of him on the wall made him look heroic, with a high brow and the nostrils of a rearing horse. He was unrecognizable. Chiselled in the wall was a remark he made during his trial: 'We loved our people.'

They were all tried and convicted, along with dozens of other young Bosnians (or Serbs) suspected of having aided them, or having transported them, or having known them, or having once considered doing the same or a similar thing themselves. A defence lawyer at the trial opened his summation by saying, 'Illustrious tribunal, after all we have heard, it is peculiarly painful for me, as a Croat, to conduct the defence of a Serb.'

Princip, Čabrinović and Grabež could not be hanged under Austrian law, because they were under twenty-one, so they were sentenced to twenty years and allowed to die of neglect in their cells. Princip was taken to Theresianstadt and put in a damp, unheated, subterranean cell, in irons. His arm, which had been injured following the assassination, was not treated. It rotted and was eventually amputated. The boy died in 1918, six months before the end of the war.

'We loved our people.' I went back outside, wondering, of course, *Which* people?

The prints of two feet were sunk in the pavement at the corner. In Rebecca West's day, children still stopped to put their feet in the assassin's shoes before running on, but now they were ignored. A plaque on the wall above read, FROM THIS PLACE ON 28 JUNE 1914, GAVRILO PRINCIP EXPRESSED, WITH HIS SHOTS, A NATIONAL PROTEST AGAINST TYRANNY, AND THE CENTURIES-LONG DESIRE OF OUR PEOPLES FOR PEACE.

I stared at the plaque for some time, wondering why it struck me as peculiar. Then I realized: it was written in the Cyrillic script, but used the Ijekavian dialect. Both Serbs and Croats had sworn to me that Cyrillic could only be used with Ekavian, while Ijekavian could only be written in the Latin script. The plaque, like the Bosnians themselves, was an illegitimate mongrel.

37

It had been the rainiest spring in Bosnia in twenty years. I walked the glistening streets. I ascended marble staircases past mud-walled houses into the clouds. Children guided me when I got lost in the straggling byways. A man called off a dog, and when I assured him I had not been worried, he assured me, 'Oh, he would have bitten you.'

Mosques stood in every neighbourhood. They crowned knolls. The more ambitious ones were of stone and stucco, with copper-sheeted central domes and porches under a line of smaller domes like offspring, while the modest ones were wooden or cement rectangular structures with hip roofs of red tiles, looking like secular buildings except for their stubby minarets. These last were often fanciful and charming, not the cool white pencils of the bigger mosques, but stovepipes of wooden slats stained chocolate, or painted green and white, with fourteen sides, rising to a platform with carved arcades under a conical cap, and crowned by a pole strung with wooden balls and electric lights that culminated in the crescent, lying on its back, the way the moon sometimes looked in Mecca and Medina, but never in Istanbul or Sarajevo.

Muslim boys saw me admiring one minaret in particular, and recognizing the tourist – and conscious of their own Otherness in the eyes of the west – they called out mockingly, 'That's not a church! That's a mosque!'

The largest mosque in town, the sixteenth-century Gazi Husrev-beg, was closed for renovations. A chart posted by the gate listed the times for each day of the month at which dawn, sunrise, noon, mid-afternoon, sunset and nightfall occurred. Traditionally, dawn was discovered each morning by a *hodža*, or imam, standing in the open air, at the moment he could first distinguish between a white and a black thread, and nightfall was judged the same way, in reverse. The times in between were calculated astronomically, so that richer mosques included in their courtyards a small building called a *muvekithana* in which the sextants, cross-staffs and astrolabes were stored. The *sahat-kula*, or clock tower, was adjusted according to the observations. Sarajevo's clock tower showed 12.00 exactly at sunset, in the Turkish manner. But now the prayer times were all calculated in advance, the muvekithana was closed, and no one paid attention to the clock tower. So that no one would have to climb the minarets, the muezzins' calls went out over loudspeakers, giving them a tinny, impersonal sound that seemed to me half-way to the brassy 'bar bar' of church bells.

On the construction barriers around the Husrev-beg Mosque were posted advertisements from travel bureaux for the *hadž*, which would take place in a few weeks. The price was a good year's salary. There were also invitations to a public lecture: 'A Bosnian Islamic State: Yes or No?' Someone had crossed out the 'No' and written 'Of course!' under the 'Yes'. I suspected one of the students who hung around the gate to the *medresa* – a school of Islamic doctrine and law – and the Islamic Theological Faculty across the street. Like the little boys who had called to me about the minaret, these older boys were conscious of their Other status, not only vis-à-vis tourists, but also in contrast to non-observant Muslims. Like the female students in their ankle-length dark coats and colourful satin headwraps, they followed an unwritten dress code that decreed blue jeans and jean jacket, white socks and loafers. They somehow made this combination their distinctive uniform, despite the fact that all young Yugoslavs wrapped themselves in denim like a protective armour against adulthood. Their haircuts, too, were the same, longish on top and short on the sides, so that they all had the same pop-out ears and the same triangular heads, from small chin to wide-set eyes to crowning shock of wavy hair. They gathered in a gaggle around the gate, clubbish, visionaries like Gavrilo Princip, and even looking like him.

At the Muslim bookstore by the gate I picked up a pamphlet in English: 'The Value of Better Understanding Among People of Various Views'.

I was, of course, infected with the western prejudice that Islam was strange and, somehow, obscurely, threatening. I had never been in a Muslim country. Travelling throughout Europe, I had never hesitated to go into Catholic or Orthodox churches, or to attend services, although I was neither Catholic nor Orthodox. But the mosques intimidated me. I feared hostility towards me as a non-Muslim. All sorts of ridiculous associations sprang to my mind, the refuse of American movies and nineteenth-century British travel narratives. I would do something wrong and be spat on, called an infidel or a dog. Benjamin was no help. He seemed to have internalized the west's wary view of his own religion. He would not have dreamed of attending a *džuma*, the principal Muslim worship service, which took place every Friday at noon, and he thought I would not be welcome at one.

On a Friday, I went to the offices of *Muslim Voice* and spoke to the Editor-in-Chief, Džemaludin Latić, one of the leaders of the Muslim community. He was a gentle, soft-spoken man with a high forehead framed by curly reddish hair. When I asked him if it would be possible for me to attend a džuma, he said, 'Of course!' He glanced at his watch. In fifteen minutes he would be going to the džuma at the Theological Faculty, and why didn't I join him? He seemed pleased when I accepted.

I was relieved. What had I expected? Anything, I suppose, except a normal, human reponse – a man's interest in my interest.

The mosque in the courtyard of the Theological Faculty was modern, boxy and low, and like many Bosnian mosques it did not have a *maksura*, the raised platform to the left of the door which could be entered directly from outside and was designed for non-Muslims attending a service. So after I had removed my shoes and washed my feet, hands and face, Džemaludin led me to the back wall of the crowded room, where I stood among the worshippers, mostly those young jean-clad men, but also older men in dark woollens wearing small caps of white cloth half-way between a yarmulka and a fez.

Although my presence seemed to be accepted, I felt intrusive none the less. The Muslim service is far more explicitly communal than the Christian. When the worshippers prayed in unison – raising open hands to their ears, bending to place hands on knees, kneeling, then rocking forward to touch forehead to ground – I had the choice either of being the only person in the room to remain standing, which seemed irreverent and left me feeling as suddenly exposed as one does in certain nightmares, or kneeling with the rest, which felt, in a way, even more irreverent. I still do not know whether I really *was* being intrusive, the politeness of the Muslims preventing them from telling me, or whether my deep, blushing discomfiture rose entirely from my own perception of Islam's foreignness, and thus my alien presence in it.

But Džemaludin, afterwards, showed no uneasiness. As we walked back towards the offices of *Muslim Voice*, he explained to me, in his slow and gracious way, the significance of some of the movements during prayer, stopping occasionally in the middle of the crowded pedestrian zone to demonstrate. 'When the hands are put up to the ears, like this, that signifies putting worldly things behind you. All of that, you discard at that moment, you forget. You must stand unburdened before God.' He stood still for a long moment, smiling, with the thumbs of his open hands touching the backs of his ears, while people streamed around him.

'That is why women cannot stand in front of men in the džuma,' he went on. 'Because, you see, men cannot concentrate on God when they see a woman. Whereas women are different, they are not disturbed by the sight of men. In that way, Islam recognizes that women are superior.'

'I noticed, actually, that there weren't any women in the mosque at all,' I said. 'Is that because there was no *mahfil*?' The mahfil was a raised platform in the back with access to the minaret, which used to be for the muezzin, so that he could unobtrusively enter the common prayer after his call, but was now often reserved for women.

'No, women are always welcome, even without the mahfil,' Džemaludin said. 'But as you could see, the room was full. There was no space for them.'

Džemaludin had spent three years in jail under the old government after his conviction on charges – which most people now agreed had been trumped up – of being an Islamic extremist plotting a coup. I asked him what he thought of the current talk of a Bosnian Islamic state.

He smiled patiently. 'That is not possible,' he said. 'Nor desirable. The only way Bosnia can survive is through tolerance between the three religions. We all worship the same God.'

I went to a Sunday service in the oldest Orthodox church in Sarajevo. Its foundations may have dated back to the earliest days of the Turkish presence, in the fifteenth century. Like the more modest mosques, it was rectangular, with a tiled roof and a square bell tower instead of a minaret, but unlike them it was built like a fortress, with thick stone walls, and iron bars over the tiny windows. Another high wall and a massive gate enclosed a cloistered courtyard. Clearly, this was the building of a religion under siege.

But if Orthodoxy feared Islam, it also imitated it, as the weak will imitate the strong. The raised gallery for women around three sides of the sanctuary may have been common in fifth- and sixth-century Christian churches, as the plaque next to the door claimed, but what was it doing here in the fifteenth century, and why was it once obscured by a lattice?

Whereas mosques strove for the lightness and airiness of tents, Orthodox churches were sepulchral. In the dim candlelight St George jabbed his needle-lance through the open mouth of a dog-like dragon, not even bothering to look. St Nicholas raised benedictory fingers while a ship foundered behind him. St John the Baptist slouched against a crossed staff, looking like a Chetnik. The icons were mostly cheap illustrations in aquamarine, flesh-tone and rose, pages ripped from a religious magazine and put under glass. The good wooden icons were protected in the museum across the courtyard.

Perhaps here, in the bomb of Yugoslavia, the Serbs actually went to church. Certainly this service was full, and included many young people. Women now stood wherever they wanted. A girl near me repeatedly kissed the icon in front of her with vigour, her hand cupping the upper frame as if it were a boyfriend's shoulder. The worshippers crossed their entire bodies, bending down to touch the floor.

After the service, many of the women went up to the gallery where, one by one, they crawled three times under a saint's relic on a raised dais. The older women struggled with stiff backs and bad knees, their heads knocking against the wood above them, hardly able to rise the third time. The relic lay in an infant-size coffin that sloped down from head to toe and was covered with a gilded red shroud. It looked exactly like the Muslim caskets in the stone mausoleums next to mosques.

Outside, I walked around the building, feeling the massive stone blocks and iron window-bars. A man was following me, and finally asked with some suspicion what I was doing.

'I'm only looking,' I said.

Another man approached. 'Is he a foreigner?' he asked the first.

The first man made a dampening motion to keep him from saying anything more. 'He understands our language,' he warned.

The two stuck with me as I circled the courtyard. They gazed at me worriedly from the gate as I walked up the street. Only a week ago a Serb minister in the Bosnian government had been beaten outside his Sarajevo apartment by unknown assailants.

I was just in time for the eleven o'clock mass at the Roman

Catholic cathedral. The building had been erected in the 1880s, or almost as soon as the Austrians had occupied Bosnia, and it might have been the cathedral of any medium-sized Austrian town: a mixture of neo-Gothic and neo-Romanesque elements, in crisp, clean sandstone, with a rose window behind Christ over the portal, and two square bell towers with clocks that showed 12 when it was noon. Inside was high blue vaulting and half-hearted Baroque.

The nave was filled with light, like the mosque. The worshippers sat, whereas in the mosque and the Orthodox church you had to stand. Catholics did not touch the floor while praying, the way the Orthodox and the Muslims did. They did not kiss icons, like the Orthodox, but they kissed their crosses and the feet of statues, and the hand of the priest who administered communion, all of which the Muslims abjured. Catholics could take communion at every service, whereas the Orthodox took it only on special occasions, and only after fasting and self-purification. The Muslims purified themselves before every prayer, but never took communion. When Catholics crossed themselves, they touched the left shoulder first, whereas in Orthodoxy you touched the right first. The Orthodox crossed themselves with three fingers, while the Catholics used the whole hand. The Orthodox sang their entire service, while the Muslims read Koranic verses in a melodic cadence somewhat like singing, and the Catholics spoke most of their service, though they occasionally broke into chant or song. The melodic modes of Orthodoxy – were they Phrygian? Lydian? – sounded exotic to me, whereas the choir in the Catholic cathedral sang in the standard majors and minors of western classical music. Islam had no choirs, only the single voice of the hodža or the muezzin. In the Catholic service, musical instruments were allowed, whereas in Orthodoxy they were not. Instruments to the Orthodox were like bells to the Muslims.

I came out of the church. I knew there was more to religious differences than what I had been mulling over. But sometimes I wondered what they were. Certainly no Croat or Serb ever spoke to me about doctrinal differences such as the *filioque* clause, or got much exercised over the fact that Orthodox priests had no choice but to marry, while Catholic priests had no choice but not to. Sometimes the Pope came up, the Orthodox exclaiming with a fair amount of passion that an infallible vicar of Christ on Earth was a blasphemy. But more often the Christians talked of right shoulders and left shoulders, or smirkingly imitated the warble of a Koranic reading. I thought – but then again, what did I know? – that surely they did not kill each other over these things. Religion was a mark of the nation, and the nations had been at odds over fundamental issues of power and privilege for centuries. But . . . weren't the nations defined, in the last analysis, by their religions? Which came first? I felt, as the groups polarized day by day, that I was watching a chemical reaction, a precipitation of hatreds resulting from interactions on a molecular level, too tiny to be visible or analysable, but inevitable and irreversible.

On the day before, I might have attended a service in Sarajevo's synagogue, except that there were not enough Jews left to hold regular services. The Jewish community of Sarajevo had once been the largest and most illustrious in Yugoslavia, dating back to the turn of the sixteenth century, when the Ottoman Empire opened its doors to the thousands of Jews freshly expelled from Spain. The community was mainly Sephardic and spoke Ladino, a form of fifteenth-century Spanish. But out of five synagogues in Sarajevo, the only one to survive the Independent State of Croatia in restorable condition was the Ashkenazic one, a large pink pseudo-Moorish oddity dating from 1902. In the sanctuary, an oriental scalloped arch formed a backdrop to the altar, and calligraphic scripts and arabesques covered the walls and ceilings, as in any good mosque.

When I spoke with community members at the centre next door it was clear they did not care whether their synagogue was Ashkenazic or Sephardic. They all agreed they were not a religious community any more, only a cultural one. Sometimes they put on a concert of Ladino songs. The old men gathered in the community building to play chess, and in the smoky back rooms men with white beards sometimes read the Torah. But the nearest rabbi was in Belgrade. Occasionally a service was held in Sarajevo, but no one could tell me when the next one might be.

At the beginning of the war, thirteen thousand Jews had lived in Sarajevo. By the end, only a few hundred were left. First they had worn the star and worked in brigades, but that had lasted only a few weeks. By the summer of 1941, the deportations had begun, and by November all the Jews were gone. The lunatic spirit of Their Most Catholic Majesties Ferdinand and Isabella, incarnate in more violent form in the ultra-Catholic Ustashas, had followed them to their refuge. The only Yugoslav Jews to survive were a few doctors and pharmacologists, whose services were needed, and some of those lucky enough to live in areas of Italian occupation, where they survived long enough so that when they finally fled to the hills after the Italian capitulation they ran into Partisan bands, which recruited them.

I went to the ancient synagogue, a sixteenth-century building which was now the Jewish Museum. From the outside it looked much like the Orthodox church, which happened to be around the corner. It was another fortress, huddled behind a wall. Inside, it was high and empty and simple, all of a white porous stone.

The exhibits on the history of the Jews in Sarajevo were in dreadful shape. Photographs had come unglued from their mountings and lay in dust in the bottoms of the cases. The texts – gold print on brown leather – had faded to the point of illegibility.

One got the impression that none of this mattered, because visitors probably came here to look at only one thing: a huge leather-bound book that hung on a long chain from the ceiling like Exhibit A lowered to eye level by the Almighty, listing the names of the twelve thousand Bosnian Jews who had died in the camps.

My eyes ran over the family names: Abinun, Albahari, Alkalaj, Altarac, Baruh, Carfati, Danon, Eskenazi, Finci, Gaon, Hazan, Israel, Jurhi, Kabiljo, Konforte, Kohen, Levi, Montiljo, Musafija, Neuer, Ozmo, Papo, Perera, Romano, Salom, Sumbulović, Tuvi, Uziel, Volah, Wasserstein, Zweigenthal. Many of the names were represented by dozens of dead, some by scores. These were the vast, extended families of ghetto life, when no one married in or out, and few moved away because there were so few places to go. The rich mix of names read like a Balkan synecdoche: the Arabic

Albahari and Alkalaj; the Hebrew Baruh, Israel and Uziel; the Ladino Kabiljo, Montiljo and Romano; the German Kohen and Zweigenthal. Sumbulović was a Turkish root with a Slav suffix. Was Danon French? Was Ozmo Turkish?

But none of it mattered. No matter what the disguise, no matter how long it had been worn, they had still been Jews.

I walked up the southern slope of Sarajevo's valley to the old Jewish cemetery. On the stone arch at the entrance someone had painted ENTRANCE STRICTLY FORBIDDEN, but the iron gate stood open, and I went in.

The older gravestones were extraordinary and, it was said, unique in all the world to Bosnia's Jews: rounded monoliths of a ton or two, of a pinkish marbled stone quarried from this very hillside, longer than they were high, flat in the front for the inscriptions, and curving gracefully on all other sides towards the ground like the backs of dolphins rising from green waves. Their solidity, their occasional mysterious bas-reliefs – on one, a folk-art hand and arm cradled the side as though a mourner had thrown herself on the stone and miraculously left her mark – and their appealing lack of geometric regularity were reminiscent of the Bogomil tombstones one ran across occasionally in the Bosnian hills. Another influence, perhaps?

I struggled through the bracken. Some parts of the hillside were empty, whereas in others the stones were crammed shoulder to shoulder. Very early Christian graveyards had that look, as the believers vied to be buried as close as possible to a recently martyred saint. Above, boys were playing soccer on a diminutive sloped field, and their ball occasionally sailed down, rebounding from stone to stone. A tiny Gypsy woman in red and green cotton swathes sat on a monolith and watched her goats and sheep graze between the rows. From the top of the cemetery, I counted thirty minarets in Sarajevo below. In the distance pinkish snow gleamed on the peaks of the mountains.

Most of the inscriptions were in Hebrew, which I could not read, but a few of the newer ones were in Croato-Bosno-Serbian. Here was Klara Josef Papo, née Levi, whose porcelain medallion photograph, cracked through the middle of her face, showed a thick-set woman with heavy eyelids turned down at the corners, giving her a worried look. She had died the year Hitler came to power, at the age of forty-six. In the museum's Book of the Dead there were 140 Papos and over a hundred Levis.

The only markers after 1941 were communal, and belated. A rough-hewn black slab said, HERE LIE VICTIMS OF USTASHA-FASCIST TERROR. Twenty people: seven unknown and thirteen named with names from the Book, aged twenty-one to sixty-four, shot on this spot, 1 August 1941. Two concrete Tables of the Law said, IN THIS PART OF THE CEMETERY LIE 900 BODIES EXHUMED FROM PITS.

The official memorial was higher up, a white and black marble block which, like the relic in the Orthodox church, strikingly resembled a Muslim casket. (Or maybe – come to think of it – that was because a Muslim casket, in the way it sloped from head to toe, somewhat resembled the old Jewish tombstones. Which resembled the Bogomil stones. Perhaps there *was* such a thing as Bosnia, and this was a glimpse of it.) The inscription on the memorial was a quotation from the writings of the nineteenth-century Montenegrin Prince-Bishop Petar II Njegoš:

SLAVNO MRITE
KAD MRIJET MORATE

'Die gloriously, when you must die.'

This struck me as a highly inappropriate sentiment, something straight from the breast of a Serb who had fought the Turks in the mountain passes. Addressed to Jews who had died crammed in cattle trucks and gas ovens like vermin, it sounded like a reproach.

Many of the newer gravestones, which were the usual tablets and were therefore kick-overable, had been kicked over. When I had come here the year before with Benjamin and Miroslav, they had gazed with me at the vandalized temple by the front gate, and the lines of fallen slabs, and Miroslav had turned to me and said with genuinely deep chagrin, 'I am ashamed.'

It had seemed to me a characteristically Yugoslav thing to say.

200

It would not have occurred to me to feel *shame* concerning the havoc a bunch of American roughnecks might wreak. I would not feel that they had anything to do with me, American or not. But if Croats had kicked over those stones, Miroslav felt implicated. And his shame forced him into denial. 'Perhaps, after all, it was soil subsidence that knocked them down,' he said, although the slabs had fallen off pedestals that remained level. 'Yes, it looks a lot like soil subsidence to me.'

This year the temple by the gate was being restored. Glass had been put back in the stars of David over the doors, and I could see fresh plaster and paint through the windows. The lower floor was now occupied by a watchman for the cemetery named Danilo, with his wife and four kids.

Danilo was stocky and grizzled, with brandy on his breath. He and his ash-blond sons had those startling Bosnian eyes. Danilo could not read the Hebrew on the stones, but he was proud of his Jewishness. He said the men at the community centre had misinformed me when they had said the Jews of Sarajevo were no longer religious. So what if they didn't have a rabbi? Jews got together at the synagogue every Saturday, from ten until one. They got together and talked about being Jews, and they felt like Jews. If that wasn't being religious, what was?

His boys shone their orbs at me from behind his legs.

Had he been born in Sarajevo? I asked.

Yes, his family had been here before the war. He did not say any more, and I did not ask.

But we walked up through the cemetery together. Danilo had painted the 'Entrance Strictly Forbidden' on the front gate, but he never locked it, and said everyone was welcome. He had painted the words in 1972, after a bunch of 'hooligans' had come and kicked over a lot of gravestones. They had been Palestinian students from the university. I made a mental note to tell Miroslav.

Danilo noticed a young couple sitting on the official memorial, smoking and hugging and sharing a bottle of wine. Drinking was not allowed, and he left me, to throw them out.

I sat on a stone. The Gypsy woman and her flock were gone. In the valley below, shafts of sunlight broke here and there through black cloud-cover. You could trace them like spotlights to the points where they fired the copper dome of a mosque, or a winking stretch of the river, or the multi-coloured mosaic of a parking lot. I pulled out the English-language pamphlet I had picked up at the Muslim bookstore, on 'The Value of Better Understanding Among People of Various Views'. The first paragraph said:

> From times immemorial it is known for the opposition of opinions and views among people on account of different motives or convictions. To activate these motives and convictions respectively, along with certain presence of instinct, internal and external doers or subjective and objective factors respectively worked or work, on the basis of deliberation which every separate individual at a certain time, place and circumstances was able and willing to use.

I glanced up. A soft rain was falling. High in the mountains, it would be new snow.

38

I went to see Alija Izetbegović.

The year before, when he had been the head of an opposition party that as yet existed in name only, he had had time for a three-hour conversation, in his cramped apartment on a street of run-down housing just north of the Presidency building. He was a short man, balding and slightly stocky, and a charming host, both effusive and attentive. We had sat with his wife and grown daughter in a room arranged in the Turkish style, with a sofa around the walls, and a low table to hold the coffee.

Izetbegović was a lawyer who had been imprisoned twice; the first time, he told me, in 1946, when he criticized Stalin among

202

friends. (He spoke two years too early; Tito broke with Stalin in 1948.) He had said that Stalin was a dictator who suppressed his people, especially the Muslims. He was sentenced to three years.

The second time came in 1983, when he was charged, along with Džemaludin Latić and several others, with calling for the overthrow of the government. The principal evidence against him was an 'Islamic Declaration' that he had written in 1970, calling on Muslims in Bosnia and world-wide to rediscover Islam as a unifying and energizing force, and to use it to take their destiny into their own hands. It could, indeed, have been interpreted as revolutionary – or, if you like, counter-revolutionary – but Izetbegović insisted that the thirteen-year-old 'declaration' had been hauled out as a pretext, and that the government had really wanted to neutralize him for his work as a defence lawyer. The Iranian ambassador told Izetbegović he had been assured by the Yugoslav government that the defendants were C.I.A. agents. The Americans were told they were Iranian agents. Izetbegović laughed heartily at the recollection. He was sentenced to fourteen years in prison, of which he served five.

What Izetbegović wanted for the Muslims of Bosnia was the freedom to define themselves as a people. Being allowed to sign themselves as Muslims in the census every ten years was not enough. The Communists appointed their own lackeys as hodžas. They confiscated the *vakufs* (endowments) of mosques in order to destroy the material wherewithal of Islam. They did not allow halal shops, which prepared meat according to Islamic strictures.

But worst of all, Izetbegović said, the Communists had taken away from the Muslims their own history. An ethnological study of the Muslims had never been undertaken. A lexicon of the Bosnian language had never been compiled. There was no History of Muslim Literature, no History of the Muslim People, no Who's Who of Muslims. In school, children were never taught poems or other works by Muslim writers. There had been many Muslim resistance heroes during the Austrian occupation, but there were no memorials honouring these people. 'The leader of the resistance was hanged three hundred metres from this house,' he said, 'and what is there now? I've been there. A trash container.'

He wanted democracy and a free-market economy and religious rights for all believers. He wanted halal shops. He wanted to increase taxes on alcohol, and ban its sale near mosques, schools and factories. He wanted to restrict pornography to special kiosks. 'The west says that women in the west are free, and that women are not free in Islam,' he said. 'But the west makes women into advertisements, into objects. Islam respects women.'

I asked if he thought women should cover up.

'Yes,' interjected his wife, who was wearing a kerchief. 'Especially the young, pretty women.' She gestured towards her daughter, who was not wearing a kerchief, and who blushed.

'Note that the *woman* says yes,' Izetbegović said. 'That is revealing, is it not?'

And would he want to establish the Shari'a law? I asked. (The Shari'a, like the veil and polygyny, had been banned in 1945.)

'No,' he said firmly. I felt he had been expecting this question. He surely knew that the Shari'a was one of the west's bugbears. 'That would not be possible in a multi-ethnic society like Bosnia. To govern here, the only possible solution is a coalition between the ethnic groups.' He thought for a few seconds. 'But if you think about it,' he added, 'what is wrong with the Shari'a? Is it less humane to cut off a man's hand than to take several years from his life in prison? You cut off the hand, it is done. I don't know. I am just thinking out loud.'

Seeing me out, he held my hand. 'There is an old Bosnian curse,' he said. ' "May God make you live in interesting times." ' He laughed. 'That is a wise curse, don't you think? Come back in a year,' he said, 'and see how things have changed.'

His wife stood behind him in the dingy hallway. I turned down the fetid dark stairs. Feral cats bolted from the trashcans below.

Now I had come back, and he was President of Bosnia-Hercegovina. His daughter, Sabina, had given up her job as an English teacher to be his personal secretary. When I reached her on the phone, she remembered me, but said her father was extremely busy. 'But come to the Presidency building tomorrow at ten,' she said. 'I will arrange fifteen minutes for you.'

The massive neo-Renaissance building stood not two blocks

from his old apartment. I left my passport at the desk, and was led up a ceremonial staircase, across a marble colonnaded hall, and down a long corridor through pair after pair of heavy red curtains held back by golden tassels. Golden numbers on cream-coloured doors counted down through the twenties, the teens, until we turned a corner and continued through another line of curtains, counting down to number one, which my guide opened. But this was only a front room, through which I was ushered to a middle room, and on to an inner room.

Here I found Sabina. She still wore no kerchief over her blond hair. She looked depressed and exhausted. She ordered coffee for me, and I sat on an over-stuffed couch. The coffee came, and half an hour went by. Sabina kept trying to talk to me, but the phone kept ringing. Another man was sitting on the couch. Izetbegović ran in, and ran out again.

'He'll have time for you,' Sabina assured me between phone calls. 'Would you like more coffee?'

Another half-hour went by. Then Izetbegović came in, pursued by three men. He looked as tired as his daughter, and he had aged considerably. He wanted to be a good host, I could see that. He took my hand and asked how I was. But he had urgent business with the other man on the couch, and then, and then, and then. Perhaps I could talk with his daughter instead?

'It's not that important,' I assured him.

He went out.

'Don't go,' Sabina pleaded. 'He'll see you.'

'It's really not that important,' I repeated. 'I just came back, as he suggested. To see how things had changed since last year.'

Sabina had promised me he would see me, and would not let me go. 'Please, please wait!'

I sat on the couch and read the newspaper for an hour. The phone rang almost continuously. Sabina spoke in French, in English, in Bosno-Serbo-Croatian. She eventually faced reality, and said unhappily, 'It doesn't look like he'll have time to see you today.'

I got up. 'Perhaps you could verify something for me,' I said. 'He told me a Bosnian curse last year that I was thinking of quoting for the epigraph for my book, but no one I've mentioned it to since then has ever heard it. "May God make you live in interesting times." '

Sabina flapped a hand in a pained, impatient gesture. 'It probably doesn't exist. Dad's always saying things like that. I think he just makes them up.'

'It was nice to see you again anyway,' I said.

Startlingly, her eyes filled with tears. Perhaps I reminded her of a happier time. 'We don't know what he's doing,' she said almost in a whisper. 'He works all the time, yet we see no results.'

The phone rang, and I left.

39

On my last night in Sarajevo I had dinner with Benjamin and Miroslav.

Benjamin talked about his family. His father had fought as a Partisan, and became a Communist Party member of good standing after the war. He had held the best opinions. He had genuinely revered both Tito and Stalin. His way seemed secure. But in 1948 Tito broke with Stalin, and one of the gods had to be a devil. In a local Party meeting, Benjamin's father had to choose, and it seemed to him that Lucifer could only be the less powerful god, the one who rebelled and fell. He cast his vote in support of Stalin. But despite the Red Army divisions massed on the border, the Soviet Union did not invade, Tito did not fall, and Benjamin's father was shipped off to Goli Otok, a small stony island in the Adriatic, along with thousands of other Stalinists, and suspected Stalinists and assorted troublemakers and inconvenient people who could conveniently be called Stalinists. Unlike many, he survived, and was released after a mere three years. He never talked about it.

The prison at Goli Otok was closed in 1987, but the island remained off limits. No boats stopped there. Then in 1990

Benjamin had chartered a boat and sailed to Goli Otok with a camera crew to shoot a television documentary. The island was treeless and virtually grassless, as barren as the Kornati islands of the northern Adriatic that the Yugoslavs considered sublimely beautiful, and which looked to me like moonscapes, pitilessly sunny and arid. The concrete barracks remained, the holding pens, the barbed wire.

The film crew's guide for the trip had been an officer at the camp in the 50s, and he had not seen the place in almost forty years. He had become lost in reminiscences. 'I remember this . . .!' he would begin, exclaiming over an office, a storehouse. He was enjoying himself as he picked over the scenes of his youth. In one room he had turned this way and that, beaming, and said, 'Yes! We interrogated prisoners in this room.'

'Perhaps you interrogated my father in this room,' Benjamin had snapped.

Now, Benjamin said to me, 'The man looked shocked and hurt, as though I had slapped him. He stopped talking.' Benjamin appeared stricken. 'I don't know why I said it! I immediately wanted to bite my tongue. He had his circumstances, my father had his. What I did . . . He felt bad, I felt bad. What good did it do?'

We kept drinking, and Benjamin and Miroslav grew lively. They recalled their years as Pioneers, members of the Communist youth group that all children aged seven to thirteen had had to belong to. In the years after the war, there were work brigades and camps, long lectures and songfests, but in Miroslav's and Benjamin's day you just signed up in school and went to an occasional meeting, and you wore the blue cap and the red scarf, and you were given a flag to wave and a chant to chant when you lined up in the streets to greet a visiting dignitary, some head of state from the Non-Aligned Movement.

'Some good democrat like Haile Selassie,' Miroslav said, his eyebrow at full cock. 'Or . . . Idi Amin. Or . . . Ceauşescu.'

Later, both he and Benjamin joined the Communist Party. 'That awful red flower!' Miroslav exclaimed, covering his eyes.

'What flower?' I asked.

'The carnation! It was the symbol of the Party. You saw it everywhere until you were sick of it.'

'When you joined the Party,' Benjamin said, 'you were given a red carnation. I remember so clearly when I joined. I had so much looked forward to getting that flower. And they gave me a faded one! I was so disappointed!' Tears formed in his eyes at the memory.

'Do you remember where you were when Tito died?' I asked them.

'Sure,' Miroslav said. 'Everybody does.'

'I don't,' Benjamin said.

'Sure you do,' Miroslav said. 'We were together, in a café.'

Benjamin appealed to me, shrugging. 'I don't remember that.'

'We got on a tram,' Miroslav continued, 'and it was full of people, but it was absolutely quiet. That was strange. Just a few whispers.'

'Ah, yes,' Benjamin said. 'I remember the tram.'

'If people came on speaking loudly, people glared at them. Some people were sitting in the seats, just crying, tears running down their faces.'

'It's true,' Benjamin said. 'Everyone was crying. I cried too.'

'So did I,' Miroslav said.

'I'm not ashamed to admit it,' Benjamin said.

'We really loved Tito,' Miroslav said to me. 'That was not a show.'

'I felt lost,' Benjamin said. 'I felt like the world could not go on without him.' He waggled his large head. 'A sort of collective brainwashing. You know!'

'What is the saying? "Sheep will respond to the loudest bark,"' Miroslav said. 'Yugoslavs were all sheep. And Tito was a hell of a barker!'

When it was time to go, Miroslav came with me. It was a cool, still night. Thousands of apartment lights rose on all sides of us as we strolled down the six-lane access road to the main thoroughfare.

'I'm sick of the Serbs!' Miroslav suddenly said. 'I'm sick of all this talk about how many of them died. It's just so they can attack us, so their offence will seem like a defence. All right, what they say about the Ustashas is right. It was one of the world's most horrible regimes.' He took my arm, stopping. 'But it's *not my fault*!'

We walked again. 'You know,' he said, 'Clemenceau said that the Serbs were like vultures. They fed on the dead left by other armies. They say they won World War I, but they *lost*! It was the English and the French armies who turned back the Germans and Austrians. The Serbs were hiding out on Corfu, and they only came back to fight once the Austrians were already beaten. And they say they won World War II, but they lost! The Partisans won, and they were as much Croat as Serb. It's all a myth, and this Serb myth is being shoved down our throats.'

We stopped by the bus shelter. I looked up and down the straight kilometres of the wide road and saw no taxis, no buses, no cars. The full moon was wrapped in a bright shawl of cloud.

'Where do you live, anyway?' I asked Miroslav.

He pointed across the access road to another gargantuan apartment complex. 'I hate Novi Grad,' he said. 'I've got my tiny cell, in my parents' tiny apartment, in these mountains of people, and nobody knows anybody else. This is a terrible way to make people live. It destroys any sense of community. You feel lost. You feel so alone.'

The road was empty and silent. Chequerboards of thousands of lights rose towards the moon. Miroslav burst out in a voice I had not heard from him before. 'I am so unhappy, Brian!' His eyebrows were still cocked and quizzical. Perhaps he had worn the expression so long he had no other.

Across the main thoroughfare was a small stand of trees. Birds were singing in the trees as though it were dawn.

'Isn't that incredible?' Miroslav said. 'I can hear those birds clearly from my window. All this – ' he spun around, and his arms took in the miles of asphalt, the seas of parked cars, the tons of concrete and glass that he was learning at the university how to build himself – 'and still the birds are here, singing perfectly.'

Part Four
In Bosnia-Hercegovina

40

I took the train south through the Neretva Gorge. The river was an opaque jade beneath the white limestone cliffs. The train was a grey ghost from World War II, trundling empty through the empty stations. No conductor came to check my ticket.

When the mountains became higher and barer, I was in Hercegovina. On every tiny plot of arable land old men and women laboured along rows of lettuce and dock. The gorge opened out at Mostar. I got off the train and found a room on the eastern slope and headed down to see the bridge.

Old centres of famous tourist towns often seem so small and fragile. I walked through blocks of high-rises and department stores on crumbling plazas; new white houses behind walls over which roses climbed; Austrian buildings with stucco masks in neo-Renaissance and pseudo-Moorish; tourist agencies, hotels, restaurants, obstacle courses made of postcard stands; finally the asphalt gave way to cut stone, and for all of fifty yards the road narrowed between stone houses, all of them tourist shops, and the river appeared on the right, and the two bridge towers, now vacant, and between them the famous bridge.

When it had been not only beautiful, but the only bridge for miles, it had made the growth of Mostar inevitable. Now its beauty alone kept Mostar growing, and I found it somewhat amazing to contemplate that all I had passed through, the shops and hotels and restaurants employing thousands of people, existed because of this one arch of stone. Even now, a few American tourists were on the streets, and I could hear them arguing with the souvenir vendors over their copper plates (engraved with views of the bridge), which were made in the backs of the shops but looked like they came from a warehouse in New Jersey.

I stood at the peak of the steep bridge. The sky over the valley was black. Rain advanced from the bare hills. Some of the thunder was real, and the rest of it came from fighter jets taking off at a nearby training base. The river did not flow so much as it heaved and boiled, as if monsters were breathing in the thick green depths, which in a sense was the true explanation. The riverbed of rock lozenges cemented together by redeposited limestone was honeycombed with caverns into which swimmers were occasionally sucked and drowned.

Sir Gardner Wilkinson visited Mostar in the 1840s for the sole purpose of drawing and measuring the bridge, but when he arrived, his attention was diverted by the Vizier Ali Pasha's practice, which he found shocking, of ringing the tower next to his palace with the heads of Montenegrins. Wilkinson had previously been in Montenegro, where he had been equally shocked at Prince-Bishop Petar II's habit of festooning the tower next to his monastery with the heads of Muslims. Wilkinson gamely entered into a correspondence with the two gentlemen, urging on them the proposition that cutting off their opponents' heads was not civilized, but his efforts came to nothing. Rebecca West quoted with glee Petar I's response to Marshal Marmont on the same subject: 'It is surprising that you should find this practice shocking, since you French cut off the heads of your King and Queen.'

When Sir Arthur Evans – interesting how many British travellers, errant colonizers of the imagination, have been knighted for their services – rode through the town in 1875, Ali Pasha was dead, having been shot accidentally through the head while in Turkish custody for having supported the Bosnian nobles' revolt against the reforms of the Porte in 1850. During Evans' visit, a rebellion of the Christian rayahs against the local magnates and tax collectors was in full flame, and the new Vizier, Dervish Pasha, assured the English consul that most of the insurgents were not Hercegovinians at all, but agitators from Dalmatia and Montenegro who intimidated loyal villagers into joining them by burning their houses and fields if they did not, and who were prosecuting the war by means of the most abominable atrocities, such as immolating entire Muslim families in their homes and roasting children alive on spits before their parents' eyes. At this point, the Pasha burst into strategic tears. Evans did not believe him.

Evans had read his Wilkinson, and so he knew the dimensions of the bridge – a peaked walkway surmounting a single half-circle stone arch, ninety-five feet from base to base and rising fifty feet above the river – but that hardly gave an idea of the work's beauty. It had the delicacy and simplicity of many Turkish bridges, plus the drama, in that single vaulting span, that they often lacked. On either side, the walkway began below the apex of the arch and rose steeply to surmount it, doing so only barely, so that the centre of the bridge was startlingly thin. It had stood for centuries, surviving several earthquakes that devastated the town, and yet it seemed as light as origami.

Both Wilkinson and Evans reverently sketched the bridge. Neither believed it could be Turkish, and their reasoning was waterproof. Evans cited 'the grandeur of the work'. In other words, he knew that Romans could build noble bridges and Turks could not, and therefore this noble 'Turkish' bridge had to be Roman, which fact furnished yet more proof that Romans could build noble bridges and Turks could not. By Rebecca West's time (Dame Rebecca West, I might add) the Turks had been gone long enough from the Balkans for the bridge to be safely attributed to them.

41

The largest and oldest mosque in Mostar, the Karadjoz-beg, had a polite sign in four languages on the gate, saying YOU MAY VISIT THIS MOSQUE. The year before, I had met the hodža, a fresh-faced young man, who had been excited about the death of godless

215

Communism and the growing numbers of Bosnians returning to Islam. Where Islam was strong and unchallenged, few disliked modern innovations that made everyone's jobs easier, like recorded muezzins' calls, but in Hercegovina, where Islam was struggling to reassert itself, even the hodža was captivated by the picturesque aspects of his culture, as though he were a tourist like me, and on any day when it was not raining he would ascend the minaret in his embroidered vest and red fez and call the worshippers to prayer from the four corners of the *serefet*. Like most hodžas, he had a beautiful voice – I always wondered what became of any tone-deaf medresa students – and I, standing below, was as thrilled as he was.

This year, the renewal of Islam continued. The Karadjoz-beg Mosque was closed for renovations. A green piece of paper on the courtyard wall announced classes after the *akšam namaz*, the sunset prayer, at a nearby mosque: 'Fundamentals of Faith: Lessons for Adults'.

I remembered liking the courtyard from last year, so I poked around again. The pavement was of river stones worn to rounded discs, embedded on end in patterns of circles and rays, making for a rough but pleasing surface. On one side stood a stone building barely taller than I was, its roofline bristling with gawky square chimneys. It had once been a *mekteb*, and students had lived as well as studied there, each in his tiny stone cell, perhaps singeing his Koran as he read huddled over the fire during the freezing winters.

By the overgrown cemetery at the back I met Danko, whose tanned, creased face sloped backward from the grey-flecked beard on his jutting chin past his hazel eyes to his receding forehead. He was reading a book entitled *Love Without Fear: A Guide to Sex Technique*, but he abandoned it to pore over my copy of the day's *Oslobodjenje*, the Sarajevo paper. He put it down a few minutes later to tell me that I was likely to get beaten up, or worse.

'Excuse me?' I asked.

'You're a foreigner, but you speak the language,' he said. 'You take notes. That makes you look like a social worker. People are nervous.'

216

He, anyway, seemed nervous. He was chainsmoking, and for each new cigarette he produced a matchbox filled mostly with spent matches, through which he rummaged with twitching fingers.

'You social workers only cause trouble,' he muttered. 'But I know you're not a social worker, otherwise I wouldn't be talking to you.'

' "Social worker?" '

'You know what I'm talking about.'

'I have no idea.'

'Agents! George Bush!'

'You mean CIA?'

He sucked on his cigarette, staring intently at me. 'Like I said, people are nervous. They think you're an agent, you might disappear. Who knows? Not here, but out in the villages. I wouldn't go there.'

'What makes you think I'm going there?'

'Social workers go there. Cigarette?'

'Thanks, I don't smoke.'

He handed me my paper. 'Nice mosque, huh?'

'Sure.'

'You want a tour?'

'It's closed. Anyway, I saw it last year.'

'This was the mekteb, here.'

'I know.'

'That's what you were taking notes about?'

'About everything. I'm a writer, not a social worker.'

'Ah.' The smoke streaming from his nostrils looked like disbelief made visible. 'A reporter?'

'No. I'm writing a travel book.'

'A guidebook? You expect me to believe that?'

'It's too long a story.'

'You want to see a Turkish house?'

'A private house?'

'No, a house for tourists. For your "book", right? It's up the street, I'll take you there. Come on.'

I followed him out of the courtyard, and we turned up the hill, through lanes boxed in by stone walls. 'You know,' he said, 'there are no real believers in Bosnia-Hercegovina any more. All those people going to the mosques are Communist agents, secret police. There isn't a single real mosque in Mostar.'

'And you're a believer?'

'No.'

'You think Izetbegović is a Communist agent?'

'Is this for your "book"?'

'Everything is for my book.'

'Izetbegović is a village boy. A puppet. Power is the key. You have to be strong to resist the Russians. The Russians can't tell the Croats what to do because the Croats are armed. Bosnia needs arms. I was born in 1939, I remember the Russians coming into our house with guns.'

'Do you mean the Serbs?'

'They call themselves Serbs, but they're Russians. They act like Russians. "You agree with us, or you can't live." Unless you have power, and then you can tell them to fuck off. Tell me, how much do blue jeans cost in America?'

'I guess a pair's about twenty-five dollars.'

'It costs fifty dollars here, and we earn a tenth of what you earn. Every Yugoslav family has a worker in the West, that's the only way to survive. But the Russians don't like it, they don't want other people to have the resources they have. So there's this Russian filter. Only one member in each family is allowed to go west. I have a cousin, nineteen years in Germany, so I can't go. Cigarette?'

'I don't smoke.'

'Here we are.'

We went through a wooden archway into a courtyard paved with more river stones, and jungly with roses. The house was wood-framed with white stucco. It had an open sitting area recessed in the ground floor and a green wooden veranda in the middle of the upper floor. Danko greeted the woman in Turkish garb who came out of the kitchen. He led me through the rooms. Divans, sofas, rugs on the floors, low hexagonal tables, ogee-arched windows in recessed bays, a water-closet entirely of stone,

218

a washroom under a dome punctured by coloured-glass circles and stars of David. It was a Turkish house all right.

'They had pipes for water,' Danko said. 'Pretty civilized. Only they couldn't control the water quality, so every fifteen or twenty years they had a cholera epidemic.'

We sat on the veranda, and the woman brought us coffee. 'This is all for the tourists,' Danko said.

'I know.'

'No one wears costumes anywhere in Yugoslavia. Except in Kosovo. The Albanians still wear costumes. But the Serbs won't let them.'

'You mean the Russians.'

'The Serbs haven't worn costumes for hundreds of years. People want tradition, but at the same time they want a modern way of life. It's universal, not just here. You see that chest? That's full of Turkish costumes. Tourists like to dress up and smoke the čibuk and take photos of each other.' He handed me a čibuk, a carved, painted pipe as long as my arm. 'You want to try?'

'I don't smoke.'

He popped another cigarette between his lips. 'We smoke a lot here.' He reached into his box and pulled out a spent match. 'Because this is a prison. Prisoners always smoke a lot. And we drink. They allow alcohol in this prison.' He pulled out another spent match.

After the coffee, we went downstairs. 'Perhaps we can talk next year,' Danko said, 'and everything will be easier. But we have to be lucky, I think. Let's see, the Turkish house, the mosque, the coffee . . . that'll be a hundred dinars.'

I had been wondering when he would get to that. By local standards, it was an outrageous sum. If any friend of mine had been there and saw me complying, he would have lunged to stop me. Yugoslavs believed it their sacred duty as hosts to protect western sheep from fleecing at the hands of their countrymen. But it was five measly bucks, and he had contributed to my 'book'. I handed the sum over without a squeak.

He tried to remain impassive, but could hardly believe it. He racked his brains. 'I can show you the Partisan memorial,' he said.

'Thanks, I've seen it. It's hideous.'

41

I had met Mustafa the year before. He lived with his mother, Behija, in a modern house in the Turkish style on the bank of the river. I often watched the news on their television.

Sarajevo TV had become schizophrenic. With the government locked in a stalemate between the nationalities, Bosnian state television, like most other Bosnian institutions, had experienced virtually no changes in personnel since the election, but many of those grey Communist journalists had colourized into Serb, Croat and Muslim journalists. All of them went their own way, and none could be disciplined by the studio bosses without provoking the wrath of their co-religionists in the government or in the streets. You could usually predict the slant of a piece by the name of the reporter at the bottom of the screen. This had the interesting effect of making Sarajevo TV coverage simultaneously narrow-minded and broad-based.

A sample of one evening's news:

A car full of Kalashnikovs had been discovered heading for Hercegovina; Serbs were suspected (Muslim reporter).

Explosions and shootings continued throughout Slavonia. Serb peasants led the camera through trashed houses, putting fingers through bullet holes in windows; Serb mothers cried about rampaging animals (Serb reporter).

Shells fired by 'the so-called Yugoslav People's Army' destroyed several homes in a Croat village (Croat reporter).

Milan Martić, leader of the illegal Serb militia of the so-called 'Autonomous Region of Krajina', marched with a column of his militant adventurists to the town of Titov Drvar, in Bosnia, and held manoeuvres, and announced the end of the border between the Croatian Krajina and the Bosnian Krajina. He was welcomed by Serb town officials, who called the Bosnian Krajina 'Serbian territory' (emphatically not a Serb reporter).

Moving to soft news: A camera followed a reporter around brushy humps and wall foundations near Gabela, a town thirty miles downriver from Mostar, which 'the world-renowned archaeologist' Roberto Salinas Price had been saying for years was the real location of ancient Troy. (Take *that*, you Romans and British, parvenu sons of Aeneas and Brutus!)

Yugoslav affairs had taken an hour. The announcer said, 'Not much of interest happened in the rest of the world today. And now for the weather . . .'

While watching, we ate the Levantine pre-meal meal of booze and bites called *meze*. In the Hercegovinian version, it comprised *loza*, a grape-stalk brandy, smoked cheese, *prsut* (prosciutto) and coarse white bread. Behija, a very short woman with a boyish cut of straight white hair and a disconcerting air of distraction, a habit of looking past your shoulder as she spoke to you, lounged in her blue bathrobe and white socks, knocking back the excellent loza, which she made herself. She liked to go to her family's old village house in the hills and slog around in wellingtons. Along with the loza, she made cornel-berry juice, elder-blossom tea and the best cherry *rakija* I had ever tasted. Now and then she cleaned, throwing everything she found in one corner willy-nilly into a different corner. While watching television, she wore a set of earphones with the volume turned up, to overcome her partial deafness.

When the war broke out Behija had been a student in Belgrade, but she gave it up to return to Mostar, where she became an *ilegala*, a Partisan courier. Her four siblings had all been Partisans.

221

Three were killed during the war, and the fourth died of tuberculosis soon after. She spoke of these things in the same hurried, dismissive way she spoke of everything else, seeming to stare at my breast pocket.

Mustafa was in his mid-thirties, stocky and round-shouldered, of gentle demeanour. He looked nothing like his mother, except for the largeness of his head, which he kept tucked and slightly forward, giving him a sheepish look. He tended to gulp when he talked. His hands wandered, looking for some haven of unself-consciousness they never seemed to find.

He took me upstairs to show me the Turkish styling of the house. It had been his father's project, and had taken years. It had been difficult finding craftsmen who knew the old techniques. His father had had to abandon the traditional stone roof, for lack of an artisan, and settle for the usual terracotta tiles.

Mustafa taught me the words. The raised sitting area in the central hall, enclosed by a railing of carved pine, was the *divanhana*. Here, the men of the house took their ease, sitting on the *sećija* – not the *sofa*, Mustafa informed me, which actually meant 'flowerbed' – and smoking tobacco or hashish in the long *čibuk* or the snake-armed *nargila*. They might also drink coffee, using the *mangala*. This large copper contraption had a rounded belly for coal embers to keep the *džezva* hot, an upper platform whose rim had depressions for holding the *fildžans*, and a hemispherical cover decorated with crescents and stars. The lower part of this particular mangala had been in Mustafa's family for years, and they had had the upper part made to match.

Off the central hall was the *ćošak*, the room in which you received guests. This was the part of a Turkish house most noticeable from the outside, because it projected over the lower floor to allow a broad bay of windows. The ceiling was made of hundreds of pieces of pine fitted into an elaborate radiating circle that nearly touched the walls – an architectural memory, perhaps, of tent-tops. The cupboard built into the wall was a *musandera*, the small copper plate was a *sahan*, the big copper platter was a *tepsija* and the engraving on it was *savat*. The carpet was a *ćilim*. The sampler was of a famous Yugoslav painting called 'The Sold

Bride' – in a ćošak much like this one, a crowd of women as colourful as cockatoos in their Turkish pants and waistcoats gathered around to adorn the girlish bride, who seemed lost in a clichéd reverie of self-consciousness, childlike pride and a soupçon of fear at the lustful Turk awaiting her.

Mustafa sat on the sećija and held a fildžan, and demonstrated how the windows were placed at a height that allowed you to turn and put your elbow on the sill and look out at the *avlija* (courtyard) below and listen indolently to the *česma* (fountain).

We returned to the concrete room off the kitchen, where Mustafa and Behija lived, received guests and watched TV.

43

The next day I met Mustafa for a drive out to the old family house in the village of Cim. He called goodbye to Behija and closed the door on her with what seemed like relief. As we climbed into his red Renault, a Yugoslav-made model, I asked, 'How old is this? What year?', thinking it was in pretty good shape for a car from the late 60s.

But Mustafa thought I had said, 'How old is this? One year?' and he answered proudly, 'No, no. It's a 1985 model. It only looks so new because I don't drive it very often.'

Mustafa bicycled to work on a ten-speed, wearing reflecting stripes and a helmet with a little projecting rear-view mirror. As we negotiated the clogged streets, he lamented the reign of the automobile – the poisonous air, the noise, the blocked sidewalks. 'And this is such a small town,' he said. 'Most people could walk to work faster than they can drive.' He was wearing his seatbelt. I wondered if he realized what an oddity he was.

We passed a tower block which housed the construction consulting firm Mustafa worked for. It had recently reduced its staff from 130 to sixty, but, instead of firing people, it had offered anyone who was willing to leave a concession stand on the plaza outside the building. The company paid half the cost of a kiosk, and gave a five-year loan on the other half. So now when Mustafa went to work he passed former colleagues selling hamburgers and ćevapčići and, since some of them were friends of his, he knew for a fact they were making more money on the plaza than they ever had inside the building.

'Food is the only thing that people are still buying,' Mustafa said. 'Well, that and weapons.'

We crossed the river to the right bank. Mostar, in one way, was a microcosm of Hercegovina. Just as Hercegovina to the east of the Neretva River was majority Serb, so most Mostaran Serbs lived on the east bank. The Catholics tended to live on the west bank and behind them, in the hinterlands of western Hercegovina, spread a nearly unbroken sea of Croats.

Dominating any view of the eastern half of the city was the Orthodox cathedral. In 1833 the Serbs had built a church on the eastern slope, but the Turks had insisted that it be partly underground, so that it would not be visible from the town. In 1873, when the Ottoman Empire could not afford such arrogance, Sultan Abdul Aziz not only gave the Serbs permission to build a new church, but helped finance it, and they promptly designed the largest Orthodox cathedral in all of Bosnia. By the time it was completed, the Turks were gone and, though the Muslims left behind still made up the largest group, their mosques seemed to cower below the dome and tower of the stone heap on the hill. I wondered if the Turks had much cared. The Bosnian Muslims, with their passionate opposition to reform, had given the Turks nothing but trouble for the past forty years.

On the west bank, we drove through the inevitable Austrian section, where the streets were lined with sycamores and horse-chestnuts and every other building looked like a ministry for the Islamic Republic of Disneyland. We passed the new Catholic cathedral and the renovated bishop's palace. The road turned upward, making its first cut into the hillside, and the concrete retaining wall was spray-painted from top to bottom with šahovnicas and HDZs.

224

'We're entering Croatia,' Mustafa said wryly. 'I think you need a passport.'

A month ago, a column of Yugoslav Army tanks supposedly heading for military exercises in fields around the Bosnian town of Kupres were blockaded for three days by the Croat villagers of Lištica, who suspected they were heading for the fighting in Croatia. At the same time, Croats in Mostar set up barricades on the road west out of the city, presumably to prevent tanks from taking this road to outflank the blockade at Lištica. Mustafa had had to drive through the barricades every time he went to his village house, and he had been disgusted and upset. The men had let him through, but had always looked him over suspiciously. Who were these self-important nobodies, who had appeared out of nowhere, toting their guns? What right had they? He was only going to Cim, to get some peace and quiet and maybe prune a tree.

'Five years ago,' he said, 'I never thought about who was who. Croat, Serb, Muslim . . . Why would I care about something like that? I didn't even *know* what some of my friends were. What really frightens me — and even more than that, what *amazes* me — is how quickly the tribal feelings have arisen. Where were they hiding, all those years?'

I expressed some facile optimism that even if violence broke out in Bosnia-Hercegovina, perhaps it would amount to no more than a few months of sporadic incidents, with a lot of the usual blood-curdling Balkan rhetoric, after which it would settle into some kind of tense but stable *modus vivendi*. Something like Cyprus, I ventured. A mess, and a shame, but not an out-and-out nightmare. Surely, I babbled on, people here had too much to lose from a full-scale civil war. They were eating, they had clothes. Many even had summer houses on the coast. Surely people would realize that their best interests lay in working together. *Surely* . . .

Mustafa waited until I had wound down, then shrugged and said mildly, 'Maybe you're right. But I don't know. I think this could become another Lebanon.'

'Lebanon', like 'Europe' and 'Balkan' and 'Eskimo', was a

word that came up often in Yugoslav conversation. There was a widespread superstition that the world, for some reason only the Almighty or the All Merciful could fathom, needed at least one Lebanon. Lebanon itself had just stopped being 'Lebanon', so Yugoslavia was taking over the role. It did not help that many of those weapons found in trucks on Bosnian roads had, in fact, been bought on the cheap from disarming Lebanese militias.

Mustafa turned on to a smaller road, which wound farther into the hills. It narrowed to a single lane closed in by wild roses and honeysuckle, which climbed and fell so steeply that crosswise ridges had been set in the concrete surface to provide traction. With a last hairpin turn and a first-gear run up a steep hillside, we were there.

We took baskets out of the car and walked up a path under dense foliage to a cluster of three stone cottages. All three used to belong to Mustafa's family, but two had been 'distributed' at the end of the war. One of the distributees greeted us, an old woman dressed in widow's black, which meant she was a Christian. Her forearms were scaly from decades of washing clothes and she walked with a teetering, arthritic gait. She served us loza and swept smashed cherries off her terrace, while the grizzled and pot-bellied man who owned the local still for making rakija sat in the doorway fixing a brass coffee mill. The old woman was one of the very few people who actually lived in Cim, Mustafa told me. Most only came up from Mostar at weekends, as we were doing.

Not very long ago, of course, Cim had been a viable village. Mustafa's grandparents had lived off the cherries, which grew abundantly here. They would spend two months in Mostar in the winter, but the rest of the year they were out here, attending to their terraces and trees. Perhaps to a romantic nationalist, a worshipper of the peasantry, the life sounded pre-lapsarian, but it had been hard. *Cim*, Behija had told me, was an old Illyrian word, meaning 'Place of many Sources', but in fact, like many Hercegovinian settlements, it had no water. The nearest spring was at the bottom of the valley, half an hour's walk away. (In many hill villages, people had to walk two hours or more for water.) Villagers would carry the water up in tall oval tanks that had straps for the shoulders and, when full, could weigh 150 pounds. Mustafa could remember fetching water when he was a boy. Now he brought it from Mostar in plastic jugs in his car.

And there were the years when the crop failed, and you went hungry. This year had been disastrous, with a warm March that coaxed out the blossoms and a cold April that killed them, but all it meant to Mustafa and Behija was that they would not be making any cherry rakija, or freezing cherry pies.

We had come to pick what there was. We continued down the path to the middle cottage. Mustafa and Behija shared it with some cousins in Sarajevo, but they rarely came. An ancient gate of sagging wood scraps opened into a courtyard, with the cottage to one side and the summer kitchen – always a separate structure in these hot parts – to the other. The cottage consisted of an entrance hall-cum-toolshed, and a single low-ceilinged room of whitewashed stucco, with two windows in deep ogee-arched recesses that showed the thickness of the walls. A stone sećija – now I knew what it was called – ran along the wall beneath the windows and I took a moment to sit on it, and turned to put my elbow on the windowsill, and looked out at a mass of obscuring foliage.

We shouldered more baskets and a ladder and headed down the slope, picking through bushes and climbing down retaining walls until we reached the terrace that Mustafa and Behija owned. Mustafa had explained to me the intricacies of this year's disaster. There were four kinds of cherries, called, in order of ripening, *aprilka* (because they ripened in April), *švabica* ('from Schwabia'), *alica* and *hruštovka*. In the luxuriating trance of a connoisseur, Mustafa had described them to me. The aprilkas were light red and sourish, not particularly tasty, but always expensive in the markets because people were eager to buy the first cherries of the year. The švabicas were black and soft, and so sweet they were sticky. The alicas were light red like the aprilkas, but sweeter (though not so sweet as the švabicas) and firm-fleshed, sometimes a little dry. The hruštovkas were hard and red-black, largest of all and second-sweetest after the švabicas. Most Mostarans preferred the hruštovkas, which I concluded must be the fruit I had always crudely called 'cherry' and bought in the supermarket at home. Mustafa's favourite was the sticky, super-sweet švabica. But the only variety to survive the spring frosts was the middling alica, and, of Mustafa's and Behija's eight cherry trees, only one was an alica.

The picking was a pleasant job. From the top of the ladder, I could see Mostar far away, and snowy mountain peaks beyond. A woman somewhere below us in the dell was laughing. A peacock cried, 'No! No!'

'I can't imagine giving up this place,' came Mustafa's voice from the neighbouring branches. 'It's so peaceful out here. No noise, no crowds.' He paused. 'No water.'

Cim now was ninety-nine per cent Catholic. The weekend villagers were descendants of the rayahs who used to work the land for the Muslim owners. Mustafa's family, the Humos, were the last Muslims in Cim, and all his grandfather's land had been reduced to one-fifth of a hectare – this terrace of eight cherry trees, a strawberry patch and a few cornel-berry bushes; the terrace below, which belonged to the cousins in Sarajevo; and the ground the cottage sat on.

'For me, that's enough,' Mustafa said, and I believed him.

'No hard feelings between the ex-labourers and the ex-landlords?'

'Oh, no. No one ever thinks about that any more.' He went on, 'In a big crop year, we invite over everybody we know, to help us pick the cherries.' He handed a brimming basket down to me. 'It's easy to get everybody to come when there are cherries to eat. But when you have to cut branches, or dig around the tree, or lime the bark to keep the rabbits away, then, hoo – it's impossible.'

We sat down for a rest. A fragile network of tiny lavender blossoms webbed the grass like baby's breath. I didn't know about the švabicas or the hruštovkas, but the alicas were delicious.

'The custom is to sing, when you pick cherries for money,' Mustafa said. 'That keeps you from eating the cherries.'

The terraces, these modest cradles of soil, had been cultivated for centuries, and the amount of labour that had gone into constructing them out of every square inch of the steep stony slopes was appalling to contemplate. As farmers in Holland or Germany named fields they had cleared, Hercegovinian villagers named each terrace, representing as much, or more, work. We were sitting on Mala Taličevina, or 'Talić's Little'. The cousins' terrace below was Velika Taličevina – 'Talić's Big'. Talic was long gone, and nearly as long forgotten, but the names remained, clustered thickly around us: 'Beech', 'Old Man', 'Stony', 'Little Girl'.

'There is an old village saying,' Mustafa said. '"*Nema Cima do Rima.*"' It could only be translated badly: 'There is not another Cim between here and Rome.' Under the blue sky, in the bower of cherry trees, among the lavender flowers, I felt I could easily believe it.

Here was a fleeting glimpse of the rural past, when the world was smaller, when every hamlet had its own traditions, its own proverbs. A man from Cim would have been called a *cimac*, and when he boasted he would have begun, 'Now, we *cimci*, we . . .' The men of Cim would have protected each other, partly because they were all cousins, partly because no man could survive alone in those hard, lawless times. You had to be as a brother to those from whom you might some day require a service only a brother could be expected to fulfil – to avenge your death, or take in your widow. To reinforce that crucial sense of solidarity, there had to be an Other, and since the world was small, that role was fulfilled by a neighbouring village, like Ilića, over the next hill. Perhaps they had red piping on their jackets over there, not the blue of Cim. Perhaps cimci looked in their coffee and called the floating grounds *iličani*. Perhaps they said the only virgins in Ilića were those girls quick enough to outrun their brothers.

How much of Yugoslavia's present turmoil could be blamed on its recent peasant past, and on that past's tribal culture? Roads had been built, and the world had been enlarged. Cimci had become Hercegovinians, who scorned the Bosnians as *šljivari* or 'plum-eaters', because figs and cherries could not grow in that colder climate. Then they all became Bosnians, and they said that when the Turks came, many Bosnians fled into the sea and drowned, but those with empty heads floated, and became the Dalmatians.

Highways joined republic to republic, but the way between the faiths remained narrow, the gate strait. Dalmatians expanded to Croats – and stopped. Cim's blue piping was gone, and the cimci with it, but Muslims, far from giving up the fez, were returning to it.

Yugoslavia had tried to move into the 'modern' world, in which you gave a job to a stranger as likely as to a brother, but it had fallen short in the transition, and few Yugoslavs, even if they lamented the tyranny of 'influence', had much respect for the cold concept that ignoring your own was some kind of virtue. The peasant tribalisms lingered. Perhaps they could be considered the genetic predisposition to cancer, while religion was the insult to the cell that triggered the disease.

'Man leans on man, as trees on trees,' runs a Yugoslav proverb. It is a comforting image. But when just the wrong wind comes, the whole forest blows down.

Cim, in any case, was dead. The last memories of its life were dying. Mustafa had been the kind of child to take careful note of his elders' world, and he was the kind of man to humbly remember what he had seen and heard. His cousins had no idea what the terraces were called. Theirs was overgrown. Sometimes they could not even be bothered to come and pick, and the fruit fell and rotted on the ground.

'Let's continue,' I said.

Mustafa climbed the ladder and I handed a basket up to him. 'There's another old saying,' he said, hanging the basket on a limb. ' "The older you get, the more you like Cim." When I was little, I hated coming up here. I thought it was boring.' He reached for a fat cluster and dropped five perfect cherries into the basket. 'Now I like it.'

'So you're getting old,' I said.

'I suppose so.'

44

On the bus to Medjugorje I saw, everywhere, private houses under construction — earthquake-proof hunks of concrete floorslabs and orange breezeblock. I had mentioned to Mustafa that Yugoslavia, despite all its troubles, appeared to be in the midst of a building boom, and he had explained to me that the boom was *because* of Yugoslavia's troubles. When dinars dissolved like sugar in the rain, you converted them into rooftiles, reinforcing-rods, bags of cement. You amassed over the years, piece by piece, several tons of solid capital. A house was better than hard currency, because the banks could not spend it.

The reasons for building applied everywhere in Yugoslavia, but along this particular route out of Mostar, into the dry hills of orange earth, there was a special incentive. Ten years ago there had not been a single bus to Medjugorje, a village of a dozen large families in a scrubby upland plain. Now there were a dozen daily. The nearby town of Čitluk had grown tentacles of *pensions* and hotels along its approaches, and in Medjugorje itself the construction fever had reached almost surreal proportions. Where ten years ago a dirt road had meandered through tobacco fields and vineyards along a stream, a line of restaurants, souvenir shops and tourist agencies now stretched, as gaudily clamorous for attention as any American strip. Where two-room stone cottages had once squatted in their cabbage and onion gardens, huge white stucco manors now loomed, muscle-bound with shoulders and wings. Yugoslavs had told me, their faces tight with envy, that these ex-tobacco farmers who recently didn't even have toilets now had lifts. They said Medjugorje had more taxis than the entire city of Split. They said the Medjugorjans were grasping harpies who would fleece me.

On 24 June 1981, five teenagers and one younger boy climbed a hill overlooking Medjugorje, and saw the Virgin Mary. She held out her arms and spoke to them. The following day, she appeared to the 'visionaries' at exactly the same time, six-forty p.m. She came on the next day, and on the next. By then, thousands of Croats from all over Hercegovina were converging on the village. They massed on 'Apparition Hill' in the hot evenings, with umbrellas and towels to protect themselves from the sun, and waited to see the children fall to their knees in unison, and stare fixedly up towards a point in the air above them, and receive a message about prayer and peace.

To the Communist government of western Hercegovina, a runaway religious movement was frightening. Tito had died the year before, and the western Hercegovinians, a tough, poor people that had been over-represented in the Ustasha movement and were still devoutly Catholic after thirty-five years of governmental atheism, looked like the wedge of a revolution waiting for a hammer blow. The police came after the children. The Franciscans hid them. The children continued having visions, every day, first in private houses, then secreted away in a chapel.

They were eventually found, of course. But the governmental actions that followed were faint-hearted. A few villagers and Franciscans were thrown in jail for a few months, and other Franciscans were reassigned. But the visionaries, curiously, were more or less left alone. And they kept having visions.

So the Medjugorje phenomenon mushroomed. Word spread, and foreigners came. First on their own, then in groups on package tours that included two nights in Dubrovnik and a day in Mostar to look at the bridge. The Virgin kept appearing, every day at six-forty p.m. You could set your watch by her.

In the ten years since the apparitions began, something between six and ten million Catholics had come to Medjugorje.

Perspectives on the phenomenon differed. For obvious reasons, it was Vatican policy not to pronounce on the authenticity of a miraculous manifestation until the visions had safely ended, and the apparitions at Medjugorje showed no sign of ending. Meanwhile, Catholics squabbled.

The year before, I had paid a visit to the Bishop of Mostar, Pavao Žanić, with an interpreter named Mili, who happened to

232

be a Muslim. Mili sweated profusely on the doorstep of the imposing episcopal palace, wondering how to address the bishop. 'Your Reverence'? 'Your Holiness'? 'Your Excellency'? We were admitted by a brawny, unsmiling priest in sharply pressed clothes, with a military bearing, who regarded the slovenly reporter and his panicking translator with some bemusement.

The first thing Žanić, a snowy-haired man of stern, impatient countenance, asked poor Mili was whether or not he was Catholic, and when Mili gulped and coloured and admitted he was Muslim, the bishop grunted disapprovingly and turned towards me.

Protestant, I apologized.

Žanić sighed. But he was willing to fulminate, even to us, on the subject of Medjugorje. The 'visionaries' said they had gone up the hill on that June day in 1981 to look for their sheep, but they had really gone up to smoke cigarettes, and had concocted the tale of the vision merely to divert their parents. It had been a childish prank that had spiralled out of control. The Franciscans had manipulated the children for their own ends, until, now, the 'visionaries' were practised liars.

Žanić gave me a booklet he had written on the subject, which I read as soon as we left. He had documented contradictions in the visionaries' accounts of the apparitions, and examples of their patently false teachings – in one instance, the Virgin had supposedly told the children that all faiths were equal – but his principal point, often repeated, was that real miracles, like those at Lourdes and Fatima, promoted healing and unity in the Church, whereas the phenomenon at Medjugorje had produced division and discord, because it had caused the Franciscans and their followers to disobey and show disrespect for their superior in the Church, i.e. their bishop, i.e. him.

The visionaries had spoken of a 'great sign' that would come, proving to all the truth of their visions, and Žanić promised that if the sign actually came he would make the thirty-kilometre pilgrimage from Mostar to Medjugorje on his knees. (However, the Virgin had said that after the sign came it would be too late to repent.)

Some people charged that Žanić had been supportive of the events at Medjugorje until the point when it had become clear that the Franciscans, and not the diocese, would have control over the show. Žanić denied this. But there was no question that the unseemly quarrel gained resonance from a long-standing power struggle between the Franciscans of Hercegovina and the diocesan clergy. (The Franciscans had been sent by the papacy into Bosnia-Hercegovina in 1260, in the hope that their more self-abnegating form of Catholicism would persuade the austere Bogomils to convert, where the sword had not. Whether or not they actually converted many Bogomils is unclear, but they became well entrenched among the Catholic population, and today ministered to over eighty per cent of the faithful in the diocese of Mostar.)

I got off the bus in Medjugorje and walked down the strip of new white bungalow shops sitting in torn-up earth and trash. I went into a tourist agency and met Veseljko. He was a tour organizer, an affable, open-faced man with a short brush of brown hair who dressed in a preppy combination of jeans, loafers and sports jacket. He had lived in California until he was ten, and spoke excellent English. His agency specialized in Irish pilgrims, several busloads of whom had been in Medjugorje for the past week.

His own perspective was that of the scheduler. The Virgin made his job easy. Although her daily apparitions were now closed to the public, she also made twice-weekly appearances on Apparition Hill, on Mondays and Fridays at ten p.m., and everyone was invited. Unfortunately, Veseljko informed me, these evening apparitions only occurred when the visionary Ivan was in town, and he had been away for a couple of weeks, 'drumming up business, because it has been a slow year'. But pilgrims could still meet the visionary Vicka every day at eight a.m. and Jakov at one p.m. (Two of the other three visionaries had stopped having visions, except on their birthdays, when the Virgin sent best wishes. The third still had visions, but no longer lived in Medjugorje.)

Veseljko said all of this in a straightforward way, without smirking. I asked him if he believed in the apparitions.

'It's not important what I believe,' he said. 'I'm here to make sure pilgrims have a successful visit, and I do the best job I can.'

But we had spent some time talking about California, and with that bond between us he could not resist adding, 'All you need to do is look at that church. It was built in the 60s, years before the apparitions. But look how huge it is! Why did they build such a big church for a couple of hundred people in a few scattered huts? I think this was all carefully planned.'

On the way out, I picked up his agency's brochure. It said, 'Although the Vatican has not officially recognized the phenomena, there is no doubt that the visions in Medjugorje are real.'

I continued along the strip, past the souvenir shops with their armies of plastic Marys, their homiletic samplers. The walls were waterfalls of rosaries. A shop sign pleaded, THE BEDROCK-PRICE ROSARY. One of the recurrent miracles of Medjugorje was that worshippers' rosaries turned to gold.

The restaurants and pizzerias listed no prices on their menus, which was illegal, and unknown elsewhere in Yugoslavia. An Irish jogger in a shamrock-green T-shirt paused to tell me he had had a fantastic week. You could feel that something special was going on here, you could feel the spirituality. About the town itself, well ... they were all crooks. 'One of my mates had a hamburger, and it cost him twelve dollars!'

The strip curved to the left. Straight ahead stood the large church with its two square towers, dominating the plain. On the shaded plaza in front, a marble statue of Mary was encircled by an iron fence, and circling the fence was an old Croat woman, crawling on her knees, her black skirt hiked so that the stones would cut into her skin. A young man with a severe limp hobbled by. On the benches under the trees sat people with St Vitus' dance and palsy, skin diseases and guide-dogs.

My tourist-agency brochure said, 'After visiting Medjugorje, approximately 500 pilgrims have reported being cured of an illness.'

Bishop Žanić's pamphlet said, 'No one knows of any healed from Hercegovina.'

Posters by the church door listed masses all day long, in English,

German, Italian and Croatian. The current mass was in German, and I went in. The church was simple and white inside, with stained-glass windows in the clerestory in colours typical of the 60s – not medieval ruby reds and Chartres blues, but pinks and lemon yellows and grass greens. Not illuminated manuscripts, but colouring books.

The pews were overflowing. The speaker was Jozo Zovko, one of the Franciscans who had been jailed briefly by the Communists. He spoke in a voice of treacly mildness. My ears pricked up when he began to inveigh against the money-grubbing restaurateurs and shopowners lining the street in front of the church, who preyed on pilgrims. They were Muslims, he said.

Veseljko, too, had said something to me about the shopowners being Muslims. Veseljko himself was Orthodox, and he had once had to translate for Brother Jozo for a Philippine television programme. As Žanić had done to Mili, Jozo first asked Veseljko if he was Catholic and, on discovering that he was not, would not let the camera team into his church. He stood blocking the doorway for the entire two hours of the interview, so that Veseljko and the crew had to remain standing in the cold rain. That was a couple of years ago. Now Jozo simply refused to talk through any translator who was not Catholic.

I went outside. Prayer meetings were going on in green tents behind the church. A long line of new confessionals stretched along the plaza, and in front of them was a field of benches with signs saying, ENGLISH, GERMAN, CROATIAN, FRENCH, ITALIAN. Priests and friars sat by the signs and waited to hear confession or to provide guidance. The Vatican had forbidden priests to lead pilgrimages to Medjugorje, so they came with 'tour groups' as 'spiritual counsellors'.

I ambled around, meeting people. A Puerto Rican woman in red described to me the miracles of the Medjugorjan sun. Sometimes it danced in the sky. Sometimes it spun, shooting off sparks. 'Wait a minute – ' she broke off. 'Is it – ?' She put on dark glasses and looked up. She turned back to me, shrugging. 'I thought it was doing it, there, for a second.'

236

I asked a group of Minnesotans if it bothered them that the Bishop of Mostar did not believe in the apparitions.

'It's a trial,' a woman said. 'This is all part of Our Lady's plan.'

Another was more direct: 'Satan is always active. He punched one of the seers just the other day.'

'Excuse me?'

'I saw it with my own eyes. One of the seers was praying and suddenly doubled over. Satan had hauled off and belted him.'

And how did they feel about the fact that the Vatican had not yet approved the phenomena? That it had, in fact, banned pilgrimages?

A man shrugged. 'The Vatican will come around. People come to Medjugorje because it delivers. I've been to Lourdes. Nothing's happening there! It's all over! This is where the action is.'

His wife told me her rosary had turned to gold.

As six-forty approached, people gathered in front of the church to stare at the sun. The first miracle of the Medjugorjan sun was that you could stare into it without damaging your eyes. The second miracle was that after you had stared for a few seconds, an image of the Host appeared in the middle of the sun, as a dark spot.

Sitting with Mark on a bench a few minutes later, I asked him what he thought about the sun miracles.

'The external signs are not the essential thing about Medjugorje,' he said. 'For example, some people say they have seen Mary. Now – I'm not sure I'd *like* to see her. I mean, I'm sure it must be wonderful. But in a way, I would find it . . . distracting.' Mark had been to Medjugorje several times. He ran a Medjugorje centre in England.

The visionaries had said that the Virgin was asking all believers to fast on bread and water every Wednesday and Friday. But Mark urged the necessity of flexible interpretations. 'An English priest has pointed out that the bread is more substantial here than it is in England. The point is to give something up, something you value, on those two days. So I don't eat chocolate.'

In my pack I had a copy of a Serbian magazine I had picked up in Belgrade with a cover photograph of a statuette of Mary, her hands pressed together in prayer, her feet lost in a puffy cloud-like pile of exhumed femurs and skulls. It was a special *Politika* publication entitled 'The Lady of Medjugorje and the Serbian Pits'. Late last year, Serbs had started opening the World War II-era limestone burial pits of Bosnia. Belgrade TV and Serbian newpapers had covered the events extensively. Experts had spoken of cubic feet and contents-settling, and come up with numbers in the thousands. Old widows broke down as the cameras zoomed in for close-ups. The bones were distributed, a few pounds each, to village cemeteries all over Bosnia for reburial. One of the caves the Serbs had unsealed was only six kilometres from Medjugorje. I asked Mark if he had ever heard anything about that.

'Yes, a couple of years ago. I always considered it just a coincidence. But word came through the Medjugorje Centre grapevine this past winter that the people of Medjugorje had been directly involved in the killings. That bothered me a bit at first. But then I realized, of course! Mary chose this place because of its troubled past. It's not just the massacres. There was discord between the villagers, too, between the different families. In one of the early services in the church after the apparitions started, one of the visionaries called for reconciliation, and one village elder got up and publicly forgave another to whom he hadn't spoken in years. They embraced. Soon, everyone was doing it! When they came out of the church, MIR was written in the sky.' (*Mir* means 'peace'.)

Mark saw in Medjugorje a great future as a force for ecumenism. 'Orthodox come here, too. A Muslim family I know in England is planning to come. "Muhammad never says a word to us!" they say. Mary is very dear to the Muslims. When one of the visionaries asked Mary to give her an example of a holy person, she named a Muslim woman. "But she is Muslim!" the visionary said. And Mary replied, "You created the divisions, not I. There is only one God." Did you know that in 1968 Mary appeared over a Coptic church in Cairo? Thousands of Muslims saw her. That's an often overlooked apparition.'

My brochure from the tourist office said, 'Many believers are

238

convinced that Medjugorje is of greater importance than Lourdes and Fatima.'

Mark went further. 'We reckon this is the biggest thing since Pentecost.'

45

The roads away from the church had recently been paths. Now they were hastily paved, heavily potholed. The Mercedes taxis wove like slalom skiers. Out where the bungalow complexes and supermarkets started to thin, where the souvenir shops dwindled to a few operations out of garages and sheds, and the vineyards came close to the road, lived the Ostojić family; so many cousins and second cousins were strewn in a score of houses that that part of the village was called 'Ostojići'. The quarter across the road was 'Jerkovići'. (Though a Jerković had recently had the nerve to build a house on the Ostojić side.)

I stayed in the house of Mate Ostojić and his wife, and their daughter Lidija, and their sons Franjo and Mićo, with their wives and half-dozen young children.

To these particular Ostojićs, a bread-and-water fast on Wednesdays and Fridays meant a bread-and-water fast on Wednesdays and Fridays. Only old, ill Mate, and Franjo's heavily pregnant wife Milena, were excepted. 'Our Lady asked it of us,' Lidija said simply. They never called her Mary. Perhaps that was too familiar. She was always 'Our Lady'.

I had got a room with them because Lidija, a slim, handsome, large-nosed woman in her twenties, worked in Veseljko's agency. I had been relieved to discover, after the first day or two, that I was not going to be taken advantage of. (The most important lesson in Yugoslavia was that you could not – *must* not – believe what one group said about another. Yet I had believed.)

The Ostojićs were themselves distressed about the image the village was getting. Lidija, like Jozo and Veseljko, blamed

Muslims, who had bought property near the church after the apparitions had begun. They did not live in the area, and did not care about its reputation.

There were no vaporizings about Bosnians. Medjugorjans were Croats, who spoke Croatian. 'Everyone in western Hercegovina would like to join Croatia,' Lidija said.

They had room for sixteen guests, but there were only me and two elderly Croat women from Sarajevo. Lidija had been explaining to me how western Hercegovina really belonged to Croatia, when one of the Sarajevan women broke in and passionately corrected her. *All* of Bosnia-Hercegovina historically belonged to Croatia.

'I didn't know that,' Lidija shrugged in my direction.

Within five minutes the woman had convinced her.

'Listen to her,' Lidija told me, giving up the field. 'She knows everything!'

Thus was the truth spread.

I asked, 'And what would the Muslims do if Bosnia-Hercegovina joined Croatia?'

'Muslims do whatever is good for them,' Lidija said. 'This way or that way. They adapt, and profit.'

I thought of the Jews of Europe; or the Chinese of Malaysia; the Palestinians of Jordan and Syria; the Phanariot Greeks of Byzantium. It seemed a universal human myth: the Yid with a thousand faces. The wily trader whose state was elsewhere, or nowhere, whose god was Mammon, and who would melt away during dangerous times but would be right back after the war, owning the store, when the famine struck.

Ten years ago, the Ostojićs, like everyone else in Medjugorje, had made their living by growing tobacco. (The Communist land-reform measures after the war placed a ten-hectare cap on a household's private holdings of arable land, but most farmers in Yugoslavia had owned less than ten hectares anyway. Mate owned five.) The tobacco harvest had been an exhausting job, Lidija said, requiring that you rise before four-thirty every morning. The pay was bad, since the state held a monopoly on tobacco. It was also a filthy job, with the tobacco juice running down your arms and getting into your hair. You lived for weeks stained brown and smelling so intensely of cigar it made you dizzy.

They had lived in a house with a kitchen and two other rooms, and had carried water from a well two hundred metres away. They had not planned their change in profession. For the first four years after the apparitions, there was no new building in Medjugorje. There were still no restaurants, no tourist agencies. The police were hostile, and the Medjugorjans kept growing tobacco.

But pilgrims began to appear, with bedrolls and Bibles. They came from the United States and Ireland and Italy, and they camped in the fields. Some came with nothing, modelling themselves on the lilies of the field. The Ostojićs let them sleep in their house, on blankets on the floors, for free.

More and more pilgrims came, and the Ostojićs, like many of their neighbours, built a bigger house to accommodate them, in 1985. The biggest room of the old house (but it was a small room) became the new kitchen and dining room, and behind was added a square two-storey structure, with living quarters for the family upstairs, and six bare white rooms for sixteen pilgrims downstairs. The family still grew tobacco.

'But guests require cleanliness, and meals,' Lidija said. 'We didn't have time for tobacco, and because of that we had to start charging. It all just happened.'

The increase in pilgrims from year to year was exponential. Medjugorje had mushroomed, and yet there were never enough rooms. The Ostojićs' neighbours were adding new wings to their houses. Lidija had worked once as an au pair in Italy, and now began to arrange tours through her Italian friends. Last year, Franjo had decided to build a bigger dining room, so that their guests would not have to eat in shifts. Then he decided, while he was at it, to build rooms for twenty more guests. This 24 June would be the tenth anniversary of the first apparition, and something like half a million pilgrims were expected.

Franjo borrowed money from the bank. Lidija borrowed money from an Italian friend. All payments from pilgrims in May and June would go directly into construction costs. Franjo took

241

two months off from his job in one of the supermarkets, and he and his brother Mićo, who was a builder by trade, hired help and set to work.

Then the fighting in Croatia started. Since the end of April, the Ostojićs had put up only me and the two women from Sarajevo.

Work was delayed as Franjo scrambled for money. The family sold their cow. Their finances were particularly parlous because Franjo had been cheated out of DM8,000 in the spring, when a Slovene who was supposed to deliver a car to him (and to several hundred other people – the deal had something to do with a lower car tax in Croatia, Franjo said), instead fled to Switzerland with DM7,000,000. The only sure income for the entire summer would be the group of fifty-three Italians that Lidija had arranged for, who would arrive the day before the tenth anniversary, barely a week away. Seventeen could fit into Mićo's house next door, and sixteen in the house built six years ago, but the other twenty had to go into the new wing.

But the new wing was barely more than a concrete shell. Lidija stood in the hot, dusty road watching the workers and said to her brother over and over, 'It *has* to be finished.'

Franjo merely frowned. He was a quiet man, of responsible mien. He picked his teeth after meals, looking stoically sick with worry. He had hired more workers. There were now fourteen of them. He didn't even want to think about how much he was paying them. All he would tell me, as we stood together surveying the chaos, was, 'A lot.' Three men were slapping on stucco with cavalier swipes of their trowels. Four others were drilling holes for the steel window frames. Two unloaded the frames. The usual five stood around doing nothing in particular. The tiles were down in the new kitchen, but nothing else had been installed. Wires hung out of the walls. The concrete, in places, was already crumbling.

They were going to run out of money. Tomorrow, or the next day. Franjo would not talk about it, but Lidija could guess. 'I don't know what we're going to do,' she said. 'Perhaps Our Lady will help.'

At one of the midday meals that was not bread and water, I

asked Franjo if he thought life was better for them now than it had been before the apparitions.

He scowled, working the toothpick in his mouth, shrugging. It was the same. You worked hard, you got by.

Mićo added, 'As long as you have enough work to do, you're OK. The worst thing is to have no work.'

The sweaty and grimy men ate, the women served. Fatty meat, bread and the fine yellow wine the family made from its own grapes and stored in vats in a sunken room off the main hall. The meal began with an Our Father and a Hail Mary, but otherwise the atmosphere was the same as at any Yugoslav table full of men. One of the workers was the designated ladies' man, joked about in terms that made him sound like a devourer, a destroyer of women. He had done construction work in Moscow (slipshod as Yugoslav building was, it was far better than Russian work, and was much in demand in the Soviet Union), and declared Russian women to be the best. They were simple, undemanding. They didn't ask for gold necklaces like Yugoslav girls. A little bit of money went a long way. I should go to Moscow, the men all agreed.

'But I'm married,' I said, following my part in the liturgy.

'What does that matter?' they all laughed, completing it.

But I have been saying 'Medjugorje' throughout, and the Ostojićs did not live in Medjugorje. There were actually two villages on this small plain. The big church had been built between them, to serve them both. (This was why the church had been surrounded only by fields, before the apparition.) Medjugorje was the village at the foot of Cross Hill, at the southern edge of the plain. This eastern end, below Apparition Hill, was the village of Bijakovići.

The visionaries were all Bijakovičans, Franjo told me. The apparition had first occurred in Bijakovići. Bijakovicans had gone to jail. Medjugorjans had not. 'Then why is the name Medjugorje the famous one?' I asked.

Franjo scowled, not his usual scowl of shy discomfort, but one of resentment. 'Bad politics,' he said.

So much for 'mir'.

The family knew I was a writer, not a pilgrim. I had lived with them for four days before Lidija finally asked me, with a diffidence I appreciated after Žanić, what my 'nation' was. She meant my religion.

Protestant, I said.

'Ah.' She digested that for a little while.

Not for the first or last time, it occurred to me to feel fortunate that I was not Orthodox, Catholic or Muslim. Protestants were so rare in Yugoslavia that my being one aroused no suspicions of my harbouring secret sympathies for one of the ethnic groups. Protestants were a mystery, something vaguely heard of in connection with faraway countries where people and the climate were cold. I had been asked if Protestants believed in Jesus Christ. More than one village sage had nodded knowingly, 'Ah, a Protestant! Joseph Smith!'

'I think,' Lidija said delicately, 'that the only difference between Protestants and Catholics is that you don't believe in Our Lady.'

'If you mean the virgin birth of Jesus, most Protestants *do* believe in that,' I said. 'They just don't believe in the immaculate conception, or in Mary as a divine intercessor.'

'Mm.' Lidija's eyes trailed away.

Honesty compelled me to admit that I was not even a practising Protestant.

She was a kind person, and we had spent much time together, talking. She seemed to enjoy my company. I could not tell how much it bothered her that not only did I not believe in the central event and personage of her faith, I didn't much believe in God either. My impression was that she preferred to think that I was searching. I knew she prayed for me. I was not honest enough to tell her the whole truth – that not only was God not a part of my life, I did not even miss His absence. That would have opened too wide a gulf between us. I found myself, in fact, shrinking from acknowledging my areligion even to myself, as it would only have made me doubt the appropriateness, even the seemliness, of my writing about this village – or, by extension, about Yugoslavia's conflict.

*

244

The days were blazing hot, so the most pleasant hours were in the evenings, when the flush of light in the empty sky gathered itself, leaving behind deeper and deeper blue as it focused to the sharp white of a lunar crescent as thin as an eyelash. You could dimly make out the rest of the moon, a grainy wafer, as its sunless plains reflected back the light of the full Earth in their skies.

> Late, late yestre'en I saw the new moon
> Wi' the auld moon in her arm,
> And I fear, I fear, my dear master,
> That we will come to harm.

The Ostojić women would sit out on the terrace, while the children vaulted around them, and out of the darkness would materialize neighbouring women in faded housedresses, pregnant or with the thick bodies of recent pregnancies, come for conversation, to pass the time until their houses were cool enough to bear. Grapes hung over the concrete walk, and out near the street was a waist-deep pothole, disguised by a potted plant, into which I fell one night. Beyond were the red dirt paths, the truck-tyre ruts, the unfinished additions. Around the corner was the concrete cowshed, sadly empty. Lidija missed the milk, and could not abide the long-life product sold in the stores.

Mate and I would be the only men. Mate was shrunken and toothless. He shook. His mouth never closed, and his uvula seemed to hang so far forward I imagined it might fall out on me each time he put his face close to mine, making earnest, lipless noises. Even his family could rarely understand him. He was perpetually miming to me an offer of wine, tilting a twitching thumb into the insatiable gape of his mouth. He seemed to lie in wait for me in the main hall, and would draw me to the wine cellar, where he would fill a tall glass at one of the spigots. He would knock on my door and hand me a pitcher.

He had spent two years in jail after the war, Lidija told me. They had thought he was a different Mate Ostojić, an Ustasha who had killed several people. They put him against a wall three times, saying they would shoot him unless he admitted to being the man they were looking for. But I'm not! he said each time, and each time they did not shoot.

Lidija thought his bad health now was the result of ill-treatment then. 'He remembers those times, and it's not good for him,' she said.

Mate gaped out at the night, either oblivious to her words, or incapable of showing any expression in response to them. Then he turned towards me and showed me a blurred, blown-up photo, which he kept guardedly wrapped in cardboard in his shirt pocket. It was the cross on Cross Hill, with people massed hazily below it like flowers. A white splotch somewhat like a robed figure, thirty feet high, hovered in the air next to the cross.

'The photographer saw nothing when he took that picture,' Lidija said. 'But when it was developed . . .'

Mate tried, I thought, to smile. He wrapped up the photo lovingly and returned it to his pocket. I wondered idly if there really had been a second Mate Ostojić.

His wife, whose name I never learned, was a tireless, cheerful woman with a doughy sun-freckled face framed by close grey curls. I thought of her as Mama Ostojić. She taught the youngest child, and me, how to greet people properly. *Dobar dan*, or 'good-day', was a 'Partisan expression', she said with a grimace. Here in Bijakovići (and, who knew?, perhaps even over in Medjugorje), one said *Hvaljen Isus i Marija!* ('Thanks be to Jesus and Mary!'), to which one answered *Uvijek hvaljen!* ('Thanks for ever and ever!')

'Hvaljen Isus i Marija!' she bellowed at me.

'Uvijek hvaljen!' I hollered back.

She squashed me in a matriarchal hug.

She had nothing against Serbs as Serbs, she told me. But Serbs were Communists, and she hated Communists.

The mosquitoes abated. The moon went down. The stars glittered. The surrounding hills were black voids.

Breaking the silence, I asked the Ostojić women, 'Why do you think the Virgin chose this place?'

But they had nothing to say.

246

I suppose I would have known, if I had been devout, that any answer would have been presumptuous.

The house was cool enough for sleep. The women gathered the children into their laps and shushed them, and Mama Ostojić led her massed daughters and grandchildren through a score of Hail Marys, which pattered against the darkness as quick and light and seemingly as instinctive as cricket-song. Mate and I, the two lost souls, just listened.

46

One morning at eight I wound through fields where men were scything the grass to Vicka's house at the foot of Apparition Hill. A couple of hundred Irish and American pilgrims jammed the courtyard, while the seer's older and younger siblings, carrying toddling and infant nieces and nephews, came and went on the long balcony above, counting the crowd, and conferring through a door to a back room. At eight-fifteen Vicka appeared, a dark-haired woman with an appealing smile, looking tired and older than her twenty-six years. The pilgrims surged forward to be touched. She came half-way down the stairs, reaching out to cup her palms around the crowns of proffered heads.

She led the crowd in an Our Father, a Hail Mary, a Glory Be and a Queen of Heaven. Then she described her visions, while a gawky man, all bobbing Adam's apple, nose and full-moon ears, translated her words into English.

'Vicka wishes to tell you that Our Lady appears to the seers in a grey dress, with a white veil. She wears a crown of stars. She stands on a small cloud which hovers above the ground. The cloud never touches the ground. She has blue eyes and black hair.

'On all the major holidays, she dresses entirely in gold. At Christmas she brings along the baby Jesus. Once, on Good Friday two years ago, she came with the adult Jesus. He was bleeding, and crowned with thorns. This was to show how much Jesus suffers for us.

'Our Lady speaks to the seers like a normal person. She asks them how they are doing, and hugs them on their birthdays.

'Now Vicka will tell you about Our Lady's messages. There are five basic themes: prayer, conversion, penance, fasting and peace. Prayer has to come truly from the heart. Many people have said they have heard Our Lady's messages, but they have not. They have not taken them into their hearts. There is only a short time left in which to turn to God. Our Lady urges us to convert to God and to peace now, because soon it will be too late. Our penance must be sincere. To do penance properly, we must fast every Wednesday and Friday. Vicka fasts three times a week, and prays for six hours a day. Most importantly, Our Lady brings an urgent message of peace to this troubled world. We must reconcile our differences and turn to God and accept God into our hearts, and embrace peace.

'Now Vicka will describe heaven to you. It is a very big space. It has a different kind of light to the light we have here on Earth. People in heaven wear rose and yellow and grey robes. They spend all their time singing, and walking around praising God. Our Lady has shown this to us, saying, "See how happy the people are!"

'Purgatory is also a big space. There are no people visible, but there is a feeling of struggle. One can feel people all around, hitting each other.

'Hell is a big fire. People are going into the fire, and coming out as beasts, as if they had never been human. The farther people go down into the fire, the more they curse God.

'She is sorry, but Vicka has no time to answer questions today.'

The crowd surged forward again. A forest of hands reached up, straining towards the beam of Vicka's smile. She came down the stairs to touch more heads, and stood next to pilgrims for photographs, and signed autographs. She did this every day, and she did it patiently, kindly. I had read that she was planning to enter a convent when the apparitions ended. I had also read that

248

she had at various time spent months bedridden because of a mysterious 'spiritual' illness.

A paper printed in South Carolina that I had picked up in the church called Vicka 'the charmer of the group, although there is nothing "put-on" about her'.

Bishop Žanić's pamphlet said, 'Vicka Ivanković is the main "seer" from the beginning and through her the creator of Medjugorje, Reverend Tomislav Vlačić OFM, has launched the main portion of falsehoods regarding Medjugorje.'

It was Vicka who told Žanić that the Virgin had weighed in concerning a dispute between the bishop and two Franciscan chaplains who had refused to vacate a parish that had been handed over to diocesan clergy. The Virgin had said the Franciscans were right and the bishop was wrong.

Žanić had responded, outraged, 'The Mother of God would never speak to a bishop that way!'

Later, the two Franciscans were thrown out of their order for disobedience – the fact that one of them had fathered a child on his mistress, a nun, also came into it – but the Virgin kept defending them. As Vicka put it, 'The Pope can say what he wants, I'm telling it as it is!'

The crowd had thinned, and Vicka had disappeared. I walked to the strip for a cup of coffee and said to the waiter, 'Everywhere else in Yugoslavia menus have prices, but not here. Why is that? I'm just curious.'

He stared at me angrily. 'What do you want to eat?'

'I want a cup of coffee. But first I want to know what it costs.'

'Ten dinars.' He spat it contemptuously, as if only the most impoverished soul – perhaps a Slovene or a German – would ask the price of a cup of coffee before ordering it.

I wanted to ask, 'By the way, are you a Muslim? That's what the Catholics all say.' Instead, I meekly said, 'I'll have a cup of coffee.'

Later I spoke with two shopowners and found them both to be Medjugorjans (or perhaps Bijakovičans) born and bred. Franjo had two cousins who ran restaurants. The souvenir shops outside the centre were obviously owned and operated by the villagers living in the houses attached to them.

Where were these Muslims? I was willing to believe there were some – or at least, outsiders – since people in such a small community would certainly know a stranger when they saw one. But the distinction they tried to draw between themselves and the profiteers was obviously difficult to maintain.

I found it interesting that they bothered to make it. Franjo, as an Ostojić, didn't much like the fact that a Jerković had built a house on what was informally thought of as the Ostojić side of the road. As a Bijakovičan, he resented the crafty Medjugorjans who had stolen his village's thunder. But the idea of profiteering was apparently painful enough to make the two villages close ranks, in a community-wide exercise in denial. Perhaps it was the result of the doubly strong anti-capitalist teachings they had grown up with, directed at them by both the Catholic Church and the Communist Party.

But, of course, the Church had always enriched itself, and so had Party bosses. Now the Medjugorjans and Bijakovičans wanted to do it too. It was thoroughly understandable, and deeply embarrassing.

By noon the sun was punishing, and I retired beneath the awning of a pizzeria and met Vaughan, a big man with a square head. His fine tan hair stood straight up in a military flat-top. He looked lonely and lost.

He had married thirty years ago, and taken a job managing a fish factory in the Yukon territory. After a few years, he and his wife moved to British Columbia, where he started his own fishing-equipment business. The marriage was childless but, he thought, happy. He thought that to the day his wife ran away with a younger man. That was twelve years ago and, even now, he could not understand it. The same year, his business went bankrupt.

With nothing to live for at home, he took to the road. He got a class-I driving licence and a job with a trucking company. He had a special arrangement with his boss. He could refuse loads. He could take off days at a time when he wanted to. In return, he did the long hauls, the irregular ones to out-of-the-way places that

250

most truckers hated. He never clocked company time or expenses in between loads, because he was never away from home. Everything he owned was in his cab. In effect, he was seeing the US in a mobile home that could carry twenty tons of steel pipe. His boss knew he wanted to see all forty-eight states, and would call him saying, 'Vaughan, sounds like we got one for you. A load of ballbearings, Truth or Consequences, Arizona, to Caribou, Maine.'

Between loads, he wandered. Nothing fancy. He would get off in a town he had never been in and walk around. Just look at people. He managed to save money. He never slept in motels, only on the bed in the back of the cab. For years, the only showers he took were in truck stops. In Miami, waiting for a warehouse to open, he woke to the sounds of a scuffle and saw a man getting stabbed to death in front of his truck. The police made him stick around for a deposition, even though he pleaded that he had a load of number-five wire due in Tallahassee. He slept in his cab around the corner from the police station. He woke to the sounds of shouting and saw another man getting stabbed to death in front of his truck. This time, he told the police he hadn't seen a thing.

He saw all forty-eight. Then the trucking industry went belly-up and the company he worked for went out of business. He got a job doing a regular run for the largest egg company in the United States (they had the McDonald's account), hauling feed to the hens.

Then he heard about Medjugorje. He was a Lutheran, and hadn't spent more than five minutes in his life thinking about the Virgin Mary. But he missed the wandering, and had sometimes thought he might like to go to Europe but never knew what he would do if he got there, and this sounded intriguing, so he signed on with a group tour and took some time off.

They had come last year, during the Christmas season. Vaughan had liked the people in his group, but felt out of place. They were all Catholics. They all saw the sun dance. The group went on an excursion to Brother Jozo's village, where they held a service. Vaughan wasn't sure he liked Jozo. The man seemed too dramatic. The group was crowded in the chapel, and Jozo was moving among them, touching people on the forehead with his index finger. The people were falling like ninepins, slain in the spirit.

This was too much for Vaughan. It was hysterical. With all these people swooning around him, he decided his job should be to watch out for their handbags and knapsacks, to make sure everything got back on to the bus. So he moved among the bodies, collecting their things. 'I'll just be by the door,' he kept assuring people, 'keeping track of the luggage.'

He turned towards the door, but the press of the crowd was too thick. So he turned another way, trying to work his way around. But every time he turned again towards the door, the crowd blocked his way, and he found himself edged, with every detour he tried, farther away from it. He turned again, and suddenly found himself face to face with Jozo. The Franciscan put his hand on his head.

'All right,' Vaughan thought, 'I'll just put up with it.' Then he looked into Jozo's eyes, and fell backward.

It felt like floating. He was aware of hands around him, lowering him. He lay on the floor, amid a great pile of luggage, and was happy. An extraordinary feeling of peace and security lingered with him for days afterwards.

On Christmas Eve, he and fifteen other people saw the Virgin Mary. It was one o'clock in the afternoon, and they were standing on the plaza between the confessionals and the church, and they saw her on the slope of Cross Hill, about a thousand yards off. She was two storeys tall. She was standing with her arms down and slightly out, and was undulating them slowly, as if to gather something into her robes, as if to say, 'Come.' One of the witnesses video-taped it, and Vaughan had a photo made from the tape, which he showed to me. On the distant, dark, grainy hill I saw once again the blurred shape, like a blue-white flame, a teardrop, vaguely robed.

Back at his job in the US hauling feed to hens, Vaughan thought of nothing but getting back to Medjugorje. But he needed $1,440 for the plane tickets, and he didn't have it. He dithered. Finally,

252

he decided he had to return. He would sell everything he had, and borrow money from friends. He asked his company for a leave of absence. When it was denied him, he resigned. The vice-president of the company summoned him to his office and said, 'Are you serious?' They talked for an hour. At the end, the vice-president said, 'When you come back from your pilgrimage, don't go to your boss. Come see me.'

Two days later, a cheque for $1,640 came in the mail. It was a reimbursement for overpayment of taxes, from several years before, discovered only now that the state was computerizing its system. Vaughan called the airline to buy the tickets, and was told the price had just gone up, to $1,640.

And here he was. He had come with a group again, but the group had left four days ago. The house he was living in was empty except for himself and his host family. He knew no Serbo-Croatian except *dobro* ('good') and his host knew no English except 'My friend!' Nothing dramatic had happened on this visit. He climbed the hills and attended services. He went to cafés at night with his host, where they tried to communicate in sign language. He had no idea what he was waiting for. He had no idea how long he would have to wait. He felt like She wanted him to be here, but She wasn't making it easy.

His smile seemed intended to say, 'Don't worry! I'm OK!' But it was ghastly in its lack of conviction.

In the afternoon I climbed Cross Hill. Cloud-masses in the distance scudded like Portuguese men-of-war, trailing their thready curtains of rain. The path, angling up through prickly bushes and low aromatic trees, was treacherous with strange smooth stones that resembled bovine skulls, all sinuous knobs and curves and sharp-edged eyesockets, easy to slip on or trip over, and waiting to cut you when you fell. Makeshift crosses by the wayside had been secured with stone cairns on which so many candles had been lit through the years that they were coated in a lava flow of sagging caramel gobs. Photographs of loved ones, or of the sick who couldn't come, or of unbelieving friends to be prayed for, were stuck in the stones, and glued in the wax, and storms had blown them across the path and into the bushes, where they snagged and fluttered. Bronze reliefs depicting the stations of the cross had been spaced out along the hike so that you knew how much farther you had to go. Elderly pilgrims who had not climbed more than a flight of stairs in forty years tackled Cross Hill in the oppressive heat. As Christ fell beneath His cross, they sweated and fainted. They sat limply beneath the crucifixion, pale and athirst.

At the top stood the thirty-foot-high concrete cross, which was visible from any point in the valley. It had been erected in 1933, for the 1,900th anniversary of the crucifixion. On the pedestal, scorched and greasy from bonfires of candles, was written, FROM EVERY EVIL DELIVER US, JESUS! One of the miracles of Medjugorje was that the cross sometimes disappeared. Another was that it occasionally glowed at night.

On the way down I met John, a big Irishman with jet-black hair and a nose that had been broken at least once. He was staggering, sweating heavily through his brightly patterned polyester shirt. 'This one was a real hard one,' he gasped to me. 'They usually get easier.' He climbed the hill every day. He was not about to let the difficulty this time discourage him, far from it. He would climb it again tomorrow, at six in the morning.

He lived in London, where he ran a branch of an organization called Aquarius, which ministered to alcoholics and drug addicts. 'Drugs is their life,' he said. 'You take it away, you have to put something in its place. That something is God.'

About Medjugorje, he was pugnacious. 'I get really upset when people talk against Our Lady here.' He must have noticed that I wore no cross. He rounded on me. 'What do you think?'

'I'm not Catholic,' I said.

He pounced. 'I didn't ask that, did I?'

I spoke carefully. 'I haven't heard any call yet.'

He turned back down the path, smirking. 'Well, I'm thinking. You come here for a chapter in your rotten book – you *think*. But you stay for five days, eh? I'm thinking Our Lady is saying to herself, "We'll let him go on for a while the way he's going, thinking he's independent. Then we'll get him." Perhaps next year you'll be living here, in a hermit's hut out in one of the fields.'

254

We reached the valley floor. 'All these houses are Muslim,' John said, sweeping his arm towards the new pensions.

'I thought only the stores were,' I said.

'Nah! All of it! This whole bloody hideous town is built out of stinking Muslim money.'

I imagined I heard in the hatred in his voice a working-class Londoner's resentment of oil-rich Arabs cruising Mayfair in their Rolls-Royces. He slowly wagged his head, and his voice began to lumber. 'These Muslims are greedy people. Very, very greedy. If I go into a shop with a twenty-dollar note, they won't want to give me change. Why don't I buy this, or this? I don't take kindly to that. It cost me a spot of money to get here from England.

'And they'll try to bribe you. I bring in groups, you see. I was invited into one of these houses. They were all smiles, they were. Come in, come in, sit down, put your feet up! Then out comes the food. Incredible spread. Soup, heaps of vegetables, three kinds of meat on a plate, baskets of fresh bread. Wine going in your glass as soon as it's half empty. Then, as if that's not enough, they heap on the ice cream. I ate till I couldn't move! Then it comes. Why don't I bring a group to stay in their house? I says, "You're trying to bribe me, you are! And if you give me a meal like this tomorrow, maybe I'll think about it." No, I didn't say that. But I could have.'

'Many of them are in pretty tough shape right now,' I said, 'with so few pilgrims coming.'

'I'm sure they are,' John said, without a trace of sympathy.

We parted by the big tents behind the church. 'There's a prayer meeting here tonight at ten,' John said. He smirked again. 'But I guess you wouldn't be interested in that now would you?'

Back at the Ostojićs', the unfinished wing stood quiet. They had run out of money.

47

The Hercegovinians were a hard, desert people, with hard, clear affections. The difference between right and wrong, between the true god and the false, was as transparent to them as the night sky, or the dry light soaking the stony wastes. Nothing grew in Hercegovina but children, and so children were made to fill the void. There was an old saying: 'Hercegovina could fill the world and still not be emptied.' Hercegovina would fill the whole world twice as fast, except that so many Hercegovinians were priests and monks.

The commanders of half of the twenty-two concentration camps of Croatia had been priests or monks.

Did I know about Prebilovci? Behija had asked.

I did not.

Until August 1941, it had been a Serb village of a thousand people fifteen miles south of Mostar. You could not find Prebilovci on any map today.

Pero, a souvenir-shop owner in Medjugorje, told me, 'The Serbs say there were two thousand in the pit. It's not possible. It was a small village. Maybe two hundred.'

At one of the tourist offices along the strip, I asked about the pit, and got an earful of history. This man's particular twist on the religious question was that he called the Orthodox, of all people, 'Protestants'. Medjugorjans had heard, he said, that the Protestants of Prebilovci had built a chute running from their village down to the Bregava River. This allowed them to hang Croats conveniently in the village square and slide them down the chute. 'Like a factory, an industry.' The Medjugorjans, terrified of these Chetniks – 'They had beards,' he said, 'like you' – were only responding.

And where was it? I asked.

'On the road to Šurmanci,' he said. 'Just ask the locals, they'll tell you.'

I walked out in the yellow afternoon along the dirt road. The big pensions fell behind. I passed a few old stone houses, a garden, an orchard. I rounded the shoulder of a hill. Beyond was only the powdered rust of the rutted road, the stale green of the shrubs' leathery leaves, the twisted trunks of the dwarf oaks. No birds sang. The only sounds were the whisper of blood in my ears, the trudge of my boots, the occasional rustle of a fleeing viper.

I had hiked into nowhere many times in my life. But this time a strange thing happened. I began to feel anxious.

Yesterday, a driver had been stopped at gunpoint near Trebinje and beaten. Another driver had been shot and killed at Split. Serbs had poured gasoline over a foreign journalist in the Krajina and had threatened him with matches for an hour before letting him go. So many people had warned me not to walk in the country on my own. To believe their tales was to be infected by their hatred. But at some point I did have to start listening, as more and more people died. The question was, when?

I found myself thinking, as I had never done before, how far I was from help. I found myself wondering whether I had told the Ostojićs, or anyone else, where I was going. (I had not, because I had been embarrassed to bring up the subject of the pit.)

The Chetniks had beards, like me.

A car approached from behind, and rumbled slowly past. The driver, it seemed to me, stared, startled, perhaps suspicious. He seemed to gape at the canteen sticking part-way out of my knapsack — the black plastic canteen that, now that I looked at it, could perhaps be mistaken for a pistol. Would he tell the villagers ahead that an armed Chetnik was heading their way?

Absurd. Yet I could not tamp down the adrenaline rush.

The road had dipped for a while, and now climbed again, to a mild rise, from the crest of which I could see far ahead. The pit was supposed to be somewhere on the right, at the foot of the range of hills, and marked so as to be visible from the road. I saw nothing. It was farther than I had thought.

In the distance, a black gnome tottered among its horned

familiars. I drew closer and saw it was an ancient woman, triangular in her flaring black skirt, out with her goats. She was hardly taller than my waist.

'Hvaljen Isus i Marija!' she piped.

'Uvijek hvaljen!' I practically shouted.

Just ask the locals, the man in the tourist office had said. But I wondered how to put it: 'Excuse me, could you point me towards the place where you people murdered a lot of Serbs in 1941?' Finally I choked out a question about the pit. But the woman seemed not to understand me. Perhaps she was somewhat deaf.

'Ask at the house!' she squawked.

The house was ahead, part of an isolated farm. A horse wearing a cowbell was eating thistles. Somewhere a pig squealed. A man stood high on a haystack, trampling the hay around the central pole. Below, his boy ran towards the stranger.

'Don't!' the man shouted.

Why? Was he afraid for his boy? Had the man in the car spread the word?

The boy ignored his father and came up to me. He saluted. I asked about the pit. He pointed and I saw, about a mile off, the stone marker. The boy ran back to his father and the other workers, yelling excitedly, 'He asked about the pit!'

I almost called after him, 'Shh!'

I walked on.

Now they knew the Chetnik was coming to see the pit. A deliberate provocation? And what did he mean to do with that gun?

A road branched to the right, and I followed it. I passed through another homestead, where large black dogs barked. The marker loomed. It was a limestone pillar some fifty feet high. The path leading to it, up the slope, was identical to the track winding up Cross Hill, a belt of brown stones between bushes, worn smooth by pilgrims' feet.

On either side, the grey, untouched rocks had been carved into arrowheads by the rain, which formed a weak acid on contact with the calcium carbonate. Down from each stone's pinprick top slanted smooth gouges, rain-gutters the width of a finger, separated by serrations as sharp as knife blades. Upon reaching the ground, the water, as often as not, simply disappeared into it, to the despair of farmers, through channels worn in the subsoil rock. All of Bosnia-Hercegovina was one vast limestone honeycomb, into which the rivers plunged and resurfaced miles away. The only way to discover which rivers were connected was by dyeing them.

The pit at the top of the path had simply been one of the larger channels, an old river tunnel. I came to the lip, at the foot of the pillar, and stared down into a bowl about twenty feet across, fifteen feet deep. The bottom looked like packed dirt, but it was a slab of concrete. I threw a rock and listened to the hollow clop. Before the concrete was there, if you happened to slip on this narrow lip, you bounced down the short steep slope and disappeared into an abyss. You fell four hundred feet. Goats had done this now and then.

Nations have their murderous specialities, influenced by their landscapes. In forested America we lynched. In urban Bohemia people were thrown from high windows. In the flat farmlands of Poland, where the groundwater was so easily tainted, the Germans had no choice but to cremate the Jews. Bosnia-Hercegovina was a mass-murderer's dream come true, a mighty necropolis of empty mass graves, high and dry, waiting to be filled.

On 4 August 1941, Ustasha forces attacked the Serb village of Prebilovci, and in the ensuing battle most of the male inhabitants were killed or carried off. The Ustashas rounded up three hundred children below the age of fifteen and two hundred mothers and unmarried women and told them they would be shipped to Serbia. Believing this, the women put on their best clothes and gathered whatever valuables they had for the trip. But after a night spent locked in the village school, they were instead sent in trucks to the town of Čapljina, where they were crammed into six railway stock cars and transported to the station at Šurmanci. There they were met by Ustashas from Čapljina, Šurmanci, Medjugorje and Bijakovići, who confiscated their valuables and marched them into the hills.

At some of the pits of Hercegovina, the victims' throats were cut at the rims. Grenades were thrown in afterwards on the heaving mass of bodies, or huge stones were rolled down. None of that was necessary at this pit, with its fine four-hundred-foot drop. The women and children were simply struck on the head, one after another, and toppled down the slope, where they were swallowed by black silence.

The tourist office man's tale of a chute in Prebilovci leading down to the black water – 'a factory, an industry' – had surely been a poetic transposition.

The bodies rotted. The bones lay in the depths until 1961, when the government, in a precise display of its schizophrenic attitude to the war, simultaneously raised a memorial to the dead and sealed the pit with concrete. The memorial proclaimed the hideousness of Fascism (and implicitly the glory of the Communist victory), while the concrete glossed over the unhappy fact that the Fascists had been Yugoslavs, their victims other Yugoslavs. While the simple pillar boasted that 'we' beat 'them', the dark cave darkly asked, Who are 'we' and who are 'they'?

As soon as the Serbs felt they could answer that question openly, they opened the pits. Last year, they had excavated twelve in Hercegovina, including this one. I could see in the concrete floor the two-by-three-foot rectangle that had been cut, through which the spelunkers had descended on ropes, to load bones into baskets by the light of their headlamps. Tents had been set up, and the dirty bones mounted on large white sheets. Afterwards, the hole was resealed, and in the new cover was embedded a black marble Orthodox cross.

Accompanied by Serbian television teams, a procession of pick-up trucks transported the bones, in hundreds of small caskets draped with the Serbian coat of arms, back the way they had come, from Šurmanci to Čapljina, and across the Neretva to the old site of Prebilovci, where a few roofless stone cottages remained. They passed under railroad trestles painted with the word, COME AGAIN! GOD AND THE CROATS! and HDZ – GOD – HDZ. TUDJMAN, YOUR SONS LOVE YOU! and, everywhere, banners splattered with the obscene šahovnica. The Serbs left a Serbian flag and a black flag on the pillar, and both, within days, were riddled with bullets.

Other than the concrete lid, the black Orthodox cross and the limestone pillar with its plaque about Fascists that someone had obscured with a shotgun blast, there was nothing for me to see but the picturesque view of the golden light slanting across the miles of scrub, the scattered red-roofed cottages, a toy-like white Catholic chapel. The sun was dropping, and I headed back.

Utter silence. Now I was afraid. I could not control it. Wild thoughts kept springing up. The Serbs had come to get their bones, and the Croats had sneered at them, and now Serbs were killing Croats, and here was this lone Serb, with his Chetnik beard and his semi-automatic, sneaking around God and the Croats' country, for the Devil knew what reason. The black dogs at the first farm howled, but no person showed himself. Were they peering at me from behind the shutters? At the next farm, they would have had time to prepare.

I came around a corner and a man stood there with a shotgun. He raised it.

'Don't!' I shouted. 'I'm an Ameri – '

Boom!

I could not stop imagining that.

I had been infected. I had a stomach ache. It became so severe, it doubled me over. I had to lie in the dirt until it subsided. At the second farm, the men were still adding to their towering haystack.

'Did you find whatever you were looking for?' the tiny old goatherd asked.

'Yes, I did.'

'*Hvala Bogu!*' she sang reedily. 'Thank God!'

I had to lie in the dirt twice more before I rounded the hill and saw Bijakovići. The sun was a fat, ripe peach sitting on the plain of Medjugorje.

Near the Ostojić house, wild honking and bellowing boomed out of a garden. It sounded like an amplified buzzhorn over which a bull that had been badly taught to speak was roaring. I would have recognized the sound anywhere. It was a Yugoslav epic song. The buzz was the traditional one-string gusle.

The famous epics were all Serbian. But in this song I could make out, brayed through the general cacaphony, the words, 'Tudjma-a-a-n is Preside-e-e-nt of Croatia-a-a-a!' Three men in the garden waved to me to join them. A cassette player sat on their table and spewed out the song.

The three men were drunk. The one who spoke to me was decrepit, though not yet middle-aged. His teeth were rotting, and his half-naked body smelled as if it were rotting too. His hair was falling out. He gripped a bottle and a cigarette, and me.

'Croatian music!' he shouted in my face.

'I thought the gusle was Serbian,' I said.

'No! No!' He shook his head extravagantly, swinging the bottle as well. His cigarette drooped wetly between his fingers. 'Croatian! It was never Serbian!'

The other men stared at me opaquely.

'*Tudjma-a-a-n is Preside-e-ent of Croatia-a-a-a!!*'

The gusle was a bee the size of a bus.

'Drink!' he yelled at me. 'Drink to Croatia!'

'My stomach hurts.'

'Anh! It's good for you!' He jammed the bottle into my face. 'I am a Croat!' he said, collapsing against me, scrabbling at my shirt-front. The wet cigarette fell.

'*Tudjma-a-a-n je Predsjedni-i-ik Hrvatske-e-e!!*'

'There!' The man flailed towards the house next door. 'A Communist lives there! And there! And there! All the houses around are Communists. This is what we'll do to Communists.' He made an oddly gentle motion, depicting a knife – or was it an icepick? – slipping neatly between ribs.

I mimicked the gesture, to see if I had seen it right, and he grabbed my hand and kissed it wetly. I had a vision of the last brown stumps of his teeth sticking to my hand.

He is one of the one-to-five per cent, I thought. The one-to-five per cent of any population, any nation, that I and Vlado on the train had agreed caused all the problems. The one-to-five per cent that became Ustasha, or Chetnik, or Partisan, not because they were afraid, or confused, or idealistic, or manipulated, but because they wanted to hurt people. They had always wanted to

262

hurt people, and until the war came they had had to content themselves with hurting animals. War was their dream come true. I did not identify with the one-to-five per cent of Americans, but Miroslav felt implicated by his one-to-five per cent, as did all Yugoslavs, which was why the one-to-five per cent was dragging all the rest down with it. In a Serb's eyes this man shrieking 'I am a Croat!' was nothing so simple as scum. He was 'Croat scum'. And from there it was a short and terribly easy conceptual step to 'Croat (scum)'.

'I have to go, my stomach hurts,' I said. I was near doubling over again.

He seemed finally to hear me. 'Your stomach?'

'Yes.'

Still holding my hand, with an expression on his face that seemed to suggest a desire to help, he pinched me as hard as he could between my thumb and forefinger.

I drew back my hand.

'No,' he coaxed, like a doctor with bitter medicine. He took my hand again. He leaned forward to gaze avidly into my face as he pinched me again, digging his nails so deeply into the muscle that my fingers tingled and sprang open. He was damaging a nerve.

'That hurts,' I said, reclaiming my hand.

'But of course,' he said.

'Tudjma-a-an is Preside-e-ent of Croatia-a-a!'

I escaped back to the road and staggered the last hundred yards to the Ostojić house, clutching my stomach. As I groped my way down the dark hallway towards my room, Mate appeared out of nowhere and thrust at me a glass of wine, tipping a jiggling thumb into the toothless gape of his mouth.

48

On my last night in Medjugorje, I climbed Apparition Hill. Ivan
was still out of town, so the Virgin was not appearing.

I had been in Medjugorje briefly the year before, and had
climbed here with a horde of thousands on a Thursday night. The
seers had played guitars and the crowd had sung songs like
'Kumbaya' while candles melted together and the stars burned
above, the village lights below.

At ten-thirty, the singing had stopped. The seers knelt and
prayed, and then fell silent. The forest of crosses twitched in the
firelight. Sparks flew upward. Wax sizzled. After ten minutes, the
seers announced that Mary had appeared, hovering over the
crowd. They said she had blessed all present. A happy sigh passed
through the multitude.

As people clambered down over the rocks, they shared flash-
lights and visions. Had anyone else seen the lightning strike the
biggest cross? How about the blue flames running up and down
it?

The singalong and subsequent had reminded me of summer
camp, when the crosses had been totem poles, and it wasn't God
in the moving shadows but the escaped convict with a hook for a
hand. Surely the world always seemed numinous when you sat
next to a fire under the stars. Later summers, too, in my
adolescence, I had stared into the flames and longed for a woman
who never came. Someone's loving, my Lord, and painfully close.
Couples were off in the darkness, kissing.

Tonight, on the quiet, black mountain, I thought of Vicka's
image of the Virgin and of heaven – the puffy clouds, the pretty
robes, the singing. A child's vision, surely. But that did not
necessarily discredit it. The lesson of Pentecost was that God
spoke to you in terms you could understand. The seers' Virgin,

after all, had black hair and blue eyes. Obviously, a Hercegovinian.

In other words – as this non-believer understood it anyway – these visions, even if you did believe, were to be taken as metaphors. The Church sanctioned black Madonnas and blonde Madonnas, and presumably did not ask of the faithful that they believe they would spend eternity literally on a cotton cloud hauling around a golden harp.

Many of the American and Irish pilgrims took the metaphor further. They came thousands of miles to hear the Word of God, and when the Virgin told them to fast on bread and water on Wednesdays and Fridays, they hosannaed and hallelujahed and spent Wednesdays and Fridays whooping it up at the pizzeria. Mark went without chocolate for the day, and perhaps the sun-boiled Irish priest who always seemed to be at the table next to mine drank only half a litre instead of his usual litre of wine.

But how far could you go with this? If the Virgin was really neither black nor blonde, were you allowed to believe she was not a woman at all, nor a personification, but the principle of forgiveness? Would you still be a good Christian, let alone a good Catholic? Many of the Protestants here would have said yes, and some of the Catholics would have agreed, but I rather doubted the Roman Catholic Church would have backed them up.

The Church's problem was that many Catholics had taken post-Vatican II ecumenism too seriously. The seer Ivanka had reported in an early interview, 'The Madonna said that religions are separated on the Earth, but the people of all religions are accepted by Her son.' Several Medjugorjans had echoed that sentiment to me in the past few days. Meanwhile, Bishop Žanić went through the roof.

The old honest talk of crusades and conversions, and entire races burning in hell, was embarrassing, but at least it was logical. Ecumenism was warm and fuzzy and, at heart, rested on fuzzy thinking. If Muslims could ignore the Pope and still go to heaven, why on earth did Catholics have to listen to him? Of *course* Muslims could not go to heaven. Truth was Truth. The difference from the old days was that the Vatican no longer explicitly consigned Muslims and Jews and the Orthodox to the flames, but let them find their way there on their own.

The ecumenism of Our Lady of Medjugorje went considerably deeper than that, but, I suspected, not as deep as Žanić feared. Ivanka's statement on the matter was a clear expression of an attitude I had perceived in the words of other Medjugorjans. 'The people of all religions are accepted by Her son.' In other words, all people worshipped the same god, but that god *was* the Roman Catholic god. Peoples of other religions simply did not realize it. Fortunately for them, God was merciful, and forgave them. (But wasn't this like the Serbs, who squashed their neighbours to their breasts and loudly announced their tolerance in forgiving them for not being Serbs?) Perhaps this was one reason why, despite proud claims to the contrary, I had met no Orthodox or Muslims in Medjugorje. But I had been impressed by the numbers of Protestants who had come sceptically, and had their lives changed.

I walked down the mountain, sharing my flashlight with a special-needs teacher from Texas. At the bottom we ran into one of Vicka's many cousins, a coltish, high-voiced lad who helped run his family's souvenir shop. He presented an image of almost comic desperation, as he flung his hands about and sputtered to us in shards of English: 'Trouble! Always! Shop! I don't! Me! Price! I know price! He doesn't know price!'

'Speak in Croatian,' I urged.

But in Croatian he was just as puzzling. 'I die every day!'

'Excuse me?'

'I try to die every day!'

Suicide attempts? But no. Apparently his family was working on a new house, and the work was hard, and he hated it, and he was tired, and no one was coming to his shop. I headed down the road.

As for myself, I liked it here, and had stayed longer than I had intended. But for the wrong reasons.

Unless John was right. Perhaps the Virgin was stringing me along with interesting human material until the moment when she would strip away my bogus observer role, my arrogant little-

266

god writer's viewpoint, and get me. I did not think so. But since I was agnostic, I believed you could never be sure.

I had written out ten traveller's cheques that day, for a thousand dollars, to pay for the Ostojić house to be finished in time for the Italian pilgrims. I had lent the money only because I was sure I would get it back. With the expanded house completed, the family would easily be able to earn what they owed me over the summer, and Lidija had agreed to bring it to me in September in Dubrovnik. The loan was an utterly painless gesture. (I would certainly not have done it if I had known the war was about to spread, leaving the Ostojićs unable to pay me back.) It had even crossed my mind that the Ostojićs, out of gratitude, would probably not charge me for the days I had stayed with them. This hardly seemed like the working of God's grace.

But Lidija had prayed to the Virgin for help, and she had prayed to the Virgin for my soul, and perhaps, in her view, the Virgin had wittily conflated the two, leaving my soul untouched but making me her agent of salvation. Why not? Why should the agent have to believe? I was playing the role of Vaughan's tax cheque, or the godless bureaucrats behind it. I had heard that sort of solipsistic miracle story many times, in which every comment overheard, every fall of a leaf or drip of a drop, was a message directed specially at the protagonist. It felt strange suddenly to be part of one such story, and not as the protagonist, but as one of the props. It was like finding myself in someone else's dream.

Through the darkness came voices. On my right was a rectangle of light – an open door. The voices were shouting. I stopped to listen. Two men. I could not see them. I saw only the silhouette of a concrete kitchen, a wash of brilliant white walls within. The voices rose and fell, in charge and counter-charge. Politics, money, a family quarrel? No. They were arguing over the nature of God.

Behind me, in the distance, a line of lights snaked up Apparition Hill. Peasants with torches storming heaven.

49

I took the bus to Lištica. It used to be called Široki Brijeg (Broad
Hill) after the Franciscan monastery on the bluff over the town,
but the Communists renamed it after the river running through
it. Now the townspeople were changing it back, but they couldn't
agree on whether it should become Široki Brijeg again (Ijekavian
– literary, historical) or Široki Brig (Ikavian – dialectical, 'pure').
Debate raged in the local paper.

The townspeople's proud nickname for Lištica was 'Little
America', because of the number of private enterprises it had
boasted even during the Communist years. In the past year, the
number had exploded. The easiest businesses to start up when
you had little capital, uncertain supply lines and no distribution
network were cafés, billiard rooms and hair salons. Lištica's one
long street was a line of nothing but. The commune, with a
population of barely twenty-five thousand, and most of those
farmers, had 120 cafés. Naturally, most of the ones I saw were
empty. All four of the cooperatively owned factories (shoes,
metalwork) were well-managed and hi-tech by Yugoslav standards, but all four were going bankrupt anyway. Seventy-five per
cent of their workforce had been laid off. Little America was in a
big depression.

I rented a room from Nikola, who had started his own
restaurant fifteen years ago, with his mother as head chef. At one
time, he had employed six waiters, but now could barely afford
one. He survived by smuggling.

'Trieste? Istanbul?' I asked.

He sneered. That was small-time stuff, for the little guys. The
real money was in currency deals and weapons. 'But I don't do
weapons,' he assured me. (Everyone bought them, but nobody
sold them.) He diagrammed the currency scam on a piece of
paper. Something about the fact that the black-market rate was

268

around 30 dinars to the dollar while the bank rate was 23, and interest on loans was 140 per cent, but if you did that and the other thing, and moved this over here . . . He circled a final figure of 50,000 dinars. 'Pure profit,' he said.

He knew of Croatians who had emigrated to America ten years ago with nothing but a passport in their pockets, who now owned hotels and restaurants, and were millionaires. How?

'I think credit is easier in the United States,' I said vaguely.

'Yes, we don't have real banks here,' he said. 'If I borrow a hundred thousand dollars from the bank and don't pay it back, they take away my house!'

'Actually, I think a bank would do the same thing in America,' I said.

'If I lived in America,' Nikola said, 'I think I would own three hotels by now.'

One of the eternally returning conversations of Yugoslavia followed. How much did an apartment in America cost? A kilo of meat? Bread? What did a waiter earn? Nikola wrote it all down, calculating how long it would take him to buy his first hotel.

At the monastery on the hill, I met Brother Jozo Pejić, fifty years old, a square-jawed man with a shy smile. He told me about Muslims in the area who were really Catholic because they crossed themselves in the privacy of their homes, and Orthodox near Jajce who were really Catholic but had left the Church out of confusion when it changed from the Julian to the Gregorian calendar. He told me that there were never more than two thousand Bogomils in all Bosnia, and all those 'Bogomil' tombstones were really Catholic, and the Muslims cooked up the story of their Bogomil heritage to obcure the fact that they, also, were all really Catholic.

He led me on a tour. The large, handsome neo-Renaissance church had only three mosaics inside. 'You see how poor we are,' he said.

It had all been restored since 1945, when the Partisans had set up cannons on the plaza and spent a lazy afternoon blowing holes through the west wall.

Outside, we descended into a depression in the grass, where a stone outcrop had been hollowed out for building material. Here in 1945 the Partisans had taken the twelve Franciscans of Široki Brijeg, aged twenty to eighty, shot them one by one, and burned them all in a pile. Brother Jozo had first crawled into the cave in 1971, risking imprisonment. All he had found were the charred remains of sandals, and skulls with small holes in the back and large ones in the front.

50

The bus climbed to the next valley, and the next, higher and higher, past Tomislavgrad. The town of Kupres was nothing more than an idled factory and grey housing blocks for its employees, farmers who had fled the tyranny of weather for something even more capricious.

The bus climbed higher, into the clouds. The driver was playing Croatian nationalist pop songs. He had taped šahovnicas to his sunguards and stuck a Croatian flag into the dashboard. I wondered how the Serbs on the bus felt.

In the cold treeless highlands, I glimpsed an army-surplus tent through the thick fog. Gypsies. What were they doing up here? Then I saw a jeep. This really was the Army. Serbian Gypsies, caravanning, headed who knew where.

'Croatia, my motherrr! Croatia, my hearrrt!'

The fog lifted for a moment. Tanks crouched all over the hills like a congress of frogs.

We topped a pass and were suddenly in the real Bosnia, of pine and beech forests as thick as stockades, and mountainsides like escarpments slanting down into seemingly bottomless moats. The driver rammed the lever into second, and the bus lurched. We began the slow grind down.

I got off at Jajce.

*

Tito's Yugoslavia had been born in Jajce. The fortress on the high rock overlooking the Pliva River where it plunged a hundred feet into the Vrbas had always been hard for invaders to conquer and harder to hold, because for forty miles in every direction there was nothing but narrow wooded gorges which, even by Bosnia's standards, presented tremendous difficulties to the movement and supply of armies. For sixty years Jajce was the last Christian hold-out against the Turks in Bosnia, and during one protracted siege the Pope promised absolution to anyone taking part in an expedition to rescue the city. When the Bosnian agas and begs revolted against the Infidel Sultan in 1851, they chose Jajce as their stronghold, and were crushed here by Omer Pasha. And here, too, the Bosnians made their last stand against the Austrians in 1878, when, after finally driving out the Turks, they found that their newly liberated land had been handed to Austria-Hungary at the Congress of Berlin.

Tanks and bombers did nothing to make the holding of such territory easier. The Germans occupied and lost Jajce several times during World War II. The town's most glorious period, from the Communists' point of view, lasted from August 1943 to January 1944, when it was the seat of the Partisans' Supreme Headquarters. Tito lived and worked in a handsome old Bosnian house directly beneath the fortress. Behind the house, steps led down into catacombs which had been carved out of the bedrock in the fifteenth century by a Bosnian duke who had been one of the twenty-four Knights of the Order of the Dragon and needed a skull-and-bones sort of place to perform his secret rites. Here, Tito could retire into the late-Gothic gloom whenever a German bombardment necessitated it. While he was waiting, he could sit on a stone throne, and perhaps wonder if the duke had been not only a secret Dragon but a secret Bogomil, as the carvings on his underground altar seemed to suggest.

On a day after one of these bombardments, 29 November 1943, the Partisans convened in Jajce the Second Session of the Anti-Fascist Council for the National Liberation of Yugoslavia (AVNOJ). Some of the delegates had walked over three hundred miles through enemy-held territory in order to attend. At the historic session, the Partisan leadership declared itself to be the country's legitimate government (thus supplanting the royalist government-in-exile), forbade the return after the war of King Petar II, drew up plans for a new Yugoslavia as a federation of six republics, introduced the title of Marshal of Yugoslavia, duly bestowed the title on Tito, and formed a commission to investigate war crimes committed by the Germans and their collaborators.

At the time – three guerilla armies and some twenty German divisions were fighting on Yugoslav soil, and the Partisans, as yet unrecognized by any foreign power save the Soviet Union, controlled only a minuscule and constantly shifting territory – this assumption of the mantle of governmental legitimacy took a fair amount of chutzpah. But Tito's self-confidence and vanity were equal to the task. Amid the rigours of running a resistance movement, he never seemed to lack the time to have his portrait sketched or his bust sculpted, or to pose for a photograph in his natty tunic, looking off into the future. (He often held a pair of binoculars, which, one imagined, enabled him to see decades farther.)

I visited the hall, preserved now as a museum, in which the second session of AVNOJ had taken place. Wooden chairs and benches faced a podium and a stage. A dusty canteen and an olive-green field coat draped over a chair represented the rough-and-ready audience. Slogans on the walls, in regulation red sans-serif letters, said, DEATH TO FASCISM, FREEDOM TO THE PEOPLE; LONG LIVE COMRADE TITO; LONG LIVE COMRADE STALIN. Perhaps needless to say, I was the only visitor. In the guest book by the door, the signatures and the ditties dedicated to Tito filled fifty pages for 1989, but only ten pages for 1990. For the first half of 1991 all of four signatures preceded mine.

I walked up to the muscular fortress at the top of the hill. A young girl showed me a collapsed tunnel through which, she said, the last king of Bosnia, Stjepan Tomašević, had escaped the besieging Turks and fled to Ključ. She showed me the spot outside the gate where the King, after having surrendered at Ključ with a promise of safe passage and a reward, was flayed alive and decapitated. Lower on the hill, I admired an Italianate campanile rising from the skeleton of a Franciscan monastery that was said to have once contained the bones of St Luke. (Queen Helen of Bosnia prudently took the bones with her when she fled the Turks, and sold them to the Venetian Republic to finance her retirement.) The rest of the old town, with its whitewashed houses under towering roofs of wooden tile or sheet metal, and the gardens of roses cascading down the abrupt slope, was quite picturesque.

It was also poisoned. Clouds billowed day and night out of a nearby ferrosilicon factory which squatted in its own blackened pit like a dragon brooding noisomely on its sterile hoard. The locals told me it produced with five furnaces what a western factory could produce more cheaply with one. It was therefore losing vast amounts of money, but could not afford to close because it employed 2,500 people. In the afternoons the gases rode up and out of the valley on sun-warmed air currents, but every night they fanned out in a creeping, clinging ground fog that smothered the town. You woke to a white chlorine haze which seemed to stick in your nostrils like gum.

I stood on the knoll above the factory one day, marvelling at the fires roaring up from the factory floor like the main thrusters of a rocket until, after a few minutes, a guard with a gun on his hip approached me and demanded to know why I was taking photographs. (Ferrosilicon is used in making steel, which means tanks.)

'I wasn't taking photographs.'

'I saw you.'

I showed him the contents of my knapsack. A semi-automatic pistol disguised as a canteen, yes, but no camera. Five more minutes and I would have had a camcorder and a sound-man.

Jajce had unusually high rates of respiratory diseases and cancer. It also had a high suicide rate, which some people blamed on nerve disorders. Tito had visited often, because of the town's glowing role in Partisan history. Swaths of mature oaks and beeches on the mountain slope above the town had been razed in order to spell TITO in three-hundred-foot-high letters. The fur-

273

naces were always shut down three days before he arrived, and kept off for the duration of his stay. Now that he was dead, the furnaces never stopped, and TITO was getting lost in bushes and saplings.

After enquiring at the offices of the Islamic Union, I attended another Friday džuma, in Jajce's main mosque, a fine, domed, eighteenth-century structure of white and green stucco, made somewhat gaudy by strings of electric lights braceleting the minaret. On the porch afterwards, Ismet introduced himself to me. He was in his fifties, a small tidy man with a short curved beak of a nose set in a flattish face of sallow skin. Over his carefully combed white hair he wore the yarmulka-like cap of white loose-knit cotton that I had seen on other Muslim men. When he found out I was a travel writer, he decided to take me under his wing and teach me everything I needed to know.

'This is called a *čulah*,' he said, indicating the cap on his head. He pointed to my notebook. 'Write it down.'

He and I and a young friend of his, a dervish named Esad, sat down for coffee in the starkly Bauhaus House of Culture. Ismet talked about what he called 'the hard discipline of Islam' – the Ramadan fast, the requirements of ritual purity. If you so much as dreamed about sex you were polluted, and had to wash before entering a mosque. He reminisced about the *feredža* and the *jašmak*, the body covering and veil that Muslim women had worn before 1946. As he drew his hand over his nose and mouth to simulate the veil, his eyes shone happily above. I noticed the stiff profile of a woman at the next table. She was listening.

'Do you think Bosnia should or could go back to the feredža and the jašmak?' I asked.

Ismet answered without hesitation. 'No. That's history.'

'Do some Muslims want it?'

'That attitude would be rare.'

Esad agreed.

'I have yet to see any women at a džuma,' I commented. 'They *are* allowed to attend, aren't they?'

'Of course!' Ismet said.

'They can, but they can't,' Esad shrugged.

274

'Meaning?'

'Of course, they're allowed. But on Fridays the mosque always fills up with men first.'

'So women, in practice, never attend the džuma?'

'Right.'

'Do they mind this?'

His eyebrows went up. 'Why should they mind?'

The next morning was the first day of Kurban Bajram, Islam's three-day 'Festival of Sacrifice', and I found myself sitting on the grassy slope behind Ismet's house drinking juice made from wild-rose petals. We were an all-male assembly: Ismet and his son Irfan, his son-in-law Fuad, the young dervish Esad, and Ibrahim, an elderly neighbour.

The day before had been the ninth day of Dhu al-Hijja, the Islamic month in which the hadž takes place. Over a million and a half Muslims – of whom 1,200 this year were Bosnian Muslims and Albanians from Yugoslavia – had performed the heart of the hadž, standing from noon until sundown on the plain of Arafat a few miles from Mecca, meditating and praising God. Today, the *hadži* were sacrificing tens of thousands of sheep, goats, cows and camels, in commemoration of Abraham's sacrifice of the ram in place of his son. (In the Muslim account, the son in question is Ishmael, founder of the Arab nation. In the Biblical account, the son is Isaac, progenitor of the Jews.) Muslims throughout the world were joining in the celebration by sacrificing animals of their own.

In Yugoslavia the *kurban*, or sacrifice, was usually a ram. According to religious law, it had to be at least two years old, and completely healthy, with no blemishes, not lame, and with fine, abundant wool. The wool was given to the mosque.

Ismet's family was well enough off to have bought two rams this year. I had arrived just after the killing of the first, which lay headless on the grass, blood dripping from the neck into a hole in the ground. The flayed skull grinned from a bucket. With a thin sharp blade, Irfan was slicing and peeling the skin back from the hind legs. He and Fuad gruntingly lifted the woolly mass to hooks hanging from the limb of a walnut tree. Something inside the body burst and a flood of green and brown bile spilled out of the neck, pooling viscously on the ground. Irfan forced the hooks between the bones of the hind feet, but one of the legs broke from the weight, and with an irritated scowl he tried to hook the limb lower down, looking for purchase, while the muscles tore and the leg slipped through his bloody fingers.

'Fuad paid six thousand dinars for this,' he said after he had succeeded, and was pulling the skin off in sheets like contact paper. He was a fat man in a white shirt, Rorschach-blotted with blood. 'He was robbed. It's worth, maybe, four thousand dinars.'

'I didn't have time to shop around!' Fuad said to me defensively. 'Haggle, pinch pennies! I'm a busy man!'

'It's not even a good sheep,' Irfan went on mercilessly. He slapped the mauve flesh. 'Thirty-five kilos, not counting wool and guts.' He threw the wool, in one piece, a shaggy slipcover, in the direction of the house. 'The second one is super, you'll see! Fifty kilos! And healthier than this one. I paid four thousand five hundred dinars for it.'

'I bought it in a village!' Fuad appealed to me. The villages were considered the best places to go for meat and produce. 'It was a good-looking sheep! I was in a hurry!'

Irfan cut off the testicles and sliced the corpse open to the sternum. The guts slid out in a purple noodly mass, which Irfan nudged with his foot into the hole near the base of the tree.

'This tree has never produced many walnuts,' Ismet said. 'But for the next two or three years it will be very fecund.'

Irfan hefted the grey bag of stomach. The tripe would be used in soup, he said. The heart would be filleted and roasted. The lungs and liver would be boiled, then cut into small pieces and roasted, and mixed with rice.

'Is Irfan a professional butcher?' I asked Fuad.

'No, he's a gourmand,' Fuad mocked. 'If you eat as much as he does, you have to buy the whole animal, to save money.'

The testicles were as large as silicon breast implants. Irfan sliced each one in half and held the soft white fillets, misted with blood, under my nose for me to admire. 'These will be fried in butter,' he said, smacking his thick lips.

'*Forza!*' Ismet said, with a gesture indicating the sexual prowess thus conferred.

Ibrahim cackled.

'Brian!' Irfan leered, gesturing to the old man. 'Guess how old he is!'

This was a conversational staple in Yugoslavia, where old men liked to show you how they could still crack nuts under their thumbs, or bend iron bars. I never enjoyed it. Once or twice I had guessed too high, hurting feelings. Ibrahim was toothless and fleshless. He looked in his eighties. He waited happily for my guess.

'Sixty-eight,' I said, absurdly.

Everyone was delighted. The hale old man!

'I'm eighty-four!' Ibrahim chirped.

'Wow!' I said.

'And still working!'

'In his garden every day,' Irfan said. 'He's amazing. Tell, us, Ibrahim: can you still fuck?'

'No!'

Irfan was taken aback. 'You can't?'

'No I can't!' Ibrahim repeated cheerfully.

'But you could last year, couldn't you?'

'Yep!'

'Brian! Can you believe it? He's eighty-five years old – '

'I'm eighty-four!' Ibrahim sqeaked.

' – and last year he could still – ' Irfan put his two fists out at waist level and pulled inward. 'Imagine that! Eighty-five years!'

'I'm eighty-four!'

The five men presented an interesting study in generational change. Ibrahim was dressed in the closest thing you saw nowadays to traditional garb – dark woollen trousers and a woollen waistcoat over a white linen shirt. He wore the black beret that was common among older Muslims. He had lived his life as a peasant. He had been born into an extended household that consisted of a *starešina*, or head man, his sons, their wives and their children, holding land in common, and all subject to the starešina's absolute authority. He was the only man here who had fought in the war, but had nothing to say about it, because he was too old, and there was no use remembering. He was a Muslim through and through, and always would be, because when he was growing up, that was all that defined you, but he had seen what religion could do, and had lived through the anti-religious Stalinist years. He had grown up accustomed to the veil, and had seen it go, and he had seen the Shari'a go. He and other Muslims of his age had given up the turban and wore berets. In the 60s, when he was middle-aged, only the old Muslims still wore turbans.

Now you virtually never saw a turban. It was the beret wearers who hobbled along the streets on their thin, bowed legs. Being a peasant, Ibrahim had no pension, and being a peasant, he would work until he died, in his 'garden', which was almost a farm, almost sufficient to his slight needs. His greatest problem was that the extended households of his youth and middle age had broken up, gone out of style, just when he needed them. He could once have expected to spend his final years in one of his sons' households, helping in the small tasks and spending the cold evenings closest to the stove in the communal kitchen. But now he lived alone. A daughter checked in on him now and then. She would probably be the person to find his body, one day.

Ismet had been ten years old when the war ended, and twenty when Yugoslavia moved away from its own brand of Stalinism. His adult life had been spent during a time of gradually increasing accommodation with national and religious feeling, and for much of it, village traditions had remained intact. Paved roads did not arrive until he was thirty; television when he was thirty-five. So he, too, was a Muslim, but without the silences, the trauma. He and his friends did not wear berets, because only old men wore berets. They sat together on the porches of the mosques in their čulahs and fezes, and talked about when they might be able to afford to make the hadž. Ismet had been saving money for over a decade and *inšalah* ('if God wills'), he would go next year, and

278

when he came back he would be able to proudly wear the golden fez of the hadži. He and his friends were not peasants, but small shopowners, teachers or civil servants in minor positions for which their religiosity did not disqualify them. Their wives did not cover their faces because it was illegal, and did not cover their hair because it was old-fashioned. The men were better educated, so they knew the Koran better. Ismet knew old peasants who could do no more than repeat the first *shahada*, or testimony ('*La illaha illa Allah*,' 'There is no god but God'), over and over again during their prayers, whereas he knew the Al-Fatiha, and the Basmala, and several of the shorter *suras*. He not only knew the festival rituals, he knew where they came from. His Muslimness was as sincere as Ibrahim's, but it was more self-conscious. Ismet would not call me by my real name. He said it was a Muslim custom to give Arabic names to guests, and he dubbed me Hašim, explaining that it was one of the noblest names in Islam. 'With that name,' he assured me, 'you are a lucky man.'

Fuad and Irfan were both in their thirties. They had grown up during a time when the traditional culture was melting under the fierce glare of television, when Yugoslavs were rich enough to hop into little Yugos and putter off to Paris for a week, or Prague for a laugh. The crypto-capitalism of Tito's Third Way accomplished what Stalinism never had: neither Fuad nor Irfan were religious.

Irfan punched the clock at a cooperatively owned factory outside Jajce. He did not need to be presentable, and he wasn't. He was extravagantly, joyfully slobby. He valued Kurban Bajram for the food and, in a recent development, for the days off. Tomorrow he was going to Neum, Bosnia's one town on the Adriatic coast, for some sun and Dalmatian seafood. His wife and two boys were already there.

His other passion was the house of concrete slabs and breeze-block he was building ten feet away from the old family house. In the old house, Irfan and his family lived downstairs, while Ismet and his wife lived upstairs. In the new house, the arrangement would be reversed, but other than that I could see little difference between the two. Irfan had shown me the cathedral ceiling of

279

wooden slats, the linoleum in the kitchen-to-be. *Fino*, eh? Super! How much would this cost in America?

His brother-in-law Fuad was an entrepreneur. He was tanned, and wore gold rings. He had a smoothly rounded, slightly pudgy build and a small-eared head of very short sleek sandy hair, all of which made him look like a seal. I had spent the night before as his guest in the café he owned, which was currently the most popular in town among the young, trendy crowd. A well-known band had played, and bouncers had vetted pleaders at the door, and gangsterish waiters had piled a lavish spread on Fuad's and my table. The floor below was a billiard room, and the one above a video-game arcade and bar, although Fuad was thinking of converting it into a whorehouse, since most of the prostitutes of Bosnia had to ply their trade by hitchhiking. (One of the best whores worked the route between Jajce and Zagreb, Ismet tipped me.) Shouting over the music, Fuad explained how he *really* made money. Again, it was through smuggling, and again, I did not understand how it worked.

'This is just a front,' he said of his three-storey establishment.

'Pretty nice front,' I said.

'Sure. But one bomb, and no more front.'

Holding up his glass of whisky that night, he explained in three words why he was not a believer. 'I am young!' For his generation, the identification of religion with the elderly was unquestioned.

But that only betrayed the fact that Fuad was not all that young any more. Esad had been only nine years old when Tito died. During his adolescence, the economy crumbled. Jobs disappeared. When he was sixteen, Milošević rode to power by exploiting Serbs' fears of the Muslim Albanians.

Esad and his friends talked about Islam. Their parents' lives were not only empty, they were imploding. Esad taught himself Turkish and Arabic. He read the Koran, and Sufi commentary, and Sufi poems. He became a dervish. He managed to find a job as an inventory clerk at a clothing factory. The job meant nothing to him, which, in his view, was as it should have been. He kept a mat in the corner of the warehouse where he observed his prayers during work hours, and tried to get to the mosque each Friday by telling his boss he had an errand in town. Sometimes it worked, sometimes not. It didn't matter. A mosque was wherever you prayed.

I had gone the previous afternoon with Esad to his house, a small old wooden structure in the traditional style. In places the floor yielded alarmingly beneath the rugs. The walls wavered and bulged. 'Muslims did not believe in building a house to last,' Esad said. 'When the owner died, the house was supposed to decay.' Instead, the owner had died, and Esad had bought it on the cheap, in mid-collapse.

His wife kept her hair covered, and stayed in the kitchen. But she was not shy. Now and then she contributed to our conversation by yelling through the wall. Things like, 'There is no problem with Islam! Only with those who don't understand it!'

Another dervish arrived, a friend of Esad's. Never having met dervishes before, I had had an exotic image of them: wild whirlers in robes, fezzed and barefoot, or something approaching street performers, who rubbed their bare arms with broken glass and stuck skewers through their cheeks. But a few minutes' conversation dissolves most exotic masks, to reveal the rather ordinary people behind them. Esad and his friend Emin thought that perhaps the dervishes in Macedonia stuck things through their cheeks. But no one did that here. Esad thought that sort of thing was unseemly. A circus act. 'Dervish' simply meant a mendicant, he explained, and in that sense, all Muslims were properly dervishes.

He and Emin met twice a week with other dervishes – most of them young like themselves – for a group prayer called a *zikr*. Some of them wore green fezes and green waistcoats, others wore their everyday clothes. In the zikr of the particular sect to which Bosnia's dervishes belonged (there were twelve), a leader chose certain phrases such as *Allahu akbar* ('God is great') or *La illaha illa Allah*, which were rhythmically chanted by the group for several minutes. Ideally, this chanting concentrated the mind, inducing a trance-like state, which allowed a more complete communion with Allah.

I said I would be interested in seeing a zikr, but Esad thought it a bad idea.

'You would see only the externals,' he told me. 'We would look like Indians to you, with feathers on our heads. It would be theatre.'

We walked to the mosque in which the dervishes held their zikr, in a small room of floor cushions and coffee paraphernalia adjoining the main sanctuary. Esad tapped out a rhythm on a *talamba* – a sheepskin stretched over a large wooden hoop – and began to sing one of the dervish songs. But he broke off, perhaps suspecting I would not understand this either.

'You see, we hit the drums, shouting, "Al-*lah*, Al-*lah*, Al-*lah*." You would think that was weird, crazy. But we are calling on the soul to wake. How would you wake me?'

'I would shake you.'

'No, you would call my name.'

'So you're waking Allah?'

Esad and Emin scowled. That was an ugly thought, a blasphemy. 'No, you're waking the soul,' Esad said.

He and Emin, like the Medjugorjans, said that all believers were one, and meant it about as much as they did. All believers were one, but the non-Muslim believers had created divisions. 'Muslims accept Christ, but Christians don't accept Muhammad,' Esad complained.

'You only accept Christ as a prophet,' I said. 'Not as the son of God.'

Esad informed me that Christians read the wrong books about Christ. The Gospels were all written many years after the fact. The account of Christ's life that Muslims read was contemporary, and in it no mention was made of him being the son of God. It always amazed Esad how little Christians knew about their own religion. Did I know, for example, how many New Testaments there were?

'I've always thought one,' I said.

'There!' Esad said. 'There's four! Matthew, Mark, Luke and John! Do you know why Christians colour eggs at Easter?'

'A vestige of spring fertility rites?'

'No! Mary proved she was a virgin by inserting an egg in her vagina, and showing that it came out coloured. Do you know why Christians light Christmas trees?'

'A winter-solstice festival of lights? To mark the fact that the days are lengthening again?'

'No! European pagans worshipped a little god, something inside the dolls they carried around. This god was so weak, in the winter they were afraid it would freeze, so they burned an oak tree to keep it warm. Christianity has preserved all this. Blood sacrifice, local gods disguised as saints. It's really a pagan religion. Who do you think discovered America?'

'The Indians?'

'No.'

'Lief Erikson?'

'No.'

'I give up.'

'You think Columbus discovered America.'

'OK.'

'But you didn't know that Columbus's navigator was a Muslim.'

'That's true, I didn't.'

'The Muslims always knew America was there. They just didn't care about it. You Christians think Muslims are dirty.'

'We do?'

'But we wash five times a day! Look at Louis XIV! He never took a bath in his life!'

'I'd heard he took one, on doctor's orders.'

'Or Queen Isabella. In Spain there was a colour called Isabella Yellow. It was the colour of her shirt. She had worn it without washing it for decades.'

Emin's scorn for Christianity was more purely doctrinal. Making his points, he drilled his index finger into the floor. 'God is three, and at the same time he is one? How can anyone believe such an absurdity? And all these people you have to bow to, the Pope and his cardinals and bishops and priests. Yes, your Excellency! Your Majesty! Your Holiness! What is that? You stand before God, no one else. And the way Christians pray!' He

283

put his palms together and waggled them above his head like a plea for help from drowning. 'What kind of way is *that* to pray? Muslims go down to the floor. That's good exercise, five times a day! Healthy body, healthy soul!'

Other things I learned: the Bogomils had been Muslims *before* the Turks came. That explained all the crescent moons on their tombstones. Christianity was a philosophy; Islam, a way of life. When a Christian went to a garden, he picked the flowers. A Muslim smelled the flowers, but left them where they were.

'So Muslims don't pick flowers,' I concluded doubtfully.

'It's an *analogy*!' Esad said, despairing.

As we parted, Emin said to me, '*Salam alejkum!*'

'*Alejkum as-salam*,' I said.

'That's an Arabic greeting.'

'I know.'

'It means "Peace be with you." '

'I know.'

'And you answer, "Alejkum as-salam." '

'I already did.'

'So let's try it. Salam alejkum! And now you say –'

We said it together: 'Alejkum as-salam.'

He clapped me on the shoulder. 'Very good! You learn fast!'

Irfan had finished cutting up the first ram. Ismet and Fuad went to the stone shed and dragged the second out by his handsome curved horns. He dug his feet in. 'He knows something,' Fuad grinned, tugging and struggling. 'Animals have an instinct.'

Ismet and Esad were chanting Allahu akbar. Fuad manoeuvred the ram beneath the walnut tree. He grasped his legs and pulled them up so that the ram fell on his side. He and Ismet rocked him until his head was over the second hole. Fuad held him down with his chest and Ismet gently stroked his throat.

Suddenly, the ram grew still. He stared quietly up at Ismet. Allahu akbar. Ismet felt along the neck, through the thick springy wool. He produced a knife. '*Bismillahi al-rahman al-rahim*,' he said, cutting with quick strokes through the jugular and windpipe. In the name of God, the beneficent, the merciful. The ram reared, frantic, for a moment, to rise. Thick scarlet blood pumped out of

284

the inch-wide vein, half a cup with every beat. The ram's eyes rolled, glistening white. He began to run. On his side, held down by Fuad, he was running for his life. His life drained into the hole. His tongue came out between his teeth. He blew red bubbles from his throat. His running faltered. His tongue lolled further into the grass. His eyes died. Irfan cut off his head.

The headless body lay still for a minute. Then it gave a slow, luxurious stretch, like a cat waking.

Ismet showed me the knife. 'Muslims love to kill,' he said. 'Especially with the knife. The Croats and the Slovenes are scared to death of us.'

'But not the Serbs,' Fuad smiled.

'In the last war, the Drina was filled with the bodies of Muslims,' Esad said. 'They floated down the Drina to the Sava, and then floated down the Sava and clogged the bridges of Belgrade, and the Serbs thought they were Serbs, and told the world they were Serbs, killed by Croats. But they were Muslims, killed by Serbs.'

Irfan brandished his own bloody knife and grinned, 'Milošević!' He mimed hanging the Serbian leader, headless, from a walnut tree. Two birds with one stone: no war, and better walnuts.

51

I stayed in Jajce for four more days.

I attended the funeral of Ismet's cousin. Men in black berets stood in the courtyard of the mosque with their hands by their ears, intoning Allahu akbar. They wiped their faces to symbolize the putting-away of earthly thoughts. They pronounced the *taslim* ('peace') on each other, looking right and left. The dead woman lay on a bier on the porch, under a green cloth. Her bier was lifted and passed from shoulder to shoulder, as though it were rolling over the men, who let go of it behind and ran to the front to take it again, until it was deposited in an old Mercedes hearse, which began the slow drive to the cemetery, the hodža walking in front with a ceremonial swing to his long grey coat. The widower came behind, with large, sad eyes, accepting condolences with tears and deep sighs. The woman's brother, thin and dark, was less decorous. He sobbed uncontrollably. His snot fell to the ground. The female mourners, farther back, were Christian friends of the deceased. The only funeral a Muslim woman was allowed to attend was her own.

At the cemetery three men stood in the grave and accepted the bier. Below the green cloth, she was wrapped in grey. She was laid against one wall of the pit, on her right side, her head pointing towards Mecca. Rough boards were placed diagonally over her as the grey fabric was unwound, so that her white shroud would not be seen. The husband and brother each threw three handfuls of dirt, and then the men crowded forward to shovel the rest in. Even the Christian women had gone by now, and the men sat for prayers, the hodža cantillating in a fine voice, followed by the husband in an uncertain one. All ended in unison with a long drawn out Allaaaahu akbar and a shouted *Amin!* The woman had died at sixty-six, and as I wandered in the cemetery I noticed many other markers for people in their fifties and sixties. Respiratory illnesses?

The next day thousands of Croats from the surrounding region gathered for the Festival of St John, at a church dedicated to the saint four miles downriver. The building was miraculous. During Turkish times the local Muslims had planned to turn it into a stable, and so, one night, the building flew to the opposite side of the Vrbas River, where it now stood. Behind the church was a statue of St John, and the masses of devout pressed forward to touch the saint, after which, like no Christians I had seen elsewhere, they wiped their faces. In the field below, šahovnica banners were flying. Racks of spits roasted a dozen whole lambs at a time.

Gypsies worked the crowd. A pretty girl in a wheelchair seemed to be missing one leg below the knee. It was tied back so tightly I wondered if the scam would eventually lame her for real. A woman crawled on her hands and bottom, one leg straight out in front of her and the other crossed over it at a sharp angle that required no more than a limber knee. If she had really got around that way, she would have had some protection for her backside, like the leather pads worn by the undeniably legless young man who was not begging, but gamely circling the church seven times on his stumps. Other Gypsies' deformities were explicit and horrible. Had the woman who was missing most of her face lost it in a fire, or from the attentions of a bear?

By tomorrow they would all be gone. Film-makers had their circuit of festivals, Gypsies had theirs.

HDZ literature blanketed the tables. One brochure was entitled 'Islamization as Cultural Enrichment'. Ah yes, the flower of the Croat nation! By the east door of the church I had paused to contemplate a fresco depicting Christ blessing two Franciscans under a ribbon banner reading *Blessed are the meek, for they shall inherit the earth*, and I had thought of Benjamin's humble smile, and the knife under the table. I could imagine the Franciscans, those dervish-like mendicants, in Ljubuški and Široki Brijeg looking around at their estates, their handsome churches, their treasuries, and smiling meekly and saying, 'You see?'

My last morning in Jajce was 26 June. The fog from the factory was especially bad. I walked to the bus station through a milky, nauseous haze. I bought a copy of *Vreme*. On the cover was a photograph of Jajce, printed upside-down: YUGOSLAVIA, 1943–1991.

The previous evening, Slovenia and Croatia had both seceded. After a long illness, Yugoslavia, aged forty-eight, was dead.

52

In a pizzeria on the hill above Travnik, I knew the waiter was Serb when he said, 'Americans don't understand Yugoslavia.'

Outside the sun shone on the thirty mosques of the former Ottoman capital of Bosnia. During the last war, a Franciscan monk with a cross in one hand and a revolver in the other had led a crowd on a massacre of the Serbs of Travnik. Afterwards, the superfluous Orthodox church had been turned into a shop.

The sun also shone on the birthplace of Ivo Andrić, the Nobel Prize winner who had been born a Catholic in a house of Muslim style, but came to identify himself with the Serbs for their suffering, and who advocated that all the (Muslim) Albanians of Kosovo be deported so that the Serbs could reclaim the land.

On the radio, the Catholic Slovenes were taking over the customs posts.

The Croats were not. The Croats were not even calling what they had done 'secession'. They were calling it 'dissociation', and assuring all and sundry that this was different from secession, although they could not explain in precisely what way. The fact was, the Croatian Parliament had dithered and squawked and strutted while the Slovenes had methodically laid the legal groundwork for secession, and when it finally dawned on the Croats that the Slovenes really *were* going to secede, and imminently, they were faced with the horrifying prospect of being left alone with the Serbs, and the Parliament had stayed up all night and passed a flurry of vague and panic-stricken resolutions, and when dawn came Croatia was 'dissociated'.

In the pedestrian zone, in the broiling sun, an entrepreneur had gathered five plastic toy cars and was offering children rides for 10 dinars. Another sold medicinal herbs from the hood of his car. There were no children, no herb buyers. The street was empty.

The radio reported wild celebrations in the streets of Slovenian cities.

A Muslim shopkeeper told me, 'There will not be war.' He did not add 'inšalah' – 'if God wills' – which was practically a blasphemous omission for a Muslim speaking about the future. The Croat woman in the tourist office also told me there would not be war. She did not add '*ako Bog da*' – 'if God wills' – which the Christians of Bosnia also usually said when speaking of the future, having picked up the habit from the Muslims. Perhaps the thought of war was too frightening to acknowledge that perhaps God *would* will it.

The next day came reports of war.

I climbed the lower slopes of Mount Vlašić. Bluebells nodded in the grass, and papery magenta blooms I did not recognize, and my feet crushed lemon thyme. Men were scything the grass on the steep slopes and tossing it down with home-made ash forks. A wiry seventy-year-old strapped together bundles of grass as large as himself, so that his head and torso disappeared when he shouldered them. A walking haystack, he descended to his cottage, where his wife was yelling at her grandchildren and a puppy wiggled.

It was 28 June – St Vitus' Day, or Vidovdan, the day on which the Serbs had lost to the Turks on the field of Kosovo, the day on which Gavrilo Princip had shot Franz Ferdinand, the day on which the Serbs had rammed through their vindictive centralist constitution for the first Yugoslavia, and the day on which the Soviets had thrown Yugoslavia out of the Cominform. This was the land of the eternal return, and Vidovdans never passed without relevant incident. Austria had chosen today to announce that, alone of all the western nations, it was considering recognizing Croatia and Slovenia. Of course this did not surprise the Serbs. Austria was plotting to become an empire again. The Serbs, in their guise as the Yugoslav Air Force, responded by violating Austrian airspace.

By the next day, the newspapers had become alarming. Tanks had gone into Slovenia. The Ljubljana Airport had been bombed. Headlines spoke of 'chaos in Yugoslavia', and described Bosnia as 'a bag of gunpowder ready to explode'. There were queues at the telephone banks in the post office. I tried to call my wife, but no international calls were going through. 'It's because we're at war,' the woman behind the counter said. Then she added almost hysterically, 'Just kidding! No war! No war!'

I had been planning for some weeks to attend a Muslim religious festival on a mountainside that weekend, and I went ahead with it, wondering what I would find when I came back down. In Travnik, I had met Sulejman, a baker and a dervish, who was also going. He was a lovely man: gregarious, emotional and kind. He had been proudly showing me the flag he had sewn

289

to wave at the gathering on the mountain-top – it was the Arabic letter ب, gold on a green background; the sweeping line stood for all-encompassing Allah, the dot below for insignificant man – when the first news came through of fighting in Slovenia.

'We'll take you hostage!' he barkingly laughed, his green-gold eyes aflame with excitement and dread. 'Bush will have to send US troops to save you, and they'll end up saving us too!' I reflected on the harsh truth that not all men were equally insignificant. I was the American, Hašim. Lucky Man.

Early on Saturday morning, Suleiman and I drove through heavy rain to the nearby village of Karaula to watch the start of the festivities. The holiday, called Ajvatovica, was peculiar to Bosnia. It had been banned from 1945 until 1990 as a dangerous manifestation of Muslim national consciousness. Long, long ago in the time of the Turks, the village of Prusac, on the slopes above Donji Vakuf, had had no water. There was a spring several kilometres away, on the slopes above the village, but a huge outcrop of rock blocked the construction of an aqueduct. A pious Muslim named Ajvaz Dedo prayed for forty days and nights, and on the forty-first morning the rock split in two.

The forty-kilometre march of horses and flags along an abandoned railway bed from Karaula to Prusac symbolized the coming of Islam to Bosnia. Each of the two hundred men in the procession had brought his own horse and flag. The men wore fezes and Turkish waistcoats – 'theatre', Esad would have sniffed – and their horses were feisty, short-tempered forest ponies who reared, and stamped in the mud puddles, and ate the flowers out of each others' halters, and bit each other on the ass, starting fights that scattered the shrieking crowd. A hodža stood on the awning of a brand-new mosque with a megaphone and boomed, 'No alcohol! No shouting! No weapons! No shooting! Applause is *not* allowed! Applause is not Muslim! Instead, say Allahu akbar! God is great!'

After the horses started off, Sulejman and I drove back to Travnik. On the way, he showed me a box of the .22 bullets he would be firing off later and I said with dismay that I thought shooting wasn't allowed.

'Not in the village,' he explained. 'But up on the mountain, sure.'

'Aren't all those bullets in the air dangerous?' I squeaked.

'Nah! They fall like rain!'

We agreed to meet in Prusac that night. I took the bus to Donji Vakuf. The town was already crowded with Muslims from all over Bosnia. Prayers were running non-stop in the mosques. Men spilled into the streets outside the coffee shops and ćevapčići joints. It occurred to me that, just as the only things Yugoslavs were buying were food and weapons, the only reasons for which they would risk travel were smuggling and pilgrimages.

Finding the railroad bed, I walked several kilometres back towards Karaula, through fields and hamlets. The rain had stopped, and it was a fresh, bright day. When I paused to lean on a gate by a field of barley, a farmer came up the dirt path. His name was Srdjan, and after a couple of minutes' conversation he invited me in. He was a Serb, as were most of the farmers around Donji Vakuf. He and his two brothers owned and worked their two hectares jointly, as all Serb peasants used to, in the old days. The difference today was that you couldn't make a decent living doing it, so the brothers had also laboured for periods in Pakistan and Iran, and had worked in factories around Donji Vakuf. All three had recently been laid off, and their savings, which at least they had been too smart to put in a bank, were now running out.

Srdjan led me past a brother's house to his own. Inside, his wife Milica was boiling milk in a broad flat pan to make kajmak. I was gestured towards the guest's place, behind the kitchen table and as far from the door as possible, and served the ritual spoonful of fruit jelly called slatko. Then I was plied with šljivovica. Srdjan's young son Igor climbed into his lap. Milica began to stack in front of me enough food for about ten football players: a pastry of greens and cheese, kajmak, slabs of a mild white cheese, a pitcher of sour milk. This milk-sodden meal was typical of the Bosnian peasantry. The brothers' cow produced twenty-two litres a day, and the family consumed it all.

'I can't!' I said.

'You can!' they ordered.

While I started digging a trench through the mound, Srdjan showed me how he had to beat his wife, or else she wouldn't work. She was a big-boned, beautiful woman, with a strong face and clear grey eyes, and she held her own, punching him back. They hugged and laughed. We drank more šljivovica. One of the brothers came in. He and Srdjan commenced pinching and pummelling Igor. He was only two and a half, but he, too, stood up to them, shouting, 'Stop it!' with his hands on his hips. He was quite the little man after that, striding up and down the room, looking for his toy gun.

Milica saw an opening, and piled more food on my plate.

'I can't!'

'But you haven't eaten anything!'

'I absolutely cannot! Not possible!'

Srdjan poured more šljivovica. People here were good, he said, everyone got along. Only the politicians . . .

And the Krajina? I asked.

He waved that away. Serbs defending themselves. A triviality.

And Slovenia?

Politics! he roared.

It was beneath his attention. What counted was his cow, and the kajmak on the stove, and his hard-working wife who gave as good as she got, and the šljivovica, from plums which were better in Donji Vakuf than anywhere else.

And Bosnia?

'What is "Bosnia"?' he said. 'Bosnia is nothing without Yugoslavia.'

'And do we have Yugoslavia?'

'Things will get better,' he insisted.

I heard horses. Igor leaped about in excitement. 'Is your camera ready?' Srdjan asked. I had told him I was a travel writer, and he thought I was putting together a picture book. We ran up the path. The horses and flags were winding along the hillside. The hodžas, with their megaphones, were intoning, 'Allaaahu akbar,' and the riders were shouting, 'Amin!' Srdjan and Milica leaned on the gate, and the riders, knowing somehow that they were Serbs, greeted them with a Partisan 'Dobar dan' instead of the

Arabic '*Merhaba*.' Srdjan and Milica nodded gravely as the green flag went by. What were they thinking? Their ancestors had been terrorized by that flag. But now there was Yugoslavia (wasn't there?), which surrounded Bosnia and with its Croat and Serb pillars held up the Bosnian roof. Srdjan and Milica had not themselves seen genocide, and it was just conceivable to them that the return of Islam, as long as it was anchored in a Yugoslav framework, could be picturesque rather than poisonous. Their son could dance and clap his hands, and a travel writer could take pictures of the handsome flags and costumes, and it might, on this bright day, worry them a little, but it did not yet enrage them.

I thanked them, and ran ahead of the horsemen down the path.

Back in Donji Vakuf, the streets were lined with thousands of Muslims. They showered the horsemen with roses, and handed up fruit drinks and squares of Turkish delight. The flags swirled, the riders shouted. Children holding out roses were lifted high. The riders beamed. Their arms spilled flowers. The crescents and stars on the horses' bridles shone in the rain-washed sunlight.

The procession continued out the other side of the town and headed into the hills towards Prusac. We passed more Serb farms, and the exchange was always the same: polite dobar dans from the riders, grave nods from the farmers. The Serbs handed up no flowers.

In Prusac, you could hardly move through the crowd. I nodded to the Gypsies I had seen begging at the Catholic festival a few days before. The cafés and ćevapčići stands and roast-lamb eateries were makeshift affairs, of folding chairs on the grass, under tarps. Some of the hand-lettered menus had no prices. Ten years from now would the Muslims here complain about the greedy Catholic merchants who didn't care about the image of the town?

I hiked with the thousands up the mountain to the split rock. In the field above, it seemed that every man had a pistol in his coat, which he pulled out and fired in an ejaculation of joy at having completed the climb. The bullets fell like rain. There would be speeches soon, and prayers, but when an old man, grinning blindly and still tottering from the ascent, fired six shots over my head I decided not to wait, and I walked back down.

That night I found Sulejman, decked out in his dervish waistcoat, and we ate roast lamb. Afterwards I finally saw a zikr; Esad had been right, it was like theatre to me. In their green vests and green fezes, the dervishes swayed forward and back, chanting in unison. They flopped their heads from side to side. I realized that it was theatre to most of the other Muslims as well. They crowded into the mosque to watch the show, like Americans gawking at a rodeo. At least now they knew not to applaud at the end.

As we also learned, zikrs go on for hours. I left long before the end. Outside, the mountain air was frigid. My knapsack was locked in Sulejman's car. I crossed to the mekteb, found a place on the floor among a tangle of denimed bodies and fell asleep.

Some time later, Sulejman shook me awake. He handed me my pack. He was laughing, his eyes bright from his brush with the godhead. 'Hey! Hostage!' he whispered. I must have smiled. I stuffed the pack under my head and fell back asleep. In the grey morning, Sulejman was gone.

Back in Travnik, the post office was in chaos. The newspapers said the war was widening. The United States government had ordered all Americans out of Croatia and Slovenia.

I came across a memorial to World War II victims in a tiny park, where a stone woman bent down with a bouquet. The inscription read:

> Yes, you hereafter, you know, it was not easy
> to defy a power which intended to crush us, but we did
>   not
> cry, we did not refuse the cup.
>
> With all of our beings we rang with the call to arms and
>   knew
> that we would die, but knew, too, that we would win.
>
> Here lies the grave. Stay, for a while,
> when the forest listens.

294

Take off your caps! Here rests the flower
of a people that knows how to die.

I decided to return to Sarajevo. Lucky Man. My landlady
shrieked as I went out of her door, 'There won't be a war!'

Part Five
Towards Kosovo

53

In Sarajevo, people were trying not to panic.

The Croatian paper *Vjesnik* predicted that the Slovenian war would lead immediately to a general Serb uprising in the Croatian and Bosnian Krajinas. Sarajevo TV chose this moment to broadcast images from the Holocaust. In over-lit black and white clips, naked bodies were being stacked, heaved on to trucks, dropped into ditches. Flattened and dried, they looked like cardboard.

I met with Miroslav during a thunderstorm, and we sat under an umbrella at a closed outdoor café in the pouring rain. Miroslav was frightened. All the non-Serb generals had been forced out of the Army, he said. This was what everyone knew would happen, as soon as real trouble began. Even the top general, Kadijević, had disappeared. He seemed to have been replaced by General Adžić. Was Kadijević dead? Miroslav would not have been surprised. Kadijević, with his Serb father and Croat mother, had at least believed in Yugoslavia, even if it meant Serboslavia. Adžić, on the other hand, was all Serb. When he was a boy during World War II he had returned home one day to find his entire family slaughtered by Ustashas.

The Dean of the Islamic Theological Faculty assured me, 'Whatever else happens, there will be no violence in Sarajevo. Serbs, Croats and Muslims live on every street. A Serb cannot blow up a Croat's house because he will kill the Serb neighbours.'

Someone had blown up the Ivo Andrić memorial in Višegrad. Muslims were fleeing the town, which was near the Serbian border, because of rumours of a Serb uprising. Serbs were also fleeing the town, because of rumours that Muslims in the Sandžak were planning an attack.

I found Benjamin. The general panic had reached the point where people were talking about which routes out of Sarajevo were safe. I had allowed the panic to infect me, and had decided to return to Belgrade. Benjamin called around for me, to find out if the trains were getting through. Turning to me, he said, 'Years ago, we would read about the terrible things going on in Lebanon. You know! "That's the Middle East," we would say, they are some kind of animals over there! Now we say, "Of course they're killing each other in the Krajina! That's the old Military Border, they're aggressive and primitive!" Maybe next week we'll be saying, "Oh that! That's *New* Sarajevo, you know what those people are like!" So what will we say when our neighbours in the next building are killing each other?'

The trains were getting through, and I got on the train.

The connection to Belgrade passed through the flat lands of eastern Croatia. In the stations, the šahovnicas had been taken down. Croatia was pulling in its head, in the hope that all the shit-kicking would happen in Slovenia. In the rich evening light, the fields of corn, wheat and sunflowers were as beautiful as ever. The high arms of wells were silhouetted against the sky. Shepherds drove their sheep down dirt lanes. Nothing could have looked more peaceful. As the train crossed into Serbia, I reproached myself for my cowardice. Why had I left Bosnia? Why had I listened to people, and not walked in this beautiful countryside?

The next morning I read that machine-gun fire had broken out along the rail line I had ridden, two hours after my train had passed.

54

In Belgrade, the news from Slovenia was startling. The Slovenes were winning.

'The only people who know what they are doing in this

madhouse are the Slovenes,' my Dalmatian friend Vanja said. He was angry at them. 'The Yugoslav Army was afraid of looking like the Russians, so it decided to go in as quietly as possible, with a very limited mission, just to secure the border stations and put the Yugoslav flag back up. So it sent in only tanks, with no air or ground cover, and with strict orders not to shoot.

'Now here's the diabolical part! The Slovene representative in the Federal Presidency was present when this decision was made, and he returned to Slovenia and told the Slovenian territorial defence commander that it would only be tanks, and the boys in the tanks had orders not to shoot. At that point, the Slovenes knew they *could not lose*. Tanks without back-up are sitting ducks! So they attacked the tanks. Easy! You fire a grenade, the tank blows up, the soldiers inside burn alive. It was in the Slovenes' interest to make the incident as violent as possible, because no matter what the death toll on either side might be, the world was bound to see it as the big bad army trying to crush brave little Slovenia.'

As it turned out, that was exactly how the world was seeing it, even though twelve times as many Yugoslav Army soldiers had been killed as Slovene militiamen (the numbers were forty-nine to four) and two thousand other Army soldiers – virtually all of them, in fact – had been captured.

The Serb generals had apparently thought that with the appearance of the first tank Slovene resistance would fold. They had been misled by their own stereotype of the Slovenes as pacifists and choirboys.

Now the Serbs of Belgrade were asking each other in hurt, bewildered voices, 'Who would have expected such savagery from the Slovenes?'

Belgrade TV broadcast footage from fifty years ago: Slovenes welcoming Hitler's army. Little children, doll-like in their Slovenian folk costumes, gave adorable Hitler salutes. Mirjana crowed with delight. She yelled at the Slovenian leaders on the screen: 'Ha! You're smiling now! Wait until you're part of Austria!'

In Republic Square, young men stood on the raised pedestal of the Prince Mihajlo statue and called for the formation of a

Serbian national guard. An open session followed in which ordinary citizens had the chance to transform themselves into demagogues. A woman screamed out her hate in the hoarse crescendoes she had learned from television. At the tables of the outdoor café where I sat, bearded young men as muscular as Olympic champions invited themselves into conversations with any foreigner they saw, and talked like Jehovah's Witnesses. 'Do you understand Serbia?'

Brother, are you saved?

Šešelj had just been elected to the Serbian Parliament, and he spent his opening speech pointing at political rivals, calling them traitors and pronouncing death sentences on them.

Croatia had installed a new, more fanatical defence minister, Šime Djodan, who spent his first speech arguing that the Croat nation went back five thousand years, and was the oldest in Europe.

Or was that in the world? Now they would have to close the Archaeological Museum in Zagreb, too.

Tell me, brother, who were multi-celled first, Serbs or Croats?

The EC, finally waking up, if not yet alert enough to think, had staggered on to the scene, in the form of a three-man delegation. The trio – an Italian, a Frenchman and a Dutchman – seemed to think that, since presidents preside over *countries*, all Yugoslavia needed was a president in order to become a country again. (The Italian, at least, should have known better.) In separate meetings with all eight members of the Presidency, they asked for, and received, everyone's word of honour that Mesić would be elected President at the next meeting. Then the three men left, and the Presidency met, and Mesić was not elected. 'Now they know who they're dealing with,' Mirjana said.

So the three men came back and asked for signed promises. They got them. They left, and Mesić was not elected. 'What's a signature?' Mirjana shrugged. 'Nothing!'

So the three men came back again and actually *sat* in the Presidency meeting and did not budge until Mesić was elected under their noses. 'What are we, apes?' Mirjana spluttered. 'Is this Togoland? Everyone talks about sovereignty, about independence! How independent can you be when three foreigners elect your President?'

She had a friend, a psychiatrist, who had just come from Slovenia. While he was there, he had believed the Slovene militia's actions were justified, but now said, 'We were brainwashed!' The Slovenian papers had warned that the Army would use chemical weapons, that infiltrators had placed bombs in trash cans and packages in the Slovenian cities. But a couple of days in Belgrade had sufficed to deprogramme him. Thank you, *Politika*.

Mirjana lamented the Slovenes' PR skills. Their military leaders charmed the foreign press by speaking in English and French, while the Yugoslav Army generals sequestered themselves. The stupid Serbs were once again losing the propaganda war. They had this naïve belief that simply because their cause was just the world would understand. But meanwhile the Slovenes and Croats were hiring public relations firms and lobbying . . .

After ten days, the war in Slovenia died down, and the Army returned to its barracks. There were no Serbs there in need of protection, and the flags flying over the customs posts were not worth the fight, nor the world's censure. The three-man team from the EC negotiated a three-month moratorium on the Slovenian and Croatian independence declarations, ostensibly to allow the laying of bilateral legal groundwork for secession, but really because the EC could not think of anything to do except postpone the inevitable, create some dithering-and-squawking room. The soldiers who had been captured in Slovenia were released. The men from the EC drank some champagne and went home.

The war continued in Croatia as if nothing had happened.

In the Serbian Parliament, a member said, 'Europe should come here and see that when we were eating with golden forks, they were still ripping meat with their bare hands off wild beasts.'

I saw Benjamin, who had come to Belgrade to mix the master soundtrack for his film. The principal film festival, at Pula in Istria, was two weeks away, and he was working frantically against the clock. He still had no idea whether the festival would actually take place or not.

If it did, there was the question of how to get there. The drive up from Sarajevo was now too dangerous, since you had to squeeze between the Serb-held Krajina and the Croat-held coast. Flying was iffy, because you never knew which airports would be closed down. They could drive to Split and then take a boat north, but there were rumours that the Yugoslav Navy might blockade the Adriatic.

He also had a more immediate worry. He had found out that morning that he could not pay his hotel bill. He carried an American Express card, but all Am-Ex cards were issued in Zagreb, and as of five days ago his hotel no longer honoured them.

Meanwhile, Belgrade was taking in Serb refugees from the fighting in Croatia. People were finding room for them in their cramped apartments. They were being put up in the hotels. They were being taken on nationalistic sightseeing tours to places like Oplenac, the family church and tomb of the Serbian royal dynasty a few miles south of Belgrade. One of the refugees I met, from Banija, in Croatia, told me that the Serbs and Croats of his village had fled *together* into the woods. They were both fleeing from the Serb and Croat militias that were fighting for the town.

I had trouble finding Vanja. He had moved out of his old place and left no forwarding address. I eventually reached him through a cousin, and found out that he was hiding from the Army. We got together for a coffee, and he lamented the fact that he would have to stay in Belgrade for the summer, where it would be hot and dull. But only Belgrade was big enough to hide in. If he went to his family's summer cottage on the island of Brač, the Croatian militia might get him. Chalk up another disadvantage of mixed parentage.

Mothers were on television every night. On Zagreb TV they were Croat mothers. On Belgrade TV they were Serb mothers. They wore black, and cried. They led sympathetic reporters through their shattered homes. They, too, finding a microphone at their lips, rose to the occasion. They gesticulated, screaming. They used the same rhetorical flourishes. 'What kind of people . . .!?' 'Never in the history of . . .!' 'Animals on two legs . . .!'

Borba, still trying to be neutral, sent a team of reporters through the lines in Slavonia. The Serbs at the first roadblock were polite to them, but admonished them not to continue. It would be suicidal. The Croats would surely cut their throats. They drove on. At the next roadblock, the Croats were also polite to them, but were amazed that they had made it through the Serbian roadblock alive.

I visited Chuck, one of the reporters for Mirjana's newspaper, and a friend of hers.

But their friendship was under strain. 'Mirjana's off in dreamland,' he said. 'You know the old saying. If you keep throwing enough shit at the wall, some of it will stick. Well, here they've been putting shit in everybody's bowls, and people are spooning it up for breakfast.'

Chuck had been born and raised in Brooklyn, and his conversation proceeded in the braying, scornful bursts of a New York City cab driver. He wore a baseball cap, and the rumpled, many-pocketed field jacket of a reporter. When Yugoslavs asked him about his background, he told them not to worry about bias: he came from a Croat family, but some of his relatives were Muslim, and he had married a Serb. His wife, Liljana, was making us tea, and their infant daughter Sara sat on Chuck's lap.

Did he and Liljana see things differently? I asked.

'Of course not,' he said. 'Of *course not*! Why would we disagree on anything?'

'Well . . .'

'I wasn't born in this goddamn country. I think both sides are fucked! I'll tell you, I'm *sick and tired* of hearing the Croats beating their chests about how all the great artists and writers of Yugoslavia were Croats. If they have so many fucking great artists, why couldn't they get together *two measly* graphic designers to come up with a new shield for the republic? But no! Instead, they had a debate in Parliament for *two days* about whether the upper left square of the šahovnica should be white or red!'

About the Serbs, however, he went on a bit longer. 'They've gone fucking crazy. Completely fucking out of their minds. There's going to be a bloodbath. Serbia will become such a pariah, it'll make Albania look like a founding member of the United Nations.'

'Come!' Liljana urged, setting tea in front of her husband. 'No more politics!'

But Chuck would not be stopped. 'The Serbs now are always talking about their poor refugees from Croatia. "Oh, look at them!"' he simpered. '"Our *poor* refugees!"' His cab-driver laugh brayed forth. 'Yeah, bu-ull-*shit*! Have you seen them? They're on a fucking vacation! They were taken out of the area so that the Serb militias and the Army can strafe and bomb the villages without worrying about accidentally killing Serbs!

'Look: Serbian culture and Croatian culture are fundamentally different. Croats are mercantile, individualistic. Serbs are totalitarian. There's an old saying: "When it comes to a fight, Croats reach for their pens, Serbs reach for their guns." The Croats are legalistic. In the Habsburg Empire, the law actually meant something. In the Ottoman Empire it never did. And so you have today's Serbia, which is basically a Fascist state.'

Liljana was shocked, 'That's too much, Chuck!'

He foghorned back at her, louder, 'A *Fascist state*!'

She turned away, sweeping up the tea things. 'I don't know what you have against the Serbs,' she muttered in a seething voice.

'Do you want to listen to your Daddy pontificate?' Chuck asked of Sara.

When I saw Mirjana again that night, she was obviously pained by the rift. 'Chuck spent too long in Slovenia,' she confided to me.

On Belgrade TV news, a Serb in Croatia, a defender of his home, had been shot through the chest. He lay crumpled on the sidewalk. His comrades were trying to lift him and turn him towards the camera. They were disturbing him in the very moment of his death, so that viewers could drink in the full horror of his gaping wound, his death grimace. But he was not cooperating. He kept turning out of their hands. He seemed to be shrinking, folding up like a flower. He curled foetally. His face was turned towards the sidewalk, and suddenly you realized he was dead, he had been dead for several seconds. His comrades were still holding up an arm and a leg.

55

I took a bus to Kosovo, where it all began.

Albanians lounged in the back; Serbs clustered around the driver. I was left in the empty middle. Outside the window, the mud-brick villages with their brush fences and high wooden gates were the most picturesque I had seen in Yugoslavia, probably because they were too poor to be able to afford any new construction. Water buffalo wallowed in the ochre puddles.

In Priština, the capital of the province, one of the Serbs attached himself to me as I headed for the cheaper of the two hotels. He was a policeman, wagging a boxy pistol on his hip. 'These are all Albanians,' he said unnecessarily, gesturing with distaste at the people on the street, who sullenly watched us walk by. He had grown up in Bosnia, and lived now in central Serbia. He had been posted down to Kosovo to keep order. He slept in a dormitory with other policemen. He missed his wife and kids, but this was important work. Had I been to Kosovo before?

Two years ago.

'It's much better now,' he assured me. 'Now it's safe. Reporter?'

'Travel writer.'

'Ah! You've come to see the monasteries!'

'Exactly.'

'Gračanica! Peć! Dečani!'

'Yes! Wonderful!' I meant it; they *were* wonderful.

'And Kosovo Polje? You must see Kosovo Polje!'

'Of course!'

From the trashy back alleys of gold-filigree shops and teahouses we emerged on to the one main street, Marshal Tito, which ran from the white-elephant prestige projects of the Grand Hotel and the ultra-modern sports complex, past the provincial parliament building and the typically ugly Brotherhood and Unity monument, to fade out uncertainly in what was left of the old bazaar. It was evening, and the *passeggio* was in full swing under the sweetly flowering lindens. Policemen strolled, bandoliered in gleaming brass-jacketed bullets, familiarly cradling their sub-machine guns in front of them like beer bellies.

Two years ago the hotel had had Albanian maids and an Albanian desk clerk, and a room had cost $14. Now the place was run entirely by Serbs.

'Not filthy any more,' my escort told me. 'Now it's a real hotel!'

It looked the same to me. Only now my room cost $41. Obviously, I was helping pay for the police.

The clerk was a passionate man. He wondered why Americans didn't understand Serbs. 'If you're going to write, do you know about the political situation here?'

'A bit.'

'These fucking Albanians. They are Muslims, you understand?'

'Yes.'

'And there are Muslims in Bosnia! So you see! The Green Axis!'

'Excuse me?'

'The Green Axis! Islam! It's aiming at the heart of Europe! Why doesn't Europe care about this?'

'What would you propose?'

'Well. You should know, I am a nationalist.' He smiled at the word, seeming both apologetic and serene. 'Maybe you will laugh.'

'Somehow I don't think so.'

'You know, the Albanians don't belong here. This is Yugoslavia! Yugoslavs belong here! Albanians belong in Albania!'

How simple! How . . . incontrovertible!

'I see!' I said.

'You understand?'

'Perfectly! And . . . so . . . with all these Albanians, we . . .?'

'Send them back to Albania!'

'Yes, of course! Although . . . It does seem like a lot of people to move. Two million . . .'

308

'Only a million and a half.'

'That's still a lot. The logistics . . .'

'Oh,' he pooh-poohed. 'It's not so hard. Look at how many people were moved during World War II.'

'By Stalin, you mean.'

'By everybody!'

I registered, and made my contribution to the costs of law and order.

56

The Sultan Murad falling like a hawk,
falling on Kosovo, writes written words,
he writes and sends to the city of Kruševac
to the knees of Lazar, Prince of Serbia:
'Ah, Lazar, Lord of Serbia,
this has never been and never can be:
one territory under two masters,
only one people to pay two taxes:
we cannot both of us be ruler,
send every key to me and every tax,
the keys of gold that unlock the cities,
and the taxes on heads for seven years.
And if you will not send these things to me,
then come down to Kosovo meadow,
and we shall do division with our swords.'
And when the written words come to Lazar
he sees the words, he drops terrible tears.

When a Serbian heroic poem first came to the attention of Europe in the late eighteenth century, it inspired a wave of Serbophilia. Goethe, Walter Scott and Mérimée all penned translations. Madame de Staël swooned. Coleridge analysed the metrics of the original, even though he did not know a word of Serbian. The literati of the salons had discovered a living Homeric world in Europe's backyard.

Like the Homeric singers, Serbia's *guslari* were illiterate. To a certain extent they created their songs anew with each singing by rearranging epithets and formulae called up from the analphabet's deep reservoir of memory. Many of them, like the Greek singers, were blind. Those that could see fought with their brethren when the Serbs rose against the Turks in 1804. They killed Turks by day and around the night fires composed ballads as hard and pure as jewels about the Turks they had killed. No savage had ever seemed more noble. No wonder Europe swooned. Serbian epic poetry is still recognized today as one of the glories of the culture. Serbs themselves revere it. Their oral poetry and their monasteries are exhibits A and B in their case for their supreme worth as a nation.

Of the three great cycles of Serbian epic poetry, one of them revolves around the events of St Vitus' Day 1389, when the Turks under Sultan Murad I engaged a coalition of Christian forces led by the Serbian Prince Lazar on the Field of Blackbirds – Kosovo Polje.

As they would later do with their defeat in World War I, the Serbs recast their loss at Kosovo as a greater glory. The Turkish multitude, like the later Austrian and Bulgarian armies, was overwhelming: 'If all of us were turned into rock-salt/we could not salt the dinner of the Turks.' And Prince Lazar, not trapped, but choosing the heavenly kingdom, was a type of Christ.

> Flying hawk, grey bird,
> out of the holy place, out of Jerusalem,
> holding a swallow, holding a bird.
> That is no hawk, grey bird,
> that is Elijah, holy one;
> holding no swallow, no bird,
> but writing from the Mother of God
> to the Emperor at Kosovo.
> He drops that writing on his knee,
> it is speaking to the Emperor:

'Lazar, glorious Emperor,
which is the empire of your choice?
Is it the empire of heaven?
Is it the empire of the earth?
If it is the empire of the earth,
saddle horses and tighten girth-straps,
and, fighting-men, buckle on swords,
attack the Turks,
and all the Turkish army shall die.
But if the empire of heaven,
weave a church on Kosovo,
build its foundation not with marble stones,
build it with pure silk and with crimson cloth,
take the Sacrament, marshal the men,
they shall all die,
and you shall die among them as they die.'

The actual military importance of the Battle of Kosovo has always been in doubt. The Serbs had fought other battles with the Turks before Kosovo and would fight more after. Their state was not completely extinguished until 1459, fully seventy years after Kosovo. But it is not hard to see why this one confrontation was chosen by the singers to stand for the destruction of the Serbian state and the fall of a five-hundred-year night. The Battle of Kosovo had poetry in it, because the leaders of both armies were killed. The Sultan was stabbed in his own tent by the warrior-disciple Miloš Obilić, who had gained access by pretending to be a Judas. As for Lazar:

> ... and in that minute the Turks came,
> and in that minute the Turks struck,
> and Lazar was scattered, nothing was left ...
> they took Lazar alive into their hands,
> took him to glorious Otmanović
> and with him brought Miloš Obilić.
> The Sultan's soul was not yet gone from him,
> he spoke to his Pashas and his Vizier:

'When I die and my soul goes from me,
cut off the head of glorious Prince Lazar
and the head of Miloš Obilić,
and bury me by Kosovo meadow
with glorious Prince Lazar under my feet,
Miloš Obilić at my right hand.'
When Miloš heard the glorious Sultan,
then sadly Miloš spoke in these words:
'O, glorious Sultan, I beg of you,
do not put my head at your right hand,
but bury my head under your feet,
Lazar, my father-in-law, at your right hand.
I have served him faithfully all my life,
let me wait on him in black mother earth.'
. . . The glorious Sultan's soul went from him.
The Turks beheaded Lazar the bright Prince,
Prince Lazar and Miloš Obilić.
They laid Lazar at the Sultan's right hand,
Miloš Obilić under his feet.

The Battle of Kosovo was the Serbs' fall of Troy. They
themselves say Kosovo is their Jerusalem. They were scattered
northward from the holy precinct, leaving behind some of their
most superb monasteries, buildings revered throughout the world
as architectural and artistic masterpieces – among them, their
patriarchate. They brought with them their songs, so that Kosovo
would never be lost to memory.

In these epics one sees the working of the Word at its most
powerful. When asked to explain Kosovo's unique importance to
them, Serbs respond that it was the heart of the Serbian kingdom.
In fact, there were other hearts as well: Raška and Macedonia.
But generation after generation passed down the songs of Kosovo,
and the great poems lit under the word a blaze of meaning, and
banked it deep in people's minds far beyond the reach of reason.

Miloš massacred Murad, Tsar of Turkey,
he massacred twelve thousand Turks;

may God be good to his mother,
he left a memory to all Serbs
to be told and told over again
while there are people, while there is Kosovo.

*

I was met outside my hotel by Gazmend, a friend of a friend. A pale man with large slate-coloured eyes, he was Albanian, a professor of electrical engineering at the University of Priština, and representative of the Kosovo branch of the Helsinki Human Rights Watch. His short hair stood up in a flat-top on his head, giving him a surprised look. 'I don't know why I still have my job at the university,' he said. 'If you're fifteen minutes late, they'll fire you. They say the university is the centre of Albanian separatism.' As we walked towards his car he gestured down the modern main street. 'They tore out the heart of the old town to build this. Your hotel sits on the site of a mosque. And they said it proved they wanted to develop Kosovo.'

The packing-crate parliament building was shut up. An advertisement for *Politika* had been placed mockingly in a window. 'The great irony of last year's independence declaration was that the Serbs had hand-picked the delegates to the Kosovo Parliament. These were the Albanians who, of all people, the Serbs thought they could trust. Toadies and idiots. But when it was discovered that the Serbian Parliament was planning to abolish Kosovo's separate status, it was these men, the weakest men, who had to be strong for us. It was they who had to pass the resolution declaring the independence of Kosovo from Serbia last July. And now they are all in hiding. Our heroes!' Gazmend smiled. 'The declaration was passed just before the weekend, so it wasn't until the following Monday that the Serbs abolished the Parliament and instituted martial law. During that one weekend of independence everyone I met in the street was so elated, so excited! Everyone was saying, "If we'd known it would be this easy, we'd have done it years ago!"' He laughed out loud.

'So, legalistically, Kosovo is independent. I mean, it was unconstitutional, but everything here is unconstitutional.'

His car was a battered Yugo, with a sun-visor that kept falling on his head. We stopped to pick up Blerim, another professor mysteriously still employed, and headed out past the apartment blocks to a weedy, empty highway. We crossed a low ridge, and in front of us stretched Kosovo Polje, an extensive rolling plain of dirty green and dun, blanketed in a dull brown haze that obscured the opposite side. Every May the plain was covered with millions of brilliant crimson flowers called Kosovo peonies. The Serbs said the colour derived from the blood of the Serbs who fell at the battle of Kosovo. But this was mid-July, hot and washed out, and the flowers were long dead. The haze was provided courtesy of two huge coal-burning plants squatting in the plain and blowing their tops through massed stacks. I had seen the sulphurous puce lignite of the area piled outside cellars, and could taste it now in my sinuses.

'Here is more of the investment the Serbs talk of,' Gazmend said. 'They have always complained that they poured money into Kosovo and that we Albanians wasted it, or stole it. But those plants send seventy per cent of their energy to Serbia, and we are left with the pollution.'

Five kilometres out on to the plain, we turned off the highway and drove up to the memorial to the Heroes of Kosovo, a stone tower, square, eight storeys tall. On the base in raised metal letters was an excerpt from one of the Kosovo poems:

> OF SERBS BY NATION AND BY BIRTH,
> AND BY THEIR BLOOD AND BY THEIR ANCESTRY,
> WHOEVER DOES NOT FIGHT AT KOSOVO,
> MAY HE HAVE NO DEAR CHILDREN BORN TO HIM
> MAY NEITHER BOY NOR GIRL BE BORN TO HIM!
> MAY NOTHING BEAR FRUIT THAT HIS HAND SOWS,
> NEITHER THE WHITE WHEAT NOR THE RED WINE!
> HIS BLIGHT ROT ALL HIS BROOD WHILE IT ENDURES!

On the viewing platform at the top, a plaque laid out where the forces had been arrayed on the field below us. The Turks, one hundred thousand-strong, had massed on one side of a small stream that I could not see for the haze, and the Serbs, thirty-five thousand-strong, on the other. The text described a Turkish advance and a retreat, and the advance of the Serbian centre in pursuit. Then the Serbian right wing failed to come forward, and the failure spread across the line as the Serbs panicked, and the Turks routed them, and cut them down as they fled.

> And in the morning, daybreak of morning,
> two black crows come flying
> from Kosovo the wide field,
> they drop down at the white tower,
> down on glorious Lazar's tower,
> one is cawing and one is speaking . . .
> 'Tsarica Milica, God is witness,
> today we came from flat Kosovo
> and we have seen two great armies,
> and yesterday they crashed together,
> and the two Tsars were killed,
> out of the Turks there are men left alive,
> but of the Serbs anyone left alive
> is a wounded man dropping blood.'

'All this is legend,' Blerim shrugged. 'A good story.' He pointed to the labels on the diagram: SERBIAN CENTRE; SERBIAN RIGHT WING; SERBIAN LEFT WING; SERBIAN RESERVES. 'Make sure you write that this is a lie.'

'Two Albanian princes with their armies were part of the Christian coalition,' Gazmend said.

'And the Kosovo peonies?' I asked.

Gazmend smiled broadly. 'The blood of Albanians.'

I laughed.

'It's true!' Blerim said hotly.

Gazmend and Blerim had their own layout of the field to show me, more important to them than the events on the plaque. They pointed out the army compound on the hill by the ridge leading towards town, and the tanks lined up just inside the front gate. 'The Serbs are ready to go,' Gazmend commented. We could make out other emplacements along the ridge, huddled conferences of tanks and artillery pieces. Clearly, they had been positioned for shelling Priština.

When the Serbs finally drove the Turks out of Kosovo in 1912, their emotions, weaned on epics, were epic in their purity and simplicity: they fell to kiss the holy ground. In a decisive battle a few miles farther south, where the Turks held a fortress that had legendarily belonged to Marko Kraljević, the greatest of all heroes in Serbian epic poetry, a war correspondent reported that the Serb soldiers disobeyed their generals' orders and excitedly charged the fortress before their own artillery had been brought to bear, but showed such unwavering determination that they overwhelmed the Turkish garrison within minutes anyway. On being asked to explain themselves afterwards, the soldiers said, 'Marko Kraljević commanded us all the time: FORWARD! Did you not see him on his Šarac?' (Šarac was Marko's horse. He was known to bite off the ears of opponents' horses. His nostrils shot out blue flames.)

Only three years later, in the Great War, the Serbs had to live the epic of Kosovo again, as if in a dream. The Serbian Army had won two stunning victories in 1914 against the larger Austrian forces which had invaded their country, but now a combined horde of Austrians, Germans and Bulgarians in overwhelming numbers was pushing them slowly down through Serbia. On Kosovo Polje, at the very edge of their beloved land, the Serbs made a final stand. But it could be no more than a delaying action. Having gained for themselves a little breathing time, the Serbs turned to the mountains at their backs. Before they wound up the first defile, they destroyed their artillery with hand grenades, and drove their lorries off a cliff.

> His eyes shed tears and he said:
> 'Deceiving world, my sweet flower,
> you were lovely, I have walked only a little,
> three hundred years is only a little.
> Now it is time to exchange my world.'
> And Marko the Prince drew out,
> he drew out the sword from his belt,

he is coming to his horse, to Šarac,
his sword takes the head off Šarac;
Šarac will give no pleasure to the Turks,
he will perform no labour for Turks,
bring no water, carry no cauldrons . . .
He snapped his razor sword in four pieces,
so that no Turkish hand should get his sword,
and that the Turks should not boast about it . . .

The Serbian poems say nothing about Albanians. The Serbs fell
to kiss the holy ground of Kosovo in 1912, but when they rose
again they saw that Kosovo cleared of its Turks was not at all an
empty land.

The Albanians had always been there, even in the days of
Serbian strength and glory. But they had lived deep and high in
the mountains, eternal refugees, an unorganized shepherd rabble,
hardly worth thinking about. For much of the Middle Ages
'Albania' was an archipelago of mountain-tops and ranges in the
seas of Serbia and Byzantium. After the Serbs began to migrate
north in the fourteenth century, the sea became Turkish, but the
Turks, for one, did not care who joined them as long as they were
Muslim. The invisible highlanders became Muslim en masse, and
dived out of the harsh hills.

From 1918 to 1941, the Serbs did their best to make these
intruders on their hallowed land feel invisible. Kosovo was the
poorest region in the country, and stayed that way. There were
no Albanian schools. The official language in all public spheres
was Serbian. When Yugoslavia was dismembered in 1941,
Kosovo and the Albanian-inhabited portion of Macedonia were
folded into a Greater Albania, under Italian protection. Today,
the Albanians of Kosovo unapologetically remember the Italian
Fascisti with fondness. For the first time, all the Albanians were
in one state. For the first time, the Albanians of Kosovo could go
to Albanian schools.

None the less, a few opposed the occupation, and joined the
Partisans. Tito promised them their own state if they would fight
the Albanian Fascists, who were called Ballists. But Tito, of

course, was not a Serb, and could not afford to push the Serbs too far, and after the war had ended everywhere else, violence continued unabated in Kosovo, as Albanian and Serb Partisans killed Ballists, and then as Serb Partisans turned on Albanian Partisans. The Albanians revolted, and were bloodily suppressed. Until the 60s, they were invisible once more.

In 1968, demonstrations broke out in Priština, in which the Albanians demanded their own republic. They did not get it, but Tito gave the province a university, language rights, its own court system, its own police force and an independent vote in the Federal Presidency. Throughout the 80s Serbia discovered that its own Jerusalem could be counted on to vote against it on almost every issue. Serbs knew that the Slovenes and the Croats liked the situation. They could almost hear the Slovenes and the Croats laughing at them. Stupid Serbs.

Worse, Serbs were leaving Kosovo in a steady stream. They told stories of intimidation by the Albanians, and of the impossibility of redress in the Albanian-run courts. Albanians countered that the Serbs were leaving because Kosovo was poor and anyone would leave who could. *We* would leave, they said, except we have nowhere to go.

The Serbs remaining in Kosovo made up only ten per cent of the population. They were frightened. They carried guns when they went out to work in their fields. They petitioned the Federal Parliament, but got nowhere. They were persecuted anew by Communist leaders who were terrified of facing the growing aggrievedness among the Serbs.

> Whoever will not fight at Kosovo,
> may nothing grow that his hand sows,
> neither the white wheat in his field
> nor the vine of grapes on his mountain.

And so the dream of Kosovo, enacted again and again, came back as a nightmare. Poetic nations can write bad poems. In Kosovo in April 1987, at a hearing of Serb grievances, one of the faceless grey Communists stepped forward and startled everyone

318

by breaking the code of silence on nationalist issues, and publicly pledging his support for the Serbs' cause. Any Serb could recite the opening lines of his speech:

> You must stay here. Your land is here.
> Here are your houses, your fields and gardens,
> your memories.

His name was Slobodan Milošević.

Everything that happened afterwards – HDZ and Tudjman, the nation-based parties of Bosnia, the secessions of Slovenia and Croatia – happened in response to Milošević. And there is no doubt that Milošević rode to power on the bronco's back of Kosovo. With that one speech, he discovered the intoxication, hitherto unknown to any of the post-Tito Communists, of genuine popularity, and he was smart enough to realize that building on and exploiting that popularity was the only way a dyed-in-the-wool Communist was going to survive the collapse of Communism. As the masses carried his photograph on their heads, and substituted his name for Tito's in the old rally ditties, calculation shaded into megalomania. By now, he took the problem of Kosovo personally. He had traced his family back to the battle of 1389.

Gazmend, Blerim and I returned to the car and drove to the mausoleum of Murad I. It was a small, well-kept domed building of wheat-coloured limestone, in a yard enclosed by a high stone wall. An enormous ancient mulberry tree grew in two fat diverging trunks like a squashed V in front of the porch.

The keeper came out from the shade and ushered us into the presence of Murad's sarcophagus, clad in green fabric and turbanned in white. As my companions had said, poetry was not necessarily history. Murad's body had not, in fact, been placed in this mausoleum, only his internal organs. His body, hollowed and thus less prone to rot, had been shipped back to Constantinople for burial. And Prince Lazar was not buried by the 'right hand' of the Sultan's liver and lights. His body and severed head were given over to his widow, the Princess Marica, who took them north with her, away from the Turks, half-way to Belgrade, and buried them in the monastery of Ravanica, which Lazar himself had founded.

But his corpse, like his people, had not thus escaped persecution. The Turks soon overran all the land around Ravanica, and made a point of vandalizing the monastery now and then, so when the great, desperate Serb migration north out of Serbia into Vojvodina occurred in 1690, the refugees carried the blackened head and shrunken trunk of their martyred king before them, and reburied him in a monastery in the hills of Fruška Gora, north of Belgrade. Two and a half centuries later, the Nazis dismembered Yugoslavia, and the Fruška Gora was incorporated into the Independent State of Croatia, and Lazar's body was transferred to the crypt of the Belgrade cathedral for safer, if only slightly safer, keeping.

After the war, the Communists left him there, trying to ignore him, but Milošević had recently sent the relics on a grand tour of Serbia, eventually redepositing them at Ravanica. And why stop there? Perhaps the future held a triumphant return to an Albanian-free Kosovo, the demolition of Murad's tomb and the construction in its place of a St Lazar Church of solid gold that would make the St Sava in Belgrade look like a music box. When the peonies bloomed in May there would be no argument over where their colour came from. Serbia would have returned to the Middle Ages, and the circle would be complete.

On the drive back to Priština, Gazmend mentioned that all Albanian doctors had been fired. Albanians were afraid to go to the Serb doctors who, like the policemen, were being sent down in shifts, so an underground network of clinics had been organized. That was how everything was working now. The Albanians had organized a shadow society. Few people still had jobs, so services and goods were bartered, and often simply given. 'It took the Serbs to teach us how to be true Communists,' Gazmend laughed.

And passive resisters. At the urgings of their leader, Ibrahim Rugova, the Albanians had started to boycott everything: the university, the elections, their jobs. They had purposely tried to become a dead weight to the Serbs, a millstone.

That was not all. The tradition of the blood-feud still ran deep in Albanian culture, but recently over a thousand feuds between families, many going back generations, had been patched up by a single man, a professor of Albanian culture, who had criss-crossed Kosovo, arguing that the Albanians had to present a solid front if they were going to resist the Serbs. The Serbs, in other words, had accomplished what Albanian nationalists had never been able to do; they had fostered a strong Albanian national consciousness in place of the traditional clannishness.

In Priština we shared a beer on the terrace of my hotel with a man named Shaqir, who had been arrested for his part in mass demonstrations calling for a separate Kosovo republic in 1981. Every few minutes a fighter jet buzzed the town, the hoarse scream of its engines blotting out conversation.

'Since 1981,' Shaqir was saying in low tones, in English, 'a hundred Albanian civilians have been killed by the police. Most were shot in the back. Fifty Albanians in the Yugoslav Army have died in "accidents" or by "suicide". From 1981 to 1989, seven thousand people have been sentenced to 20,840 years in prison. If you're caught with a photograph of Ibrahim Rugova in your pocket you get two months. If you say "Kosovo Republic" you get two months. If you order Kosovo Riesling in a bar by saying "KR", you get two months.'

As for Shaqir himself, the police had broken down his front door in 1981 and put him in solitary for two months, then released him, and then imprisoned him again for two years.

'Did they torture you?' I asked. I never liked to ask this, but I always had to. No one ever volunteered the information. 'If you don't want to talk about it – '

'No, why not?' he shrugged easily. 'People should know.'

But then he paused, and in the long seconds of that pause an expression that I had seen many times before slowly consumed his face. So many people in Yugoslavia had been tortured at one time or another, and every one I had met – Serb, Croat, Muslim, Albanian – had been seized with the same expression. The face

321

set slowly, like a pudding congealing, and a flush rose, and the eyes went through an extraordinary transformation – they locked on to yours, and deepened, and turned inward, trance-like, as tears welled up around the edges of a brutal clamping-down of the will. It was a terribly intimate look, a defenceless, childlike look, and, I'm convinced, unfakable. Perhaps this was how you looked at your torturer as he avidly, lovingly scanned your face to see how you would respond to . . . this.

'They beat you every day,' Shaqir said quietly. 'They beat you until they're afraid you will die if they beat you more. So they send you to the hospital and fix you up and send you back so they can beat you again.' He started to say something else, but stopped. 'I'm sorry. To talk about it is to remember.'

About life after prison, he could speak more or less matter-of-factly. 'My kidneys are ruined. I'm crippled by rheumatism. I had a wife and two children, but you have a choice: you can live with them and bring them trouble, violence at school. Or if you love them, you leave, so they can get work, lead some sort of normal life. So I divorced my wife.'

'To say the Serbs are Fascists is an insult to Fascism!' Blerim burst out loudly.

We happened to be surrounded by Serbs in police blue and army olive green. Their beers glowed, their bullets shone, their pistols bulged, their walkie-talkies made eerie robotic burbles.

'Come now,' Gazmend demurred.

'Really!'

'He's joking,' Gazmend assured me.

'I am not!'

'Have you seen Gračanica?' Gazmend said, changing the subject.

Gračanica was a famous Serbian monastery outside Priština. 'I have.'

'It's a beautiful building.'

'It is indeed.'

'Albanians kept those monasteries in good repair for five hundred years. Just like the keepers at Murad's mausoleum.'

On the monastery's famous frescoes, the eyes of the sainted

Serbian King Milutin and Queen Simonida had been gouged out. The Serbs said Albanians had done it. Albanians said Serb peasants had done it, out of a folk belief that plaster rubbed from a saint's eyes could be applied to your own to cure various ocular ailments.

'You probably didn't see many Serbs at Gračanica,' Gazmend commented.

'No.'

'You never do. Serbs build churches wherever they go, but it's not so they can attend church. It's so they can say, "This must be Serbia, it has a Serbian church."'

One of the policemen was roaring drunk. He was waving his fat pistol and shouting, a short man, challenging all comers. Two of his colleagues were trying to calm him down.

My eyes were glued to the pistol. I quailed each time the barrel foreshortened to a black hole. The walkie-talkies sang to each other. The hotel restaurant's stereo system was pounding out a Serbian national song, a basso male chorus on the march. On the street under the lindens a line of crouching Gypsy boys polished the shoes of policemen and soldiers, swinging their brushes in time with the music.

57

In the shade of the fountain of the Sultan Murad Mosque I met Jakub, a burly man of hazel eyes and white hair wound in tight curls. He introduced me to his young son, Durim, who was transfixed by my beard. (In Kosovo too, a beard meant 'Chetnik'.)

We had been talking for only a moment when another man hurried over to us and spoke anxiously with Jakub in Albanian.

'He heard you speaking Serbian,' Jakub explained to me. 'He thought you had come to poison the fountain.'

The man apologized profusely to me for thinking I was a Serb.

Jakub showed me proudly around the mosque, which was indeed beautiful inside, its whitewashed dome painted with a great crimson wheel of arabesques drooping teardrop spokes like a firework. Then we went to a teahouse, where the tea was served with lemon wedges in plain glasses you had to hold gingerly by the rim. It was so strong it made my teeth squeak.

The Serb and Albanian communities were so antagonistic now, so fearful of each other, that no Serb would dream of going into an Albanian teahouse, unless it was to order everybody to the floor. Out of the corner of my eye, I could see the almost comically violent double-takes of the Albanians who came in the door and saw this bearded stranger speaking Serbian in the corner. They went into wide-eyed huddles with other customers who, I could only hope, were disabusing them.

Xhevdet came over for a chess game. He was an elementary-school teacher and parachutist. I had seen him before, he said.

I had?

He had been a member of the team that formed the five Olympic rings in free-fall over Seoul. The photograph had appeared all over the world.

Yes, I had seen it. And he had been . . .?

Part of the black ring.

Ah yes, of course.

Xhevdet and Jakub got into a game. They played with abandon, bringing their queens out immediately, sacrificing with élan. Within five minutes one was chasing the other around the board in a Tom-and-Jerry endgame. Meanwhile, I taught Durim how to count to twenty in English. He also wanted to know the word for beard.

A gnarled old man with a village-drunkard's crazed grin joined us. He embraced his friends and patted me warmly on the shoulder for not being a Serb. He turned to the board for a brief histrionic look of deep concentration, and then grimaced proudly and pulled from a hidden pocket in his jacket a home-made dirk with a thin five-inch blade. A puncturer, a quick in-and-outer. He passed it around for our admiration.

Xhevdet had won the game, and he turned to me while waiting for Jakub to set up the board. 'Parachutists have to be very close.

They trust each other with their lives. The Serbs and Albanians in our parachuting club are still friends. That's unique!'

'Your start,' Jakub said. He gestured towards Durim. 'A bright boy, eh?'

'Very.'

'*Durim* is an Albanian word. It means "patience". My generation was given a lot of Arabic names. Like Xhevdet. But now we give Albanian names. Or Catholic.'

'Catholic?'

'Our leaders recommend it. To play down the oriental connection. So Europe will be more likely to help us.'

He sent his queen flying into a thicket of knights and bishops. The old man was fondly patting the pocket to which he had returned his knife. Out of another pocket he pulled a second knife, a huge Bowie type, single-edged, with a thick spine, for good hacking and hewing. We handed it around. Xhevdet tested it against his fingernail and nodded.

'We could solve all our problems here,' he said expansively, 'if everybody just went parachuting together.'

'Sure,' Jakub said. 'And packed the Serbs' parachutes wrong.'

'No, I'm serious.'

'Your move. Where was I? Oh yes. Some Albanians are even converting to Christianity. I mean, some Albanians have always been Catholic, but some of the Muslims are converting.'

'That's going too far,' Xhevdet said. 'It doesn't look good.'

'It looks opportunistic,' Jakub agreed.

'The Serbs would say the Albanians' original conversion to Islam was opportunistic,' I said.

'Maybe they're right!' Xhevdet said cheerfully. 'Why not? We Albanians aren't so devout. We have Catholics, we have, what, twenty per cent or something who are Orthodox.'

'Greek Orthodox, not Serb Orthodox. Check.'

'For us, it has always been more important that we are Albanians.'

'Yes, we kill each other irrespective of religion.'

The old man was pulling a tyre iron out of his jacket. One end had been sharpened into a spike.

'Check.'

'James Baker was in Albania a few weeks ago,' Xhevdet said excitedly. 'Thousands of people were lining the streets, cheering him. He gave Albania six million dollars in aid.'

Whistles.

'And this wasn't government money. This was out of his own pocket.'

'I . . . don't think so,' I said.

'I heard it! He just pulled it out. It's nothing to him, he's from Texas.'

'Checkmate.'

I had figured out by this time that Durim could not speak a word of Serbian.

'He's not going to learn,' Jakub said with finality. 'French, English, German are important. Who speaks Serbian?'

'The problem with Serbs,' Xhevdet mused, 'is that they have no history.' He pronounced this with slow relish, probably imagining a Serb hearing it and choking apoplectically. 'When we had a kingdom, they were still monkeys, swinging in the trees.'

58

Voices on Kosovo:

Slobodan, a civil engineer in Belgrade: 'Albanians are the most primitive people in Europe.'

Slavko, a Belgrade news photographer: 'I know a man down there who has two wives, and from those two wives he's got twenty children. I know another who has ten. That's two men, thirty children. That's how they are taking over Kosovo. It's a deliberate policy, directed from Albania.'

Drago, a Serb who was born in Kosovo and now works at the port in Rijeka: 'When you go to Priština, you will see all the Albanians dressed as though they are poor. But they have gold sewn in the linings of their jackets. They get this from drug-smuggling and gun-trafficking.'

Milica, a Serb shopkeeper in Kragujevac, a town in central Serbia where many Serb refugees from Kosovo have settled: 'Both the Albanians *and* the Serbs from Kosovo are primitive. Few of them have even finished elementary school.

'They'll be sitting around in a café, and one of them will say, "Let's go to a football match," and they'll all say, "Yeah, let's go," and they go. They don't know *what* they're going to do next. Primitive!'

Mirjana, a translator in Belgrade for a western newspaper: 'When you go down there, go to the villages and look at their houses. My God! They are fortresses! They have high walls all around them, with no windows, just little slits for shooting out of. It is expressive of their whole mentality. They are closed off from the world. First of all, *this* must change.'

Zorica, a student of dentistry in Belgrade: 'When you visit the Serb areas of Kosovo, you will see that their yards are open. I mean, yes, they are enclosed, but only by concrete or steel fences. The important thing is, you can see *into* them. That's normal!'

Fadil, an Albanian translator, in his natal village: 'This is the part of town where the Serbs live. Note that they have high walls too. It has nothing to do with the nation, it is simply a custom in this part of the Balkans.'

Miroslav, a Serb who has travelled in the United States: 'What impressed me most about America was the way the yards had no fences at all. It seemed so civilized!'

Azem, an Albanian artist who lives half the time in Priština, half in Belgrade: 'Look at the older houses in Belgrade. They are arranged around a courtyard, with windowless backs to the street. Or look at the high walls around the houses in Dalmatia. Those are splendid Venetian houses. They are primitive?'

A Serb sidewalk sociologist: 'The Albanians rape Serb women and young girls as a calculated form of terror. You see, in the Muslim mind, the best way to humiliate your enemy is to rape his women, because it brings shame on the whole family.'

Isuf, an Albanian journalist living in Priština: 'The rapes are grossly exaggerated. If you look at the police statistics, they show that in all of 1987 there were only two rapes, and in 1988 there were a couple of attempts but no successful rapes.'

Dimitrije, an ethnomusicologist in Belgrade: 'The police in Kosovo used to all be Albanians, so the rapes were never reported, or if they were, the case went to an Albanian judge who threw the case out. That's why *we* had to throw all the judges out.'

Isuf: 'The Serb press has created such a climate of fear that the Serbs here see rapes everywhere. I no longer get into an elevator with an unknown Serb woman or even a Serb woman I know a little, because I am terrified she will say I tried to rape her.'

Vuk Drašković, the main opposition leader in Serbia, anointed by the western media as the 'democratic' alternative to Milošević: 'What we would do in Kosovo would be simple and fair.
'One. During World War II, the Italians and the Germans brought 120,000 Albanians into Kosovo as colonists. All of them, including their children and grandchildren – about four to five hundred thousand people – will be returned to Albania.
'Two. Also during World War II, the Italians and the Germans expelled two hundred thousand Serbs from Kosovo. Tito promulgated a special law in 1945 prohibiting them from returning to their homeland. We are proposing that all of those Serbs, and

their children and grandchildren, would return to Kosovo. (You should write "allow", but we will persuade them.)

'Three. After World War II, another forty thousand Albanians came into Kosovo from Albania. All of those who have attacked Serbs, or desecrated Serb graves, will be sent back, along with their children. The rest can stay, because they did not come into Kosovo during a war situation.

'Four. After World War II, more than three hundred thousand Serbs have left Kosovo, because of Albanian terror. All of them will be "allowed" to return under the same conditions as the Serbs I mentioned in point number two.

'Regarding the high birth rate among the Albanians. Depending on the resources of the Serbian state, we will pay benefits for the first two, three or four children, regardless of race. But if you have more than that, say, five children, you will lose all benefits on the first four, and you will be taxed for the fifth. You will pay a double tax for the sixth, a quadruple tax for the seventh, and so on. If Allah orders Albanians to have twenty children each so that they can take over the Serbian state, then Allah must find the money for them.'

Azem: 'The high birth rate among the Albanians is a direct result of the fact that until the late 60s there was a virtual apartheid situation in Kosovo, with Serbs living in the towns and Albanians out in the rurul areas. It's the village people who have ten kids. The Albanians who now have been living in towns for a couple of decades have two kids, like everybody else. Two generations ago, the Serbs lived mostly in rural areas, and they had large families, too.

'Serbs and Albanians are like two brothers, one thirteen years old, and the other ten. The thirteen-year-old is embarrassed by everything the ten-year-old does, because it reminds him of what he used to be like. But he doesn't know this consciously. He just hits his younger brother.'

A Serb sidewalk sociologist: 'Albanians have no concept of the rule of law. They live according to an old tribal code. You can't imagine how impossible it is to impose any kind of control down there. When they kill each other, they don't go to the police, they settle it themselves. A slit throat, a bullet in the back.

'They don't pay for their electricity, they simply tap into lines illegally. There's no way of knowing who owns which piece of land, none of it's on paper. If a couple of Albanians run down a Serb woman in a truck, you can't trace the truck. It has no licence. Even if you find the truck, you can't find out who owns it. Nobody owns it. There's no title. There's no insurance. Nobody talks.'

Fadil: 'Even Hitler couldn't change the situation here, and even God couldn't help it. So what can Milošević do?'

Shkelzen, a former professor and current political organizer in Priština: 'In 1956, the Serb police went from house to house, confiscating weapons and torturing people. But Albanians today have ten times as many weapons as we had then. We Albanians are renowned for our skill in black market weapons smuggling.'

Fadil: 'As Camus said, "You can kill me, but you can't beat me."'

Gazmend: 'We are completely unarmed. We are totally defenceless.'

Serb conductor on a train, with a reasonable shrug: 'I think the simplest thing is probably just to kill them all.'

59

Fadil lived near the centre of Priština, down a dark alley, in a room that was six feet square. When he had answered the ad for the room, the Serb landlady had said, 'What do *you* want?'

'A room,' he said.

'You're Albanian!'

'Yes,' he admitted.

She harrumphed. 'Only for two months then.'

'If I'm good,' Fadil said sweetly, 'can I stay longer?'

He had been good, and he had been living in the room for several years when I first met him two years ago, although he suspected that his rent, at DM30 a month, was higher than it was for the Serb students in the similar cubicles opening off the dank courtyard.

He kept the location of his room secret, even from most of his friends, which meant that he could receive no mail there, and he had no phone, so I had had no way of contacting him before my arrival this year. But in a city where many people had no phones, and many more had phones that did not work, Marshal Tito Street operated like a party line, and if you just wandered up and down it long enough you eventually came across everyone you knew, and I found Fadil after an hour or so.

He looked exactly the same, with an abundant mop of curly ash-blond hair, a full uncombed beard, and steel-rimmed granny glasses with darkened lenses. The index finger and thumb of his right hand were stained nicotine-orange. Anywhere else in the world, he would have looked like a Beat poet or a Lennon wannabe. Here, he was obviously a Chetnik.

I think he enjoyed it, the surreal conversations with Serbs about the fucking Albanians, the near-confrontations with Albanians who did not realize he was Albanian. He liked the feeling of marginality. He felt safer out there, beyond group feeling. He felt less compromised.

His room looked exactly the same, too. A bed took up half of it. Stacks of books took up another quarter. The rest was filled by a shallow table with a typewriter, a hotplate for making coffee, and a palm-sized television set his father had given him four months previously, which for the first three months had lacked an adapter, and for the last month, thanks to a friend's return from abroad, had had one which, unfortunately, did not fit.

His landlady had wanted to kick him out during the demon-

strations last year – she said she feared reprisals from other Serbs
– but he had persuaded her to raise his rent instead. Now he paid
DM50 a month. That was virtually his only expense. He went for
days at a time on nothing but coffee and cigarettes, and his
friends often paid for those anyway. Sometimes he was treated to
meals by journalists for whom he translated. When I had first met
him, someone had given him a packet of Dunhill cigarettes, which
he promptly traded at a kiosk for ten packs of the locally
produced filterless sticks of tarry junk. His expenses were actually
less than two years ago, because he had stopped his week-long
drinking sprees. When I had first met him, after he had been 'lost'
for a few days, he had said, 'Life is dead here. There's no culture,
only bad theatre, and I can't afford to buy books, and there are
hardly any books to buy anyway. So I drink.' But it eventually
got to the point where he could imagine himself becoming one of
those teary wrecks with rotten teeth you could see in every
Kosovo bar, and of all the groups he did not want to belong to,
he least wanted to belong to that one.

In Kosovo, Fadil looked like a Chetnik, but in fact he *was* a
Beat poet, or at least a translator of Beat poetry, which was not
only popular all over Yugoslavia, it was virtually the only
American literature anyone knew (which perhaps pointed to
certain similarities between the Tito era and the Eisenhower era).
Four years ago Fadil had met Ginsberg at a reading in Macedonia,
and later published his interview with him in a Priština arts
magazine, and translated 'Howl' and 'America'. Since then, he
had written to the City Lights Bookstore in San Francisco several
times, explaining his situation, enclosing his clippings and suggesting they send him some books for free, which they had done.
His last letter had gone unanswered though, and he was wondering if his mail wasn't getting out of Kosovo.

Most of the other books he had in his room – a collection so
eclectic as to seem castaway – he had stolen from the university,
where for years he had been an on-again, off-again student of
American literature. He was a little embarrassed about the thefts,
but told himself, and me, that the English department had been
lousy, and the professors had been idiots, and the entire depart-

ment library had fitted into one glass case, which had always been kept locked, and you often couldn't find the professors to get the key because they had often not bothered to come to class, so actually, in a way, more people had access to the books once Fadil had stolen them, since he loaned them out to friends.

His translations were tacked all over his walls: typescript on cheap greyish bond, and yellowing squares of newsprint torn from the arts magazines. Among them were photographs of other bards: John Lennon, Bob Dylan, Jim Morrison. Fadil's latest translation was of Bruce Springsteen's 'No Surrender' (he had been making a point). His work hadn't appeared all last year, because for a while the magazines only wanted Albanian poems and Albanian folklore. He didn't like that sort of cultural chest-thumping and had got depressed and stopped working.

Currently, his great passion was Morrison, which put him squarely in the Yugoslav avant-garde mainstream. All over the country I had met serious poets who, on finding out I was a writer, had wanted to know with what degree of extravagance I admired the poems of Jim Morrison.

But Fadil drew a sharp distinction between worshipping the man's works and worshipping the man. He knew people who said they loved Morrison, but didn't seem to know much of his poetry, and didn't seem to understand what they knew, and those people made him shudder. They reminded him of the people at rallies who held photographs of Tito or Miloševcić over their heads. So on his one trip abroad, several years ago, he had gone to Paris, and had made a point of visiting the cemetery where Morrison was buried, and had had a friend take a photograph of him pissing on Morrison's grave.

He locked the room and we wandered off to look for acquaint-ances, and eventually found a couple at a table outside a café in a mini-mall under the crumbling concrete plaza of the sports centre. They were professors at the university, and Fadil sat over his coffee, making fun of them to me: 'They sign a loyalty oath every morning. They have to be there at exactly seven a.m. and they have to stay until three p.m. If they go out for coffee, they have to check out, and come right back. If they have to piss, they have to raise their hands and say, "Excuse me, I have to go piss." If the Serbs tell them they have to come in at five a.m., these guys will say, "Sure." ' Fadil saluted. ' "Just tell us when you want us to show up, and we'll be there." '

His friends smiled and nodded at me. I wondered if they understood much English. After they left, Fadil spoke more seriously. He found what they had done, in fact, incredible. 'When the Serbs introduced the loyalty oaths last year, our leaders and our intelligentsia told people not to sign, so many workers were fired. Then it was the turn of the intelligentsia to sign, and suddenly there was talk about "pointless gestures", and a lot of them signed.'

We continued the conversation while strolling back up Marshal Tito. Fadil said that now a person could sign the oath and not lose all his friends, because once people started to go hungry they understood that you couldn't always be 'pure'. Fadil's brother, who worked in a tax office and had a wife and children, had signed an oath, and Fadil didn't blame him.

Fadil was scornful of Ibrahim Rugova, the President of the Democratic Alliance of Kosovo and the unofficial leader of the Albanian popular resistance. 'He can talk for pages in interviews, and never say anything. Yet he's extremely popular.' Indeed, I had been seeing Rugova's photograph on walls everywhere, like a new Tito: male-pattern balding, a tired face, a rakish scarf. 'He keeps telling everyone to keep quiet, to wait, to put up with all the bullshit. So that we don't give the Serbs an excuse for killing us all. Maybe it's the right strategy, but I don't know. I think he's overestimating Europe's willingness to help us and underestimating the Serbs' willingness to keep right on kicking the shit out of someone who's lying motionless on the ground.'

'Were you involved in any of the demonstrations last year?'

He laughed. 'Me? Forget it! It's crazy to protest against somebody who is perfectly happy to kill you. Some people were walking along a road towards my parents' town to go to a demonstration, and a policeman shot and killed five of them. I see him every day when I'm back home.

'It's strange to think that my life isn't worth anything. They

334

don't need an excuse. A Serb in the street could shoot me at any time, and nothing would happen to him. At least if he killed somebody's chicken he'd have to pay for it.'

We ducked into the alley leading to his room. 'But if war really comes here,' he said, 'the Serbs can't win. There are two million of us. What are they going to do? Kill a million? There would still be a million left. I don't have a gun, but I can carry a few litres of gasoline. I can burn down houses.'

Fadil found Lindita waiting for him in his room. She was the reason he didn't tell many people where he lived.

Lindita was a beauty, tall, with beige skin and glistening black hair. Her mother was Albanian, her father Montenegrin. She thought of herself as Albanian, but her brother had a picture of Milošević on his wall.

Fadil had known her since he was seven years old, when she was born to the family living next door in his home town of Rahovec. While they were growing up, she had always asked him what kind of girl he liked, and when he was twenty-four and she was seventeen, he said, 'All right, if you think you're old enough, let's start.'

But when her family found out, her father was angry, and her brother hit her, and tried to drive matchsticks under her finger-nails. When she told Fadil, he cornered her brother and punched him, knocking him down. A few days later, Fadil's mother heard from Lindita's mother (the Albanian in the house breaching Montenegrin security) that two of Lindita's uncles were waiting in Priština to beat Fadil up. She begged him not to go back for a few days longer. Fadil walked down the alley to Lindita's family's door and shouted over the garden wall, 'Tell them I'm taking the seven o'clock bus tomorrow!' The two men were waiting for him at the bus station, but they only glared.

Fadil and Lindita told their respective families that the relationship was over, and continued it in secret. In Priština they never met on the street. They never spoke to each other, except in Fadil's six-by-six room, which he had carefully chosen for its Serb landlady and Serb neighbours, to reduce nearly to zero the possibility of anyone he knew accidentally meeting any of them.

In Rahovec, when Fadil and Lindita happened to meet each other, they enquired politely after each other's health, as neighbours will do, and continued on their ways. The only other thing Fadil could do in Rahovec was sit and read by the window on the upper floor of his parents' house, where he could sometimes catch sight of Lindita in her parents' garden. Of course, she never looked up, and he never waved. Being Albanians in Kosovo, they were well versed in circumspection. Their secret was eight years old.

It was pleasant to see Lindita again, but I had to wonder if they had planned a tryst (and how rare were they?) that my unexpected arrival had disrupted. Perhaps she had been waiting here for some time while Fadil, obeying the iron dictates of Albanian hospitality, had taken me out for a coffee. I made a move towards absenting myself for a decent interval, but Fadil would have none of it. He was making more coffee and pulling out his translations. All three of us could barely fit in the room, and Fadil didn't seem to think Lindita would have much to say about poetry, so after a few minutes she left. 'She's a fiery one,' Fadil said proudly. 'And jealous as hell.'

He pointed to a translation over his desk of Corso's poem 'On the Walls of a Dull Furnished Room':

> I hang old photos of my childhood girls –
> with breaking heart I sit, elbow on table,
> chin on hand, studying
> > the proud eyes of Helen,
> > the weak mouth of Jane,
> > the golden hair of Susan.

'When she saw that, she hit the roof,' he said. 'She kept demanding, "Why *that* poem?" I told her there weren't many Beat poems about being faithful to your girlfriend, but it didn't help.' He had, in fact, cheated on her a number of times. But he didn't really look at it that way. He had needed to, that was all. Of course he had not told her. Her jealousy did not permit it.

Eventually, he would have to steal her. In Bosnia brides were stolen all the time – it was in fact a custom, and there were prescribed, orderly ways in which the offending family and the injured family re-established good relations. Among Albanians it was not as common, and their families might not reconcile for years.

But all that was still in the indefinite future. Fadil thought he should have a job first. Just last year Lindita had said again that she was willing to wait, but she was twenty-five now, and Fadil sometimes wondered if he was asking too much of her. He had not even finished his studies. 'It's easier to get into prison here than it is to get out of college,' he said to me ruefully. Whenever people asked him what he was planning to do about his future, he would only answer, 'I'm planning to stay alive.'

But enough of women! Fadil poured the coffee and lit a cigarette, and pulled out two translations of 'America', one by him and one by some idiot who translated for a different magazine and had written to Fadil's magazine saying there were seventy-seven mistakes in Fadil's translation. Fadil had fired back a letter pointing out the 122 mistakes in the idiot's published translation, and they had been furiously polemicizing against each other ever since.

'Just *look* at this! Ginsberg's line is "America I'm putting my queer shoulder to the wheel," and he has "strange"! But "queer" also means homosexual, doesn't it?'

'Yes.'

'Of course! So I have "pederast". Much better! Now look at *this* line . . .'

60

Serbs despised the Croats, but they were haunted by the Albanians. Croats were their twins who had gone bad, the unsettling image in the mirror of what the Serbs might have become had not God, in His grace, granted them their Serbness. The Albanians were bogeymen.

I was struck by a story told to me by Jasminka, an office worker in the Serbian tourist bureau in Belgrade. Her father had been born in Kosovo, and when he was nine years old – this was during World War II – his entire family had been murdered by Albanians. The killers had not harmed him, however, and Jasminka explained the omission by saying, 'They let him live so that he would remember.' It was simply inconceivable to her that those particular Albanians just might have spared her father because they, being perhaps human, could not bring themselves to kill a young boy. No, their 'mercy' was in fact an extra twist of the knife. In Jasminka's face, I could see a sort of awe at the contemplation of such evil genius.

Some stories Serbs believed about Albanians were literally medieval. I had been told more than once about the Serb children of Kosovo, whom Albanians had roasted on spits in front of their parents' eyes. This tale has had great staying power. You can read it in histories of the Crusades, where both sides accused the other of it. The Pasha of Bosnia told Arthur Evans in 1875 that the Christian rebels were guilty of doing this. The presence of the parents is almost always a feature.

A story I heard even more often concerned the young Albanian hooligans who took a Serb baby into a cemetery and tossed it back and forth until it died. The first time I came across this lurid little piece of theatre, I was struck by its incongruity. Now who, I wondered, had thought *that* up? The answer was, no one in this millenium. As I later discovered, the tale goes back far beyond the Middle Ages, back to the early Christian centuries. Interestingly enough, according to Umberto Eco, it was first spread around by Armenian bishops, who said it about the Bogomils. In earlier versions, the little body is torn apart after its death, and its blood mixed into the flour for the sacred host, which detail, of course, has survived in the perennial slanders against the Jews and their preparation of the Passover meal. This element was lacking in the version I heard about the Albanians, probably because Muslims don't use sacred bread in their ritual.

Was a child ever roast on a spit in the Balkans, or tossed

around like a rag doll and torn apart? If it happened, surely it was the result of an application of *lex talionis*, the horrified participants steeled to it by the conviction that it previously had been done to one of theirs. Thus do the ghouls of the imagination rise up to walk the earth. The Word becomes flesh.

The most unsettling aspect of all of this was the unanimity of Serbs' opinions about the Albanians, from drunks to bartenders to journalists to university professors. Even people who managed to be rational about the Croats, like Mirjana, could not speak of the Albanians without sounding as though their skin was crawling.

Vesna and Aleksandar, therefore, had seemed to me like a breath of fresh air. I had met them two years ago in Priština. They were Serbs who actually liked Albanians. And unlike the Slovenes and Croats, who embraced the Albanians the way northern white American liberals in the 60s embraced the safely distant southern blacks, Vesna and Aleks liked the Albanians even while living with them.

Vesna had been born in Priština and she spoke fluent Albanian, which was a rarity even among Kosovo Serbs. She was a sociologist in a country where the discipline hardly existed, and she could talk about Albanian culture and family structure without the Serbs' usual moral dread, their fastidious skirt-lifting. Her husband Aleks, who had been born in Bosnia, was the only Serb in the Union for Culture and Education, but got along well with his Albanian co-workers. When I had first met them, Vesna had just finished a job translating for an opinion poll among Serbs and Albanians in Kosovo. The first ever attempted, it showed that Albanians and Serbs didn't agree on much. It also showed how materially poor the Albanians were, and when Vesna invited me and a journalist from *Die Zeit* to a restaurant in Priština where we could eat traditional Albanian food, she talked at length about how much the Albanians' conditions moved her. (The directors of the survey – a bunch of Slovene agitators – were later arrested by the Serbian police.) 'You would never believe the absurd things that go on here,' Vesna had said over *flija*, the Albanian national dish. 'Just recently I read about a

Serb quarter in one of our towns which would not allow a *single Albanian family* to move in!'

'Actually, I don't have much trouble believing that,' I had said.

This year, when I told Fadil I was going to visit Vesna and Aleks, he said, 'They have changed.' He would not elaborate. 'You talk to them, and see.'

Two years ago, they had been living with Vesna's parents in the town of Kosovo Polje, a Serb enclave, but since then they had acquired their own apartment near the university, and I called to get directions. Vesna met me at the door. She introduced me to her eighteen-month-old son, Petar, and took me on a tour of the apartment: the master bedroom, the children's room, the kitchen, the dining room. The tour was quick, because these were all different parts of the same room. Two years ago, Vesna had always had on hand a reference book on the code of Leka Dugagjini, the basis of Albanian common law. I noticed now that the book prominently placed on their coffee table was a large and expensive publication on the medieval frescos of the Serbian Patriarchate in Peć.

We sat for coffee. Vesna told me that her parents still lived in Kosovo Polje. I remembered that two years ago they had been looking forward to getting out of Kosovo (they had never shared their daughter's fondness for the Albanians). They had been building a house in Kragujevac with money Vesna's father had earned from a decade of work away from his family in Baghdad. Now the house was finished, but stood empty. A new Serbian law prevented Serbs in Kosovo from selling their property. 'We are hostages here,' Vesna said.

She and Aleks seemed the same, she fluttering nervously with an air of being anxious to please, and he with his quiet, monkish demeanour, his charming opaque smile. His beard was trimmer. Perhaps that was in keeping with his new position as head of the Union for Culture and Education. His job entailed organizing public readings of books by Serb authors and arranging trips for Serb folk-dance troupes. But his favourite days, he said, were the ones in which he had nothing to do, and could sit at his desk and read German literature. There were a lot of those.

And Shkelzen? And Isuf? I asked.

Aleks said they were no longer working at the union. 'When the government started firing Albanians, it justified its actions on the grounds that they were separatists,' Vesna said. 'Why even get into that? All they had to say was that the Albanians hadn't shown up for work in a month! Isn't that a good enough reason?'

What had happened to change their opinions? I asked.

'You're not here as a reporter this time, are you?' Vesna asked.

'No.'

'You remember Helga, the journalist from *Die Zeit*?'

'Yes.'

'When she was here two years ago, she was taken by an Albanian translator to a few villages, and the Serbs kept behind their doors and wouldn't talk, while the Albanians invited her in and gave her presents – jewellery, clothes, food. So she went back to Germany and wrote about how wonderful the Albanians are and how terrible the Serbs are. So I don't talk to reporters any more.'

'I'm not a reporter. But I *am* writing a book.'

'I will talk to you as a friend.'

'I shouldn't put any of this in my book?'

'No. Well . . . Don't use our real names.'

'I won't.'

'Aleks and I have been disappointed in our Albanian friends. I got very angry when the demonstrations were going on in Albania against that terrible Stalinist government. A lot of the Albanians here in Kosovo signed a declaration in support of the President, Ramiz Alia!'

'Why do you think they did?'

'They didn't want to confront the horrible conditions there.'

'And you don't think that's understandable?'

'Albanians are *only* Albanians. That's the only way they define themselves. In Belgrade, a Serb is a Serb, but he's also a Communist, or a democrat. Or he's religious, or he's atheist.'

'Perhaps Albanians in Albania are like that,' I said.

'An Albanian can go to Belgrade or Slovenia and meet other people, become cosmopolitan. But when he comes back to his house in the village, he is exactly as he used to be. He's back in that rigid system. It's a closed society.'

'But you already knew that,' I said.

'I think it's the most closed society in Europe. My field as a sociologist is the role of women in Albanian society. But they won't let me talk to them any more! If an Albanian sociologist was interested in Serb culture, I would be absolutely delighted! The more we understand each other, the better. But the Albanians don't want me to do my work.'

Was this the crux of the problem? Had the Albanians closed ranks, leaving Vesna, who no doubt had prided herself on her almost unique access, feeling rejected, betrayed?

'They live in extended families of forty or fifty people, all in a single compound,' Vesna was saying. 'The head man is called "the god of the house", and the head woman is "the goddess". Each member is absolutely circumscribed by his or her role in the house.'

'But you already knew that,' I said again.

'The Serbs gave up that system forty years ago! Serb families are normal now! *Little* families!'

Her angry gesture took in Aleks and her son. The three-member family in the one-room flat: the twentieth century. The things she had always known had once given her pleasure *because* she had known them. The expert, she had told others. Now those very elements had locked her out, and she could only hate them in return.

'What really opened my eyes,' Vesna went on, 'was this farce about the poisoning.'

Ah, yes. I had heard both Serbian and Albanian accounts, and had come away with the feeling, as one so often did in Yugoslavia, that there was no way of knowing what had really happened. In March of the previous year, thousands of Albanian children and teenagers had suddenly become ill. They had fallen down in heaps on the playgrounds. Albanians had told me that the symptoms, which lasted from five hours to two days, were shivering, confusion, loss of consciousness, and blackened and bloated faces. No one had died, and recovery had been complete for all except a

342

few children who still experienced occasional relapses. Since no Serb children had been affected, the Albanians said the illness was a result of deliberate poisoning by the Serbs.

The Serbs scoffed. The children had been faking it, they said. They fell in unison, on secret command, and lay limply as they were taken to the infirmaries, and recovered sufficiently to sit up when reporters were present, to gasp that they had been poisoned, before falling melodramatically back.

Albanian doctors found poison. Serb doctors didn't even find symptoms. A French medical team was called in, and in the western press I had read that the team had found no clinical evidence of poisoning, but had been convinced that the Albanian children sincerely believed they were being poisoned, and ascribed this mass hysteria to the enormous pressure the Albanians were under in Kosovo. I had quoted this account to Albanians, and they had insisted I had it wrong. The French doctors *had* believed there was a poison, they said. But on their way back to France with blood samples for analysis, they stopped in Zagreb, and their samples were stolen from their hotel room.

How could we have poisoned only Albanian children? the Serbs demanded.

The Albanians had several theories. Time-delay 'vaccinations'? A certain food in the public supply poisoned, with secret instructions to the Serbs not to eat that food? The Albanians also pointed to the fact that two months before the incident, the school schedules in Kosovo had been changed. Instead of Serb and Albanian children attending school at the same time, as they had always done, Serb children went in the morning shift, and Albanian children in the afternoon. Gas in the classrooms? A poisoned powder on the desks?

My own doubt, which I voiced to Fadil, was: Why on earth would the Serbs execute this elaborate poisoning scheme, if it didn't kill anybody?

Fadil shrugged, unfazed: 'They were trying to provoke Albanians into a rebellion, so they could crack down.'

The 'poisoning' had happened only a year before, all over the province, in the most public manner possible, in front of thou-

343

sands of witnesses. And yet the divergence of opinion was absolute. Every Albanian I had met was convinced there had been a poisoning. Every Serb I had met was convinced there had not been. Both sides were sincere in their conviction. How could anyone, in the face of this phenomenon, hope to ever find out whether Albanian men really raped Serb girls? Kosovo was a house of mirrors.

Vesna: 'I watched young men as they looked around, and saw their friends on the ground. I could see them *decide* to become sick, and then become sick, and I could see that seconds after they had decided to become sick, they believed they were sick. I found it very frightening that they were capable of this.'

Depressed, I made ready to leave. Vesna and Aleks had been hospitable, and I thanked them.

'We want to move to Belgrade,' Vesna said. 'But there's no chance. I wonder about Petar growing up in Kosovo. Who will he play with? At the hospital, I was the only Serb giving birth. There were forty Albanian mothers.'

'It's a deliberate policy,' I said bleakly.

At the door, Vesna spoke lightly but searchingly. 'You're not CIA are you?'

'No. But I suppose if I were I wouldn't admit it.'

'A friend of mine says you must be a spy. How do you know I'm not working for the secret police?'

'I'm sure I've talked more than once to the secret police without knowing it.'

'I'm not working for the secret police.'

'I'm not a spy.'

'I've lived here for twenty-seven years. Perhaps I'm paranoid.'

She closed the door.

61

On a hot hazy day, Fadil and I went to Rahovec, his home town. As the smoking bus churned over the last brown hill and the town appeared below us, sprawled across the valley and stretching up the far slopes in a jumble of stone walls and alleys and clawed-out patches of earth, Fadil sighed and said, 'This must be the dirtiest place in the world.'

We walked up towards his parents' house from the bus station. Red dust swirled in the street, mingling with black smut from the few cars whose drivers had found gasoline, and flies from the horses pulling low wooden wagons loaded with hay and manure. In the lots between the collapsing slate-roofed houses and the unfinished breezeblock ones, mounds of trash towered over our heads. Two years ago the town had been neater, but the Albanian street cleaners, like everyone else, had stopped showing up at work and, like everyone else, they had been fired.

Fadil and I turned up a steep alley between high stone and mud-brick walls. The infamous walls. They reminded me of the old mountain towns of Bulgaria, or the villages of southern France, or the estates of Vojvodina, or, indeed, the monasteries of Serbia. Never had I encountered something as simple as a garden wall invested with so much sinister meaning.

'Here's one of the holes for shooting out of,' Fadil said, pointing to a tiny chink.

'So that's really true,' I said.

'If the Serbs had any brains at all, they'd give us guns and leave us alone, and we'd go back to killing each other.'

'*Samo sloga Albanca spašava*,' I said.

'Seriously though, there has naturally been less and less of the blood feuding as the years go by, even without this recent reconciliation drive. People could always stop a blood feud by bringing in a mediator who would set a settlement price, and now

345

a lot of families do that right away, instead of spending a few generations ambushing each other.'

Fadil's family had last been involved in a vendetta in the time of his father's father. The situation then had been rather complicated because in the previous generation a young member of the family had marched off to a neighbouring village to avenge a death, and had rashly shot and killed the first two men he met there – neither of whom belonged to the right family.

We passed the green metal door of Lindita's house, and a few feet farther on opened another green door, and passed into a dim garden of pear and apple trees, and flowerbeds marked off with pickets made of half-buried liquor bottles. We were greeted by Fadil's sister-in-law, Violeta, a young barefoot black-haired woman. Fadil's mother, Drita, set about making us coffee.

The house was a spacious, two-storey concrete structure that Fadil's parents had built some thirty years ago when they had moved into Rahovec from their ancestral village, about ten kilometres distant. The downstairs sitting room was furnished with a wrap-around sofa covered in alarming lime-green polyester hair, facing a television set. The upstairs sitting room had another sofa (less unkempt), and one of those massive dark shelf-and-wardrobe combinations so popular throughout Eastern Europe. Fadil's bedroom was a larger version of his Priština cubby-hole, with a collage of rock posters on the walls and stacks of stolen books. His two sofabeds were the most hirsute of all, exhaling thirty years' worth of cigarette smoke and sweat, winter mildew and summer dust.

That night the family welcomed me with a meal that must have cost Fadil's brother, the only wage-earner in the house, more money than he made in a fortnight. The low table in the upstairs sitting room disappeared under platters of grilled beef, whole grilled chickens, cheeses and cow's brains. Fadil and I had been dispatched to pick up the brains, which a butcher-friend of his had hacked out of the skull with an axe, bone chips tapping off the walls, while we waited. The brains were a special treat, I knew, and particularly expensive, so I ate the sickly rich, jelly-

346

soft curds with what I hoped was a look of unsqueamish gusto stapled to my face.

Perhaps because these were townfolk, the family's size was 'normal'. Fadil had only two siblings, a married sister who lived in a different town, and his brother Xhevdet, Violeta's husband, who worked in the tax office and 'earned ten litres of gasoline a day', as he put it.

Xhevdet was also a poet. (If in the rest of Yugoslavia every young person seemed to be an engineer, in Kosovo a random table at the teahouse usually proved to be filled with poets and philosophers.) His first collection of dense, elliptical poems had just been published in a thin paperback with the trademark bright yellow cover of Kosovo's only publishing house. As he tried to do with Jim Morrison, Fadil admired the poems without much admiring the poet. He considered Xhevdet a bit of a bore.

Although Xhevdet was the younger brother, he looked considerably older. Grimacing perpetually, with a light sheen of sweat across his brown, stubble-shadowed face, he seemed always to be undergoing abdominal surgery without anaesthesia. Perhaps he had an ulcer from the responsibilities he had taken on. What he thought of his layabout older brother, stuck in his young-rebel time warp and not even writing his own poetry, I could never detect.

The two women of the house, Violeta and Drita, had a table of their own, lower and smaller, like a children's tray, at which they knelt and nibbled pretzels when they weren't restocking the men's plates. The fifth member of the family was four-year-old Gent, Xhevdet's and Violeta's son. Like the Serb boy I had met outside Donji Vakuf, he had learned early what it meant to be a man. He liked to stand in the doorway with his fists on his hips, surveying the room with a know-it-all's imperviousness to curiosity or surprise. He slept every night with his grandmother, having announced to her that he would protect her until her husband came home.

The exact whereabouts of Fadil's father were unknown. A prominent photograph in the downstairs sitting room showed a man with Latinate good looks; the only soft lines of his face were in the well-formed lips. He had fought as a Partisan during the war. For most of the war, the Albanian Partisans thought (understandably, since Tito had promised them) that their reward for resisting the aggressor would be an Albanian state that corresponded to the extent of the Albanian nation, or at least an Albanian unit in a Balkan Communist federation including Yugoslavia and Bulgaria. Whatever Fadil's father may have thought when those promises evaporated in the last days of the war and Serb Partisans took to killing Albanian Partisans, he never told his family. He remained a Communist, and after Yugoslavia's expulsion from the Cominform in 1948 he became an unswervingly loyal Titoist.

In the Soviet Union, deep roots in the class struggle were often rewarded with a trial and the noose. Communism in Yugoslavia was never that psychotic, and old warriors didn't die, they just fell into sinecures. After a two-year spell of trouble with the new Serbian rulers during which he was not allowed to work, Fadil's father became a Party functionary, and eventually rose to become Chairman of the Rahovec Town Council. During the hard years of strong Serbian rule in Kosovo in the 50s and 60s, any Albanian Communist must have looked like a quisling to his fellow-nationals. Then came the golden 70s and early 80s, when the Albanian Communists were allowed to go local in a long, fine wallow of public spending and ethnic quota-filling that made them both comfortable *and* popular. Then Milošević appeared, and in March 1989, the chairmen from all the city councils of Kosovo witnessed, as 'guests' of the Serbian Parliament, the promulgation of the new Serbian Constitution which annulled much of Kosovo's autonomy. Throughout all these changes, Fadil's father must have shown a certain pragmatic flexibility, because when the new, pliant Kosovo Parliament was constituted the Serbs allowed him to become a member.

He was, in other words – although neither Fadil nor Xhevdet said this – one of the 'hand-picked' men, one of those the Serbs felt they could trust, one of the 'toadies and idiots' as Gazmend had harshly put it. He may not have deserved such scorn; he may have been a decent man. But clearly he felt his fights were behind

348

him. If youth thought him too compliant, then let youth fight as he had fought.

But the Serbs passed a referendum signalling their intention of abolishing Kosovo's autonomy altogether, and Fadil's father, sixty-five years old and with a family to support, and not in good health, had to become a hero again, as he had not been since he was twenty. In July 1990, he had voted to make Kosovo an independent republic of Yugoslavia, after which, along with his fellow-parliamentarians, he had gone into hiding. When the news reached Rahovec, his Serb neighbour across the alley was heard to yell over the wall, 'I'll kill the whole family!' In September Fadil's father and his paunchy, flabby conspirators gathered again in utmost secrecy in a town near the Macedonian border for a constitutional convention, and after a long day's work they held a twenty-minute public ceremony in the town's Hall of Culture, in which they officially proclaimed the Republic of Kosovo. Then they fled into Macedonia. Fadil's father eventually made his way to Slovenia, where he considered himself safe. Then Slovenia seceded and the Serbian tanks rolled in, and he fled again. The last the family had heard, he was headed for Germany.

Between tentative spoonfuls of bovine grey matter I gently enquired of Fadil and Xhevdet how it might have been that their father had been considered safe by the Serbs. But no stories were forthcoming. They preferred to remember that once *in* the Parliament, their father had been the first to stand up and say, 'I did not fight as a Partisan for this.' By 'this' he had meant the oppression of the Albanians in Kosovo, Fadil said. That had been clear to everyone.

When the meal was over, the women began cleaning up while the men headed for cigarettes and the evening news in the downstairs sitting room. In the hall, I noticed the complete works of Tito, in a long matching set of massive red volumes, probably the man's weight in words.

'See?' Fadil grinned. 'He must have been great. He wrote more than Shakespeare.'

349

62

Since they were all out of work, the men of Rahovec were
fortunate in being naturals at hanging out. Fadil and I would
walk down a hot bright street, and within a few yards he would
meet someone he knew, and you never met someone you knew
without retiring to the nearest teahouse for a Russian tea or a
Schweppes or a beer (no one bought the beer from Peć any more,
because the factory had been taken over by Serbs), and a long,
aimless conversation in the fuggy shade.

We met Idriz, who had been arrested the previous year during
a one-day general strike. Two policemen took him up to the
fourth floor of the police station and swung him by his hands and
feet in front of an open window. Then they tried to break his
wrist by tying his hand back against his forearm, but since he was
a butcher he had strong wrists. Then they hit him on the head a
few times so that now, ten months later, he still had a buzz in his
ears.

We met the black-toothed, wiry Korab, who used to be 'the
biggest drunk in town', as he said himself.

'Bigger than me,' Fadil agreed.

'Fadil? Anh, he was nothing!'

Korab had stopped drinking two years ago, and was now
drunk on Islam. He told me that Judaism was to be reviled
because it claimed the Jews were a chosen people. Their two
thousand years of homelessness was a punishment for their
hubris. Islam was for everyone.

'There's a Ginsberg line, "Jahweh fights Allah,"' Fadil commented, *à propos* of that. 'I'm having trouble translating it. I have
"*zot*" and "*perendia*", but I think that means more "God" and
"Lord".'

'Jahweh and Allah are the same,' Korab said.

350

'But in the poem, Ginsberg is referring to the Jewish god and the Arab god.'

'But they are the same god!'

'I'm not talking theology, I'm talking literature. "Jahweh" and "Allah" mean two different things.'

'You can only say that because you are not a believer!'

'Even if I *were* a believer, I'd still have to translate the poem!'

'Allah is Allah! He is Lord and God!'

'Brian, help me out here.'

'Forget it.'

We met the muscular, blond Osmand, who did a hilarious imitation of Serb policemen: the swagger, the menace, the ostentatious display of heavy weaponry. '"Hands up!" "Lie down!" "Over there!" "Back up!" Pah! They are Rambos! We Albanians are different. When we take out a gun, it is to shoot somebody. Very simple, I pull out the gun, bam bam, you fall over dead.'

We met Selim, who recalled the days when Albanians said 'Father Hitler' and 'Uncle Mussolini'.

Fadil wondered aloud why, if we say that Napolean was great, and Alexander was great, we don't call Hitler great?

'I suppose I would argue for not calling any of them great,' I said.

'We need a second Hitler,' Selim said. 'Someone to bomb the hell out of Belgrade.'

We met Anton, a teary, slack-jawed wreck, slugging brandy out of a bagged bottle. He was the last Albanian still working at the police station. The Serbs had kept him on because he was the only person who knew how to work the telex machine.

Fadil quoted Jim Morrison: 'Here every day is a century.'

We met Ramadan, who said, 'It's natural that Albanians look to America, because the Serbs are looking to Russia. Russia has always supported Serbia. An old Serb saying is "God in Heaven and Mother Russia on Earth." I think Albania will become a second Israel for America.'

'I'm not sure we could afford it,' I said.

'I heard the US is going to open up an American Centre in Priština!' said Ramadan.

'Next step, it will be a US consulate!' said Fadil.

'Third step, an embassy!' said Ramadan.

I was now in a part of the world where the guest was never allowed to pay for anything, under any circumstances. 'We are poor,' the Albanians always said, 'but we are not so poor as that.'

In fact, they were so poor that many of them could not pay for themselves. Others at the table would pay, or the waiters, who turned out to be friends, would not present a bill. Since everyone chainsmoked, cigarettes seemed to be an alternative currency, functioning as a social lubricant. A new arrival at the table would toss a couple of cigarettes to every person seated, or he would tuck one behind a friend's ear or into his breast pocket. Fadil was so pleased to be so many more cigarettes away from destitution that he would line them up next to his tea glass where he could gaze on them. The first time someone offered one to me, I said I didn't smoke, but Fadil interjected considerably less than half jokingly, 'Give it to him anyway. He'll give it to me.'

Back out on the street, we did occasionally pass people Fadil did not know, and they invariably stared angrily at our two beards. More than once a child mimed violence, either cradling forward with a gurgle of pain from a knife in the gut, or jolting backward from the impact of a sniper's bullet.

'Doesn't it start to get on your nerves?' I asked Fadil.

'What?'

'The stares.'

'If I paid attention to what was going on around me, I'd have to kill twenty people between here and the centre of town.'

Back at the house in the evenings, we would listen to Fadil's rock-and-roll records ('People here say that Mick Jagger had Brian Jones killed') while Violeta brought us dinner and coffee. Or we would listen to Xhevdet, while Violeta brought us dinner and coffee. Xhevdet seemed burdened by armies of interlocking theories about art and politics. He would grimace, lounging barefoot on the hairy sofa, and unburden himself on us. Violeta had caught me one day washing my trousers in the bathtub, and had taken away all my dirty clothes to do herself. When everything else was done, she and Drita would sit with the men and

352

knit socks and crochet table coverings. Violeta usually had a textbook open next to her. After all, she was a medical student.

On the television, members of the Serbian Parliament were locked in a long debate about whether there was any such thing as Serbo-Croatian, or whether everyone in Yugoslavia spoke Serbian. Meanwhile, Serb mothers were storming the parliament building, demanding the return of their soldier sons from the fighting in Slovenia and Croatia.

'These are the same mothers who marched to the Parliament four years ago and said, "Give us arms to fight the Albanians,"' Fadil said. 'Now they see. I am sorry for them, but they asked for this. Everyone in the world knows that war is terrible, except for the Serbs. They think it is glorious. But if they want a war in Kosovo, we will show them that it is not glorious. As Jim Morrison says, "They've got the guns, but we've got the numbers."'

By the time we stretched out on Fadil's sofabeds long after midnight, I was always exhausted. 'I like to live each day on ten coffees, two beers and two hours of sleep,' Fadil said. 'Training for becoming young.'

'I'm training to grow old,' I yawned.

'You don't have to train for that.'

Fadil had offered to take me to see the village his family had come from. When we left Rahovec, Violeta gave me what she had been knitting. Wedding socks, for my wife. The new Vesna would have known that Violeta was merely buying a journalist.

63

The seven a.m. bus to Malisheva would not stop in the street for a couple of Chetniks, so Fadil and I caught the seven-fifteen at the station. It was filled with workers going back to their jobs in Austria. These were the people who were keeping Kosovo from complete economic collapse. They were taking the seven-fifteen bus because the driver was Albanian, and he would not charge them for the Kosovo portion of their trip, saving them each about $6. On his cassette deck he played Albanian folk songs, which sounded like overlapping muezzin's calls except for the frenzied accompaniment of twanging strings and tambourines. 'This one is about the new bride in the house who doesn't satisfy the mother-in-law,' Fadil said with an embarrassed twitch of his lips. He didn't like the stuff. If he wanted orientalism, he listened to Deep Purple.

Our driver stopped on a hill for a chat with a bus heading the other way. The other driver was a Serb. As the two men eased out their clutches to go on, the Serb handed across two cigarettes. Our driver tossed an entire packet. He had a dozen more packets under a towel on his dashboard, for later encounters. Perhaps it was why he still had his job.

At Malisheva, the weekly fair was in progress. The older men wore pocketless wool pants that rode low on the hip, and the distinctive Albanian skullcaps of pressed white wool that looked like volleyball halves. Their beetling brows obviated the need for hat brims. Ash pitchforks were for sale, and smuggled clothing, and tambourines made of sheep skin stretched across rings cut from steel barrels. The food section was large but unvaried: thousands of peppers, tomatoes and cucumbers. 'We are *used* to living without meat,' a seller told me. (Implication: The Serbs aren't; we are tougher than the Serbs.) Fadil met a friend at the fair who passed him the message that his father had reached Germany and was staying with distant cousins. He was all right.

We walked out of Malisheva, on the road towards Lubishta. It was already hot. The occasional car sped by very fast, and the heat was greater on the asphalt, but Fadil did not want to take the old dirt road under the poplars by the river because, he explained, we would be walking past isolated farms, and if two Chetniks were seen approaching, well . . .

'So you're admitting there *is* Albanian terror against Serbs,' I said.

'No, no! But people are nervous.'

We left the asphalt near Lubishta and took the dirt road into the village. The stone walls were punctuated by beautiful ten-foot-high gates made from closely woven saplings, like Cyclopean wickerwork. I followed Fadil into a low concrete shed that turned out to be a tiny grocery store, and we sat on milk crates sipping tonic water. Fadil knew everyone in Lubishta, because the only regular job he had ever had was a two-year teaching stint in an elementary school just behind the village. Excited word went out that Fadil had arrived with an American in tow, and soon a number of friends had gathered. By the time we returned to the blinding heat, we were a small crowd. One man ran off to chase a water buffalo out of a cornfield, and another dug up half a dozen potatoes and filled my pockets with them.

The school was a bare concrete box in a pitilessly shadeless field. Fadil had hated his two years there. 'If you have no tail, they'll pin one on you; if you do have a tail, they'll chop it off,' a friend warned him of the dimwit Communist school bureaucrats. Fadil's main problem, in their eyes, was that he did not beat the children.

'I came to teach them, not to beat them,' Fadil said.

'But they're not afraid of you,' the school officials said.

'I came to teach them, not to make them afraid of me.'

An argument developed on our way back through the village over which person in the group would have the honour of being our host. 'It's always like this,' Fadil said. 'We'll have to promise whoever loses to have meals in their houses on the way back tomorrow.'

At length we were captured by a fellow named Ismet, a hollow-cheeked man with a great half-dome of sun-freckled forehead and a dense black beard. (His was the only beard in the village. Now we were *three* Chetniks – an army.) Fadil winced. 'Ismet *clings*,' he said to me.

Like all the family compounds in the village, Ismet's was behind a high wall. The building in which guests were received was in its traditional place, just inside the great wooden doors, on the right. Under the arch over the gateway, a round pan of flija was cooking unattended on an open fire. Straight on was the courtyard, and the several living quarters, in ochre brick. What the Serbs never said when they talked about these 'fortresses' – or perhaps they simply didn't know, never having been inside one – was that quite often the only real wall was the one facing the street. The backs, as in this case, often opened directly out on to the fields, and compounds were often separated from those next to them only by low walls or brush fences.

The population of Ismet's household currently numbered seventeen. Ismet was one of four brothers, each of whom had a house in the compound, as did their father, who was still the head of the household. 'But we can disagree with him, and sometimes get our way,' Ismet assured me, no doubt familiar with the things the Serbs said. One brother had four children, another had two. Ismet had an infant daughter. The household had divided twice in Ismet's lifetime. When he had been in elementary school, an uncle had split off, taking half of the family's twenty hectares. (He was a son from a previous marriage, and each marriage counted as an equal inheritance unit.) Then a few years later his father's full brother took half of the remaining land. So the current household of seventeen had only five hectares, and I asked the obvious question. Since Albanian common law had no principle of primogeniture, how did they prevent the land being broken up into impossibly small holdings?

'We force the Serbs out and take *their* land,' Fadil deadpanned.

Ismet jumped. Then he laughed nervously. 'Of course, he's joking.'

'Of course,' I said.

'Fortunately, many sons don't want to stay in the village,' Ismet said. 'They sell their rights to their brothers and go to Priština, or they go abroad to work.'

But you could see the awkward results of land division in this case. The household's courtyard ran straight back from its street frontage in a long narrow band. The uncle who had broken off lived with his sons in the band next door. The two households did not get along very well. Across the sluggish creek at the back were the real fields, which were divided higgledy-piggledy into plots with no natural borders. Much of the tension originated here, as one household's planting, say, 'accidentally' encroached

356

on the fallow plot of another, or one household diverted more than its share of water from the creek. I noticed a wall of cinderblocks was being erected between the two courtyards. At least there were no holes for shooting through.

We returned to the building by the gate, took our shoes off in the small outer room, and went on into the *odë*, where guests were entertained. The odë was empty of furniture except for a low round table. The whitewashed walls were bare. Thin cushions ran around the edges of the room. The guest's place was on the cushion in the middle of the far wall, facing the door – at the centre of attention, and farthest away from chores. He was supposed to repay hospitality by telling good stories, a custom that always made me nervous.

Only males entered the odë. The females of the household delivered food to the outer room, knocked on the door and departed. The food was then brought in by one of the men. Some Christian monasteries had similar arrangements, to prevent the monks lusting after the cooks. After several months of solitary travel, I felt a little like a monk myself, and when I was afforded a second's glimpse of a pretty, long-haired girl in Turkish pants who had not vacated the outer room fast enough after bringing flija and roasted peppers, I suppose I felt in a pale way what a man born to the life would have: the mere sight of her, fleeting and taboo, felt charged, erotic.

For the meal we sat on the floor around the low table. A large cloth spread beneath the table was brought up over our laps like a common napkin. There were no plates. The crisped oily peppers were piled on the table in front of each of us, and we pulled the thick doughy layers of flija with our fingers from the common pan. As a national dish, flija said something about the poverty of the Albanians. Made out of nothing but wheatflour and milk, it went down like successive flaps of rubber matting. Fadil held back until we neared the bottom because he thought the slightly burned parts were the best. 'At least they taste like *something*,' he said.

Afterwards the cigarettes were passed around, tucked behind ears. 'Smoking is good for you after a meal,' Fadil explained to

357

me. 'It clears the lungs.' We sat back on the cushions and drank quarts of sweet, strong lemony tea. I told a lame story or two. Ismet brought out some Skenderbeg cognac, which all present agreed was the finest in the world. It came from Albania. After my second glass I refused repeated urgings that I accept another. But Fadil announced, '*I* will have another, anyway,' and poured liberally. Ismet was unable to suppress a glare, into which Fadil smiled serenely, saying, 'Because it's rare.' And to me: 'And because it's *expensive.*'

The patriarch regarded me with his deep blue eyes, meditatively smoothing his snowy moustache, and asked, through Fadil, why I didn't build a munitions factory in Kosovo.

'He assumes every American is a wealthy capitalist,' Fadil explained.

I apologized for not being able to do so.

And why didn't America give Albanians the atom bomb? That was what they really needed.

I explained that the current thinking in Washington was that such a move would be destabilizing.

Fadil and I made our apologies and rose. We still had a number of miles to walk. Ismet announced that he would come with us. '*Clings!*' Fadil groaned to me. At the gate, one of the boys handed me a bag from the kitchen. The women had cooked my potatoes.

We made our way across meadows of flowering camomile, bird's-foot and chicory. Flocks of jackdaws chipped and beeped in the willows, and rose en masse to fan out and wheel in the white sky. Distant brown slopes rose up into broken-rocked hills.

Looking up at the trees, Fadil said, 'I want to be buried under two trees. Not with one of these stone chunks stuck in my mound. I want a birch at my head and a linden at my feet. The white birch for my pure thoughts, the fat linden leaves for my sure feet.'

'That's nice,' I said.

'Thank you.'

Ismet took a picture of Fadil standing in front of two trees, which happened to be willows. A creek had cut a ditch behind him, and it looked like a trench for a mass grave.

358

We waded barefoot across the creek, and beyond lay another village, and another concrete shed, where we sat again on milk crates in the dark and drank tonic while people gathered. It so happened that a journalist was in the village who had lost his job when the Serbs closed down the main Kosovo newspaper. He was privately shooting a documentary on some massacres that had occurred in the vicinity in 1919. Fadil generally hated journalists and this was no exception. 'Where was this guy five years ago?' he growled to me. 'And what's the point anyway of talking about seventy-year-old deaths?'

The journalist wanted a shot of his source – a fleshy, toothless ancient – tottering down the village street, as though deep in melancholy remembrance. The old man tottered, alone in the dust between the stone walls, and the journalist crept along behind him, and the whole village stampeded on the heels of the journalist. The old man pointed his cane out over the meadows that Fadil, Ismet and I had just crossed and the ditch that perhaps *was* a mass grave, and described how the Serbs had thrown children in the air and caught them on their bayonets.

'The rape of Belgium!' I said.

'What?' asked Ismet.

'That's an old story.'

'It's true!' Ismet said indignantly.

'The killings I can believe. Not the bayonets.'

'It *must* be true! He saw it!'

But it turned out that the old man had *not* seen it. He had been born on the first anniversary of the massacre. And Fadil's question lingered. Why do this? If it were just to remember, that was one thing. But it was not just to remember. The baby of those bitter times was now barely holding on to life, and the greedy camera had had to search him out and prod him with questions. Did the Albanians really need more reasons to hate the Serbs? This only reinforced the appalling Balkan belief that seventy-year-old murders were set right by sparkling fresh ones.

We set off again into the hills, through watermelon fields. At the upper end of each field stood a grass wigwam on stilts, wide enough for a man to lie in, tall enough for him to sit up in. In a few days, a three-week vigil would begin, as one man from every household would move out into his wigwam to guard the melons from the cowherd boys through the thirsty days and the temptingly dark nights.

I remarked that it sounded gruelling.

Oh no, they rejoined. It was a coveted job: you just sat all day, and the women brought you food and drink.

Fadil quoted Pink Floyd: ' "So you think you can tell/heaven from hell? Blue skies from pain?" '

We continued up through brush and stone, and cleared the top of the hill. Below us spread the valley in which Fadil's ancestral village, Ponorac, lay. 'The most beautiful village in the world,' he said, with an uncharacteristic lack of irony.

We followed a dirt road down into the valley, and traced a serpentine course between the brush-fenced fields. A boy, catching sight of three Chetniks, leaped comically in the air and sprinted full-tilt away from us. He reappeared at a couple of distant curves, still running madly, and was gone.

We came into the most beautiful village in the world. And it seemed, indeed, a competitor, with the sun finally shading orange and sliding off our backs, the white walls snaking along the contours of the land like mini-Great Walls, the intricate sapling gates, the mountains rearing up behind. Fadil pointed out which houses used to shoot at which others.

We sat on milk crates and drank tonic once more, and then pressed on to Fadil's uncle's house for tea in the odë. Fadil's father had given up his portion when he moved to Rahovec, but one of the brothers had recently given him back a plot, saying he or Xhevdet or Fadil should build a house on it one day. Fadil showed me the grassy place, and fantasized about the rooms he would have, filled with books. He would have the peace and quiet to carry out his next translation project.

'Which is?'

'*Finnegans Wake*.'

He had already stolen a crib and a concordance.

With a dozen friends, we walked up a narrow valley to the source of the stream that watered the village. On the way we passed through the small bit of woods that had been left standing by general agreement, so that the shepherds and cowherds could have a shaded place in which to nap. Fadil pointed out a large field above, which as far back as anyone could remember had always been common grazing land, until the village woke one morning a couple of years ago to discover that one of the households during the night had marked off a plot for itself, and within hours the entire population was out there in tractors, furiously marking off plots before it could all be taken, and now there was no common grazing land. Fadil shook his head. 'Do you think the Serbs could be right about us?'

We all took a ritual drink from the stream where it bubbled up cool and clear from the hillside, then walked back down through the growing dusk. Someone climbed a wall, and came back with an armload of cucumbers, passing one to each. We sat in the grass eating the cucumbers, watching the stars come out.

Conversation turned to imponderables, as it will do under the stars. Golden past, leaden present, nameless dread, precarious life, transient youth, inevitable women.

It turned out that all of us were married except Fadil. About half the men had had arranged marriages. Most had not expected companionship, did not want it and did not have it. Marriage provided sustenance and community ties. It made as much sense to talk to the food on your plate, or to the gift a man gave you. I wondered what the others would have made of Fadil whispering on his parents' phone to Lindita.

'May Fadil's bride stand still all night long,' someone said. It was an old blessing, describing an ancient but still current custom. On his wedding day the groom danced and drank, and the more extravagantly he did so the better he showed himself. The bride's duty, meanwhile, was to turn herself into an icon of the marriage commodity: she was to stand stock-still for hours, with her eyes almost closed, her hands in front of her, one palm up, the other palm down, the fingers lightly touching.

It occurred to me that for all the self-vaunting talk in Yugoslavia about the Croat/Serb/Muslim culture that I would find out in those pristine Croat/Serb/Muslim villages, only in Kosovo were the old rural traditions still more or less intact, and all they aroused in the Serbs was hatred, and in Croats and Slovenes a vague unease about 'backwardness'. Perhaps the other Yugoslavs really did want their tradition to consist of costumes and coffee-making and nothing more, the waxwork kitsch that Nino had spoken of, so many weeks ago.

Or perhaps they despised Albanian tradition only because they recognized in it no high culture. Fadil himself had admitted to me, with endearingly frank ruefulness, 'OK, I know we've been here the whole time, fine. I *know* that. But you can see the Roman baths, the Turkish mosques, the Serbian monasteries. Where are *our* buildings?'

The answer, of course, was everywhere — in the mud-brick villages, with their high walls and shooting holes. And it brought you back face to face with the question haunting all of the Balkans: Once you decided that civil rights were nationally based, you inevitably ended up arguing about competing national rights, and therefore more deserving nations. And what more indicative of just deserts than high culture? Did not glorious epic poetry and glorious monasteries permit you to supplant a people who built no glorious monasteries, who wrote no glorious poems?

I recalled a conversation I had once had with a tourist guide on the Croatian island of Korčula. During the war, she had said, the Italians had randomly picked up several young men off the streets whom they were going to shoot as hostages. One of the men happened to be a talented sculptor. 'They said he would have been another Meštrović!' the guide said, stricken. 'So the towns-people said they would give the Italians *ten* other boys to shoot, if only they would not shoot that one.' She wailed, 'But they did not listen!'

I slept that night in Fadil's uncle's odë. The next day we hiked to a swimming hole, where some of us swam, while Fadil chased his friends with a stinging nettle. A cousin took us on a sightseeing trip in his car; many miles from the village the car ran low on fuel, and all the filling stations were empty. The rumour was, gasoline was being diverted for Army use.

'It usually disappears right at harvest time, anyway,' Fadil said. 'So that our food will rot in the fields.'

We hitched a ride on a truck. The driver would never have stopped for two Chetniks, he said, but he recognized Fadil's cousin. It was his own truck he drove, mostly hauling sand for private construction projects, but he couldn't make a decent living any more. His licence last year had cost 100 dinars, but this year the Serbs raised it to 5,000. And then there were the police, who stopped Albanian truck drivers so often for unspecified 'violations' – it happened to him about once a day – that the 'fine' was a standard 200 dinars; and to save time, whenever he saw a cop signal him over, he just slowed down and held the money out of the window.

The Serbs were calling Albanian reserves into the Army, he went on. Friends of his who had been called were hiding, driving only on back roads.

'Why would the Serbs want potentially unreliable Albanians in their army?' I naïvely asked.

'To get the men out of the villages,' Fadil said.

'Ah. So they won't be able to fight if the Serbs crack down.'

'Well, mainly to get them all into a camp somewhere, so the Serbs can shoot them all *before* they crack down,' the driver said.

He dropped us off twenty kilometres outside Djakov. 'The police have a roadblock up ahead,' he apologized, 'and they would give me trouble for transporting you. A bus stops here sometimes.' He headed off, calling out the window to Fadil, 'See you when we're free!'

We were in the middle of fields. Two young men had been waiting at the bus stop for a couple of hours. Fadil fell into a conversation with them about Ibrahim Rugova. One of the youths expressed the commonly heard doubt about whether Rugova knew what he was doing when he kept advising the Albanians to wait, to ignore all provocations.

'Patience, sure,' the man said. 'I will be patient.' His face became anguished. 'But the question is, patient *for how long*?'

64

My bus ground up out of Kosovo, passing long lines of tractors with boys sitting glumly in the intense heat, waiting at empty gas stations for a miraculous tanker.

The passengers were Serb, the driver was Serb. Over the loudspeaker came Serbian folk music. The only Albanian, Shkelzen, was sitting next to me. He told me a complicated, improbable story about a job he had in Niš, and I concluded he was on a smuggling trip. An intimidated couple across the aisle were Serb neighbours from his little village. They were heading for Soko Banja, where the ailing woman – she was suffering from 'nerves' – would see a specialist and take the curative radon baths. They had rarely been out of their village, and never out of Kosovo, and were relying on their more worldly Albanian neighbour to pilot them through the terrifying wider world.

We stopped at an isolated roadside inn, where the driver could eat a meal for free while the passengers paid for it with premium prices on Cokes and coffees. A shell game was in process in the parking lot. Of course, all of the men around the table – the kibitzers, the stupid oaf who always lost, the regular joe who picked the obvious shell and won – were in league. The marble really *was* under the obvious shell, but if you were fool enough to bet on it the man knew how to squirt it into his palm.

I went to the toilet, and by the time I came back the men had scored.

'I beg of you!' The husband of the sick woman was pursuing one of the conmen around the lot, weeping. 'Please! I beg of you!'

The big man pushed him away. 'Fuck off.' His colleagues were throwing their things into a car.

In the space of two minutes, the husband had lost all of his hard currency – DM100. He had needed it to pay the doctor in

Soko Banja. His Albanian protector had not been worldly enough: Shkelzen had been cheated too, out of another DM50.

The conmen had jumped in their car and taken off. The husband was crying for a policeman. The bus driver was telling him to get back on the bus or be left behind. His wife was collapsed in her seat, sobbing, 'Thieves everywhere! That's why Yugoslavia is falling apart!'

The husband was cowed by the driver into getting on board. He cast about for sympathy, but the other passengers clucked their tongues disapprovingly. They wondered how he could have been so stupid. So did his wife, who would not let him sit next to her. Shkelzen huddled next to me. 'How did he do it?' he asked of no one in particular.

The two country bumpkins, Serb and Albanian. I delved into my emergency stores of hard currency and handed $60 to Shkelzen. He passed every dollar of it over to his Serb neighbours.

Part Six

The Impossible Country

65

After a few days back among Serbs in Niš, I came to the conclusion that their mood was rapidly hardening, and at the same time becoming clearer, like glue drying. Now when I admitted I was an American they would either grunt and fall silent, their customary hospitality struggling with their fury at Washington's tilt against them, or they would back me into a corner and let me have it with both barrels: the history, the martyrdom, the glory, the inability of the world to understand. The degree to which one furious interlocutor and the next were interchangeable was positively spooky. Pausing to think of an example of how Tudjman was changing the language *exactly as the Ustashas had done*, three people in a row, who did not know each other, chose the same word, out of dozens of possibilities. Had the example been printed in *Politika* that morning? Maybe an American could never actually *understand* Serbs, but after a few days in Serbia he would at least have learned the lesson by rote.

This repetitiveness was ominous for politics, problematic for the travel writer. I took to noting down any departure from the standard tirade. One man in a kafana saw me writing with my left hand, and leaned over my table to say bitterly, 'All Americans are left-handed!' In a country where they still slapped toddlers for reaching with their left hands, he meant it both literally and figuratively.

The wheel was coming around again, and this time the Serbs would have to fight for right entirely on their own. As they had once borne the full weight of the Turks and had heroically endured, they would now bear the full weight of world censure.

369

'Speak in Serbian and the whole world will understand you,' was an old saying of theirs. What they really meant was, God would understand you.

I caught up on the news, which had been hard to come by in Kosovo.

The Yugoslav Army had agreed to a complete withdrawal from Slovenia. In other words, Slovenia was going to get away. Croat leaders had fought the decision to withdraw, because they had feared it meant the Army would concentrate its powers on *them*, and they were probably right. The televisions in the bars were reporting five-hour gun battles in Slavonia that resulted in three dead, five dead. The men in the bars clucked their tongues in disbelief. A militiaman was interviewed live from his hospital bed and when he was asked how many had been killed that day in his unit he began, 'About sixty – ' but the transmission was cut off. Even the Serbs were having some trouble with young men hiding from the reserves – soft city boys, the curse of modernity – and it would be much worse if people knew how many were actually dying in Croatia. Were there really refrigerated trucks leaving the battlefields, secret mass-burials in the dead of night? Were Serbs and Croats now dropping their *own* into pits, and sealing them away? The possibility seemed worse than death itself. It conjured up unquiet thoughts of armies of unquiet spirits abroad in the night.

The much-publicized 'mothers' movement' was continuing. Serb mothers had been invading the Serbian Parliament, Croat mothers the Croatian Parliament, each group chanting that nationalism was nothing to them compared to the lives of their sons. 'Idiocy!' they cried. 'A men's war!' 'Listen to the mothers!' To better dramatize their message, the Serb mothers and the Croat mothers had joined forces. They had rented buses, planning to ride together from Zagreb through the battle zones, picking up mothers as they went. When they arrived in Belgrade they would descend on the Federal Parliament, an irresistible moral tide of black-clad women. The convoy began, and two hours later it stopped. The Serb mothers and the Croat mothers had fought on the buses. After a delay, the motorcade went on, with all the Serb mothers in one set of buses, the Croat mothers in another.

On a radio talk show, a Serb called in to say that if Serbia had not sacrificed itself for the west at the battle of Kosovo Polje in 1389, the world today would have three superpowers: the United States, then Russia, then Serbia. A second caller responded angrily – that should be Russia, then Serbia, then the United States!

On the evening news, crying women were wandering through a field of high grain. They were picking up pieces of bodies. A hand, a head. More purple, noodly viscera. Serb mothers, Serb innards? The television said so. Was Zagreb TV showing the same footage at that same instant, and calling it Croat mothers and their fragmented sons? This was the only practical advantage of looking exactly like your enemy, and speaking like him. It had been exploited for years. I had a Tito-era book at home with a dramatic photograph of a young man getting his head axed off, and the caption read, 'Partisan executed by Germans'. I had another book published recently in Belgrade that showed the same photograph, over the caption 'Serb youth killed by Ustashas'.

Niš had all the elements of a typical Serbian city: a few bare outlines of Roman remains, a solid Turkish fortress, a preserved concentration camp in which German Nazis and Bulgarians had held about thirty thousand hostages, a pleasant flowery meadow up on a hill where about ten thousand of those hostages had been shot, and a lot of post-war buildings, since the Allies had bombed Niš thirty-two times.

Niš also had something unusual: a Turkish tower built out of Serb skulls.

'To understand the Serbs, you must see . . .' This was a modern epic formula that Serbs used frequently. They applied it to places where the Serbs either suffered gloriously, or created gloriously –

places such as Kosovo Polje, or the Serbian monasteries, or the memorial of the concentration camp at Jasenovac. The Ćele Kula, or Skull Tower, was one such place.

The Serbs had been in full revolt against the Turks for five years when the battle of Čegar Hill was fought four miles north of Niš in 1809. The Serbs lost, and the Turks – who were getting mighty tired of this rebellion – cut off the heads of 952 of their fallen enemy, stuffed the scalps with cotton and shipped them to Istanbul for the enjoyment of the Sultan, and built a squat square tower out of the skulls. Standing just outside the city on the road towards Istanbul, it was supposed to be an object of terror, a discouragement to shepherds thinking of becoming insurgents, but when Alphonse de Lamartine saw it in 1833 he showed again that marked correspondence between Serb and French feeling by writing:

> *Qu'ils laissent subsister ce monument! Il apprendra à leurs enfants ce que vaut l'indépendance d'un peuple, en leur montrant a quel prix leurs pères l'ont payée.*

The Serbs took this sentiment to heart, and after the Turks were driven out of Niš in 1877 they built an Orthodox chapel completely enclosing the tower, both to sanctify the unburied remains and to protect this monument to Serbian glory from the elements. (At the same time, all of the mosques in Niš, as in every other Serbian city, were being systematically destroyed. As one man put it to me, 'Their buildings were here for five hundred years. That was long enough.')

I entered the chapel to examine the tower. It certainly no longer had the power to terrify. Most of the skulls had disappeared over the years to relatives, souvenir hunters and reliquaries, leaving behind empty niches in the crumbling brickwork. A wall of plexiglass protected the fifty or so that remained from further plunder.

'To understand the Serbs . . .' What message was I supposed to read in this wreck, cowed by its Orthodox frame and protected from my prying fingers? That by seeing proof of the peculiar

372

barbarity the Serbs had suffered under for so long, I would better understand their simple hardness, their Homeric ideas of heroism and justice? But this barbarity was not at all peculiar to the Turks. The Austrians cut off nine hundred Turkish heads and entombed them in the foundation of the fortress of Karlovac. The Prince-Bishop of Montenegro could look out the window of his episcopal fortress and count the heads he had had stuck on pales like lollipops. The centuries-long German and Russian occupations of Poland included every barbarity imaginable, and yet the Poles did not hold up their hideous suffering like a Medusa's head and expect the rest of the world to turn to stone. It was probably not the Turks who had made the Serbs warlike. It was perhaps worth keeping in mind that both the Croats and the Serbs had been invited into the Balkans by Byzantium specifically as warriors, to keep the Avars in check. As a Sarajevo friend of mine once put it, 'We are not South Slavs for nothing. We came all the way down here from the north because we kept causing so much trouble we had to move on.'

At the ticket booth outside, I stopped to ask for some historical information, and unleashed one of those torrents. The man stepped out of the booth, the better to harangue me. He began in a friendly enough fashion, but as the subject possessed him he grew angry with me for being an American who did not understand Serbs, and hate twisted his features at the mention of Croats and Slovenes, who had killed Serbs so many times in the past, and were killing Serbs again. In America, we were ignorant or, more probably, under the influence of a disinformation campaign by the Albanian and Croatian lobbies. The west called the Serbs primitive, but did I know that when Barbarossa met the Serb leader Stevan Nemanja in this very city in 1189, the western emperor had –

Never seen a fork before?

Exactly! So I knew!

Yes. (I had heard the story a dozen times. Nemanja's fork was usually golden, and Barbarossa gaped like a bar-barbarian.)

If you counted correctly, the medieval Serbian state had lasted from the seventh century to the fall of Smederevo in the late fifteenth century. The Croats, on the other hand, had had a state for only 150 years. What was that? Nothing! The Serbs had never lost a war in their entire history. In 1804 they rose and beat the Turks but were betrayed by Europe, and so they rose in 1815 and beat the Turks again, but were sold down the river again, and in 1878 they threw the Turks out once and for all, and in 1912 they freed Kosovo and in 1913 they beat the shit out of the Bulgarians, and in World War I they fought the battle of Kolubar which was taught in all the military schools all over the world – West Point, the Royal Military College, etc. – as a perfect example of how to fight a battle against numerically superior forces with better equipment, and at the London Conference of 1915 the Serbs were offered a sweet deal, but they turned it down for the sake of the Croats, who showed their gratitude in 1941 by setting up concentration camps for the Serbs, some of them especially for children, a war crime that was unique to the Croats, even the Nazis never did that, and in the various concentration camps they killed over one million Serbs, no, more than that, because *one million* Serbs were killed at Jasenovac alone, the total was probably one and a half million! No, two million! This was a shattering blow to the Serb nation because Serbs did not reproduce so quickly, not like the Albanians, who bred like ants. One Albanian, with neither money nor a job, would have seventeen children! But Kosovo had always been Serbia, it was the cradle of Serbian nationhood, it was the Serbs' Jerusalem, and it would always remain a part of Serbia, it would never be separated, never!

But I had asked about the Battle of Čegar, and he would tell me. The Serbs had been outnumbered, as always, and yet they might have won anyway were it not for the incompetence of one of their leaders, who failed to bring his men to bear at the crucial moment. But the Serbs, although they lost, won eternal glory. (Čegar, in other words, was a type, in the biblical exegetical sense, of the Battle of Kosovo Polje – Ed.) The hero Stevan Sindjelić offered his men the opportunity to abandon the fortification receiving the main brunt of the Turkish attack. Not a single Serb absconded, even though to remain meant certain

374

death. As the Turks pressed closer and the end was obviously near, Sindjelić's crowning deed of heroism was to fire his pistol into the gunpowder magazine, causing a titanic explosion which killed all of the remaining Serbs plus a number of Turks.

When I thanked the man, the fury that had possessed him seemed suddenly to disappear. He gave me an absent-minded, slightly rueful smile, looking like someone with a bad hangover who needed to ask, a trifle anxiously, what he had done the previous night. He shrugged, glancing away. 'My pleasure. Any time.'

I walked away with that final image in my mind, of the Serb blowing himself and his comrades sky-high. A brochure I had picked up said, 'That heroic deed [of Sindjelić's] has inspired generations to come to follow his example.' It occurred to me that a people who did not mind losing battles – who in fact saluted the genius of their nation for losing battles – were dangerous indeed. When the ticket man had pointed to Čegar, I had turned to see two combat helicopters flying low over the hill. Perhaps they had been bringing wounded Serbs back from Slavonia to the military hospital next to the Skull Tower. When the Serbs said they would take on the world, I did not doubt them.

During my days in Niš, I was hearing more and more frequently another epic formula of the Serbs. It was the one that, in its bare-bones form, ran: 'The Serbs are tolerant.' Elaborations included, 'The Serbs are the most tolerant people in the world,' and 'The Serbs are too tolerant for their own good.' Sometimes instead of 'tolerant' singers substituted 'forgiving', or 'peace-loving'. A three-line version of the forgiveness motif ran:

> The Serbs even forgive the Croats,
> and a people that can forgive *those* monsters
> is a forgiving people indeed.

In a manner typical of oral poetry, formulae came in blocks, and these three lines tended to appear in conjunction with another triad:

375

The west says Serbia attacked the Croats
but see how safe Serbia is, how peaceful!
No one will touch you here.

This last was irritating enough in its illogicality for me to have
my own formulaic response:

The reason for Serbia being so peaceful
is nothing more
than that it's winning the war.

I chatted one day with three old women sitting in a row on a
park bench. They all wore black skirts and shoes, on top of which
one had a pink blouse, one a black, and one a green.

Pink: First we took down the statue of King Aleksandar and
put up a worker instead. Now we have to take the worker down,
and put the King back up. Serbs are so stupid!

Black: Serbs are good people!

Pink: Good and stupid.

Black: But, sister, they're not the same thing.

Pink: Listen to what I'm telling you . . .

Green: Perhaps George Bush will come, and he'll realize we're
good people, and then maybe he'll help. Or that Russian. What's
his name?

Black: Gorbachev.

Green: Right, Gorbachev.

Black (to me): Serbs have always loved the whole world, why
does everybody hate us? Where are you from?

I: The United States.

Black: God help me, son, you say a beautiful thing. We Serbs
love Americans, we love the whole world.

A passing man: Are they going to change the statue?

Pink: They say they're going to put the King back. Fuck your
mother – excuse me – but fuck your mother, nobody knows what
they're doing, they don't have any idea.

Green: Someone should line up the members of the Presidency
and shoot them all.

376

(Smiles and nods all round.)

Green: But not Milošević. He's changed a lot since last year. People still don't accept him – [to me] he's a former Communist, you know – but he's a good man. As for the other politicians, it's impossible to say who's better, they all change their opinions so fast.

Black (to me): We let Croats, Slovenes, Macedonians, Albanians, all live here, we don't touch them. They have their rights, exactly as we do. But look what they do to Serbs over there! They kill them, they burn their houses. They're going to cut us off from Europe! We'll need a visa to go through Zagreb. And you can bet the Croats won't give out many, not to barbarians like *us*.

Pink: But, sister, that's why I say Serbs are stupid!

Green (to me, about Pink): Her only brother was killed by the Germans. She still can't look at Germans without getting angry. For example, in a movie, if Germans appear she has to leave. She loves everybody, except Germans. And these Croats and Slovenes want to go back under them, after we saved them!

Black: They're separatists. You simply can't live together with separatists.

(All agree.)

I was curious to test this pedal-point about tolerance. There was one working mosque in town, mainly for Albanians, but also for a smattering of Bosnians and Turks. I had trouble finding it. I went to a tourist office off the main square and found two grizzly bears behind a counter.

'The mosque?!' one growled, in gruff amazement. 'Why do you want to see the *mosque*? Are you a Serb?'

'An American.'

'Have you seen the Skull Tower?'

'Yes.'

'The Roman remains?'

'Yes.'

'The concentration camp? The hill where the Nazis shot everybody?'

'I've seen everything except the mosque.'

Speak Serbian and the whole world will understand you. The

bear turned out to be gentle. He came out from behind the counter and held my hand, led me out to the street and gave me directions.

The mosque stood on a main street. It was a stucco square with a red-tiled roof and a brick minaret. A sign on the door said it was only open from eleven to two on Fridays. Graffiti on the stucco said: GET OUT, MUSLIM DOGS! and DEATH TO MUSLIMS!

From there, I wandered through back streets to the Catholic church. A storm broke just as I reached it, and I went into the courtyard and stood under an awning. After a few minutes, a priest came out of a nearby door to look at the rain, and when he caught sight of the bearded stranger he nearly jumped out of his skin. I came forward, speaking reassuringly bad Serbo-Croatian. We sat in his office, where he explained that someone had written CROATS WILL GET THE KNIFE! on the church, but he had painted it over. Only a few of the Catholics in Niš were Croats anyway. The rest were Slovenes, Albanians and Czechs. There were only four hundred in the whole area. He had received threatening letters, signed 'Šešelj'. But the most disturbing incident had been the bomb, which someone had thrown at the front door in May. The building shook and glass blew out, but no one was hurt. He showed me the spot.

I went looking for someone I had met in Niš two years ago. At the bookstore where he had worked, his colleagues said he had been called into the reserves, and was training up north. But later his wife came in, and I found out from her that he happened to be in town for the next two days, on leave.

Srdjan was a poet. Two years ago, he had been excited by Milošević and his dangerous ways. 'With him, we're probably going to hell,' he had told me, and then smiled, 'but we were going to hell anyway.' But now that he was staring hell in the face, he evidently preferred fantasy. He had become a royalist. The magazine he wrote for conjured up visions of a Greater Serbia that would be allowed to come into existence peacefully because the other nations would simply recognize the rightful claims of good King Aleksandar II. (As opposed to the land-grabbing shenanigans of the discredited former Communist Milo-šević. Aleksandar II Karadjordjević is the grandson of the king who was assassinated in Marseille. A London businessman, he could be heard regularly opining that he was just the figure of reconciliation and legitimacy that Yugoslavia needed. He was said to be hard at work learning Serbian.)

I met Srdjan that evening at his favourite watering hole, and he looked the same: slender, hyperactive, with a face of delicate, inexpressive features. The difference was the deeply frightened look that came into his eyes when he talked about the 15th of August, only a few days away, when his unit would go into battle. You could tell that he simply could not believe what was about to happen to him. 'That's the way it is,' he murmured to himself several times – a mantra.

He told me and his friends around the table about Army life. He was in an artillery unit, so every morning he got up at six a.m. – he hated that the most, the early rising, he was a poet, he had always drunk and wrote till four and slept till noon – and spent the day trying to hit things with shells. When he went to war, he would be several kilometres back from the line, which arrangement would hopefully save his life. There were a hundred soldiers in his unit: seventy Serbs, fifteen Albanians, ten Croats, four Slovenes, one Macedonian. Non-Serbs throughout the Army tended to desert, and one of the desertions from his own unit, Srdjan said delightedly, was 'a symbol of Yugoslavia today'. Two Slovenes and two Croats had deserted together. One of the Slovenes had arranged for his father to meet him with a car in some woods near the training camp. All four deserters made their way to the rendezvous point, and the father drove away with the two Slovenes, leaving behind the two Croats, who were caught.

Two years ago, Srdjan and his wife, Jadranka, had been renting a single room without running water or electricity in an otherwise abandoned building, but they had not been able to afford even that, and had since moved back in with Jadranka's parents, who lived on the edge of town in an old farmhouse surrounded by modern high-rises. I had lunch there the next day. The guest room was just inside the front door, on the right, like an Albanian odë. Jadranka brought us our food but did not eat with us. Srdjan dandled his three-year-old son, whom he had named after a Serb poet. He and Jadranka would have three children at the very least, he said – if he survived this war – because it was a man's duty to increase his race. He then talked about Milošević. His theory was that the entire family was psychotic. Milošević's mother, father and uncle had all committed suicide, Srdjan said. It was in the genes. But instead of killing himself, Milošević was having the infinitely greater satisfaction of killing his own nation.

Srdjan telephoned his best friend, Dragan, and we all drove out to the country house of an older man, a political columnist, whom they knew and respected. His house was extremely luxurious by Yugoslav standards. We were ushered into the guest room, which was just inside the front door, on the right. The columnist smoked a pipe professorially, and kept an expensive chessboard in a prominent place, set up part-way through a grand master's game he let us know he was examining. He was a pontificater, a portly paterfamilias in his Roman villa. He lectured to us younger men as acolytes, and my mind wandered. But I remember his long, heavy, smoulderingly resentful description of Milošević as a man utterly devoid of ideology or principles, a man of merely pointless, reflexive cunning. He was almost a simulacrum, an eerie blank, leading his people in jerking steps towards the precipice. And by the way, he was impotent. And his wife was a nymphomaniac.

My ears pricked up. Say what? How did he know *that*?

'Because he's a diabetic,' the paterfamilias said.

'I didn't know there was a connection,' I said.

'And anyway, he's a tyrant, and the connection between tyrants and impotence is well established.'

When we got up to go, the paterfamilias told Srdjan to desert. 'This is not your war. This is one set of liars against another. All of the leaders supporting this war have sent their own children abroad.'

Srdjan was silent.

In the car on the way back, we passed long lines of vehicles

380

waiting at empty gas stations. All the gasoline was going north to the fighters in the Krajina.

'Why weren't *you* called up?' I asked Dragan.

'When I got out of the Army, I was assigned to a different reserve, with a different function.'

'Which is?'

'External threats. I'll get called up when we get into a war with the United States.'

Srdjan was sunk low in his seat, silent, his hands between his knees. 'What is the punishment for desertion?' I asked him gently.

'I don't know. Five years in jail, maybe. But I wouldn't desert if it was only five days in jail.'

Dragan took a hand off the steering wheel, and caressed his friend's head.

'Why not?' I asked.

'Because Serbs are threatened. Regardless of the idiotic politics, Serbs there are threatened.'

The next day, Srdjan returned to his training camp and I, trying to escape politics for a little while, went into a Putnik tourist office to ask if there was any concert, lecture, movie – anything – going on in town. But when the man behind the desk (who survives in my notes merely as 'Putnik') found out I was American, he was not about to leave me in my Croatian-lobby-induced state of misapprehension. He was articulate and well-educated, and spoke with energy, pulling maps out from a drawer when necessary to make his points.

The western papers said the situation here was complicated, but that was wrong. Things here were very simple! Life in Serbia was paradise, because Serbs knew how to live. He had his job, but he didn't work too hard. Croats and Slovenes were good people, but Serbs were better. Croats and Slovenes were hard workers, whereas Serbs had soul. Look at the Japanese, who didn't want to take vacations . . . Fuck your mother, that was crazy! Or look at the English, with their buttons buttoned and their long ties, their long looks, their long hours. Or the Germans, who wouldn't know fun if they fell into it, he knew what he was talking about, he had to deal with Germans. The only material difference was, a German had a BMW, he had a Yugo. Otherwise, he had everything – good coffee, good brandy, radio, TV. He worked from seven to one, he had lots of free time, he played tennis, he enjoyed himself. Things in Serbia were *solid*. They were made out of concrete and wood. (Slap, bang.) He'd been in Australia, there was nothing there. He didn't mean history. Everything in Australia was made out of cardboard. If you leaned against a wall, you would fall right through it. Fuck your mother . . . All this nationalist talk – it was all on the other side. Serbs had never cared about that. Serbs never noticed. He had these Croat friends, and they were always hitting their chests and saying 'I am a Croat!' OK, so they were fucking Croats, what was he supposed to do about it? Now if I looked on this map . . . His wife came from this little Serb village on the coast. It was surrounded by Croats. All the people in her village had to climb into the hills at night and sleep in caves because the Croats were getting ready to attack. The new Serbia would solve that problem. The new Serbia would include a long arc reaching through Bosnia all the way to his wife's village. Bosnia would be cantonized. The Muslims would get the Sandžak, the Serbs would get western Bosnia, and Dalmatia would go to Italy.

'Italy?' I said.

'Of course. Venice had Dalmatia for centuries.'

'But what about all the Croats living there?'

'They *want* to belong to Italy.'

Putnik invited me to dinner that night with his wife, Milica. We met at an Italian restaurant. Putnik was dressed in a flowing open-necked white shirt and white trousers, and reeked of cologne. 'Did you hear on the radio?' he asked excitedly as we sat down.

'What?'

He was bubbling with satisfaction. He kissed his fingers. 'Massive battles all through Slavonia. We rolled over the Croats. We destroyed them! Thousands! The tanks are heading for Zagreb! Maybe we'll go all the way!' He pulled a map out of his pocket, to show me how far the Serbs had advanced. Croatia was nearly cut in half. 'What did I say about my wife's village? Now Serbia will have some beaches! Surfing! Sand volleyball!'

'He's joking!' Milica giggled.

He tapped a village in the middle of Bosnia. 'This is where I was born. They're all Muslims in there. We'll clear that out, too.'

Milica giggled again. 'He's joking!'

Later they showed me a photograph of their six-year-old son, Stevan, who was at home with the grandparents. 'He plays piano,' Putnik said. 'He's a genius. Of course!'

This led, naturally, to the Albanians. For Putnik and Milica they were not ants. They were rabbits. Milica's opinion was professional, since she was a sociologist.

'Tell me, I'm curious,' Milica said. 'Are the niggers taking over America?'

'You know, it's interesting,' I said. 'A lot of people in Yugoslavia have asked me that.'

'Don't the niggers have a higher birth rate than whites?'

'You might find this hard to believe, but I have no idea.'

'Why are you writing about Yugoslavia?' Milica asked. 'I was in China two years ago. *That* was interesting. Yugoslavia isn't interesting.'

'Of course we're interesting!' Putnik exclaimed. 'Look! We're killing people every day while I play tennis! Isn't that interesting?'

Over coffee, I lobbed the grenade on to the table. 'Kosovo costs Serbia a lot of money it can't afford. There's nothing there but Albanians, and you hate Albanians. What would be so terrible about giving it up?'

The reaction was instantaneous. Putnik was enraged. 'What if a bunch of Serbs came to America and fucked all the time, and took over Virginia, and said they wanted to secede? What would the US do?'

'I'm . . . not sure.' I was still trying to absorb the hypothesis.

'Maybe you're not sure, but *I* am sure. You wouldn't allow it! You have no idea what the Albanians are like.'

'Ants? Rabbits?'

Our evening was suddenly over. Putnik no longer wanted to talk to me. He said something about my being CIA and handed me a matchbook to talk into as though it were bugged. Milica stared at me unhappily. Putnik paid the bill and walked me to a bus stop.

This was not the first time I had tried suggesting, purely for the sake of discussion, that Kosovo be let go, and the result had always been the same. Instead of an argument, I got ostracism. I had let slip the fact that I was an agent for the other side.

While Putnik kept watch over me at the bus stop, the sounds of a radio drifted down from an open window. The Yugoslav Army had been attacked in Kosovo by snipers . . . An Albanian had been wounded in the return fire . . . He died on the way to the hospital.

Putnik laughed. Still enraged at me, he poured his rage into that loud laugh. 'You know what that means don't you? They shot him in the head!' He laughed again, both delighted and enraged, and mimed the shot, downward, in the back of the head of a kneeling man. Then a hand gesture: Get the fuck out of here. He meant it for me too. My bus had arrived.

I spent a final day in Niš. On the hill where the ten thousand hostages had been shot, three giant concrete fists punched up out of the ground and towered over the trees. In the villages in the hills around the city, I walked through the overgrown graveyards, reading the usual Yugoslav tragedies in stone. The limestone slabs from the 40s – there were always lots of them, men and women, young and old, all the children of broken-hearted old couples, brothers and sisters dead of torture within days of each other – were wrapped with barbed wire, perhaps to symbolize the bitter pain of so much senseless loss. Or perhaps the wire was a secular crown of thorns for a people's martyrdom. On the more recent graves lay cups of coffee, evaporated or spilled by the rain, sodden cigarettes, greasy plates from which some animal had eaten the kajmak or the kiflica, and left the tomato and banana to rot. Many country Serbs still believed in a very concrete way that the living owed much to the dead. The dead had to be nourished, or they would restlessly walk the earth. In some cemeteries you saw entire houses built for the comfort of the dead, complete with refrigerators and television sets. You heard stories of this or that dead uncle or father (males seemed to be harder to satisfy) appearing before his terrified kin and moaning that meat was not

384

being left for him in sufficient quantities. 'Vampire' is a Serbian word.

On the bank of the river that flows through Niš, I stopped to look at a monument, a tilted brown-black steel beam a foot wide and eight feet tall. The brief text printed on it said it had been erected in 1989 to mark the eight hundredth anniversary of the meeting in Niš of the Emperor Frederick I, known as 'Barbarossa', with the Serbian leader Stevan Nemanja. I puzzled over three deep parallel indentations in the top of the beam. Then I figured it out. The damn thing was a fork.

66

I had intended from the beginning to finish my trip where I had started it, in Zagreb, but I discovered in Niš that it was no longer a simple matter of heading north. The railway lines between Belgrade and Zagreb had been repeatedly bombed, so no trains had made the run for weeks, and the Highway of Brotherhood and Unity connecting the two cities was littered with mines. (Ironies now were a dime a dozen.) I could either make a detour through Hungary, or head west through Montenegro and take a boat up the coast. The second option was a little iffy – the Yugoslav Navy, which like the Army was Serb-controlled, had been making moves towards closing down coastal traffic, and the bus routes from the coast to Zagreb were constantly in danger of being cut off by Serbian advances – but I chose it anyway, because it would keep me in the former Yugoslavia.

So I turned around and took a bus back through Kosovo and up the Rugova Gorge, the same through which the Royal Serbian Army had retreated in 1915, before the dirt road was put through. The hot, crowded, dusty bus swayed over the immense precipices, stopping at hamlets hidden in the high crags to pick up strong, tall, handsome, black-clad women carrying buckets of cheese to markets on the other side of the mountain. These were already

Montenegrins, although we did not officially cross into that republic until shortly before the Čakor Pass.

I rented a room for the night in Plav from a big-boned, loud, opinionated, black-haired woman with piercing blue eyes, and we were visited by her brother-in-law, who was returning grandly drunk from his nephew's wedding with a gun tucked in his belt. The two of them seemed to revel consciously in the larger-than-life stereotype that was supposed to characterize them. 'We are Montenegrins!' the man grinned wolfishly. 'We eat stones!'

I left the next day, wondering about the sentiment that had often been expressed to me by Serbs, most recently and succinctly by Putnik's wife Milica over her spinach *calzone*. 'Montenegrins are insulted if you call them Montenegrin!' she chirped with childlike glee. ' "No, we are Serbs!" they say!'

I stopped off in Cetinje, which had been the capital of Montenegro during the centuries in which the mountain men were continually fighting off the Turks. Graffiti said, DOWN WITH GREAT SERBS! and CHETNIKS, CETINJE IS YOUR DEATH. The Serbian cross with the four Cs had been transformed into a swastika. After weeks among Muslims, Croats and Albanians wondering if I should shave off my beard, I finally ran into unpleasantness in the land of the super-Serbs. A young man in the street came straight at me with burning eyes and pulled on my beard, saying, 'What does this mean? Get the fuck out of here!'

'But you have a beard too!' I said.

'Yeah? Are you calling me a Chetnik?'

'I don't know what you are. I'm an American.'

He stared at me blankly. 'American?'

'Yeah.'

'Oh.' He let go of my beard. 'Forgive me. I thought you were a Chetnik.'

'Apparently.'

He threw his arm around me. 'Come on, I'll buy you a drink.'

Over Johnny Walker, he explained that there had been a Chetnik rally in Cetinje a couple of months ago, and the Chetniks had been chanting, 'This is Serbia,' and there had been some violence. Nothing much – some gunfire, a few wounded – but people here were still angry. He hoped I didn't take the beard-pulling personally. A man thought of Chetniks, a man drank . . . These things happened.

He and the barman discussed how many Montenegrins mistakenly thought they were Serbs, and settled on twenty per cent. They agreed that Montenegrins had never had anything to do with those abject slaves of the Turkish Empire. They agreed that Montenegrins were the most honourable nation in Yugoslavia. They also agreed, startlingly, that Serbia had no business fighting in Croatia. That was how most Montenegrins felt, they said.

'But the pro-Serbian government here just won an election,' I objected.

Anh! That didn't mean anything. They were a bunch of Communists. They controlled the newspapers, the television. *Manipulacija!* Let's drink!

The first morning bus to Kotor was cancelled because the driver was drunk. The second one ran out of fuel five minutes outside town. It took an hour for our driver to flag down a trucker willing to sell him a few litres from his own tanks.

In Kotor, the priest of St Luke's showed me proudly around his ancient stone church. He was from central Serbia, and his assistant was from Niš, and both were categorical about Montenegrins who said they were not Serbs. They were agents of the Vatican, pure and simple. They were probably getting paid.

I continued around the Bay of Kotor, past Herceg Novi, and started up the famous tourist coast of cypresses and figs and lavender, and thousands of summer homes. A few miles south of Dubrovnik, the bus crossed from Montenegro into Croatia. Anti-tank barricades stood ready by the side of the road. A mile farther on, we passed the first demolished summer house. A bomb had blown the roof off and chunks of concrete clung like scared cats to the twisted reinforcing-rods of the shattered walls. This had been happening all summer. It was probably a Serb's summer house blown up by Croats, but it might have been the other way around. Or it might have been a Serb's house blown up by Serbs, to make the Croats look bad. (Yugoslavs loved these theories.

Putnik had explained away atrocities committed by the Yugoslav Army in Croatia by saying he had read that Croatian forces had donned stolen Yugoslav Army uniforms and attacked their own villages.) So much for a second house being a hedge against inflation. Fuad's pessimistic view had turned out to be more accurate: 'One bomb, and no more front.'

At the Dubrovnik bus station, two women got into a shoving match over which had been the first to offer me a room. I spent only one evening in Dubrovnik, one of the most beautiful walled cities in the world. The fat creamy limestone paving-blocks of the streets had been polished by millions of feet until they shone as if wet in the rosy sunset light. The narrow alleys rising in stone staircases from the spine street were so clogged with potted trees they seemed like streambeds at the bottoms of gorges. Cats lolled on every sill, and waited patiently for scraps in every restaurant. I thought of Rebecca West's comment, that you could measure a city's level of civilization by the contentedness of its cats. A door in the seaward wall led to steps down the rocks to the sea, where I watched the red sun float down and drown in a peach sparkle.

I wanted to stay longer. Like the Dubrovnikans, I felt that this city, of all cities, would be relatively safe. Virtually no Serbs lived in Dubrovnik. It had never belonged to Serbia. And its fame would surely protect it. The Serbs had everything to lose in world opinion, and nothing to gain strategically by attacking it.

But I had to leave the next morning because I was due in Zagreb. I took the bus farther up the coast, and crossed over to the island of Korčula. My landlady made me basil tea out of her war reserves. (The radio had advised islanders to lay in three months' worth of oil, flour and canned goods.) She was a talkative, sweet, elderly woman with far-sighted eyes swimming behind wide-screen glasses. Her husband was handsome and dashing in his lieutenant's uniform in the wedding photographs on the walls, and red-faced and pot-bellied in the flesh, snoring on the couch in his socks and underwear with the newspaper over his face. She put fresh flowers every morning in each one of her immaculate lace-curtained guest rooms, all of which were empty except for mine. She laundered the unslept-in sheets once a week.

388

She complained to me that Tudjman had misspent Croatia's money. Whereas Nino in Zagreb had said the HDZ had not put enough money into economic restructuring, she had a simpler criticism: he had not bought enough guns.

On the walls of the medieval town, posters instructed people on how to black out their homes. Other posters ordered all those over eighteen years of age who were not already in the National Guard or the Territorial Defence or the Civil Defence or the police to register for the People's Defence, the last-ditch local guard. The radio reported that Macedonia had declared independence from Yugoslavia. Milošević was planning a trip to Athens, where he would meet with Greek and Bulgarian leaders, and Korčulans were sure, and were perhaps right, that the purpose of the meeting was to discuss the division of Macedonia.

The church towers and keeps were draped with banners carrying the protective Unesco symbol for a cultural monument, a blue quartered square with a dependent triangle. 'Serbian target practice,' the townspeople said. It was true that the Serbs were deliberately destroying Croatian cultural monuments as they swept through Slavonia. The Croats – and the western press – were decrying it as senseless, mad. It was anything but. When nations argued for their superior rights over other nations on the grounds that they possessed a superior culture, or laid claim to a piece of land by pointing to the buildings they had built on it, they were making culture a weapon. At that point, it also became a legitimate target.

At the refugee office, donated food was being packed in boxes and loaded on vans. A volunteer told me there were about 150 refugees on the island, and more coming in every day. Commune officials were saying there was room for as many as two thousand refugees but he, the volunteer, knew they could accommodate much more. For example, Serbs' summer homes alone could house about 2,500. He called a driver to take me to meet some refugees, and then embarked on an interminable diatribe, touching all the bases: Serbs were oriental, Croats were western; Serbs were despotic, Croats were democratic; Serbs didn't work, Croats did; et cetera.

I was saved by the arrival of the driver. He was Ivo, a broadly built man of medium height and age. We took off in his tinted-glass van. 'What do you do?' I asked.

'I am a volunteer.'

'For what?'

'For killing!' He spoke with boyish gusto. 'I am a *specijalista*!' He twirled a finger around his crown. 'We're the ones who wear the black headbands! You have heard of the Borovo Selo massacre?'

'Yes.'

'I was there!'

I was interested. 'Tell me about it.'

He squeezed out a tight smile, slightly shaking his head. 'Maybe later.' He had been in the hospital after Borovo Selo, and since then he had been working on the island.

'Doing?'

The same smile, of secrets happily held back. 'Working for Croatia. I am up all night! I am very tired!' He drove fast, not looking at the road, holding a walkie-talkie in one hand. 'I want to go back and fight again.'

The refugee couple we were looking for were not in, so Ivo drove me down to the Hotel Korčula for a drink on the terrace. He had been the first HDZ man in Korčula, he bragged. A year and a half ago, he had raised the tricolour with the šahovnica on a tower in the old town. It was the first šahovnica raised in Croatia since World War Two! And he had gone to prison for it. He had had the flag made secretly in Split, and in the middle of the night he had scaled the tower with a rope, had gone down the inside stairs to barricade himself in, and had raised the flag for all to see when dawn came. The fire brigade had to be summoned to take it down. The fire chief called it a Fascist flag! And he was still the chief, could I believe it?

'How long were you in prison?' I asked.

There was a small pause. 'A couple of hours. They made me sign something, admitting that what I had done was wrong.' He grimaced. 'Communists! That's how they operate! The flag was in prison for two days. Then it was given back to me.' (This would have been shortly before the elections, and the authorities were no doubt cravenly feeling their way through a minefield of changing definitions of vandalism and patriotism.) 'I have the flag at home. It is a piece of history. No other foreign reporter has seen it, but I will show it to you. Some people say it is anti-Serb. It is not! It is pro-democracy. This is a fight for western values. The Serbs have an eastern mentality. They don't work! ...' Et cetera.

After the flag incident, he was constantly harassed. People would not speak to him. His hair turned grey in six months. But the western part of Korčula – the neighbourhood of villas on the slope facing the old town – they were all 'pure Croats', and they stood behind him. ' "You are a hero!" they said. "Just tell us what you need!" ' He appeared moved by the memory.

Then he became bitter. Korčula was still full of Communists, did I know that? It was a stinking nest of Communists. It had always been that way. During the war, it had helped the Partisans! And changes since the election had been damned slow. The old police chief was booted out only a month and a half ago.

We went into the old town, through a courtyard and up three flights to his apartment, a small place with the usual crowding of chairs and cupboards, the room-filling table. His wife brought out the precious relic and he held it up for me, his eyes brimming with pride. Friends had written encouraging messages like *Thank God!* in the white squares of the šahovnica. 'You understand that you are the first reporter to see this,' he repeated. 'The first Croatian flag raised in a public place! This is *history* I'm holding in my hands!'

'I feel very lucky,' I said.

It was folded and put away. 'I probably seem very calm to you,' he said.

Not at all.

'But the anger is always here.' He tapped his chest. 'Anger at the Serbs, at Croats who are traitors, at the Communists who are still persecuting me. It is not easy being a patriot in a time of quislings. At night, I explode. My wife must spend a long time calming me down. I had a heart attack two years ago, and now I have to carry emergency medication with me at all times.' He pulled a vial out of a pocket. 'At any moment I could – ' he snapped his fingers. 'Gone! So every day here seems like a year to me. I am only waiting to get back to my unit. I have two sons – one is twenty-two, one eighteen. They are Croat patriots, too. They would fight if I let them. They are eager to fight! But I will not let them. "No!" I say. "You must stay and protect your mother and sister! I will fight! I alone!"'

He had ended in a ringing voice, his finger in the air. I was not sure what to say, so I said nothing. He brought his finger down and rubbed his eyes. 'I am very tired. I have to sleep.'

We made arrangements to meet later that day, and I spent a few hours in purely touristic pursuits – looking at the cathedral, taking a swim. It gave me an odd feeling. They were killing people every day while I swam! Wasn't that interesting? I sat in a doorway on the cathedral square and watched children play football. Two boys picked on a girl until she ran away crying.

When Ivo picked me up in his van, he announced right away, in the operatic manner I was getting used to, 'I have decided! In two days, I return to the fight!'

We drove again to the Bon Repos Hotel, where refugees were being housed in detached bungalows. This time, we found the couple Ivo was looking for. Ivan and Katica had a kitchen, and two rooms filled with institutional furniture. Ivan was short, round and balding. He spoke in a thick clotted voice while waving thick short fingers. Katica was equally short and round, but had a bird-like voice. They were from an area of Croatia near the Bosnian border called Banija. Their village was Staza, population about five hundred, nearly all Croats, but completely surrounded by Serb villages. Ivan had been a signalman on the railway, and even after his retirement had stayed close to his former colleagues, most of whom were Serbs. So when other Croats were leaving Staza, frightened by what they had heard was happening to other Croat villages, Ivan and Katica stayed, confident in their friends. Finally, one Serb friend pleaded with Ivan, 'Get out while you still have a head on your shoulders.' But they still didn't leave. It was not until a mortar from a nearby battle landed in their garden and wounded their pigs that Ivan realized they were not safe.

First, though, he killed the pigs and cured the meat. 'A crying shame to waste pork! And they had been killed prematurely!'

He and Katica could not believe that they would be gone more than a few days – the battle would pass on, and they would return – so they just threw a couple of pillows in their small car, and one change of clothing. Their sixteen-year-old son took his accordion and his parrot. They left on the 7th of September, four days ago, and stuck to the back roads, afraid of running into either the Army or the vigilantes. They first headed north, hoping to reach friends in Zagreb, but fighting blocked their way, so they turned south, into Bosnia. They could think of no one that they knew in that direction except for a couple they had met the previous summer, when they had holidayed on Korčula. So they drove to Korčula. Their friends had no room, but the refugee committee had taken them in, and here they were.

'Thank God I came among these people!' Ivan said, gesturing towards Ivo. 'Just tell us what you need, they told me. I tell you, I cried. The tears were streaming down my face. It's hard for a man to accept help.'

They had called back to Serb friends in Staza, and found out that half of their house had been destroyed, and the other half was being used as some sort of Chetnik headquarters. There had been a brief shot of Staza on the television news, and Ivan had seen bodies lying in the street. Neighbours? Old friends? Only God knew. Ivan and Katica knew they had nothing to go back to. All they owned in the world was the car, the pillows and one change of clothing each.

Ivan's face turned plum. 'And my son right now is very upset.'

'Oh yes, my God,' Ivo said, signalling to me that I should listen, this was horrible, the world must know.

The entire family of a friend of their son's had been butchered. They were Serbs, actually, who had refused to kill their Croat neighbours. So other Serbs had killed them – father, mother and daughter – and stuck their heads on stakes outside the house. (Dead, mutilated Serbs? I had no trouble guessing how the story was reported on Belgrade TV.)

'How can Chetniks do such horrible things?' Katica said.

'They must be drugged,' Ivan said. 'Humans could not do what they do.'

Yes, Ivo had seen something about that on Zagreb TV. The commanders were slipping some drug into the soldiers' tea. It turned men into raging animals. Yes, the Croatian doctors knew all about it, they even knew the name of the drug, but Ivo could not remember it.

The conversation turned away from such horrors, to more pleasant things. Ivan and Katica were good people, Ivo said to me. The right kind of refugees, not throwing themselves on Korčulan hospitality and moaning, but doing what they could to help. Ivan was handy with tools.

'I fix things that I find at the dump,' Ivan said, 'or things that Korčulans need fixed. I refuse their money. "No!" I say. Why should they pay? I will do whatever they need of me, help where I can. Because they have taken us in! They have helped us, person to person, from their hearts.'

Katica proudly brought out a hairdryer that Ivan had found at the dump and fixed. She turned it on to show me how strong the fan was, how hot it got. 'These are not cheap! Someone threw it away, and all it needed was a little part. Crazy!' She went back into the kitchen and came out with an electric coffee mill. 'Ivan fixed this, too.' She turned it on and it hummed for me.

So they had the car, one set of clothes, two pillows, a hairdryer and a coffee mill.

'I don't want money!' Ivan repeated, louder. 'I don't want to be on the backs of the Korčulans!'

'See!' Ivo exulted to me, throwing a hand towards Ivan. 'He is that kind of man!'

'If I fix a TV, I don't ask for anything! But if they want to give me something, say, three hundred dinars – that is good for ten days of bread. That's all I need!'

Katica was wheeling in a television. 'Ivan found this in the dump and fixed it!'

'We are satisfied to have a place to sleep!' Ivan was announcing to the world. 'I make myself useful! I have ten fingers!'

'He's *that* kind of man!' Ivo said.

Ivan was waxing rhapsodic. 'One person to another! I help you, you help me! No money! We are humans! What is more important? We do what we can! I help in my own little way! People come to me, I don't turn them away!'

'In fact,' Ivo said, 'I have a hairdryer *myself* that doesn't work!'

'Bring it! Bring it!' Ivan shouted.

'Don't be shy!' Katica sang.

'Now, the man who lives in Viganj, *on the other hand*,' Ivo said, suddenly glowering. 'He is the bad kind of refugee. He whines. He expects hand-outs. He has two young children, but he drinks. He drinks, and beats his wife!'

The heads around the table waggled in disgust.

'He asks for money, and then wastes it!'

'We buy underclothes,' Ivan conceded apologetically.

'Of course!' Ivo said. 'You need underclothes!'

'Because we left only with the clothes on our backs. So we bought one set of underclothes for each of us. That's all!'

'Of course! While he buys liquor! And beats his wife!'

'And she with two children!'

'And I'm – asking – myself,' Ivo ground out furiously, leaning across the table, 'why isn't he defending Croatia? He is not ill, he's got two arms and two legs! I'm out there fighting for my homeland while he drinks and beats his wife! My wife says to me, "Go! I will care for the children!" And do you know what I say? I say, "Thank you! Thank you for being the kind of wife a man needs in these times!"' His finger was in the air again.

'And *we* thank *you*!' Katica trilled.

'You see this man?' Ivan shouted to me, grabbing Ivo by the shoulder and shaking him. 'Do you see this man? Croatia needs more men like this!'

'And men like *this*!' Ivo bellowed back.

They crushed each other in an embrace.

On the way back to town, I told Ivo I wanted to hear about Borovo Selo.

He allowed a pregnant moment to pass. 'Listen. I will tell you.

Ten minutes! I have nothing to hide. But quickly.' He pulled the van into an empty car park and we went into an empty bar. He rustled up a bartender and a couple of beers. 'I had to call command headquarters this afternoon, to get permission to speak to you,' he said.

'They gave it to you, I presume.'

'Yes. As long as you are a reporter.'

'I'm not a reporter. I'm a travel writer.' Have incomprehensible mission, will travel.

'Oh. Well . . . That's all right. I'll tell you anyway. First, you should know something about the specijalistas. We are an élite force! We wear black headbands and black gloves.' Again, the boyish grin, the hand circling the crown. 'We have crucifixes on our chests. And a specijalista code! A specijalista never retreats! When we come, it is a fight to the end. That's it! It will be settled right there! We only cross ourselves, go forward, and kill!'

He had been trained as a specijalista during his regular stint in the Army years ago, he explained. So he had already known the techniques. Camouflage. Sneaking up on a man. The knife in the boot that you whipped out in one smooth motion and threw through a throat at thirty paces. The five fastest ways to bleed a man to death. Garrotting. Windpipe-crushing. Blows to the temple. In the Army, of course, it had been dummies. Now it was Serbs, that was the only difference. 'But it's better not to talk of those things,' he said, after having talked of them. 'You understand me. War is war.'

Not that they did not carry firepower. They had far better guns than the lousy AK-47s the Army and the militias had.

'May I ask what make?'

The happy, tight smile, the head-shake. 'You may ask! But I won't tell you! Secret!'

'All right.'

'I *can* tell you, they are American. They are shipped to us by a California businessman. A friend of Croatia. Very powerful, quiet, with nightscopes.' He kissed his fingers. 'Beautiful! I was sitting next to a friend when he picked off seventy-five Chetniks with one of these rifles in twenty minutes.'

'Pretty slick. All killed?'

'I didn't go out and check.'

Ivo was the oldest by far in his unit. The others were just boys. They amazed him. They went out on a mission, crossing themselves and going forward, knifing and garrotting, and when they got back they put on headphones and listened to rock music. They were a different breed.

'Borovo Selo . . .' I prompted.

Right. Borovo Selo. His unit had been stationed in Zagreb. Word came in of the initial trouble there, and they were sent in. He had spent four and a half hours pinned down in that famous ditch. His buddy next to him had been hit in the leg by a dum-dum bullet. The bones were still there, but all the flesh had been blown away; as though it had been melted off. Ivo had been shot in the head. But he had been lucky. The bullet had glanced off. His clothes were soaked with blood. He was brought into the hospital, and the next twenty-five people they brought in were all dead. He could have been one of them. He stayed in the hospital for three months, and then came back to Korčula.

'So twenty-five Croats were killed,' I said. 'First I heard twelve, and then twenty-five, and then thirty-five.'

'No. All in all, seventy-five Croats were killed.'

'Seventy-five? I thought you just said twenty-five.'

'Twenty-five were killed in the battle. Afterwards the Serbs killed fifty prisoners.'

I wrote down the number. 'And as I understand it not many Serbs were killed.'

'That is wrong! Many were killed.' His eyes narrowed voluptuously, in what seemed almost sexual pleasure. His mouth caressed the word again: 'Ohh . . . many!'

'How many?'

He looked at my pen poised over the pad. 'Seven hundred and fifty.'

'Excuse me? Seven-five-oh?'

'Seven hundred and fifty. You can probably double that. But I didn't tell you.'

'You're telling me that 1,500 Serbs died at Borovo Selo?'

397

'I didn't tell you anything.'

That clinched it. I had doubted him virtually from the beginning. A middle-aged man in the special forces who carried around heart medicine? And why would the special forces be sent into the centre of Borovo Selo on a bus? These were the guys who were supposed to be crawling around in the forest with leaves sticking out of their black turtlenecks. And if he had been in the hospital ever since Borovo Selo, the first big skirmish of the war, when had he seen his friend pick off seventy-five Chetniks in twenty minutes, or got to know the young men who killed all day and boogied all night?

He had a scar on his throat. It was not big, and it looked years old. I was curious to see what he would make of it. 'I couldn't help noticing that scar,' I said. 'Is it from . . .?'

But this time, there was no bragging, no heroic posturing. His response shattered my conviction that he was a fraud. His face took on *that expression*. The convulsive set of the features, the flush, the eyes locking on to mine and deepening, turning inward, trance-like. He started to slowly shake his head. Tears welled. He was wrestling with some horrible memory. 'Yes,' he said. 'In Borovo Selo. They came through the trench killing the wounded. They hit me with a rifle butt.' Kundačiti! He opened his mouth wide to show me the row of missing molars. 'Then they held me up by the hair and . . .' He could only motion it. 'But I was lucky . . .'

Ivo dropped me off near my room. Returning to cheap theatrics, he heartily clasped my hand, declaiming, 'I am off in two days! To fight for Croatia!' He knew I was leaving before then. 'I will tell you one last thing.' He turned my hand and pointed to my ragged fingernails. 'You should never volunteer for fighting. You cannot survive in the killing business if you suffer from nerves. I have been in a war, and look – ' he held out his hands. His nails were sleek, shining.

He vaulted back into his van. A final salute, a jaunty smile, a roar away. Hi ho, Silver! So many things in Yugoslavia were unknowable. Ivo was just one more.

I took a boat to Split, but it was no use getting off there because all the roads from Split to Zagreb were closed down by the fighting. The boat continued to Rijeka, where the bus station was mobbed with people trying to get to Zagreb. I got the last seat on a bus. The route the driver took hugged the Slovene border, but still passed through towns that had been hit with Serbian mortar fire. Croatia, in places, was only a couple of kilometres wide, just as it had been in the Middle Ages.

Only a few days later, the Yugoslav Navy closed down the coast. Split was blockaded and bombed.

Dubrovnik fared worse. The Serbs cut it off for three months. Despite its world-wide fame, its cultural worth had proved too provoking, and the shells rained down. The people of Dubrovnik were not islanders, and had not been urged to stockpile food. They were reduced to living in their cellars, drinking puddles, eating rats, while their stone city, which had talked its way out of so many wars and survived so many earthquakes, was brought down around their ears.

67

Sandbags were piled in front of the shop windows of Zagreb. Long passageways deep under the old town had been opened for the first time in decades, so that the populace could hide in them if the city was bombed. The statues in the cathedral were being winched down from the walls, for transferral to safe storage. In the courtyard behind, refugees, some of them wounded, were lined up outside the Caritas office. A woman who had been cut by flying glass had a face like a completed jigsaw puzzle.

Zagreb TV was now broadcasting war news all day, interspersed with music videos, such as one I saw of Croat soldiers running through fields of grain in slow-motion like lovers rushing to an embrace, except that they were firing AK-47s, the empty bullet casings somersaulting balletically out of the magazines and over their shoulders, all to the tune of 'Men at Arms'. (The name

399

of the song was brave enough, but that of the group performing it was unfortunate – Dire Straits.) The main news concerned the city of Vukovar in Slavonia, which had been pounded mercilessly by Serbian artillery for weeks, and was little more than a pile of rubble. But it had not yet fallen, and Croats were calling it 'Croatia's Stalingrad'. I had never been there, but I remembered once noting down lines from a speech that Ante Pavelić had given in Vukovar on 14 August 1941: 'This is now the Ustasha and Independent State of Croatia. It must be cleansed of Serbs and Jews. There is no room for any of them here. Not a stone upon a stone will remain of what once belonged to them.'

I found Nino, Nataša and Silvija in their apartment, and we drank coffee in the sunshine out on their rooftop terrace, catching up, while shouts of 'Potatoes!' from itinerant sellers drifted up from the streets below, and helicopters flew in the wounded – most were missing one or both legs, Nataša said, as the Serbs liked to aim for the knees with dum-dum bullets, and follow up with a knife to the throat – to the hospital on the ridge, which sported a brand-new red-cross banner on its roof. 'Serbian target practice,' Silvija said, demonstrating the wide dispersal of the joke.

All three had returned just days before from vacations on the coast, where, as I had done in Dubrovnik, they had allowed themselves to believe that the war existed only on the radio, and all you had to do was spin the dial over to music to impose a cease-fire. Now they were looking around in blank disbelief at Zagreb digging itself in, and were saying to each other, and to me, struggling to get out of first gear, 'Can you believe this is happening? In the heart of Europe? In the twentieth century?'

They were acutely aware that in the months since we had last met, Yugoslavia had stopped being a country hovering vaguely in the corner of the world's eye and had become an object lesson, a warning of the worst that could happen, that was *waiting* to happen, among many other peoples struggling through the thicket of autonomist passions of the post-Cold War world. Concerned as they were about Croatia's image in the west, this profoundly embarrassed them. With deep sighs, they gave me recent examples. The President of Chad had said: 'We won't allow the Balkanization of Chad.' The head of the government of Papua New Guinea had said: 'We will not allow Papua New Guinea to become another Yugoslavia.'

Chad! *Papua New Guinea*!

'In the heart of Europe? In the twentieth century?'

Nino's broadcasts about Eogen Ćiro Piček had been interrupted by his holiday, and he had no plans to start them again. There was no longer any decent way to wring humour out of Croatia's situation. He had also left the Naughty Boys, so he had no money.

None of them had enough money, in fact, to pay the rent, since they could not get as much hard currency for their dinars as they had in May. They were negotiating with their landlord, who, fortunately, was unlikely to find anyone else able to pay the rent either. They had also taken in a fourth rent payer to spread the burden, a Slovene-English journalist named Chris, who was reporting on the war for a British paper.

Another new tenant was Maška, a refugee from Slavonia. Silvija had found her wandering the streets in the small town of Tenja, near Osijek, when she had gone there to report on the aftermath of a battle. Tenja had been deserted, and down a street littered with corpses just beginning to rot, Maška had been picking her way in a sort of dainty daze. Maška was a cat.

Life went on at the radio station. Silvija had given up trying to keep the newsreaders from inserting the words 'so-called' in front of references to various Serbian institutions. Director Ćopo, safely protected from being drafted into the reserves by his position, had told the recruitment office that Radio 101 could do its work fine with its female reporters, so all the men were available for military service.

And it came, as if on cue. I had been back for only an hour. The phone rang. Nino went to answer it. When he returned, he was pale. It had been his mother. The militia had caught up with him. He was being ordered to report for assignment in three days.

He proposed we go out for pizza. The idea was to take his mind off his fear, but of course it didn't work. He sat in the stall with his shoulders hunched as though to protect the back of his head, his eyes darting, looking for a door to escape through. Nataša anxiously held on to his arm.

'I always used to be angry with America, the way it was always barging around the world and interfering,' Nino said. 'But now I pray that America will come and occupy this country, and write a constitution for us as they did for Japan after World War II.'

When we had finished, I said, 'Why don't I pay?'

'Fine, if you insist,' Nino responded unhesitatingly. 'The cash register is up front.'

We split up, Silvija going to the radio station, Nino heading to his mother's to get more details on his doom and possible extrication therefrom, and Nataša and I returning to the apartment, where I met Chris, a soft-faced young man in jeans and loafers.

'I was completely neutral when I came down here to cover the war,' he told me. 'I was always telling Nino and Nataša and Silvija that they were simply paranoid about the Serbs, they were just being bloody biased Croats. Then I went to Glina with some other journalists. The battle line was supposed to be a few kilometres away. We were in a car with white press signs all over it, and yet mortars started raining down all around us. We fled the car and leaped into a ditch. There was a break for a few seconds, and I ran into a farmhouse. I huddled in there for the next six hours, while this unbelievable shelling went on. I mean, the Army had gone absolutely *berserk*. It was shooting at everything that moved, at fleeing civilians. Four mortars hit the roof of the house I was in. Fortunately none penetrated to the ground floor. Then the tanks rolled in, and blew up everything with the word "Hrvatska" [Croatia] on it, or just an H, and then a tank sat in the square and proceeded to blow holes in the cathedral. The Croatian militia was completely overwhelmed. They simply fled. The only way they managed to stop the Army was by blowing up the bridge on the road out of town.'

Thus had the Serbs warded off another potentially sympathetic voice in the media. It had by now become a truism among journalists, including veterans of Vietnam, Angola, Cambodia and the Gulf War, that Yugoslavia was the most dangerous assignment any of them had ever had, the principal reason being that the Serbs seemed to be deliberately targeting them. Croats and Albanians had a history of getting what they wanted by ingratiating themselves, sometimes shamelessly, with one or another of the great powers, and so, by extension, their natural inclination was to seduce journalists. But the Serbs, used to relying on themselves, felt such calculation was beneath them, so at first they had simply shut western journalists out, while Croats and Albanians had taken them to dinner. (It is no accident that the only refugees described in this book are Croats. I had run into Serb refugees in Belgrade, but they had been suspicious of my intentions, and refused to talk to me.) Then, when the Serbs perceived in western newspaper reports what any fool could have predicted, namely a preponderantly Croatian and Albanian point of view, they could only conclude that journalists were enemy agents, and the only reponse they could think of was to start shooting. In short, of all the elements of the Serbs' self-serving self-image, the truest was that they were stunningly stupid in their straightforwardness.

But Chris, perhaps, remained more neutral than he had made himself out to be. When Nataša left the room for a moment he immediately spoke to me as westerner to westerner, gentleman to gentleman, in a tone of bored superciliousness: 'Frankly, I think all the people down here, both Serb and Croat, are nasty pieces of work. I mean, this is the Balkans, isn't it?'

He elaborated on this theme until Nataša returned. Then he asked, 'What are you doing here, anyway?'

'Working on a travel book.'

Since he was from England, he actually understood what I was talking about. 'Right. The sort of book where you make fun of everyone you meet.'

'That's it.'

'I can't stand the genre myself.'

Late the next morning I made my way up the hill to the old town. I was curious to see the ceremonial presidential guard, which Tudjman had recently established for himself.

403

Nino: 'We don't have Baranja any more, or Slavonia, or the Krajina. But we have the presidential guard!'

The changing of the guard occurred each day at noon, outside the presidential palace in Stjepan Radić Square. I arrived just in time, joining a crowd of about thirty people, wrapped in coats against the chill and threat of rain. The old stable doors on the ground floor of the palace swung open, and out popped the little corps of trumpets and drums, tootling its short fanfare over and over again, followed by the guard in all its peacock glory: the rank and file in red tunics with gold frogging and black trousers, their superiors swirling black capes over cream tunics. They jerked forward in a stilted gait, with an odd, fey, lilting motion of their white-gloved right hands, raised to shoulder height. Tape on the pavement showed them where to wheel and stamp, where to line up like chorines and swing out the bayonets of their bolt-action rifles with another awkward flourish, of bird-like white gloves. A choreographer at the National Theatre had dreamed all this up. The costumes were based on those of Maria Theresa's personal guard, and included, of course, the cravat, which was named after the Croats, who invented it. (The Serbs contributed the neck sucker to world currency, whilst the Croats gave the neck tie. It seemed appropriate.)

One elegant window of the presidential palace stood open above the square, and the plush curtains behind it were slightly parted. Was Tudjman standing in there, watching, just out of our sight? Rumour had it that he almost never left the palace any more. He had had gold coins struck with his portrait, and he had taken to strutting around in a presidential sash. This reminded the Croats of Tito. But Tito's vain theatrics had at least had a real army behind them. Tudjman, who outfitted his soldiers with Rayban sunglasses but no bullets, reminded me more of Mussolini.

The dolls had completed their transfer of mock power, and marched back to their shelves, the doors swinging shut behind them. The crowd was unsmiling. One old woman clapped vigorously and long, but the applause did not spread. The scattering of men in camouflage carrying submachine guns – the guard for the guard – relaxed, and their commander gathered them to give out orders.

I realized that I recognized him. He was a fattish, bristle-headed man, with a bar moustache and a pistol the size of a small cannon on his ample hip. I had seen him last year at the HDZ rallies, where he had bellowed like a performing bear in a business suit, warming up the audience for the shrieking monk or the twitching Tudjman. On one occasion, as he ended on his customarily frenzied note, as though in some cheap television parody his arm came up in a Nazi salute, only belatedly bending at the elbow and shooting out two fingers to form the victory V. In those days he had seemed constantly enraged, his hair on end and his face an apoplectic purple. Now, in his camouflage trousers stuffed into shiny black boots, his rakish beret, bustling around with his orders backed up by a gun that could blow a plate-sized hole through flesh and bone, he looked deeply happy. Nino and his friends would die because of men like this, who would not die.

I met Nino and Nataša at a café. Nino was still exploring his options. Someone he knew who was a police informer had recently tried to recruit him to monitor the movements of Serbs living in Zagreb. The theory was that the Serbs would get advance word of any impending attack on the city, and would quietly start absenting themselves. Nino had turned the offer down, but was now considering it, as a way of keeping out of the militia, even though the thought of spying revolted him. Another possibility was to escape to South Africa. Since I would be in Vienna in a few days, he asked me to enquire at the South African Embassy there (obviously, he could no longer contact the one in Belgrade) about what he had to do to get a six-month visa. 'Be sure to tell them that I've been there before, and I have about forty relatives, all rich, who will support me.'

But even if he obtained the visa, he was not sure he would go. The pressure to stay and fight for his country was, of course, strong. People who left were traitors, cowards. At the same time, he could see no reason to fight for Croatia, if all Croatia could give him was an old gun, and three bullets to share with three other people. That wasn't fighting for Croatia, that was merely dying for Croatia.

We sipped our *cappuccini* from heavy porcelain cups, and nibbled dainty squares of mint chocolate, and Nino, for the first time, talked to me in detail about his family. 'At the end of World War I, my grandmother danced in front of the Croatian Parliament holding a Serbian flag. Whenever I think of that, I find it nearly impossible to believe. She can't believe it either. Twenty years of Yugoslavia later, and she was whole-heartedly Ustasha. Her husband was an Ustasha judge in Karlovac, and perhaps he was sending Serbs off to be executed.'

Nino fidgeted with the card summoning him in two days to the militia office. The text on the card talked only about the settling of 'administrative issues'. Rumour had it that a white card was not so bad, while a yellow card meant trouble. Nino's card was yellow.

'I want to explain why I'm so frightened about going to the office with this card on Monday. My family has a deep appreciation of the random chances of war. My grandmother and the Ustasha judge had two children. One was my mother, and the other was a boy named Rajko. They both grew up in Karlovac. My mother was eleven when the war started. Rajko was a little older, maybe fifteen. When he was sixteen he was put in the Domobran, the Croatian Army. But he defected, and escaped into Bosnia, and joined the Partisans. Towards the end of the war, he came back into Karlovac as a liberator, with his Partisan unit. Everything was in chaos then. People were burying their uniforms, and stealing different ones, and no one knew who was who. People were settling private scores. Someone on the street pointed to Rajko and said, "His father is Ustasha!" My mother heard through friends that Rajko was in trouble, and she came with other friends, people who could vouch for him that he had fought as a good Partisan. They arrived three minutes after Rajko had been put against a wall and shot.

'That was what it was like. Anyone might point. Enemies were everywhere, there was no time to investigate anything. Meanwhile, thousands of people were fleeing Karlovac, going north to

Zagreb, which had not yet been occupied by the Partisans. My mother's parents were already there. She managed to get on one of the trains. But by the time she reached Zagreb it was on the verge of falling. Allied planes were flying overhead, the armies were closing in. The city was overflowing with Croats who had fled to it, and now they were fleeing from it. It was a mass movement of hundreds of thousands, going north to "seek help from the West" – that's what my mother remembered people saying. The Communists were coming, and the West would save them. She headed for the train station, but on the way, by pure accident, she was spotted by her grandmother, who lived in Zagreb, and pulled out of the crowd. Her grandmother told her it was ridiculous to look for help from the West, Croatia had been against the Allies for the entire war. She was taking my mother back to her apartment. But – by another accident – they ran into my mother's father, the judge, who was calmly sitting in a park reading a newspaper, while the artillery shells were coming in. And *he* said no, it would be safer for my mother to go north, and he led her back to the station. But by that time the last train had gone.

'And of course, we all know what happened to those people who fled north. They ended up being massacred at Bleiburg.

'Fifteen days later, my mother's father was dead, executed by the Partisans. During the days he was in jail, he had written notes secretly to my grandmother, on toilet paper. The last one said, "Thank God, Rajko is still alive." My mother and grandmother had never had the courage to tell him that Rajko had been shot.

'People vouched for my grandmother, saying she had never been involved in politics, and she was left alone. My mother, though, since she was young, was a target for re-education. A Partisan from Dalmatia was put on her case. The Dalmatians knew all about the lie of the Independent State of Croatia, because Pavelić had handed Dalmatia over to the Italians. Over fifty per cent of all the Partisan dead were Dalmatians. You can look it up. So this fierce Partisan from Dalmatia had a dossier on my mother and everything. He saw she was a real tough case, a daughter of an Ustasha judge, whew! But instead of re-educating her, he married her. I like to say that I'm the child of tolerance.

'And now my father, who was anti-Ustasha, hates Serbs. And my mother, who was Ustasha, says there's no difference between Serbs and Croats where she came from, they're all animals, they'll drink coffee with you, smiling, and shoot you around the corner. And her mother, who danced with the Serbian flag and then was the wife of an Ustasha judge, says that people have no idea what they are doing when they support the HDZ, it has nothing to do with whether HDZ is right or wrong, it has everything to do with war, and all she can see is her son Rajko lying dead in the street.

'I understand better now what she and my mother have been talking about all these years when they said how crazy war is, how nothing is predictable. It's like an earthquake. You run to the left, you die. You run to the right, you live. I got a card, but Robbie didn't. Why? It just happened that way. A friend of mine has already been rotated once, into the police reserves. They gave him fifteen days out at a frontier post. There were five of them, out there without any training, and only one gun to share between them, and one box of bullets. If the Serbs had attacked, they would have died, for certain. But the Serbs did not attack, and after fifteen days he came home.

'My friends tell me not to worry about Monday. Some have already gone, and they say someone will get me to sign a list, and they'll take my telephone number, and tell me they'll call me when they need me. But I have this horrible fear in my mind. I will go to the office on Monday. Everything will be going all right, I'll be filling out the papers. And suddenly this man will come in, and he'll look around and say, "Who's here right now? I need some men. OK, how about you. And you, and you." And they'll tell me I have to follow the man, and I'll be taken out the back, and they'll hand me an old gun and two bullets, and push me through a door, and wham! – ' Nino's face went blank with terror. He stared across the marble-topped café table, across some wasted no man's land in his mind's eye. 'Serbs!' he whispered.

We walked out of the café into a light rain.

*

408

Can you believe this is happening? In the heart of Europe? In the twentieth century?

When had Croatia graduated from 'Europe' to 'the heart of Europe'? Well, yes, Serbia and Greece were on the other side. But I had thought Serbia, in any case, was not Europe.

Still, I knew why the Croats said it this way. They wanted to believe that surely, *surely*, Europe would not let this continue. Not in its own 'heartland'. Surely Europe would intervene.

But what, instead, was happening? Europe was horrified and, being horrified, was distancing itself. It was the reflex Benjamin had predicted, and Chris had obligingly displayed: 'I mean, this is the Balkans, isn't it?'

Everyone played that game. People said, 'It's the politicians, not the people.' But politicians were simply lightning rods for the people's submerged hatreds, just as the 'frontier' Croats and Serbs, those 'primitive' and 'aggressive' people, were nothing more than surrogates for their more civilized countrymen, who hid the cold logic of their nationalism behind masks of flabby ecumenism and brittle shells of tolerance, and were discomfited at the sight of their own faces laid bare. Just as all Croats, about whom the crusaders had said, 'God save us from war and the Croats,' had been surrogates for all Catholicism, and were therefore fanatical Catholics, while Bosnians were fanatical surrogates for Istanbul. And the western press today was recycling the same brainless condescending trash that the west had always pronounced about the Balkans, about it being a powder keg, about its having already once in this century 'dragged' Europe into a general war, as if it were not the rabid nationalisms and military enthusiasms of the Great Powers that had turned an assassination in a small city very far from the heart of Europe into a continent-wide cataclysm. Who was the adolescent here, embarrassed by his pre-adolescent brother?

Can you believe this is happening? In Europe? In the twentieth century?

Of all the centuries and all the continents to mention.

Nino, Nataša, Silvija, Robbie and I spent my last night in Zagreb at the apartment of Danko, the basketball player. None

409

of them watched much news any more. Instead they spent the evenings, especially Nino and Robbie, playing a video game on Danko's wide-screen television which involved hitting coloured lozenges with a bouncing ball. Nino had decided, after all, that he could not abandon his country. But his mother, the crafty old Ustasha judge's daughter, had pulled strings, and had got a friend of a friend at the militia office to pull Nino's file and assign him to the unit that would defend Zagreb itself, so that he would be brought into action only if the Serbs were actually fighting their way, on the ground, into the city. 'And if that happens, I may as well fight,' he said. 'Because, if the Serbs occupy Zagreb, it will be like the Chinese occupation of Tibet.'

He turned back to the bouncing ball. He and Robbie had been competing for hours, and they were neck-and-neck. Nataša was hungry and wanted to get something to eat. Nino ignored her. She complained. They fought. She left angry. Nino and Robbie played on, occasionally leaping up from the sofa in victory, or throwing down the joystick in defeat, and they were still playing when I crept into a back room and fell asleep.

68

My train into Slovenia passed another train heading in the opposite direction, a long succession of flatcars carrying Army trucks, tanks and field artillery. On the cobbled streets of the Baroque capital Ljubljana, a glossy coffee-table book entitled *The War for Slovenia* was on sale. I attended a 'Service for Peace and Justice in the Homeland' at the cathedral, and only fifty people came – perhaps because the Slovenes already had peace. In one of the squares, some Croats had set up a booth from which they were selling the usual collection of Croatian flags, badges, belts, armorial shields and black headbands. The Slovenes gazed with some bemusement at this gaudy mass of Croatology without buying anything. One tall blond Slovene jogging by in a brand-new running suit stopped to say, with that Swiss sort of dismissive self-confidence that other Yugoslavs had found so irritating in the Slovenes for so many years, 'You can't buy your freedom! You have to earn it!'

I got together with an old acquaintance, a Slovene radio journalist who was also a friend of Silvija's. We sat in a lovely old square, drinking beer, while Slovenes rode past on bicycles. Igor shook his head, in contemplation of the Croats. 'I made a bet with Silvija that I could find *somewhere* in the new Croatian Constitution some provision for legally ousting Tudjman. She bet that I couldn't. I looked for two hours, and there was nothing.'

That evening, Slovenian radio reported artillery fire near Zagreb, and a gun battle at the Army barracks on the city outskirts. The Croatian government had initiated a blockade of the barracks just as I had been getting on the train for Slovenia, and this was the Serbs' response. The following night came reports that the Yugoslav Air Force was dropping bombs on the hill over Zagreb where the main radio transmitter was located, and that the populace was in the bomb shelters, and the city had been blacked out. I tried to reach Nino *et al.*, but there was no answer that day, nor the following.

On the third day I reached Nataša. She said that on the first night of the black-out she had come home in a tram with its lights off. Cars had been creeping along, using occasional bursts of their side-lights to check for obstacles. The whole city had been dark except for the neon Levis sign over Jelačić Square, which apparently no one had known how to turn off. Now there was sniper fire at night, and even during the day around the presidential palace and the train station, and people stayed wherever they happened to be when darkness fell. Some mortars had come in the previous night, and a few people had been injured. She and Nino and Silvija had gone down into the basement, where they had spent the night playing cards.

With a twinge of guilt, I wondered if I should go back. For a day or two anyway. I knew these people. They had given me a bed to sleep in. Was I going to flee to Vienna – to Europe! – while mortars fell on them?

411

'If I were not here, I would certainly not come,' Nataša said wearily. Perhaps she sensed my desire for her to absolve me. 'We'll keep in touch, won't we?'

'Of course,' I said. After a pause, I added lamely, 'Good luck.'

'Thanks.'

I hung up. I was not a Croat or a Serb, trapped by loyalties. I was the American, Hašim. I could escape, and I did.

Postscript

I am a slow writer. It is June 1993.

For the past twenty months, along with everyone else, I have listened to the horrors on the radio, and read about them in the newspapers. I am unqualified to express an opinion about what could or should be done to save Bosnia, or punish Serbia, or warn Croatia, or protect Kosovo. I think most of the commentators on the radio and in the newspapers are similarly unqualified.

I have not gone back. But I have kept in touch with the people of this book and can speak of small things:

The bombardment of Zagreb turned out to be brief, although the war continued savagely elsewhere in Croatia. Nino, Nataša and Silvija had to give up their flat in the spring of 1992 because they could no longer afford it. Silvija now lives alone. She remains the News Director for Radio 101. After a few dangerous assignments in late 1991, she decided she would do no more reporting from the front. 'It was not that I was afraid,' she says. 'I just couldn't stand to be in the afternoon in a place where people were killing each other, and in the evening to be drinking a beer with friends in Zagreb.' Of her relatives in Sarajevo, one is wounded, one missing. Another relative is missing in Vukovar, and is presumed to be in one of the mass-graves. Her sister has fallen in love with an American mercenary. Robbie is ancient history. 'After all that has happened, it's funny. I don't hate Serbs. I truly think I don't hate them. I just don't want to know anything about them.'

Nino and Nataša are sharing a flat in New Zagreb. In early 1992, Nino went to work for Sky News as a 'fixer' for correspondents in the field. This work kept him out of the militia, but it put him in places like Slavonski Brod during a massive artillery attack. Two camera-men who were friends of his have been killed. Nataša still prepares news reports for Radio 101. She also worked on a British television documentary about the refugees in Croatia (there are one hundred thousand in Zagreb alone) and won a summer internship in Atlanta with CNN. 'Everyone knows she is the best reporter at the station,' Nino tells me over the phone. 'Ah, she is rolling her eyes.' Igor Ćopo, the Director of 101, supported Nataša for the internship, even though she comes from a Communist family. Ćopo has surprised Nino. He seems now to recognize the need for an independent radio, and is no longer unquestioningly supportive of Tudjman. As for HDZ, Nino reports that, under the guise of converting state enterprises to private ones, it is looting the country.

In April, he and Nataša went to London for the broadcast of the documentary, and he spent a week making contacts for documentaries he might do himself. He ran into young exiled Yugoslavs everywhere, working in Pizza Huts and washing dishes. When his friends in London asked him what he thought of the future of Europe, he had a standard answer: 'I think World War Three will start here.'

Danko joined a Spanish basketball team, and he and Nika have emigrated. They live in Madrid, and have a baby boy.

Belgrade has changed dramatically, Mirjana tells me. Thousands of students and intellectuals have fled, and the streets are filled with soldiers. Since the blockade began, forty children have died in the Belgrade hospital for lack of proper medicine. Mirjana has no gas, which means she has no hot water, and she cannot cook. Electricity has become so expensive that she heated only the library last winter, and spent her days in there, wrapped in a blanket, watching the news on television. Leni had his own blanket. Her car has finally been fixed by her mechanic friend, but now there is no gasoline to put in it.

When pressed, she will admit she is angry about what she

perceives as an anti-Serb slant in the western media, including the newspaper she works for. She believes the three sides of the Bosnian conflict are equally guilty of atrocities, and in any case Serbia has not been supplying or supporting the Bosnian Serbs since the earliest days of the war. She thinks the Vance-Owen peace plan is unfair. She argues that, since the Muslims are mostly town dwellers, the Serbs have always been in the majority on about seventy per cent of the land, even if they make up only thirty-five per cent of the population. Still, she was exasperated when the Bosnian Serbs rejected the plan. 'When your back is to the wall, you can't go through the wall, you have to submit.' She scoffs at predictions in the west that the fighting may spread to Kosovo. 'If it starts there, I can tell you, it won't be Serbs who start it. It will be foreign agents.'

She assures me that she doesn't need anything. With the warmer weather, she has been freed from the library, even if she can't drive anywhere, and none of the buses in downtown Belgrade are running.

Leni is ageing. Mirjana's daughter tells me she is planning to buy her mother a puppy.

Vojislav Šešelj's party is now the second-largest in the Serbian Parliament, holding a third of the seats.

Vanja avoided both the Yugoslav Army and the Croatian militia by enrolling as a foreign student at the University of Amsterdam.

He feels somewhat guilty about this. He is aware that many Croats would call him a traitor and a coward for having left. (An old girlfriend sends him letters to this effect.) But he has no intention of returning. 'The Dutch are very tolerant, very accepting,' he says. 'This is a good country for foreigners.'

Maja has spent the past year in China. Vanja misses her. He invited her to come and live with him in Amsterdam, but she responded that although she might visit him she no longer wanted to live in Europe.

Vanja's mother received her Croatian citizenship automatically with the declaration of independence, but since her husband was a Serb it took him two years, several trips to the police station and several loyalty oaths. Vanja's parents assure him that the threatening midnight phone calls have stopped, but he worries that they are lying to him.

In the weeks after the Serbs began shelling Sarajevo in April 1992, Benjamin roamed the streets with a television crew, filming the carnage while trying not to get blown up or shot himself. Mirjana's daughter Marina, who is a good friend of Benjamin's, talked to him in June 1992, when he reported that he and his family had been forced to move from their flat to a safer part of town. He said he was waiting for the airport to open, so that he could put Radina and Mak on the first plane out. Then, in June 1992, all the phone lines were cut. Mirjana and Marina tried sending messages via ham radio. They asked the Sarajevo correspondents of Mirjana's newspaper to bring out some word. But months passed, and they heard nothing.

In April 1993, Mirjana decided to accompany a correspondent to the Serbian front line in Sarajevo. She went on her own responsibility, without a flak jacket. She had thought that surely now she would learn something about Benjamin, but when she had got within half a mile of the city centre, a no man's land two hundred yards wide prevented her from continuing. For two days, between translating for the correspondent and taking cover from snipers' bullets, she stared across this deserted band. She could clearly see the old town, the market, the destroyed parliament and presidency buildings. But there was no way to cross, no way to call. She returned to Belgrade.

At last, in May, a message was brought out by a reporter. Since anyone coming in or out of Sarajevo is asked to carry dozens of messages, they are usually very brief. Benjamin's was: 'We are here. We are all OK.'

I have not been able to find out anything about Miroslav.

416

Mostar has been almost completely destroyed. In the summer of 1992, Serbs in the hills east of the city shelled the right bank of the Neretva, where Mustafa and Behija were living. They fled across the river, and moved in with a cousin whose house had a good, strong basement. Then, in April 1993, the Croats attacked the Muslims of the left bank, hoping to force them out and thus gain control of the city, which the Vance-Owen Plan had designated as the capital of a future Croat province. Mustafa and Behija fled back to the right bank, along with their cousin, and took shelter in the remains of their traditional Bosnian house. As of three weeks ago, they were still alive.

The men of Medjugorje (and Bijakovići) take turns fighting Muslims down in Mostar: one week on, one week off. No one from either village has been killed, which strikes the Medjugorjans as miraculous, but Franjo was hurt when a window in Mostar shattered from an explosion and landed on his head. He spent several days in the hospital.

Lidija explained to me in a distressed voice why Croats had to fight the Muslims in Mostar: the Muslims had lost so much territory to the Serbs, they were desperate, and they wanted to take Mostar as recompense for all they had lost. So they attacked the Croats. But Mostar had never been more then ten per cent Muslim! It was a difficult situation, and she felt sorry for the Muslims. She sounded genuinely distressed. But Mostar could not be theirs.

There are few pilgrims in Medjugorje and no money, so Lidija has been working as a housekeeper and nanny in Italy for two years, and sending her wages back home. She tells me that for this entire war there has been a zone of peace around Medjugorje, stretching twenty kilometres in all directions. Another woman, a tour guide, tells me that a captured Serb pilot said he and his comrades had special orders to bomb Medjugorje, but every time they passed over the plain they saw nothing below them but thick clouds. Miracles.

There is an alternative explanation, however. Since Medjugorje has many more bungalows and pensions than any other town in

417

western Hercegovina, it was chosen to be the Hercegovinian headquarters for both the UN forces and the Red Cross.

The Virgin is still appearing every day at six-forty p.m.

The Croats and Muslims of Jajce, working together, succeeded in defending their town for several months against a determined onslaught by the Serbs. But in the late summer of 1992, they began to fight amongst themselves, and within days the Serbs had overrun the town. Thousands of Muslims and Croats fled east, across the mountains to Travnik. In May 1993, fierce fighting broke out between them. It began over a flag. I know nothing about the fates of Fuad, Ismet, Irfan, Esad, Emin and Ibrahim.

In Kosovo, Gazmend and Blerim were fired from their jobs within weeks of my visit. Gazmend now teaches in private homes and is paid, in Deutschmarks, out of a Solidarity Fund established and maintained by contributions from Albanians abroad. His wife gives piano lessons. They get by.

The police have killed twenty Albanians in the last year. An illegal election was held on 24 May 1992, and Kosovo now has a president, Ibrahim Rugova, and a parliament. But the Serbs have said that if the Parliament convenes every member will be given a five- to fifteen-year prison sentence.

Fadil jokes that Kosovo now has two parliaments, one in exile and one in limbo. He is living alone in the house in Rahovec. The rest of the family is in Skopje, with Fadil's father, who moved there as soon as Macedonia became independent.

Fadil, too, is teaching, in an elementary school five minutes from his house. He is paid DM30 a month from the Solidarity Fund, which means he is richer than he has been in years. But he still doesn't like teaching, and wouldn't mind getting as far away from Rahovec as possible. Lawrence Ferlinghetti has told him he'll always have a free place to stay in San Francisco. He asks me to send him works by Ezra Pound, James Joyce, Walt Whitman and Jim Morrison.

418

He is still with Violeta. His immediate plans are the same as always. He plans to stay alive.

Vesna and Aleksandar are still living in Priština. Petar is three and a half. Vesna has taken up a new speciality in sociology that has nothing to do with Albanians. Aleksandar has taken a job now at the university library. It's better than the work at the cultural union, he reports, because he has even more time to sit around reading books.

Srdjan survived his stint in the Serbian artillery. He fought for six months, and was one of the gunners who helped flatten Vukovar. Fifteen of his friends were killed.

He is no longer a royalist. Aleksandar II, he now says, is too 'cosmopolitan'. He is looking for a leader who is a Serb, and who thinks of himself as a Serb, and as a Serb *first*, and then perhaps as a cosmopolite second, who has never been a Communist, who is a nationalist without being a nut. He has had a devil of a time finding such a leader, but there is one man who is currently giving him hope. He will keep me informed.

There is a cashier at the supermarket near my house in Ithaca. His name is Miroslav, and he is a Serb from Belgrade. His wife, Vesna, is a Fulbright scholar at Cornell University. She is Slovene, but she has lived all her life in Belgrade. They have two daughters. Their visas will expire in two months. They cannot return to Belgrade because Vesna, as a Slovene, will not be allowed to return to her post at the university, and Miroslav will be looked on as a 'bad Serb' for having married a Slovene, and the two girls will be mistreated at school for being half Slovene. They cannot go to Slovenia because Miroslav, as a Serb, would not be allowed to work, and even Vesna would have trouble finding a job because she doesn't speak Slovenian very well. Miroslav says that, if they are forced to return, they will have to split up the family.

He thinks the west has made a big mistake in acceding to the division of Bosnia along nationalist lines. But, he says, if they are going to divide Bosnia, let them divide it into *four* parts, not three: one part for the Serbs, one for the Croats, one for the Muslims – and the fourth part for the people who still want to live together.

'There are quite a lot of those,' he says. 'More than anyone knows. People will come from all the other pieces of the wreckage. And there will be a place you can point to, and say to the nationalists, "See? It can be done."'

Miroslav and Vesna and their two daughters would live there, in the fourth part of Bosnia, in the soul of Yugoslavia.

Bibliography

I refer the interested reader to the following books, which aided me in the preparation of this book:

Banac, Ivo, *The National Question in Yugoslavia: Origins, History, Politics*, Ithaca, NY: Cornell University Press, 1984

Doder, Dusko, *The Yugoslavs*, New York: Random House, 1978

Durham, M. Edith, *High Albania*, London: Edward Arnold, 1909

Evans, Arthur J., *Through Bosnia and the Herzegovina on Foot During the Insurrection, August and September 1875*, London: Longmans, Green & Co., 1877

Gazi, Stephen, *A History of Croatia*, New York: Philosophical Library, 1973

Glenny, Misha, *The Fall of Yugoslavia: The Third Balkan War*, Harmondsworth, Middx: Penguin, 1992

Koljević, Svetozar, *The Epic in the Making*, Oxford: Clarendon Press, 1980

Lockwood, William G., *European Moslems: Economy and Ethnicity in Western Bosnia*, New York: Academic Press, 1975

Magris, Claudio, *Danube: A Journey Through the Landscape, History and Culture of Central Europe*, trs. Patrick Creagh, New York: Farrar, Straus & Giroux, 1989

Paris, Edmond, *Genocide in Satellite Croatia, 1941–1945: A Record of Racial and Religious Persecutions and Massacres*, trs. Lois Perkins, Chicago: American Institute for Balkan Affairs, 1961

Pennington, Anne, and Levi, Peter, trs., *Marko the Prince: Serbo-Croat Heroic Songs*, with introduction and notes by Svetozar Koljević, New York: St Martin's Press, 1984

Pfaff, William, *Barbarian Sentiments: The Clash of Nations, Nationalisms, and Ideology*, New York: Hill & Wang, 1989

Rothenburgh, Gunther Erich, *The Austrian Military Border in Croatia, 1522–1747*, Vol. 48 in Illinois Studies in the Social Sciences, Urbana, Ill: University of Illinois Press, 1960

Rusinow, Dennison, *The Yugoslav Experiment 1948–1974*, Berkeley, Ca: University of California Press (for the Royal Institute of International Affairs, London), 1977

Stewart, Cecil, *Serbian Legacy*, London: George Allen & Unwin, 1959

Tolstoy, Nikolai, *The Minister and the Massacres*, London: Century Hutchinson, 1986

West, Rebecca, *Black Lamb and Grey Falcon: A Journey Through Yugoslavia*, New York: The Viking Press, 1941

Wilkinson, Sir J. Gardner, FRS, *Dalmatia and Montenegro with A Journey to Mostar in Herzegovina and Remarks on the Slavonic Nations; The History of Dalmatia and Ragusa; The Uscocs; &c., &c.*, 2 vols., London: John Murray, 1848